From
Yorktown
to
Valmy

From Yorktown to Valmy

The Transformation
of the French Army in an
Age of Revolution

Samuel F. Scott

University Press of Colorado

Copyright © 1998 by the University Press of Colorado
International Standard Book Number 0-87081-504-0

Published by the University Press of Colorado
P. O. Box 849
Niwot, Colorado 80544

All rights reserved.

The University Press of Colorado is a cooperative publishing enterprise supported, in part, by Adams State College, Colorado State University, Fort Lewis College, Mesa State College, Metropolitan State College of Denver, University of Colorado, University of Northern Colorado, University of Southern Colorado, and Western State College of Colorado.

Library of Congress Cataloging-in-Publication Data

Scott, Samuel F.
    From Yorktown to Valmy : the transformation of the French Army in an age of revolution / Samuel F. Scott.
    p. cm.
    Includes bibliographical references and index.
    ISBN 0-87081-504-0 (cloth : alk. paper)
    1. France. Armée—History. 2. United States—History—Revolution, 1775–1783—Participation, French. 3. France—History—Revolution, 1789–1799. I. Title.
UA702.S386 1998
355'.00944'09033—dc21   98-28519
                                                                                                 CIP

For Denise

Contents

Preface ix
Introduction xi

Part I
The American Revolution and the Last War of the Old Regime

Chapter 1 The Special Expedition 3
Chapter 2 Early Experiences in Rhode Island 17
Chapter 3 Mounting Frustrations and Tensions 31
Chapter 4 March to Victory 47
Chapter 5 Yorktown 67
Chapter 6 The Long Journey Home 93

Part II
The French Revolution and Revolutionary War

Chapter 7 Between Revolutions 117
Chapter 8 The Royal Army Confronts the French Revolution 135
Chapter 9 Disintegration and Partial Recovery in 1791 151
Chapter 10 War and the Transformation of the Army 165
Chapter 11 In the Aftermath of Revolution, 1794–1815 187

Conclusion 213
Bibliography 217
Index 239

Preface

THIS BOOK IS THE RESULT of many—perhaps too many—years of research and writing. It has suffered from numerous postponements for various professional and personal reasons. Ideally, it should have been published a decade or two ago, during the bicentennial celebrations of the American and French Revolutions; however, it was not ready then. I hope it is ready now.

I consistently derived pleasure from working on this project. No matter what the causes or duration of the interruptions, I always enjoyed returning to it and savoring the human dramas that emerged from the research. I still do. Some readers might object to the number of examples I use to elucidate certain points in this study. I am unwilling to let these human beings fade into historical generalizations or statistics. I feel this all the more strongly because the great majority of the examples are drawn from the lives of ordinary people—that is, obscure individuals who otherwise seldom or never emerge from historical records. At the same time, I believe that it is ahistorical or excessively ideological to treat the officers and soldiers whose experiences I describe and analyze as either idiosyncratic anecdotes or the passive victims of great historical movements. These men played a direct and immediate—albeit limited—role in the most important developments of their time. For those who still find my examples excessive, I offer one optimistic note: They could have been multiplied many times over!

The primary goal of this work is to improve understanding of the closely related phenomena of revolution and war in the late eighteenth century. Both activities were conducted in the name of the highest principles. Both entailed extensive violence and suffering. And both involved the mass participation of

PREFACE

individuals. What follows is an attempt to translate these important historical developments into more human terms by examining a few thousand officers and soldiers: how their lives were influenced by political and ideological upheavals and how their actions, in turn, affected events.

To complete this study, I needed the assistance of many institutions and individuals. The National Endowment for the Humanities provided the funding that allowed me to conduct the original research that provided the groundwork for the project. Later research and travel grants from Wayne State University permitted me to extend my research and to fill the inevitable gaps that became evident. Although the resources and staff of many archives and libraries in the United States and France were essential to this study, a few deserve special acknowledgment: the Purdy Library of Wayne State University, the Rhode Island State Archives, the Newport Historical Society, and the Archives Division of the Virginia State Library in the United States; in France, the Archives de la Guerre and the Archives Nationales.

It is even more difficult to single out specific individuals, because scores of people have contributed to the completion of this work. To satisfy the demands of brevity and justice, however, I would like to identify a few. Delinda Neal has persevered through all the interruptions and literally countless revisions to produce the final manuscript. In contrast, I became acquainted with Bob Selig only toward the completion of this study, but his generous sharing of his own fine scholarship led me to investigate new sources and modify old conclusions, thereby improving the final results. Barry Rothaus, an old friend, colleague, and sometime collaborator, gave advice and encouragement at various times. Henry Narducci provided essential research assistance at early stages of this study. Bob and Dewey Morton supported my writing not only by furnishing the best of all locations in which to write but also by their interest in what I was writing. My scholarly debt to Jean-Paul Bertaud is exceeded only by my personal debt; he and Michèle have provided me and my family with a true "home" in France for three decades. Finally, every accomplishment in my professional life has depended upon the love and support of Tim, Rob, and Denise.

INTRODUCTION

ON NOVEMBER 5, 1780, François Gogue, a drummer-boy in the Regiment of Soissonnais, died at the French military hospital in Providence, Rhode Island. He had been born thirteen years earlier in a village in the province of Dauphiné. Following the death of both his parents on August 13, 1777, when he was ten, he was enrolled in the Soissonnais Infantry where his older comrades, with that combination of humor and affection typical of French soldiers of the period, gave the apparently pesky orphan the nom de guerre, or military nickname, "Go-away."[1]

Gabriel de Queyssat was born into a noble family of Protestant background in rural Guyenne in southwestern France. As had four of his brothers, he entered the army as a junior officer when he was sixteen years old. After sixteen years of service he was discharged as a captain in 1775. Recalled to service five years later, Queyssat resumed his rank and participated in the American War of Independence, during which the British made him a prisoner of war. When the Revolution broke out in France after his return, he supported it, joining the Paris National Guard in 1789. He returned to regular duty as a battalion commander in August 1791, fought at Valmy, and within two years was promoted to brigadier general. Suspended from his functions in July 1793 after being denounced as a noble and an "accomplice" of Lafayette, he was imprisoned from January to November 1794, when the Revolutionary Tribunal absolved him of all charges. He retired the following April and died near his hometown on April 30, 1837, three months after his ninety-fourth birthday.[2]

A former wig maker whose father was a small winegrower, Alexis Morge was born on March 8, 1759, at Landrecourt in what would later become the department of the Aisne. At age twenty he enlisted in the artillery regiment of Auxonne where he rose to the rank of corporal only after nearly twenty years of service. On January 13, 1809, after taking part in twenty campaigns and five sieges in the United States and Europe, he was "killed by a shot from a musket pointed at him by accident."[3]

Nicolas Tribout, a native of Lorraine, enlisted in the Royal Deux-Ponts Infantry, a German regiment in the service of France, in June 1775 when he was eighteen. Like the others mentioned here, he fought in the French forces that aided their American allies in the United States, where he was wounded (at Yorktown) and promoted to corporal and sergeant. Although he reached the rank of sergeant-major after returning to France, Tribout advanced rapidly only with the French Revolution; commissioned as a second lieutenant in April 1791, he had become a colonel by the end of 1794. He fought in every campaign of the Revolutionary Wars between 1792 and 1801. He retired on March 28, 1807, but was reactivated in late 1809. After serving in Spain in 1810 and 1811, he again retired. Dissatisfied with inactivity, Tribout asked to return to duty in March 1812, a request granted five months later. His last campaign was the ill-fated invasion of Russia, in the aftermath of which he died on January 23, 1813.[4]

These sketchy and disparate careers appear to have little in common. Certain factors do, however, tie them together. All four men served in military units that participated in both the American and French Revolutions. Although each individual's experiences were unique, they were not atypical of those of scores of other soldiers for whom comparable examples could be given. Finally, none of these men was very prominent; one can search history books long and hard—and usually in vain—to find any mention of them. For their time and place, they were rather ordinary people, yet they played an active role in some of the most extraordinary events of the period.

What follows is an attempt to provide a collective history of these men, and thousands like them, during what has been called the "Age of Democratic Revolution." This began as a study to determine what concrete, human links—if any—existed between the two great revolutions of the eighteenth century. As will be seen, such connections were limited; neither the spirit of liberty nor the contagion of revolution (depending upon one's attitude) was readily transferred across the Atlantic. Like most negative conclusions, this one is probably somewhat disappointing to reader and writer alike. Nevertheless, negative conclusions, no matter how unexciting, contribute to our knowledge. Beyond that, these men—around six thousand soldiers and nearly five hundred officers—and their units, in spite of some peculiar characteristics, constituted a reasonably representative sample of the entire French army during the most

INTRODUCTION

radical transformation in its history; studying them in detail affords insights into the larger institution of which they formed a microcosm. Perhaps most important, the story of these soldiers suggests how great events in history affect and are affected by ordinary people.

To elucidate this last point and, it is hoped, clarify the processes involved, this study will deal with events on two levels: analyses of general situations, particularly political and military developments, and descriptions of what these circumstances meant to the soldiers and officers responsible for implementing decisions. Despite the obvious and often drastic differences between these two levels, it must be continually borne in mind that both were equally part of the historical reality. The personal conduct of Sergeant Nicolas Tribout at Yorktown and of Lieutenant Colonel Gabriel de Queyssat at Valmy cannot be disassociated from those crucial military victories and their momentous political ramifications.

Notes

1. Information on young Gogue comes from the regimental troop register, or *contrôle de troupe*, for the Soissonnais Infantry in the Archives de la Guerre (henceforth A.G.), 1 YC 966.
2. See André Lasseray, *Les Français sous les treize étoiles (1775–1783)* (Paris: Protat, 1935), vol. 2, pp. 379–385.
3. A.G., uncoded contrôle for the 6ᵉ Régiment d'Artillerie à pied, vol. 3 (26 Août 1811–1 Septembre 1813).
4. See A.G., 1 YC 869, 14 YC 144 and 145, and Classement général alphabétique, Officiers, carton 3797.

From Yorktown to Valmy

Part One

THE AMERICAN REVOLUTION
AND THE LAST WAR OF THE OLD REGIME

1
The Special Expedition

THE AMERICAN REVOLUTION had entered its sixth year and the Franco-American alliance its third when a French fleet carrying an expeditionary force of over five thousand men under the orders of Jean Baptiste Donatien de Vimeur, comte de Rochambeau, dropped anchor off Newport, Rhode Island, on July 11, 1780. Both the war and the alliance were going badly, and the success of both would depend heavily upon the performance of this small army, the only substantial force of foreign allies ever to serve on U.S. soil for an extended period.

Ironically, it was the decisive defeat suffered by France at the hands of England in the Seven Years' War that had furnished both the incentive and the opportunity for the French to renew their old struggle with the English during the American Revolution. Military and government leaders in France were eager to avenge this humiliation and to restore the balance of power that had been upset by the international predominance Britain enjoyed after 1763. Simultaneously, the conquest of Canada finally removed a long-standing threat to the British colonists in North America, making them much less dependent on military support from the mother country. Mounting tensions between the colonists and the home government during the 1760s and 1770s were followed with considerable interest in France.

When hostilities erupted in 1775, political, strategic, economic, and ideological considerations all ensured broad French sympathy for the American cause. A year after the fighting broke out, the French government began to send substantial military supplies to the rebels through a "private" merchant house, Roderique Hortalez and Company, established by Caron de Beaumarchais with 1 million *livres* from the king of France. Congress sent unofficial representatives, notably the charming Franklin, to encourage further assistance and cooperation. American ships were afforded safe haven in French ports, while France undertook a major naval buildup. Meanwhile, French agents visited the United States, and French officers—some with and some without royal approval—volunteered their services to the inexperienced American army, where they encountered receptions as mixed as the various motives that had brought them to America.[1]

By the beginning of 1778, France was already deeply involved—albeit unofficially—in the American Revolution. At the same time, French preparations for war were complete; the battle of Saratoga in October 1777 had not only encouraged expectations of an ultimate American victory but had also increased the possibilities for a British compromise, contrary to French interests. Consequently, Louis XVI formalized the existing cooperation and intensified the French commitment by signing Treaties of Amity and Commerce and of Alliance with the United States of America on February 6, 1778. The following month Anglo-French relations were officially broken. The American rebellion became a global war, and the French monarchy entered the last phase of its ancient rivalry with England.

The early results of the new alliance, which was enthusiastically received on both sides of the Atlantic, were disappointing, and the resulting frustrations led to mutual recriminations. The first American appearance of the French force came with an expedition of a dozen ships of the line and nearly four thousand troops under the command of Charles Hector, comte d'Estaing, which arrived off Delaware and proceeded to New York in July 1778. Unable to advance because of the deep draft of his vessels, d'Estaing went off to attack the British garrison at Newport, Rhode Island. After muddled attempts at coordination with local American forces under General John Sullivan, d'Estaing began to disembark his troops on August 9. The sudden arrival of a British fleet, however, led the French commander to reembark the men and hastily put to sea. A summer storm scattered the opposing fleets, and when d'Estaing returned to the Rhode Island coast, it was simply to announce that he had been forced to put into Boston for extensive repairs to his ships. Sullivan was incensed and publicly complained of having been betrayed by the French. These irresponsible accusations perhaps contributed to a dockside brawl between Frenchmen and Americans that resulted in the death of a French officer. Official visits and informal apologies were exchanged, and the authorities managed to hush attempts to publicize the incident; when d'Estaing's fleet departed from Boston harbor for the West Indies in early November, however, the only results for the alliance were frustration and bitterness.[2]

After some success in the Caribbean against the islands of Saint Vincent and Grenada, d'Estaing returned to North America in early autumn of 1779. This time his objective was Savannah, Georgia, held by a British force of twelve hundred men under General Augustin Prevost. After landing most of his four thousand troops south of the city and effecting a junction with General Benjamin Lincoln's Americans, d'Estaing summoned the English to surrender on September 16. The British commander requested a truce, and with typical eighteenth-century noblesse oblige d'Estaing granted it—during which around eight hundred reinforcements arrived to bolster the British defenses. When the truce expired and the garrison refused to accept terms, d'Estaing opened the siege and on October 9 launched a massive attack on the town. Despite very heavy losses (d'Estaing himself was wounded twice), the allies were unable to take the enemy positions. During the last week of October the French broke camp, boarded their ships, and once more sailed away.

As after the Newport affair the previous year, a residue of resentment remained following the French departure. Over twenty months had passed since the signing of the treaties, and although the presence of French forces in American waters had created considerable consternation among the British, the only direct results of the military alliance had been worse than negligible: They had further discouraged a people who were approaching exhaustion after four and a half years of inconclusive warfare.[3]

In their conception—and consequently their strategy—of the war against Britain, French and American authorities had entirely different approaches. In contrast to the Americans, the French did not conceive of this conflict as a war waged solely for U.S. independence; for them, the stakes involved the balance of power in Europe and in the European-dominated world. As far as Americans were concerned, the struggle was confined to North America. For the French, the scene of operations stretched from India—where Pierre André, bailli de Suffren, won some of the most impressive victories of the war near the end of hostilities—to Africa, where a French expedition succeeded in recovering Senegal from the English in late January 1779; from the Caribbean, the most crucial region for French interests at that period, to Nova Scotia, which throughout the war remained a potential area for French operations; and from North America, where the French hoped to alternate the employment of West Indian garrisons during appropriate seasons (as in the case of d'Estaing's expeditions), to Europe, where a cross-channel operation against England continued to attract continental strategists.

5

The last of the Old Regime's projects for an invasion of Britain (anticipating Napoleon's plans by a quarter of a century) was a Franco-Spanish project that antedated Spain's entry into the war against England in July 1779. Typically, the extensive preparations for this attack were frustrated by Spanish slowness, disease, and weather. As a result, the entire operation was called off indefinitely in fall of 1779. Before this decision was made, a sizable French army had been assembled in Normandy and Brittany, the advance guard of which was under the orders of the comte de Rochambeau.[4]

Even before the British project had been canceled, the French government was receiving proposals to dispatch an expeditionary corps to serve in North America for an extended period. Marie Joseph Paul Yves Roch Gilbert du Motier, marquis de Lafayette, who was in France on leave from the American army and who entertained ambitions to lead such a corps, submitted a memoir urging this course of action to Foreign Minister Charles Gravier, comte de Vergennes, in mid-July 1779. The king agreed to the plan in February 1780 but considered Lafayette too young and inexperienced for the command. Instead, Lafayette returned to the United States to inform the American authorities and make preparations to receive the French army, and the comte de Rochambeau—who was fifty-five years old and had combat experience dating back to 1742—was promoted to lieutenant general and appointed commander of the *expédition particulière* at the beginning of March 1780.[5]

There followed the massive task of assembling troops, transports, and supplies for the transatlantic crossing that would originate from the port of Brest.[6] The selection of the troops was not difficult since Rochambeau had his pick from the thirty-two thousand men who had been assembled for the aborted English invasion. A real problem arose, however, over the number of troops to be included. Rochambeau, who at first had been allotted only four thousand men, convinced Louis XVI to increase his command to approximately seventy-five hundred. Vessels—both transports and fighting ships—were collected, outfitted, manned, loaded, and made ready for sea. Food, clothing, equipment, weapons, ammunition, and horses were sent to Brest and stowed on the waiting ships. Throughout these preparations Rochambeau had to contend with shortages, bad weather, slow transportation, and bureaucratic red tape. Nevertheless, progress was slowly made.

Rochambeau originally selected six infantry regiments (the Regiments of Neustrie, Bourbonnais, Soissonnais, Anhalt, Saintonge, and Royal Deux-Ponts), Lauzun's Legion (a mixed unit consisting of hussars, infantrymen, and cannoneers), and one of the two battalions of the Regiment of Auxonne Artillery to form his little army. Insufficient transports, however, necessitated leaving behind the Regiments of Neustrie and Anhalt, along with three hundred of the nine hundred men of Lauzun's Legion and about one hundred artillerymen from the Auxonne battalion. These twenty-five hundred soldiers were intended to form a "second division" that would follow the main force to America at some indefinite time; in fact, these units would never leave France. In addition, Rochambeau had to restrict each infantry regiment to one thousand men, "chosen among the most robust"; the remainder would stay in France under a handful of officers and noncommissioned officers (NCOs) to enlist and train recruits. The total enlisted strength of the corps, then, was slightly more than five thousand men, selected primarily on the basis of their readiness for combat. One other consideration also played a role in the selection: Royal Deux-Ponts was a German regiment in the service of France, and Lauzun's Legion included a significant minority (one-fifth of the total strength) of German soldiers, since both units were expected to be able to enlist foreign recruits—particularly German deserters from the British army—in America.

In all, the soldiers of Rochambeau's command constituted a fairly typical cross-section of the French regular army toward the end of the Old Regime.[7] None had volunteered to fight for American independence; indeed, they were at sea for seven weeks before being informed of their destination. Although the troops greeted this announcement with loud cheering, the response was one of relief that they were *not* bound for the West Indies, whose inhospitable climate had been deadly to tens of thousands of their comrades, rather than of enthusiasm for the American cause.[8]

Although the expedition included a slightly high proportion of foreigners, the regional background of the French troops reflected the composition of the entire army: a large percentage (around 40 percent) from the frontier areas of northern and eastern France and comparatively few from the southern (about one-eighth of the total) and western (less than 10 percent) provinces. Likewise, the proportion of Rochambeau's soldiers from cities and towns was basically the same as that in the army as a whole, approximately one-third; and a significantly larger percentage of the sergeants (over 40 percent) came from urban areas, where literacy—required for their administrative duties—was higher. The social origins of Rochambeau's enlisted men, like those of most of the line troops, were rooted in the popular classes—rural and urban workers, peasants, artisans, small shopkeepers, and members of the petit-bourgeoisie—yet virtually every group in society was represented, from migrant laborers to nobles (who were officially prohibited from serving in the ranks).[9] An example of the latter was Louis d'Aigrefeuil, a twenty-eight-year-old native of Martinique who enlisted as a private in the grenadier company of Lauzun's Legion the month after its arrival in America and was discharged "as a gentleman" on October 31, 1780.[10]

There was also a wide range in the soldiers' ages. The oldest enlisted man in the expeditionary corps was Jacques Feyolard, a sixty-one-year-old sergeant major in the Bourbonnais Infantry; the youngest member was Jean Baptiste Leroy, coincidentally in the same regiment, who was only four years old.[11] The latter was one of the *enfants de troupe,* sons of members of the regiment who were enrolled as children at half pay and who would normally serve as drummer-boys until they enlisted as ordinary soldiers for full pay at age sixteen; customarily, there were about a half-dozen such enfants in each regiment. Since marriage was officially discouraged, only a handful of soldiers' wives accompanied the troops; like their sons, they usually performed some service for the military, particularly as laundresses and sutlers.[12]

Most of the army, however, consisted of young, single men, over half of whom were between ages eighteen and twenty-five and less than one-fourth of whom were older than thirty. In fact, as a group they were slightly younger than their counterparts in the army as a whole—almost certainly the result of the selection process before embarkation. Closely related to their age was their length of service, which was generally shorter than the army average, although about three hundred and fifty men had served for twenty years or more and fewer than one soldier in ten had been in the army less than a year.[13]

Like the men whom they commanded, the officers under Rochambeau's orders accurately reflected the general composition of the French officer corps of which they formed a portion, despite certain peculiarities. Most of these four hundred or so officers participated in this mission simply because they happened to be members of the units selected to go to America, although some staff officers had used their influence to get their appointments and others would later travel across the Atlantic independently to join Rochambeau's corps.[14] Nearly nine out of ten were aristocrats; the length of their noble genealogies, however, varied from as recently as the previous decade (as in the case of Pierre-Charles Tuffet de Saint-Martin, a lieutenant en second in the Auxonne Artillery) to more than eight centuries earlier (the marquis de Montmorency-Laval, commanding colonel of the Bourbonnais Infantry, who dated his family's nobility to 955).[15]

More than the longevity of their noble lineage differentiated some aristocratic officers from others, thereby disrupting the apparent homogeneity of the officer corps. Most important was the distinction between court and provincial nobility: Since 1760, only those aristocrats who had been formally presented at court could expect to achieve the rank of colonel and above.¹⁶ Rochambeau's officers exhibited the same stratification that existed generally in the Royal Army.¹⁷

Whereas a few young scions of the upper aristocracy dashed through the various grades of lieutenant (sous-lieutenant, lieutenant en second, lieutenant en premier) and captain (capitaine en second, capitaine commandant), most country nobles spent their entire careers in those ranks, although a handful became majors or lieutenant colonels toward the end of their military service. In contrast, colonels, who might number as many as three per regiment (proprietary, commanding, and colonel in second), were normally young court aristocrats on their way to becoming general officers.

A brief statistical profile of Rochambeau's officers, mirroring the general situation in the army, might elucidate these circumstances. Among all lieutenants in the line regiments of the expedition, the average age was slightly over twenty-eight and the average length of service nearly eleven years. Captains averaged thirty-eight years of age and twenty years of service. Majors were, on average, forty-three years old and lieutenant colonels between forty-four and forty-five, with twenty and twenty-seven years of military experience, respectively. Colonels commanding regiments, however, had an average age of between thirty-two and thirty-three, with over eighteen years of service. Colonels in second were only twenty-five years old and had spent nine and a half years in the army. The comparatively youthful age and lengthy service of colonels were the result of the custom of commissioning court nobles while still boys and assigning them to the entourage of a senior officer, frequently a relative or a family connection. Although a somewhat extreme example, the career of the comte de Custine typifies this practice. Adam Philippe de Custine became a lieutenant in 1747, four months after his fifth birthday; he fought in his first campaign the following year. A captain before he was twenty, he became a colonel in the Custine Dragoons two years later. In March 1780 he was named to command the Saintonge Infantry and promoted to brigadier general.

Staff assignments expedited the advancement of court aristocrats. The captains on Rochambeau's general staff were, on average, more than a dozen years younger than captains in the line regiments, and over half would become colonels by 1789. Although experienced professionals, like Colonel François Marie d'Aboville of Artillery and Colonel Jean Nicolas Desandrouins of Engineers (both in their early fifties), provided necessary expertise on Rochambeau's staff, it is difficult to determine what Colonel Jacques Anne de Vauban, age twenty-six, and Colonel Jacques Boson de Talleyrand-Périgord, eighteen years old, contributed beyond their illustrious family names. Similarly, one is hard put to explain the appointment of

Lieutenant Charles Gabriel du Houx de Vioménil (at thirteen the youngest officer in Rochambeau's command) except that he was the son and nephew of two major generals on the staff.

The service of young Vioménil in the same unit as his father and uncle was by no means an unusual phenomenon. Three brothers from the Irish-French family of Dillon, Lieutenant François Théobald (called Frank), Captain Guillaume Henri (known as Billy), and Colonel in Second Robert Guillaume, were members of Lauzun's Legion. Rochambeau's son, Donatien Marie Joseph de Vimeur, vicomte de Rochambeau, served under his father as second colonel of the Bourbonnais infantry and later of the Saintonge Infantry. This practice was more than a form of institutionalized nepotism and was by no means restricted to the upper aristocracy. Georges Balthazar Edme Chandron de La Valette was a lieutenant in the Saintonge Infantry of which his uncle, Charles François, was lieutenant colonel. Lieutenant Bessonies de Neuville of the Soissonnais Infantry, who succumbed to smallpox at Yorktown in 1782, was the fifth brother of Charles Marie Martial Bessonies de Saint-Hilaire, also a lieutenant in the same regiment, to have died "in the service of the King."

For the lower nobility, military service—even with its limited opportunities for advancement—was their ancient heritage and often the only suitable career available. Lieutenant Gabriel François de Silly, the elder of two brothers in the Regiment of Bourbonnais, exemplifies the situation of many provincial nobles. In 1786 he applied for a royal pension, noting that the recent death of his father, an army officer with over forty-five years of service, had left him and his three brothers (two in the Regiment of Béarn) "with no fortune" and two sisters to support.[18] Officers from different levels of the aristocracy naturally gravitated to the same units as their kinsmen, even though this gave provincial nobles no ostensible advantage.

Clearly, whereas noble officers shared many common characteristics and interests, there were also important distinctions among them. The differences among officers, however, paled in comparison to the gulf that separated officers and men. For example, nearly twice as many of Rochambeau's officers than his men came from an urban environment. Less than half as many officers as soldiers were natives of the northern and eastern frontier provinces, but nearly twice as many officers were southerners. The importance of such differences is impossible to evaluate precisely; nevertheless, in an era when society was extremely localized, when one referred to one's native region or province as one's "country" (*pays*), and when traditions, customs, dress, eating habits, and even language varied substantially from one area to another, they certainly increased the distance between officers and soldiers.

SPECIAL EXPEDITION

Social distinctions were more fundamental. In practice, few commoners could aspire to be commissioned as officers, and in May 1781, while Rochambeau's army was stationed in America, this practice was formalized in the Ségur decree, which required four generations of nobility for a direct commission as an officer. Despite a few very limited exceptions, this legislation effectively prohibited nonnobles and the recently ennobled from receiving direct commissions and firmly established a caste system within the military hierarchy.[19] Army routine reinforced the separation of officers from soldiers. Officers were quartered apart from their men, usually in private homes; they had separate meals and entertainment; whenever possible, they traveled by themselves. Few officers, usually the most junior in rank, personally conducted the drill and training of the soldiers in their unit. Whereas only a small number of soldiers could go on leave during their enlistment (most commonly, eight years), officers were entitled to frequent and extensive leaves.[20]

The one possible bridge between officers and men consisted of the "officers of fortune," the only substantial group expressly excluded from the provisions of the Ségur decree.[21] These were men commissioned from the ranks, usually senior NCOs in their early forties with one to two decades of military service. Most were from the better-off popular classes (artisans, craftsmen, shopkeepers) or the lower middle class (small merchants, the liberal professions), although a few were unskilled laborers or poor peasants and even an occasional petty noble. Almost all were comfortably literate. Normally, they were in charge of routine administration; indeed, the chief administrative officer in the regiment, the quartermaster treasurer, was invariably an officer of fortune. They were also primarily responsible for the onerous duties of drill and discipline. Few were promoted beyond first lieutenant, and virtually none were accepted as genuine equals by their fellow officers. Officers of fortune constituted about one-tenth of the French officer corps, although Rochambeau's forces contained a slightly higher proportion.

Such, in sum, was the small army of the comte de Rochambeau, around fifty-five hundred officers and men in all, that embarked from Brest between April 4, when the first elements of the Regiment of Royal Deux-Ponts began to board ship, and April 17, 1780, when the commander established his headquarters aboard the *Duc de Bourgogne*. On the whole, they formed a fit but otherwise unremarkable contingent of the French army of the period. Each unit of the expedition left behind in France a regimental depot, including between three and six officers—usually among the oldest (mostly officers of fortune) and youngest (cadets recently assigned to the unit) officers—to recruit and train reinforcements for the regiment during its overseas assignment.[22] Nearly left behind also was Colonel Dillon of Lauzun's Legion. The comte de Dillon, who had participated in the French reconquest of Senegal the previous year, had become involved in an "affair of honor" at Nantes, in the course of which he received two sword wounds. When Dillon finally arrived at Brest on April 20, Rochambeau wisely confined him to his assigned ship under arrest "to care for his wounds and punish him for his mistake."[23] Archaic noble traditions still survived.

On May 2, 1780, Rochambeau's corps finally sailed from Brest. The Atlantic crossing was not unusual by eighteenth-century standards; by twentieth-century criteria it was terrible.[24] Even before departing from France, some regiments began to report large numbers of men incapacitated by illness. After only a few days at sea, one soldier noted that some of his comrades "wished that they had never in their lives become soldiers and cursed their first recruiter. This was only the beginning—the really miserable life was only beginning." Drinking water soon became so unpalatable that one had to hold one's nose while swallowing it; adding wine simply postponed the transition to straight wine. The staple food consisted of unappetizing hardtack and heavily salted meat. Vermin, especially lice and fleas, abounded. In addition to seasickness, disease—particularly scurvy—became rampant; within a month ships were counting their sick by the scores, within two months by the hundreds. By the time the convoy reached Rhode Island, more than thirty soldiers had died, only one of whom was killed in action during a minor skirmish with some British ships on June 20. What is perhaps most horrifying about the accounts of this suffering is the pervading sense that much of it was accepted as normal for such an undertaking.

On the morning of July 11, following a voyage of exactly ten weeks, the French convoy anchored off Newport. In one respect, Rochambeau's expedition was nothing more than the latest episode in France's long colonial struggle with England; over the previous century many thousands of French troops had undertaken comparable missions against the same foe. In retrospect, however, these men were about to become directly involved in some of the most remarkable developments of that, or any other, age.

Notes

1. The background of French intervention is discussed in many sources; most useful here were Claude H. Van Tyne, "Influences Which Determined the French Government to Make the Treaty With America, 1778," *American Historical*

Review 21 (1916): 528–541, and "French Aid Before the Alliance of 1778," American Historical Review 31 (1925): 20–40; Jonathan R. Dull, The French Navy and American Independence: A Study of Arms and Diplomacy, 1774–1787 (Princeton: Princeton University Press, 1975), pp. 27–81; Edward S. Corwin, "The French Objective in the American Revolution," American Historical Review 21 (1915): 33–61; Neil L. York, "Clandestine Aid and the American Revolutionary War Effort: A Re-Examination," Military Affairs 43 (1979): 26–30; and Durand Echeverria, Mirage in the West: A History of the French Image of American Society to 1815 (Princeton: Princeton University Press, 1957), pp. 36–81.

2. Paul F. Deardon, "The Siege of Newport: Inauspicious Dawn of Alliance," Rhode Island History 29 (1970): 17–35; and Fitz-Henry Smith Jr., "The French at Boston During the Revolution, With Particular Reference to the French Fleets and the Fortifications in the Harbor," Bostonian Society Publications 10 (1913): 9–75. A British view of this episode can be found in Frederick Mackenzie, Diary of Frederick Mackenzie, Giving a Daily Narrative of His Military Service as an Officer of the Regiment of Royal Welch Fusiliers During the Years 1775–1781 in Massachusetts, Rhode Island and New York (Cambridge, Mass.: Harvard University Press, 1930), vol. 1, pp. 268, 283–285, and 315–405.

3. Alexander A. Lawrence, Storm Over Savannah: The Story of Count d'Estaing and the Siege of the Town in 1779 (Athens: University of Georgia Press, 1951); and Charles C. Jones Jr., ed., The Siege of Savannah in 1779, As Described in Two Contemporaneous Journals of French Officers in the Fleet of Count D'Estaing (Albany: Joel Munsell, 1874).

4. More detail on this operation is provided by Alfred Temple Patterson, The Other Armada: The Franco-Spanish Attempt to Invade Britain in 1779 (Manchester: University of Manchester Press, 1960); and C. R. Fonteneau, "La Normandie et la Manche pendant la guerre de l'indépendance américaine," Revue internationale d'histoire militaire 41 (1979): 131–140.

5. James Breck Perkins, France in the American Revolution (Boston: Houghton Mifflin, 1911), pp. 290–297; and Claude Manceron, Les hommes de la Liberté, vol. 2: Le Vent d'Amérique: L'Echec de Necker et la Victoire de Yorktown, 1778–1782 (Paris: Robert Laffont, 1974), p. 239.

6. To best appreciate the immense efforts involved in preparing this transatlantic expedition, one should read Rochambeau's correspondence, which is preserved in the Library of Congress, Manuscript Division, The Papers of Jean Baptiste Donatien de Vimeur, Comte de Rochambeau, 1777–1794 (henceforth Rochambeau Papers), in fifteen volumes; vol. 2, pp. 36–37, 44–49, 66–72, 81, 87; vol. 7, pp. 9–18, 27; and vol. 8, pp. 2–3, provided the information in the following two paragraphs.

7. Data on the soldiers and noncommissioned officers of Rochambeau's corps are based on a quantitative analysis of all the enlisted men in the force, whose records appear in the following regimental contrôles: A.G., 1 YC 188 (Bourbonnais), 1 YC 966 (Soissonais), 1 YC 932 (Saintonge), 1 YC 869 (Royal Deux-Ponts), and 10 YC 1 (Auxonne). Similar information on the men of Lauzun's Legion is in Archives Nationales (henceforth A.N.), D^2 C 32. Comparable data for the French army as a whole in the 1780s are drawn from my

dissertation, "The French Revolution and the Line Army, 1787–1793" (University of Wisconsin, 1968), pp. 136, 144, 163–164, 185.
8. Jean Jacques Fiechter, "L'Aventure américaine des officiers de Rochambeau vue à travers leurs journaux," in Michèle R. Morris, ed., *Images of America in Revolutionary France* (Washington, D.C.: Georgetown University Press, 1990), pp. 67–68.
9. The occupations of these men were not listed in the contrôles but can be found, in collective form, in later inspection reports in A.G., X^b 25, 53, 104 and X^c 83, which have been compared with similar reports for the army as a whole, cited in my book *The Response of the Royal Army to the French Revolution: The Role and Development of the Line Army, 1787–1793* (Oxford: Clarendon, 1978), p. 7n.
10. A.N., D^2 C 32.
11. For Feyolard and Leroy, see A.G., 1 YC 188.
12. For a general discussion of *enfants* and soldiers' wives, see André Corvisier, *L'Armeé française de la fin du XVIIe siècle au ministère de Choiseul: Le Soldat* (Paris: Presses Universitaires de France, 1964), vol. 2, pp. 757–771. For the number of women accompanying Rochambeau's corps, see Evelyn M. Acomb, ed. and trans., *The Revolutionary Journal of Baron Ludwig von Closen, 1780–1783* (Chapel Hill: University of North Carolina Press, 1958), p. 85n.
13. Besides the obvious correlation between age and military experience, another factor that decreased the soldiers' average length of service was the fact that Lauzun's Legion was a new unit, formed only in 1778.
14. Gilbert Bodinier's work on French officers in the American and French Revolutions provides the most comprehensive biographical material available; on this point, see his "Les officiers du corps expéditionnaire de Rochambeau et la Révolution française," *Revue Historique des Armées* 3 (1976): 142. One example of an officer who went to America on his own is Louis Alexandre Berthier, later Napoleon's chief of staff, who sailed to the United States by way of Martinique, arriving to join Rochambeau's staff at Newport two and a half months after the main party; see Howard C. Rice Jr. and Anne S.K. Brown, eds. and trans., *The American Campaigns of Rochambeau's Army, 1780, 1781, 1782, 1783* (Princeton and Providence: Princeton University Press and Brown University Press, 1972), vol. 1, pp. 222–225.
15. This and the following information on Rochambeau's officers in America has been extracted from Gilbert Bodinier, *Dictionnaire des officiers de l'armée royale qui ont combattu aux Etats-Unis pendant la guerre d'Indépendance, 1776–1783, suivi d'un Supplément à Les Français sous les treize étoiles du commandant André Lasseray* (Vincennes: Service Historique de l'Armée de Terre, 1982), unless otherwise indicated.
16. Arthur Chuquet, "Roture et noblesse dans l'armée royale," *Séances et travaux de l'Académie des sciences morales et politiques* 175 (1911): 237.
17. The general condition of the French officer corps in the 1780s, which serves as the basis for comparison with Rochambeau's officers, is described in Scott, *Response of the Royal Army*, pp. 19–26, 190–206.
18. Besides Bodinier's *Dictionnaire*, see A.G., X^b 25, 53, 91, and 104 for requests for gratifications and pensions, which tell a good deal about the families and financial situations of many officers like Bessonies and Silly.

19. See Georges Six, "Fallait-il quatre quartiers de noblesse pour être officier à la fin de l'ancien régime," *Revue d'histoire moderne* 4 (1929): 47–56; André Corvisier, "Hiérarchie militaire et hiérarchie sociale à la veille de la Révolution," *Revue internationale d'histoire militaire* 30 (1970): 86; and David D. Bien, "La Réaction aristocratique avant 1789: l'exemple de l'armée," *Annales, Economie, Société, Civilisations* 29 (1974): 36–41, 515–530.
20. For further information on army life in the 1780s, see Scott, *Response of the Royal Army*, pp. 32–45.
21. The best available treatment of this topic is Charles John Wrong, "The Officiers de Fortune in the French Infantry," *French Historical Studies* 9 (1976): 400–431, which provides the basis for the following discussion.
22. Details on the officers who remained in France (the only group about which Bodinier is mistaken) can be found in A.G., X^b 53, 91, 104; X^c 83; and X^d 24.
23. Rochambeau Papers, vol. 7, pp. 48–49.
24. Firsthand accounts of the voyage can be found in ibid., pp. 49–50, 64–66; Claude Blanchard, *The Journal of Claude Blanchard, Commissary of the French Auxiliary Army Sent to the United States During the American Revolution, 1780–1783*, trans. William Duane (Albany: J. Munsell, 1876; reprint New York: New York Times and Arno Press, 1969), pp. 15–33; Gilbert Chinard, ed., "Journal de Guerre de Brisout de Barneville, Mai 1780–Octobre 1781," *French American Review* 3 (1950): 229–238; Warrington Dawson, ed., "With Rochambeau at Newport: The Narrative of Baron Gaspard de Gallatin," *Franco-American Review* 1 (1936–1937): 328. The quotation is from an unpublished paper, "The American Campaigns of Georg Daniel Flohr, Fusilier, Regiment Royal-Deux-Ponts, 1780–1784," generously provided by Robert A. Selig who is editing Flohr's journal, a remarkable source for Rochambeau's American expedition.

2
EARLY EXPERIENCES IN RHODE ISLAND

IN SPITE OF PREPARATIONS to receive Rochambeau's forces in America, the arrival of the French was less than auspicious. Lafayette had returned to the United States in late April 1780 to inform Washington of Rochambeau's coming and to help get things ready for his army; with him had come Dominique Louis Ethis de Corny, a commissary charged with procuring supplies and provisions. Corny was to arrange for quarters, food, forage, bedding, firewood, horses for riding and hauling, wagons, and other necessities and—in anticipation of the effects of the ocean voyage—to provide hospital facilities.[1] One building Corny selected for this purpose belonged to the College of Rhode Island (now Brown University) in Providence. The college authorities, however, were opposed to the plan, and the citizens of Providence formally protested against it as a threat to public health, suggesting that tents would serve as well. Ultimately, it took an order from the Rhode Island Council of War to put the edifice at Corny's disposal.[2]

Rochambeau's personal introduction to the United States was no happier. After anchoring in Newport harbor on July 11, he had gone ashore to find "not a person in the streets, gloomy and dismayed looks from the windows." Shortly afterward, when French officers were observed publicly socializing with English officers who had been captured during the voyage, local inhabitants were outraged and local officials protested that these mutual enemies should be put away in cells on the French ships; similar resentments would reappear later in Franco-American relations.[3]

Yet, there were some encouraging signs of cooperation. Governor William Greene gave Corny his full support and assistance. General Washington sent Dr. James Craik, his assistant director-general of hospitals, and recalled General William Heath from leave in Massachusetts to aid in the preparations for the French.[4] Conforming to a resolution passed by Congress on May 27, 1780, the General Assembly of Rhode Island declared that anyone encouraging desertion or harboring a deserter from the armed forces of an ally of the United States would be subject to the same penalties as those encouraging or harboring an American deserter. At the same session, the assembly appointed inspectors to supervise markets in Newport, Providence, Bristol, and Warren to ensure that French purchasers would not be overcharged or cheated.[5]

These early experiences typify the bittersweet relations between Americans and the French throughout the sojourn of Rochambeau's army in the United States. Often, the primary impetus for unity between the allies was simply the threat from their common enemy. Such a threat appeared within ten days after Rochambeau had landed at Newport: An English fleet of twenty-two ships under Admiral Marriot Arbuthnot was sighted off the coast, where it soon established a blockade of the seaport.

The appearance of the English compounded Rochambeau's already formidable problems. To begin with, he had to check the sites where his forces would be lodged, hospitals for the sick, and encampments for the healthy. Then came the disembarkation, which began with the elite companies of grenadiers and chasseurs from his infantry regiments on July 13 and continued for three days until all able-bodied troops were landed. On July 16–19 the sick were taken ashore. Meanwhile, these thousands of men had to be nourished, especially with fresh water, vegetables, and fruit, to halt the ravages of scurvy. Illness was reaching alarming proportions: Around seven hundred soldiers were incapacitated, and between their arrival at Newport on July 11 and the completion of disembarkation eight days later an additional thirteen men had died.[6] Hospitals were set up not only at Providence but also at Newport and Poppasquash.[7] Simultaneously, the French commander had to oversee the establishment of defensive positions around Newport, which the British had evacuated the previous October when d'Estaing's expedition had posed a threat to all British posts along the coast. Beyond that, the *Isle de France*, carrying three hundred and fifty men of the Regiment of Bourbonnais (one hundred of whom were on the sick list) had been separated from the convoy and forced to put into Boston, and the French artillery had yet to be unloaded.[8] The presence of enemy ships, carrying more troops than Rochambeau could muster, jeopardized the expedition at its inception.

EARLY EXPERIENCES IN RHODE ISLAND

Frantic measures by the allies and indecision on the part of the English avoided potential disaster. The French troops quickly dug entrenchments and landed their cannon, and the French fleet under Admiral Charles Louis d'Arsac de Ternay prepared for combat. Local militia from Rhode Island and nearby Massachusetts were called up and put under General Heath's command to reinforce the French, although Rochambeau soon sent more than half of them home "to gather their harvest" while retaining two thousand of the best fit and equipped to assist in the defense. Meanwhile, Washington made a feint against New York that created concern for the security of the major English base in North America. On the other side, Arbuthnot overestimated the allies' strength, delayed taking any action, and failed to coordinate plans with the British commander at New York, Sir Henry Clinton.[9] By early August the French positions were strong enough to resist attack, and the British opportunity was lost.

In the midst of this crisis, Washington's emissary, Lafayette, had arrived at Newport on July 24. The defenders' frenzied activity prevented him from discussing any general strategy with Rochambeau for four days. On July 28, however, he advanced a plan he had been advocating since May, a plan that would remain Washington's pet project for ending the war until the Yorktown campaign the following year: a joint attack on New York at the earliest possible moment. Rochambeau, an experienced and cautious commander in a precarious and unclear situation who had begun his military career fifteen years before Lafayette was born, responded to the brash young general kindly but firmly. He pointed out that his force had hundreds of men hospitalized, that he was in serious need of additional supplies, that the general military situation in America was worse than he had expected, and that a military setback under these conditions might be irretrievable. His dispatch to the chevalier de La Luzerne, the French minister to the United States, in early August tersely summarized his evaluation of the situation: "We cannot afford a repeat of the Savannah episode" (*il ne faut pas faire ici des affaires de Savannah*).[10]

As their leaders debated strategy, the French troops performed mundane but essential tasks. The soldiers had to pitch tents and make camp southeast of Newport. Rochambeau's staff and senior regimental officers, above the rank of captain, had to be assigned lodgings in privately owned houses in Newport.[11] The French had to purchase, transport, and distribute food, firewood, straw, and other necessities on a regular basis. Great effort went into the construction and improvement of defensive works, necessary not only for strategic purposes but to provide self-protection. French soldiers had to dig trenches and shore them up with timber, build earthworks reinforced with fascines, and haul the necessary materials, tools, and men to where they were to be used. Guard details had to be posted around the camp, at headquarters, in outposts, at magazines, and elsewhere. These arduous duties were made more difficult by the summer heat, which the French found excessive; to deal with this problem, on July 27 Rochambeau ordered that reveille would be at four A.M. and that work would be suspended from 10:00 A.M. to 2:30 P.M. More routine military activities, such as drill and inspections, were resumed.[12]

Meanwhile, the grisly effects of the voyage continued after disembarkation: Eighteen soldiers died between July 20 and 31 and 66 more in August; the death toll reached its peak in September when 70 men perished; and although the mortality rate declined thereafter, losses continued through the end of the year, reaching the appalling total of 265 deaths from natural causes between May and December. These grim statistics, symptomatic of colonial warfare in the eighteenth century, tend to mask individual, personal tragedies. A few examples among the many possible suggest the human reality behind the cold figures. Nineteen-year-old François Denis Regneauld, who had enlisted in the Auxonne Artillery the month before his unit sailed from Brest, "died in America at the hospital of Newport" five weeks after landing, an abrupt end to a short career and a short life. Dominique Verette, a native of Saint Léonard in Normandy and the same age as Regneauld, also died at Newport on December 11, 1780, only twelve days after his older brother, twenty-three-year-old François, who had enlisted with him on the same day in the same company of the Saintonge Infantry.[13]

Disease, heat, and demanding duties were not the only problems with which the French had to contend in America. Most Americans held ingrained anti-French sentiments, bred by generations of Anglo-French hostility and fed by periodic armed conflict; the recent alliance could not hope to alter those opinions substantially in a few months or even years. Religious differences had long fostered suspicion and antagonism, and the Loyalist press frequently warned of "Papist" intentions to supplant native Protestantism with an alien Catholicism.[14] To avoid giving offense, Rochambeau severely restricted public religious ceremonies and forbade all of his corps from entering Protestant churches during services, even going so far as to post special sentries on Sundays to prevent any incidents.[15] Often tied to the religious issue was the preconception that the French were the slaves of a despotic prince, bent on destroying the traditional political freedoms enjoyed by Americans. For those whose prejudices took a less general, more personal form, there was a host of other perceptions: Frenchmen were often physically deformed, they were sissified dandies, their tastes in dress and food were disgusting, they had no sense of morality.[16]

Official relations, emphasizing mutual confidence and cordiality, ignored such popular attitudes. Local authorities in Rhode Island quickly made amends for the cold reception Rochambeau had originally met; within forty-eight hours they extended a formal welcome to the French and ordered the illumination of Newport in their honor. General Heath paid his respects and exchanged dinners with the French leaders. The General Assembly congratulated Rochambeau and Ternay on their safe arrival and guaranteed them full support; Rochambeau replied in kind, saying his troops would "live as brothers, in the best discipline" with their "faithful allies."[17] Patriot journalists and clergy, especially dissenters like Dr. Samuel Cooper, used their influence to foster warm relations between the allies, praising the excellent qualities of the French and muting differences between them; a number were well rewarded by the French government.[18]

The dichotomy between popular suspicion and official confidence persisted during the entire U.S. stay of Rochambeau's army. Personal contacts, however, would change individual opinions and even modify—but seldom reverse—more general attitudes. Perhaps the most immediate and concrete fear of Americans was the danger French troops—or soldiers of any nationality, for that matter—posed to public order and morality. Interestingly, in no other area did the French prove American fears more groundless. Virtually all sources agree that the French displayed exemplary discipline; American public documents are unanimous on this point. French participants—including Dumas, Fersen, Lafayette, Montesquieu, and Robin—agree, and their accounts cannot be completely dismissed as self-serving.[19] Most impressive in this regard is the private correspondence of Americans who had no personal stake in the issue yet testify to the good conduct of the French.[20] For this performance Rochambeau deserves primary credit. On June 8, while still at sea, he issued a general order requiring that all observe "the most exact and severe discipline in all respects" and prohibiting anyone from taking so much as "a piece of wood, a bunch of straw, or any kind of vegetable except after mutually agreed upon payment." Transgressors would be punished to the full extent of military justice.[21] Within a week after arriving at Newport, Rochambeau proved that he intended to apply this order literally; he condemned a servant to twenty-five strokes of the cane for stealing a piece of cheese.[22]

Rochambeau was particularly sensitive to New Englanders' concern for private property. On July 30 he forbade the officers to hunt and threatened that anyone discovered hunting or on their way to hunt would be taken into custody, although this prohibition appears to have been in effect only during the harvest season since in November permission to hunt was "continued." Subsequent orders warned soldiers to respect fenced land, to refrain from using wood taken from American property, to keep to "beaten paths" and not cut across cultivated areas, and to stay out of all gardens and enclosures.[23] Such concern should have been especially appreciated after the depredations committed by the British during their occupation of Rhode Island when they confiscated livestock and destroyed houses, bridges, mills, military stores, and ships.[24]

Rochambeau's principal means of protecting his hosts was to isolate his soldiers from native inhabitants as much as possible. Sentinels guarded the French camp, and every member of the corps needed a pass to leave its confines. Soldiers could not go into town without being accompanied by a noncommissioned officer. Drinking was confined to the regimental sutlers' establishments; drinking elsewhere was punishable by "twenty-five blows with the flat of a saber."[25] The segregation of French enlisted men from local women seems to have been nearly complete; there is no record of treatment for venereal disease or of the birth of any children—legitimate or illegitimate—of French military personnel while the French were at Newport.[26]

These measures drastically curtailed friction between American civilians and French soldiers; they did not, however, totally eliminate incidents. In August 1780 a French corporal, Pierre Antoine Bonichon, killed an American; Bonichon was subsequently tried by French court-martial, condemned to death, and executed by a firing squad. Some months later an American was apprehended in connection with the shooting of a French sentinel. The details in both cases are vague, and neither affair was publicized, presumably because the authorities on both sides managed to hush them up.[27] Similarly, there are no records of litigation between French and Americans, perhaps because local courts refused to hear such cases.[28]

One aspect of the French presence in Newport that was very attractive to most citizens was the boost it gave to the local economy. The number of officers and men of Rochambeau's command was approximately the same as the population of the town, around fifty-five hundred, and they were all consumers. Furthermore, despite the destruction and disruption caused by the British occupation (December 1776–October 1779), Newport was still an important commercial center.[29] The French represented a very attractive market that local merchants did not hesitate to exploit. Within a few days of their arrival, newspapers in Newport and Providence began to encourage nearby farmers to furnish meat, poultry, milk, vegetables, hay, straw, cider, and other products to sell to the French and promised that they would "receive a generous Price, serve their Friends, and benefit themselves," although the hope was expressed that "no Person will be sordid as to demand extravagant Prices from our great and generous Allies, who have come so great a Distance to our Relief."[30] Business prospered—all the more so because the French paid in specie rather than with the rapidly depreciating American paper money.

This profitable trade was not without disadvantages, however. The French were offended by the cupidity of American merchants, a sentiment that would be frequently reinforced in future transactions.[31] Furthermore, U.S. suppliers were not always reliable or their goods always acceptable. Although the latter problem usually occurred because the goods were of inferior quality, occasionally the Americans were not at fault. An amusing example of this difficulty was the inability of French drivers to control the first horses provided in Rhode Island—apparently because the horses could not understand commands in French![32] More serious was the effect French purchases had on the American army. Within a few weeks after the French had landed at Newport, U.S. troops were having difficulty purchasing supplies because American merchants infinitely preferred the hard cash of the French to the nearly worthless paper of the Americans. Soon, U.S. units in the area were suffering shortages; even Lafayette complained that his forces lacked meat and suggested that French payments in specie were responsible for the situation.[33]

On the other hand, once the shock of the arrival of the French army had worn off and the hectic activities following the arrival had been completed, cordial social relations developed between the French and Americans. Differences in language presented difficulties but did not constitute an insurmountable barrier. By mid-November the French had set up a printing press and begun publication of the *Gazette françoise*, which appeared weekly until January 1781. Essentially, the paper was a digest of news translated from American newspapers, particularly the *Newport Mercury*, which also included a healthy dose of pro-American propaganda. The new paper helped to acquaint the French with their new environment.[34] The *Newport Mercury* also helped to foster closer relations by carrying advertisements in French, including some for English lessons and a French-English dictionary.[35] All of these efforts were aimed at the French officers; English lessons for the enlisted men were largely limited to practical matters, such as instructing sentinels to translate their challenge, "Qui vive" to "Ou is dair" (Who is there).[36]

A few soldiers such as Georg Daniel Flohr of the Royal Deux-Ponts attempted to learn English on their own to converse with some "beautiful

American maidens" near their encampment. Flohr was encouraged by his conviction that the men of his regiment "were particularly well liked by the girls since we were Germans, and they hold the German nation in very great esteem."[37] Two significant considerations emerge from Flohr's comments: First, the isolation from the civilian population imposed on Rochambeau's soldiers was never total; second, the Germans serving in the French forces enjoyed a somewhat different relationship with the Americans than did the native French troops.

In their personal contacts with inhabitants, officers were generally much less restricted than the soldiers. Announcements in the *Gazette françoise* (December 22, 1780) and *Newport Mercury* (June 16 and 23, 1781) invited them to attend the local Masonic lodge; some accepted.[38] Furthermore, the French officers who were lodged in American homes had almost daily contact with their hosts and hostesses. Many Frenchmen were quite taken by the natural beauty of young American women, who, in turn, seem to have been charmed by their guests' continental manners. At the least, many French officers found the ladies of Newport an added inducement to learn or improve their English language skills.[39] Rochambeau even had a hall, complete with gaming tables, constructed on the grounds of the Vernon mansion to accommodate large social gatherings, although he later became concerned about his officers' excessive gambling there.[40]

Public events also brought American citizens and French military men together.[41] On August 24 and 25, 1780, Rochambeau held a review of his army, followed by a parade and the firing of salvos by both artillery and musketry to celebrate the feast of Saint Louis, namesake and patron saint of the French king.[42] On August 29, a delegation of nineteen Indian leaders (Oneidas, Tuscaroras, and Caghnawagas) visited Rochambeau, who urged them to support the allies and mistrust the English; they were lavishly entertained, treated to exhibitions of French military might, and given gifts by Rochambeau.[43] Certainly, this constituted an unusual break from normal routine in Newport! A less happy occasion for military ceremonies was the unexpected death of Admiral Ternay, whose funeral took place amid pomp and solemnity on December 16, 1780.[44]

The most important and impressive festivities at Newport during the French stay came with Washington's visit, March 6–13, 1781. The commander in chief's arrival was welcomed with an illumination of the town (in which more candles were used at greater public expense than in greeting Rochambeau's forces). Inspections and reviews of the French troops, an elaborate ball, and a number of banquets and speeches followed to celebrate the event.[45] Although the precise effects of these ceremonies are impossible to identify, they obviously brought the French and Americans together in mutual enterprises and familiarized them with each other.

Throughout the winter of 1780–1781, many French officers traveled within and beyond Rhode Island for pleasure, to improve their knowledge of this new country, and in the performance of official missions. More than a score of Rochambeau's officers, including Claude Blanchard, Armand Charles de Charlus, Adam Philippe de Custine, Joseph Louis de Damas, Robert Guillaume Dillon, Mathieu Dumas, Hans Axel de Fersen, Frédéric Charles de Haacke, Louis Armaud de Lauzun, Anne Alexandre de Montmorency-Laval, Louis Marie de Noailles, Jean Baptiste de Saint-Maisme, and Dominique Sheldon, made trips in the northeastern United States. The most inveterate voyager, Jean François de Beauvoir, marquis de Chastellux, subsequently wrote an important description of America in the late eighteenth century that consolidated his reputation as a scholar. Rochambeau and some members of his staff were required to travel to keep track of his scattered forces—for example, the sick at Providence and Lauzun's Legion in its winter quarters in Connecticut—as well as to coordinate strategy with Washington. Christian Forbach, comte des Deux-Ponts, whose family exercised hereditary command over the German regiment of the same name, was sent to Pennsylvania to counter the anti-French propaganda being spread by the English among German settlers there. One officer, Charles Louis de Secondat, baron de Montesquieu, estimated that he covered five hundred leagues (fifteen hundred miles) in the course of two months during that winter.[46] Regardless of their purpose, these trips not only broke up the monotony of garrison life but also expanded the French officers' acquaintance with the American environment.

Another form of Franco-American contact—of an entirely different nature—involved desertions by Rochambeau's troops. A continual plague in eighteenth-century armies, desertion was a comparatively minor, albeit not negligible, problem among French soldiers in America. The alien atmosphere in the United States inhibited, but did not preclude, desertions. The first men to leave their units did so only two months after their arrival at Newport. Between September 1780 and the end of that year, thirty soldiers left their colors to seek refuge amid this new society; double that number would desert Rochambeau's corps before it left Newport.[47] Whether the attractions of their new environment or the unacceptable conditions of their familiar employment were primarily responsible cannot be determined (a perennial problem in identifying motives for desertion).

Meanwhile, Rochambeau's forces began to recover from the effects of their sea voyage; simultaneously, measures were taken to combat new health problems. Fruits and vegetables, notably onions, were distributed to the troops to counteract scurvy. Local fresh water intended for the same purpose, however, contributed to a new threat—dysentery. To combat this, rum and vinegar were issued to be mixed with water; in addition, the soldiers were instructed to drop a piece of toast or a hot iron into their water to "purify" it before drinking. Military hygiene and health were further improved by orders requiring that new latrines be dug frequently and that soldiers be fully clothed before emerging from their tents for reveille, since morning mists were considered a major source of respiratory illnesses. By October 1780, the number of men hospitalized had declined by half the figure of three months earlier.[48]

Despite its inauspicious beginnings, the presence of a French army on American soil encouraged hopes for the success of the Franco-American alliance. At the same time, some circumstances augured ill for the future of Rochambeau's expeditionary corps in America.

Notes

1. See the instructions for Corny in Rochambeau Papers, vol. 7, p. 6.
2. See Providence Town Meetings, vol. 6 (1772–1783), preserved at the Providence Public Library, the sessions of June 15 and 19 and July 1, 1780; and Rhode Island State Archives, Records of the Council of War, 1779–1781, meeting of June 25, 1780.
3. Rochambeau to Montbarey, July 16, 1780, in Rochambeau Papers, vol. 7, p. 66; and Lee Kennett, "Le bilan d'une rencontre: l'armée française en Amérique (1780–1783)," *Annales historiques de la Révolution française* 48 (October–December 1976): 532.
4. John Russell Bartlett, ed., *Records of the State of Rhode Island and Providence Plantations in New England*, vol. 9, 1780–1783 (Providence: Alfred Anthony, 1864), pp. 75, 87; and William Heath, "The Heath Papers," part 3, *Collections of the Massachusetts Historical Society*, 7th series, vol. 5 (1905), pp. 70–72 (henceforth, "Heath Papers").
5. Bartlett, *Records of the State of Rhode Island*, vol. 9, pp. 86, 92.
6. Accounts of the disembarkation include Dawson, "With Rochambeau at Newport," pp. 326–329; William de Deux-Ponts, *My Campaigns in America: A Journal Kept by Count William de Deux-Ponts, 1780–1781*, trans. Samuel Abbott Green (Boston: J. K. Wiggin, 1868), pp. 90–92; and Bibliothèque Nationale (henceforth, B.N.), Département des Manuscrits, Nouvelles Acquisitions Françaises 17691: "Journal de l'armée aux ordres de Monsieur le Comte de Rochambeau pendant les campagnes de 1780, 1781, 1782, 1783 dans l'amérique septentrionale par le général Lauberdière," pp. 9–13. A microfilm of this last, very useful but unexploited source was generously provided by Dr. Robert Selig. Figures on the number of deaths, like all statistical data on enlisted men, have

been extracted from the contrôles of all the units in Rochambeau's corps—
A.G., 1 YC 188, 1 YC 966, 1 YC 932, 1 YC 869, 10 YC 1; and A.N., D² C 32.
7. Rochambeau Papers, vol. 7, p. 69; and Edwin Martin Stone, *Our French Allies, Rochambeau and His Army, Lafayette and His Devotion, D'Estaing, De Ternay, Barras, De Grasse, and Their Fleets in the Great War of the American Revolution, From 1778 to 1782, Including Military Operations in Rhode Island, the Surrender of Yorktown, Sketches of French and American Officers, and Incidents of Social Life in Newport, Providence, and Elsewhere* (Providence: Providence Press, 1884), pp. 217–218. Despite its excessive and lyrical title, Stone's book contains much useful—and some useless—information, often utilized by subsequent authors.
8. Rochambeau Papers, vol. 7, p. 69; and Dawson, "With Rochambeau at Newport," p. 329.
9. Rochambeau Papers, vol. 1, p. 234; "Heath Papers," pp. 91–93 and 100–102; and William B. Willcox, "Rhode Island in British Strategy, 1780–1781," *Journal of Modern History* 17 (1945): 310–313.
10. Rochambeau Papers, vol. 7, pp. 81–138. An outstanding example of Rochambeau's attitude toward and treatment of Lafayette is seen in his letter to the latter, dated August 27, 1780, and reproduced in Henri Doniol, *Histoire de la participation de la France à l'établissement des Etats-Unis d'Amérique: Correspondance diplomatique et documents*, vol. 4 (Paris: Imprimerie Nationale, 1890), pp. 380–381n.
11. For the assignments, see Newport Historical Society, Town Proceedings, vol. 1, p. 5; and Stone, *Our French Allies*, pp. 221–224.
12. The best source for the daily life of Rochambeau's troops is Archives départementales de la Meurthe-et-Moselle (Nancy), E 235, Armée de Rochambeau, Livre d'ordre contenant ceux donnés depuis le débarquement des Troupes à Newport en Amérique Septentrionale, 1780. Lee Kennett very generously loaned me a microfilm of this useful document. Kennett's own book, *The French Forces in America, 1780–1783* (Westport, Conn.: Greenwood, 1977), is easily the most thorough study of Rochambeau's army in America; it is impossible to avoid repeating much of the material contained there.
13. The total figures are from the contrôles indicated in note 6 in this chapter; information on Regneauld is in A.G., 10 YC 1 and on the Verette brothers in A.G., 1 YC 932.
14. Kennett, *French Forces*, p. 38; and William C. Stinchcombe, *The American Revolution and the French Alliance* (Syracuse: Syracuse University Press, 1969), pp. 107–108. An example in the *Pennsylvania Ledger* is quoted in Frank Moore, *The Diary of the American Revolution 1775–1781* (New York: Washington Square Press, 1967), p. 299.
15. Livre d'ordre for November 2 and 14, 1780.
16. William C. Stinchcombe, "Americans Celebrate the Birth of the Dauphin" in Ronald Hoffman and Peter J. Albert, eds., *Diplomacy and Revolution: The Franco-American Alliance of 1778* (Charlottesville: University Press of Virginia, 1981), pp. 45–46; and Abbé Robin, *New Travels Through North America: In a Series of Letters; Exhibiting the History of the Victorious Campaign of the Allied Armies, Under His Excellency General Washington and the Count de Rochambeau, in the Year 1781. Interspersed With Political and Philosophical Observations, Upon the Genius, Temper, and Customs of the Americans; Also Narrations of the Capture of*

General Burgogne, and Lord Cornwallis, With Their Armies; and a Variety of Interesting Particulars, With Occurred, in the Course of the War in America (Philadelphia: Robert Bell, 1783; reprint New York: New York Times and Arno Press, 1969), p. 19.
17. Newport Town Proceedings, vol. 1, pp. 11–13; William Heath, *Memoirs of Major-General William Heath* (New York: William Abbott, 1901; reprint New York: New York Times and Arno Press, 1969), pp. 225–226; Bartlett, *Records of Rhode Island*, vol. 9, pp. 158–160.
18. Stinchcombe, *American Revolution and French Alliance*, pp. 91–119. Typical pro-French propaganda can be found in the *Providence Gazette and Country Journal* and *Continental Journal and Weekly Advertiser* (Boston) during summer 1780. Rev. Cooper, for example, began receiving a stipend (in specie) from Louis XVI in January 1779; see Charles W. Akers, *The Divine Politician: Samuel Cooper and the American Revolution in Boston* (Boston: Northeastern University Press, 1982), pp. 278–280.
19. See Mathieu Dumas, *Memoirs of His Own Time, Including the Revolution, the Empire and the Restoration* (Philadelphia: Lea and Blanchard, 1839), vol. 1, pp. 67–68; Axel de Fersen, *Lettres d'Axel de Fersen à son père pendant la guerre de l'indépendance d'Amérique* (Paris: Firmin-Didot, 1929), pp. 72–73; Louis Gottschalk, ed., *The Letters of Lafayette to Washington, 1777–1799* (New York: privately printed, 1944), p. 104; Emmanuel de Lévis-Mirepoix, ed., "Quelques Lettres du Baron de Montesquieu sur la Guerre d'Indépendance Américaine," *Franco-American Review* 2 (1938): 203; Robin, *New Travels*, p. 21.
20. Two examples include a letter of William Channing, dated Newport, August 6, 1780, quoted in Ezra Stiles, *Literary Diary of Ezra Stiles*, vol. 2, Franklin B. Dexter, ed. (New York: Charles Scribner's Sons, 1901), p. 459; and a letter of James Jarvis, dated Boston, February 5, 1781, Boston Public Library, Manuscripts, R.1.1.91.
21. Copies of this "Order Prior to Disembarkation" can be found in Rochambeau Papers, vol. 2, p. 100a; and Livre d'ordre for June 8, 1780.
22. Livre d'ordre for July 17, 1780.
23. Ibid. for August 5 and 12, 1780, and April 9 and May 1, 1781.
24. Mackenzie, *Diary*, vol. 1, pp. 279 and 285, and vol. 2, p. 391, where he notes that these actions "have thrown great disgrace on our arms."
25. Kennett, *French Forces*, pp. 57–58, as well as Livres d'ordre for July 30, October 31, November 13, 1780, and January 3, 1781.
26. Kennett, *French Forces*, p. 167; Fiechter, "L'Aventure américaine," p. 78; and James N. Arnold, *Vital Records of Rhode Island, 1636–1850. First Series: Births, Marriages, and Deaths*, vol. 4: *Newport County* (Providence: Naragansett Historical Publishing Company, 1893), pp. 18–24, for births and deaths between March 1, 1781, and April 1, 1782.
27. Kennett, *French Forces*, pp. 57 and 81.
28. Newport, Rhode Island, Inferior Court of Common Pleas, Court Records, 1767–1783, vol. H-1 1/2, no. 945820, preserved on microfilm by the Newport Historical Society, for sessions from May 1780 to May 1782.
29. John Austin Stevens, "The French in Rhode Island," *Magazine of American History* 3 (1879): 402; and Rice and Brown, *American Campaigns*, vol. 1, pp. 123–125.

30. See the *Newport Mercury* for July 15, 22, and 29 and August 12, 1780, and the *Providence Gazette and Country Journal* for July 15 and August 5 and 12, 1780.
31. An early example can be found in Jean Edmond Weelen, *Rochambeau, Father and Son: A Life of the Maréchal de Rochambeau and the Journal of the Vicomte de Rochambeau*, trans. Lawrence Lee (New York: Henry Holt, 1936), p. 205.
32. Durand Echeverria, ed. and trans., "The Iroquois Visit Rochambeau at Newport in 1780: Excerpts From the Unpublished Journal of the Comte de Charlus," *Rhode Island History* 11 (1952): 73; and Heath, "Heath Papers," p. 103.
33. Rhode Island State Archives, Letters to the Governor, vol. 15, items no. 17 and 18; and Waldo G. Leland and Edmund C. Burnett, eds., "Letters From Lafayette to Luzerne, 1780–1782," *American Historical Review* 20 (1914–1915): 371.
34. The Rhode Island Historical Society possesses a full run of the paper; see also analyses of it in Allen J. Barthold, "*Gazette Françoise*, Newport, R.I., 1780–81," *Papers of the Bibliographical Society of America* 28, part 1 (1934): 64–79; Jacques Godechot, "*La Gazette françoise*, ancêtre des journaux d'armées publiés sous la Révolution," *Annales historiques de la Révolution française* 52 (1980): 118–125; and Jacques Godechot, "*La Gazette Françoise*: First of the Army Newspapers Published in the World, First French-Language Newspaper Published in the United States," in Nancy L. Roelker and Charles K. Warner, eds., *Two Hundred Years of Franco-American Relations: Papers of the Bicentennial Colloquium of the Society for French Historical Studies in Newport, Rhode Island, September 7–10, 1978* (n.p., n.d.), pp. 78–92.
35. See the issues of November 23, 1780; January 15, April 14, and May 5, 1781, for examples.
36. Livre d'ordre for February 13, 1781.
37. Robert A. Selig, "A German Soldier in America, 1780–1783: The Journal of Georg Daniel Flohr," *William and Mary Quarterly*, 3rd Series 50 (1993): 580.
38. Stone, *Our French Allies*, p. 337.
39. Comments along these lines appear in Dawson, "With Rochambeau at Newport," pp. 333–337; Lévis-Mirepoix, "Lettres du Baron de Montesquieu," p. 196; Acomb, *Journal of Von Closen*, p. 49; and Stone, *Our French Allies*, pp. 256–274 and 329–330.
40. Stone, *Our French Allies*, p. 227; and Livre d'ordre for January 19 and February 22, 1781.
41. Brief summaries of these social activities are found in Mary Ellen Loughrey, *France and Rhode Island, 1686–1800* (New York: King's Crown Press, 1944), pp. 27–30; Stone, *Our French Allies*, p. 296; and Perkins, *France in the American Revolution*, pp. 307–308. Contemporary references to them abound in the newspapers and personal accounts of the time.
42. See Livre d'ordre for August 21 and the coverage of these activities in the *Providence Gazette and Country Journal* for August 26, 1780.
43. Rice and Brown, *American Campaigns*, vol. 1, pp. 121–123; B.N., N.A.F. 17691, "Journal par Lauberdière," pp. 15–17; and Armand Charles Castries, "Dans l'armée de La Fayette, souvenirs inédits du comte de Charlus," *Revue de Paris* 64 (1957): 108–109.
44. Livre d'ordre for December 15 contains detailed instructions for the conduct of the ceremony.

45. Newport Town Proceedings, vol. 1, pp. 17, 19, and 34; Rice and Brown, *American Campaigns*, vol. 1, pp. 241–244; and Stone, *Our French Allies*, pp. 362–369.
46. See Howard W. Preston, "Rochambeau and the French Troops in Providence in 1780–81–82," *Rhode Island Historical Society Collections* 17 (1924): 7–9; Kennett, *French Forces*, p. 85; Rochambeau Papers, vol. 7, pp. 191, 211–212, and vol. 14, pp. 31–33, 38; William Heath, *Memoirs of Major-General William Heath* (New York: William Abbot, 1901; reprint New York: New York Times and Arno Press, 1969), pp. 244–253; Lévis-Mirepoix, "Lettres du Baron de Montesquieu," pp. 200–201; and Marquis de Chastellux, *Travels in North America in the Years 1780, 1781, and 1782*, 2 vols., ed. and trans. Howard C. Rice Jr. (Chapel Hill: University of North Carolina Press, 1963).
47. From the contrôles cited in note 6 of this chapter.
48. For the health problems of Rochambeau's army in 1780, see Livre d'ordre, July 31–August 29, 1780; Kennett, *French Forces*, pp. 58 and 63; Blanchard, *Journal*, pp. 63–64 and 72; Rochambeau Papers, vol. 15 (unpaginated) for August 25, 1780; Stone, *Our French Allies*, pp. 232 and 532; Gaston Maugras, *Le Duc de Lauzun et la cour de Marie-Antoinette* (Paris: Plon, 1913), p. 218; Amblard-Marie-Raymond-Amedée de Noailles, *Marins et soldats français en Amérique pendant la Guerre de l'Indépendance des Etats-Unis (1778–1783)* (Paris: Perrin, 1903), p. 204; and Jean des Cilleuls, "Jean François Coste (1741–1819), médecin en chef de l'Armée de Rochambeau, premier maire de Versailles (1790–1792)," *Revue Historique des Armées* 4, no. 1 (1977): 17n.

3
MOUNTING FRUSTRATIONS AND TENSIONS

EVEN BEFORE ROCHAMBEAU'S CORPS had settled at Newport, the allies were anxiously awaiting the second division that had been left behind at Brest. The French commander, whose already small army had been further weakened by casualties sustained during the voyage, was preoccupied with the speedy and safe arrival of these reinforcements. Lafayette, Washington, and other American leaders were equally concerned as rumors circulated that this force was in the Bermudas, that it had arrived at Charleston, or that it was not coming. Despite plans to embark the twenty-five hundred men in autumn 1780 and despite expectations of their coming as late as the following April, the continuing English blockade of the harbor of Brest prevented their departure.[1]

The failure to dispatch additional troops adversely affected Franco-American relations. Rochambeau, together with the commander of the French naval forces at Newport, Admiral Ternay, and officers of their staffs, met with Washington and his staff at Hartford, Connecticut, on September 20, 1780, to discuss plans for allied military operations. Both commanding generals were disappointed with the strength of their ally's forces and were dubious about the amount of cooperation they could expect from the other. Washington was impatient for some military action before the end of the year to bolster flagging U.S. morale; Rochambeau feared the consequences of precipitous action.

The conference did, however, result in general agreement on major objectives. It was recognized that New York was the key to the British position in North America, but its capture would require at least twenty-four thousand—preferably thirty thousand—troops, as well as naval superiority in nearby waters. To achieve such a goal, Rochambeau was to appeal to his government for further military and naval assistance while remaining on the defensive in Rhode Island.[2] Although outward appearances of cordiality were maintained, disappointment and suspicion persisted.

On one issue there was no ambiguity: His discussion with Washington confirmed Rochambeau's conviction that substantial reinforcements and additional supplies were essential to ensure allied victory. Having received no official communication from France, Rochambeau ordered his son, the vicomte de Rochambeau, back home on October 28 to present his case at court.[3] The French government was not blind to the problems. Ten additional officers had been sent to Newport in late June 1780, and a special detachment of approximately six hundred troops, drawn from various regiments, was assembled in November, although it would not leave France until the following March.[4] Meanwhile, the second division waited and was awaited—interminably.

Another means of strengthening the French army in the United States was to enlist deserters—particularly Hessian mercenaries—from the British forces. Scarcely two weeks after Rochambeau's arrival in Newport he was corresponding with Anne César de La Luzerne, the French minister to the United States, regarding this prospect; within a month sergeants from the German Deux-Ponts regiment and from Lauzun's Legion were selected "to receive the Hessian deserters" whom La Luzerne had attracted to Philadelphia. By the end of August 1780, a dozen of these men had been enrolled in Lauzun's Legion and another half-dozen in Deux-Ponts. Although Rochambeau described this practice as a double benefit—adding a trained soldier to one's own army while depriving the enemy of the same—within weeks after enlisting, a number of these recruits deserted from their new units as readily as they had left the British ranks. For example, Frédéric Wilhelm Punchelet, who was born in Berlin in 1755, was enrolled in Philadelphia as a hussar in Lauzun's Legion on August 26, 1780, arrived at his unit on September 22, and deserted on October 3; Jean Klein, a native of Hungary, enlisted in the same capacity, joined his squadron on the same date, and stayed only four days longer before he deserted. In spite of the unreliability of some of these men, the French enlisted a total of 160 deserters during their stay in America, but this was not nearly enough to compensate for the lack of reinforcements from Europe.[5]

The French government's neglect of Rochambeau's corps can only be understood by placing this particular expedition within the context of France's overall war effort. The scope of French military and naval commitments was literally worldwide, as exemplified by the departure of a fleet from Brest in March 1781 (composed of 190 warships, transports, and merchantmen) whose destinations included the West Indies, South America, Africa, and the Indian Ocean, as well as the United States. Even in the New World, North America ranked well behind the Caribbean in French priorities. Between the time of France's entry into the war against England and the fall of 1782, twenty-nine battalions of infantry were sent to Martinique, Guadeloupe, and Saint-Dominque to join the nineteen battalions already garrisoning those islands; Rochambeau's army, in contrast, contained eight infantry battalions. To put this in another framework, the budget for the French navy in 1780 and 1781 was approximately 160 million livres per year; Rochambeau's annual budget amounted to only about 4 percent of this figure (6.6 million livres). As one final example, between March and December 1781, Admiral de Grasse's fleet suffered over five thousand casualties, roughly the number of enlisted men in Rochambeau's entire force.[6] As essential as French support may have seemed to Americans, it constituted but a portion—and not the most important portion—of France's war with England. Nevertheless, French activity beyond the United States forced the British to extend their own efforts considerably, thereby contributing to the American cause—a contribution few Americans appreciated, however.

Like most Americans, the French in Rhode Island found little encouragement in the grand strategy of the war; their concerns were more immediate and more mundane. In addition to coping with a language that was alien to most, Rochambeau's personnel had to deal with other foreign elements in American society. The severe—and, in French eyes, gloomy—observance of the Sabbath in Protestant New England puzzled and offended some of the Catholics who were accustomed to *celebrate* holy days. Even the Quakers, who were idealized in enlightened circles in France, were found to be "as hypocritical and as vicious as the rest of humanity." And the multiplicity of religious sects provided diversity but did not guarantee tolerance, since each group despised the others.[7]

Although many French had little or no reaction to the ways in which religion was practiced in America, all were affected by differences in eating and drinking habits. Americans normally ate much more meat than the French, and it was prepared much more plainly; although in the course of their stay the French consumed tons of cornbread, they never accepted it as a genuine substitute for their customary bread. Similarly, Rochambeau's officers found the Madeira and Port wines of their hosts too sweet and were continually amazed at the vast quantities of tea Americans consumed. These cultural differences surprised, annoyed, and even alienated a number of the

French, but the officers politely disguised their reactions, and the soldiers had no opportunity to express them.[8]

Far more fundamental problems than differences in customs faced Rochambeau. One of the most pressing was finding lodging for his army. Within a week of landing, Rochambeau determined that because it would be "impractical and even impossible to winter in the Antilles," he would have to provide his troops with more suitable quarters than the tents they had pitched after disembarking. As in Europe, the officers would be housed in the homes of civilians who were able and willing to provide lodging. Quartering the troops constituted a much greater difficulty. Although Rochambeau would have preferred to build separate barracks where the soldiers would be concentrated (and more easily controlled), after consulting with his top aides he decided instead to lodge them in separate houses that had been seriously damaged during the British occupation and would be repaired at French expense. This situation would ultimately benefit the local inhabitants, who could reoccupy the buildings after the French had departed, and would be half as costly as new construction (no minor consideration). Although less expensive, the repairs still required large amounts of material, including eighty thousand bricks, six hundred cartloads of sand, eighty hogsheads of lime, one hundred and fifty thousand feet of one-inch planks, one hundred thousand shingles, and over two hundred thousand nails; the total cost would exceed eighty-eight thousand livres.[9]

Before the repairs could be completed, new problems arose. Some local people began to move into the houses as soon as they became habitable, and Rochambeau had to send detachments of soldiers to occupy the buildings and evict the squatters. More troublesome were several storms in October that scattered the French tents and disorganized the camp. Consequently, at the beginning of November the French troops were ordered to abandon their encampment and move into town, although not all repairs had been finished. The two hussar squadrons of Lauzun's Legion constituted a special problem, since Newport lacked sufficient forage for their horses; these cavalrymen were to be sent to Providence where they could be maintained more easily. When news of these plans reached Providence, however, local merchants increased their prices so much that Rochambeau decided to send most of his cavalry to Lebanon, Connecticut, about eighty miles from Newport, where plentiful fodder was available at reasonable cost.[10]

Lauzun's hussars—around 240 strong—together with artillery horses, reached their winter quarters in late November; there they would remain, isolated from most of their comrades, until the following June. Governor Jonathan Trumbull did what he could to lodge the troops, who took over barracks of the state militia, and entertain the officers; his efforts were only partly successful. The duc de Lauzun, the proprietary colonel of the unit and a court favorite at Versailles, was gracious to his hosts but bored with his surroundings, which he described as "a few huts scattered among vast forests."[11] When he received news of mutinies in the U.S. army in January 1781, he used this as an occasion to ride to Newport to inform Rochambeau; he remained there, with a much more active social life, through the winter.

The troops of his command had no such opportunities to seek diversion elsewhere. For them, escape lay in desertion; more than a score of men deserted between November 1780 and June 1781, three-fourths of whom were defectors from the British army. Not all of these men succeeded in their attempt, and when apprehended they faced harsh punishment. Christophe Hand and Joseph Franck, both corporals, were condemned to be hanged for desertion, but in the absence of an executioner (the expeditionary corps included "one hangman," who probably remained with the main party in Newport), the two were executed by a firing squad in April 1781.[12]

Although conditions were less primitive in Newport, life was not without difficulties for the French garrison there during the winter of 1780–1781. Moving into the recently and sometimes incompletely repaired houses in the town improved living conditions for Rochambeau's forces; at the same time, the move expanded and complicated the duties of the troops. Nightly guard duty outside the town required hundreds of soldiers to watch various posts and provide patrols for rapid communication (a task performed primarily by mounted couriers from Lauzun's hussars who had not been sent to Connecticut). Within Newport itself, the primary concern was the danger of fire. Guards were to undergo full inspections under arms at sunset and sunrise; pickets were to sleep fully clothed; each building in which troops were lodged was to have casks and buckets of water (with care taken to break any ice in them both at night and in the morning), as well as saws, ready for use in fighting fires; a sentinel was posted in a church steeple on Spring Street to sound the alarm in case of fire. In addition, chimneys had to be swept at least every six weeks; no cooking stoves were allowed within quarters; officers had to visit the billets of the men in their company each night between seven and eight to ensure that all fires were extinguished; and in the event of fire, all French military personnel were to provide the local *gardiens du feu* with their assistance and full cooperation. Other duties included the maintenance of clean latrines, the disposal of waste away from thoroughfares, and the regular sweeping of streets. Simultaneously, drills and training, inspections, the distribution of supplies, and the ongoing improvement of defenses continued to take up the soldiers' attention and energy.[13]

These regular routines helped to keep the troops occupied with, if not interested in, their duties. Their commanders, above all Rochambeau, were preoccupied with other issues, especially provisions. The day after the French arrived at Newport, Rochambeau called his general officers and chief financial and supply officials to the first of many meetings about this matter. Their major concerns focused on foodstuffs (meat, bread, vegetables), other supplies (such as forage and straw), and services (carpentry, masonry, laundry, hospital care). In addition, they discussed the purchase of horses for hauling and riding, cattle, firewood, and rum and cider. Intimately involved was the issue of finances, since American prices were high, inflation was mounting, and concerns were increasing about the reliability of the purchasing agents employed by the French government.[14]

The purchase of supplies by the French involved substantial quantities of money and goods. Ten days after the arrival of the French fleet, an agreement was signed with a Hartford merchant, Josiah Blakely, to furnish the French forces with 300 cords of wood, 1,000 barrels of "first quality" flour, 30 oxen (15,000 pounds), 3,352 tons of hay, 613 tons of straw, 30,000 bushels of Indian corn, and 37,125 bushels of oats. A supplementary contract committed Blakely to provide live cattle and sheep to be butchered for fresh meat.[15] Even before Rochambeau's forces reached America, Lafayette had entered into an agreement with Jeremiah Wadsworth, commissary general of the Continental Army, to furnish supplies to the French (at a 5 percent commission). Wadsworth subsequently formed a private partnership with a "Mr. Carter" (John Barker Church) for this purpose and ultimately emerged from the Revolution a very wealthy man.[16] The official French purchasing agent in the United States, charged chiefly with the acquisition of transport, was John Holker, whom Rochambeau never trusted.[17]

The form of payment for goods and services was also a major problem for the French. Benoît Joseph de Tarlé, intendant in charge of the finances of Rochambeau's army, had been instructed to use paper money as much as possible for purchases; in fact, Tarlé was usually forced to pay in specie, since it was much more readily accepted and did not threaten to undermine further already shaky U.S. finances.[18] By mid-1780 American paper money was worth less than 1.5 percent of its face value. In addition, the bills of exchange the French expedition had been given had lost one-fourth of their value even before the French had landed and one-third of their value by the time they had been in America for three months. Lack of cash forced Rochambeau to take "very onerous loans," and he urged his government to send specie lest French credit in the United States collapse and discipline among his troops disappear for lack of necessary supplies, because Americans would "provide nothing, not a house for lodging, nor a field for camping without hard cash."[19] In light of the vast problems it faced, the French government was reasonably responsive to Rochambeau's pleas; it sent nine shipments of specie, the first arriving in Boston at the end of February 1781. Each shipment then had to be safely and laboriously transported from its port of arrival to Rochambeau's corps—wherever it might be.[20]

Compounding Rochambeau's financial difficulties was the fact that the French forces in the United States were required to pay top dollar for whatever they purchased, which resulted in general resentment. Americans were offended because the presence of the French—or, more accurately, French cash—drove all prices up. The French were convinced that they were being "fleeced." Swedish nobleman Axel de Fersen, one of Rochambeau's aides de camp, was outspoken but not atypical in his evaluation of American cupidity: "Money is their God."[21] A number of the higher-ranking officers, also court aristocrats who were accustomed to out-of-pocket expenses beyond their army pay, complained of the excessive costs of their service in the cause of American independence. For example, the baron de Vioménil, a general on Rochambeau's staff, claimed he had to borrow thirty thousand livres to support himself in the United States, and the colonel of the regiment of Soissonnais Infantry, the comte de Saint-Maisme, estimated that he spent forty-five thousand livres of his own funds because of the dearness of goods in America.[22] Other officers tried expedients to cope with high prices. Claude Blanchard, a commissary officer, speculated in bills of exchange. Claude Marie, chevalier de Tressan, among others, had goods shipped from France for sale in the United States at a considerable profit.[23] Some of the French even improved their financial status by selling slaves.[24]

The poor quality and inadequate quantity of certain supplies turned an objectionable situation into an intolerable one for the French. Rochambeau frequently reported that Holker was trying to charge far more than he should for inferior goods; for example, the French officers refused to accept every single saddlehorse Holker sent them. In another instance, Rochambeau refused to sign for two hundred wagons furnished by Holker, since they had been rented for three months and were delivered more than seven weeks late. Other charges—for wood, transportation, lodging, and commissions—were also considered excessive. Rochambeau had no doubt that John Holker was simply "a greedy merchant and no friend of the King." Jeremiah Wadsworth was no more reliable; his firm consistently delivered insufficient or unacceptable supplies. By mutual agreement, the Wadsworth contract was canceled after July 1780.[25]

For the soldiers in the ranks, these thousands of livres and hundreds of tons were translated—literally—into their daily bread. By regulation, each soldier was entitled to a daily ration of twenty-four ounces of bread (for which twenty ounces of flour or eighteen ounces of biscuit could be substituted), eight ounces of fresh or salted beef, and one ounce of rice, as well as one pound of salt per month; a deduction was made from his pay for the cost of this food (amounting to nearly 40 percent of a private soldier's wages).[26] The distribution of these rations and other necessities (such as straw, vinegar, firewood) took place on a regular basis, forming an important part of the troops' routine; normally, meat was distributed every two days and bread or a substitute every four days, although the quantity and type of foodstuffs available and weather conditions could modify those arrangements.[27]

Within a month of the arrival of the French at Newport, conditions in America required modifications in the rations of Rochambeau's soldiers. The most significant change was the use of cornmeal to supplement bread flour (officially, two-thirds wheat and one-third rye), which constituted the most important staple in the soldiers' nutrition. Rochambeau, like the rest of his compatriots, was uneasy about the introduction of this change in the soldiers' diet, for, as he gently explained, corn was a food "to which they are not accustomed."[28] Indeed, the financial situation of the French forces in the United States can be gauged by the proportion of corn in their rations, which usually had an inverse relation to the funds available. Other changes in rations, such as the relative amounts of rice or of fresh and salted meat, also varied according to conditions; for example, salted beef and rice, which stored well, became more common in the French diet during the winter of 1780–1781.

The needs of the French troops were not limited to food. Fresh straw, used for bedding, was essential less for comfort than for hygiene, and Tarlé sought the cooperation of state authorities to encourage local farmers to bring all the straw they could to Newport for "a Generous Price."[29] Firewood was necessary for cooking and, especially from the autumn on, for heating. This commodity was particularly scarce in and around Newport because the British had denuded area forests; in addition, firewood was bulky and costly to transport. Consequently, scores of French soldiers were regularly assigned to cut, stack, load, and unload wood throughout the winter months.

The transportation of firewood and other supplies, in turn, required the purchase or rental of vehicles, in particular wagons and boats. As always, Rochambeau was concerned about all of these expenses and asked the governor of Rhode Island to issue orders that the French should pay no more

MOUNTING FRUSTRATIONS AND TENSIONS

than the American army was charged (a request Governor Greene pointed out was beyond his authority to enforce).[30] In addition to such basic necessities as food, straw, and wood, the French also required a regular supply of candles, bedclothes, drinks (such as cider, rum, and wine), cooking and eating utensils, fodder, and other provisions that fell between absolute necessities and luxuries.

As the French settled in at Newport, they faced problems besides those involving the supply and cost of provisions. Once the feeling of relief following the trying voyage had passed and the frantic preparations to organize defenses against enemy attack had been completed, routine activities were resumed, albeit in an alien environment; simultaneously came a growing sense of boredom and tension. According to a number of the officers (Lafayette, Fersen, and Montesquieu, among others), the army felt frustrated because it wanted immediate action against the enemy.[31] Although such testimony may contain a bit of aristocratic bravado, inactivity contributed to a growing ennui. In addition, more than six months passed before the first mail arrived from home and although less striking in the eighteenth than the twentieth century, such a lengthy gap in communications could hardly help morale.[32]

Strains were reflected in mounting friction among the officers. Lafayette, who had hoped to command the expeditionary corps, seldom let an opportunity pass to criticize Rochambeau, although his criticisms were more insidious than blatant.[33] Although most of his officers respected Rochambeau, Lafayette was not alone in finding fault with him; Major General Chastellux wrote to La Luzerne, complaining of Rochambeau's "unbelievable ignorance" about the United States.[34] But Rochambeau was hardly the sole object of criticism among the French officers. One unidentified officer in the expedition made the following comments about some of his comrades: of the baron de Vioménil, "no ideas, no talent . . . only zeal and bravery"; of the comte de Vioménil, younger brother of the baron and an inspector general, "will always be incapable of leading or inspecting [as many as] four men"; of the comte de Saint-Maisme, "his great incapacity and lack of abilities . . . leave no hope for the future"; of the comte de Custine, colonel of the Saintonge Infantry, "[he has] the ardent desire to be something, using violent and extraordinary means in the absence of talent"; of the comte de Charlus, son of the minister of marine and colonel in second in the Regiment of Saintonge, "[he has] very little ability and a great opinion of himself."[35]

Some officers simply got on the nerves of others, especially in the restricted confines of Newport. Personal animosity sometimes took petty forms; for example, the officers of Lauzun's Legion so resented Major Pollerescky, apparently for some of his financial dealings, that they refused to dine with him. Virtually any special reward—such as a bonus (*gratification*), promotion, or pension—would set off a chorus of complaints about injustice and offended honor. Some officers protested what they felt were unfair orders or assignments.[36] In March 1781, when Rochambeau had to select a contingent of troops for an expedition to the Chesapeake region, the officers competed so intensely to participate that violence resulted.[37] Is it any wonder, then, that by spring 1781 not a day went by without two or three officers being under arrest?[38]

The most dangerous and disruptive form this rivalry took was physical violence, particularly dueling, a tradition that survived from the chivalric past despite prohibitions against the practice. Because some duels took place clandestinely or remained unreported, it is impossible to know how many occurred.[39] Claude Etienne Hugau, lieutenant colonel of Lauzun's Legion, claimed one-fifth of his unit's officers were involved in duels over the period of a few months. Often the issues were minor. Captain Louis Henry de Beffroy and Captain Henry Esclent, both in Lauzun's Legion, fought with pistols because the former ripped up the passes Esclent had given to two hussars. The vicomte de Noailles, colonel in second of the Regiment of Soissonnais, had a duel with his counterpart in Lauzun's Legion, Robert Guillaume Dillon, the scion of that Irish-French family who had almost been left in France because of another duel in April 1780; the subject of this affair of honor was, according to commissary Blanchard, so insignificant as "not to deserve mentioning."

Whatever the specific issues in these conflicts, inevitably an offended sense of honor was the basic cause. When Lieutenant Colonel de La Valette of the Saintonge Infantry passed over Lieutenant Claude François Bernardin La Chesnaye for assignment to a combat mission, the lieutenant was bitterly disappointed. To console himself, La Chesnaye went drinking with some fellow officers, in the course of which he verbally attacked La Valette, calling him, among other things, "a dirty bugger." The lieutenant colonel's nephew, also an officer in the regiment, overheard this remark and challenged La Chesnaye to a duel. Lieutenant La Valette was wounded; La Chesnaye was arrested and subsequently shipped back to France, where a few years later he wounded another comrade in another duel. A similar sense of outrage led the marquis du Bouchet, a major on Rochambeau's staff, to fight Captain de Lauberdière, an aide de camp of the commanding general. Du Bouchet had been ordered to remain behind in Newport when most of Rochambeau's corps began its movement to join Washington near New York in June 1781; Lauberdière offered to buy his horses, since he

MOUNTING FRUSTRATIONS AND TENSIONS

would not be needing them. Humiliated by what he regarded as an intentional insult, du Bouchet responded angrily, offending Lauberdière. Both parties were wounded in the ensuing duel but made peace during their mutual convalescence.

Duels were not severely punished, whatever the laws and regulations might be.[40] Indeed, since relatively few resulted in fatalities, the continued observance of an archaic code of honor at a tolerable cost was allowed. A controversial incident in March 1781 showed that other responses to perceived dishonor could be more deadly than most duels. Captain André de Bertrier des Forêts (or Forest) of the Saintonge Infantry had a disagreement with his commanding officer, Colonel Custine, as a result of which des Forêts was reprimanded and felt he had been gravely insulted. The captain appealed to General de Vioménil, who supported Custine and ordered that des Forêts be arrested for insubordinate behavior. In despair, the thirty-eight-year-old captain—whose service dated to 1759—returned to his quarters and blew his brains out with his pistol. Many officers condemned Custine's conduct; at the next general formation, Captain Alexis Dujuast de Vareilles, who was des Forêts's cousin, began to draw his sword and had to be physically restrained from attacking Custine.[41]

The mounting friction among French officers during the winter of 1780–1781 is obvious. The effects of the situation on the soldiers—who almost never emerge from anonymity in the records—are more difficult to document; nevertheless, their behavior also exhibited growing stress. The dull routine and onerous duties of the French troops undoubtedly contributed to a desire to desert; however, the foreign environment kept the number of deserters rather low (around fifty from September 1780 to March 1781, two-thirds of whom had been recruited in America).[42]

Other evidence attests to disciplinary problems in the winter quarters. For example, beginning in mid-November, a detail had to be regularly posted at the guardhouse (*la prison*) to supervise military prisoners; in early January, Rochambeau reiterated a regulation of the previous October, prohibiting soldiers from drinking anywhere but at the sutlers' establishment under penalty of twenty-five blows with the flat of a saber; and on January 9, an order from the commanding general warned that not only would soldiers who engaged in fighting be punished "to the full extent of the regulations" but that their company officers would also be put "under arrest for a very long time."[43] The most serious incident took place toward the end of the French stay in Newport. During the evening of May 28–29, 1781, Sergeant Claude Cornevin, a fifteen-year veteran in the Auxonne Artillery, attempted to murder a captain in the same regiment, Jacques François Alphonse Pilotte de la Barollière, for reasons unknown. Although the captain eventually recovered, the sergeant was condemned to death after having his hand cut off; his execution took place on June 1.[44]

Severe discipline was routine in the French army of the period. At times, however, it declined to the level of sadism. During autumn of 1780 the superior officers of the Regiment of Bourbonnais decided the traditional corporal's saber was inadequate for administering punishments that called for blows with the flat of a saber and had a new saber made of iron to beat the unfortunate soldiers. Even other officers disapproved of such conduct. Captain de Lauberdière on the general staff, who had witnessed soldiers "spitting up blood after a beating," complained that "severity, properly applied, and firmness are qualities in an officer, but inhumanity, unreasonable harshness should never occur." He also criticized applying this punishment to the buttocks of offenders as if they were "school boys," thus adding insult to injury.[45]

The winter of 1780–1781 was depressing for the French on a much grander scale as well. Despite the outbreak of hostilities between England and the Netherlands in December, the prospect of Franco-American success was growing dimmer. General Benedict Arnold's treason in September 1780 was a bitter shock to Americans and their allies; more ominous was the fact that this was only the most spectacular expression of a more general disillusionment within the U.S. army, perhaps within American society as a whole.[46] By 1781 the British had greatly strengthened their position in the South, controlling South Carolina, Georgia, and much of North Carolina and threatening Virginia. Developments in Europe further increased uncertainty. In October 1780 the French cabinet was changed, and the ministers of both war and marine were replaced. In December Empress-Queen Maria Theresa died, and no one could predict what directions Austrian policy might take under her successor, Joseph II. Meanwhile, France's ally Spain was concentrating its military and naval efforts against Gibraltar and pressuring the French to do the same.[47]

On top of all this, in January 1781 units in the Continental Army from Pennsylvania and New Jersey, composed of long-suffering veterans whose patience had finally run out, mutinied en masse and demanded long overdue pay and supplies. The French government, already disturbed by the situation in the United States, became seriously alarmed; the entire French commitment in North America was subjected to review. On March 9, 1781, Foreign Minister Vergennes wrote La Luzerne that not only had Louis XVI decided not to send Rochambeau the additional reinforcements, munitions, and supplies he had requested through his son but that the king would not even dispatch the second division, which had been waiting to join Rochambeau since the previous spring; furthermore, Vergennes ordered that if the American army continued to disintegrate, Rochambeau was to keep his entire corps concentrated in Rhode Island, prepared to sail for the West Indies whenever notified. Simultaneously, the new minister of war, the marquis de Ségur, sent the same instructions to Rochambeau.[48]

In early 1781 it appeared that direct French assistance, perhaps the Franco-American alliance, and possibly American independence itself were in jeopardy. One military commander wrote in September 1780, "I have no money, no provisions . . . no army. I have nothing left but hope for better times."[49] Whereas Washington or Rochambeau might have been the author of this lament, these were the words of the British commander in chief in North America, Sir Henry Clinton. Fortunately for the Allied cause, the English were also experiencing difficulties that left them unprepared to take advantage of their enemies' weaknesses. Beyond that, just when the French court was beginning to despair about conditions in America, the situation of the small French expedition in New England was starting to improve.

Notes

1. Rochambeau Papers, vol. 7, pp. 69–133, 152, and 201, vol. 2, p. 112, and vol. 14, p. 78; Leland and Burnett, "Letters From Lafayette to Luzerne," pp. 369–371; Stiles, *Literary Diary*, vol. 2, p. 459; and Robert C. Bray and Paul E. Bushnell, eds., *Diary of a Common Soldier in the American Revolution, 1775–1783: An Annotated Edition of the Military Journal of Jeremiah Greeman* (DeKalb: Northern Illinois University Press, 1978), p. 185.
2. Rochambeau Papers, vol. 7, pp. 157–160; Kennett, *French Forces*, pp. 59–61; Stephen Bonsal, *When the French Were Here: A Narrative of the Sojourn of the French Forces in America, and Their Contribution to the Yorktown Campaign, Drawn From Unpublished Reports and Letters of Participants in the National Archives of France and the MS Division of the Library of Congress* (Garden City, N.Y.: Doubleday, Doran, 1945), pp. 37–40; and Arnold Whitridge, *Rochambeau* (New York: Collier, 1965), pp. 99–102.
3. Rochambeau Papers, vol. 1, p. 237.
4. Ibid., vol. 2, p. 119, vol. 3, p. 282, and vol. 8, p. 99, as well as Boston Public Library, Ms. f Fr. 160, Langeron Papers, 1778–1785, vol. 2, pieces 31, 49, 64, and 65.
5. For the Rochambeau-La Luzerne correspondence on this topic, see Rochambeau Papers, vol. 14, pp. 8–10 and 49; for the men's military service, see the contrôles for Deux-Ponts and Lauzun's Legion, A.G., 1 YC 869 and A.N., D^2 C 32, respectively.
6. The best discussion of France's efforts in the American War can be found in Dull, *French Navy and American Independence*, especially pp. 143–144, 167–

168, 198, 224, 347–349, 377; see also J. G. Shea, ed., *The Operations of the French Fleet Under the Count de Grasse in 1781–1782, As Described in Two Contemporaneous Journals* (New York: Bradford Club, 1864; reprint New York: Da Capo Press, 1971), p. 165.
7. See, for example, Robin, *New Travels*, p. 13; and Lévis-Mirepoix, "Lettres du Baron Montesquieu," p. 198.
8. Robin, *New Travels*, pp. 16 and 36; Rice and Brown, *American Campaigns*, vol. 1, pp. 20–21; Preston, "Rochambeau and French in Providence," p. 9; A.N., M 1036, Anonymous, "Manière de vivre des Américains"; Louis Philippe, comte de Ségur, "Extraits de lettres écrites d'Amérique par le comte de Ségur, colonel en second du régiment de Soissonnais, à la comtesse de Ségur, dame de Madame Victoire, 1782–1783," *Mélanges publiés par la Société des Bibliophiles françois*, deuxième partie, pièce no. 6 (1903), p. 176; and Lee Kennett, "L'expédition Rochambeau-Ternay: un succès diplomatique," *Revue Historique des Armées* 3, no. 4 (1976): 100.
9. See Rochambeau Papers, vol. 7, pp. 67–68 and 146, and vol. 15, record of the staff meetings of August 25, 1780, and February 23, 1781 (no pagination); and Rhode Island State Archives, Letters to the Governor, vol. 15, no. 68, and Petitions to the Rhode Island General Assembly, vol. 18, no. 29.
10. Livre d'ordre for October 21, 1780; Dawson, "With Rochambeau at Newport," p. 336; and Rochambeau Papers, vol. 7, pp. 165 and 167.
11. Armand Louis de Gontaut Biron, duc de Lauzun, *Memoirs of the Duc de Lauzun*, trans. C. K. Scott Moncrieff (London: George Routledge and Sons, 1928; reprint New York: New York Times and Arno Press, 1969), p. 194.
12. On the stay of Lauzun's Legion in Connecticut, see Stone, *Our French Allies*, pp. 301–308; Maugras, *Lauzun*, pp. 228–234; and Frances M. Fransson, "The French at Lebanon, Connecticut: November 1780–June 1781," *Daughters of the American Revolution Magazine* 108 (1974): 454–456. The fate of hussars Hand and Franck is recorded in A.N., D^2 C 32.
13. The basic source for soldiers' duties in Newport during this time is Livre d'ordre, October 29–November 21, 1780. A duplication of most of the standing orders can be found in Chevalier de Chastellux, Instruction pour le service de l'armée pendant le Quartier d'hyver in Houghton Library, Harvard University, Autograph File. The former source provided the basis for the discussion of this subject.
14. These concerns were expressed at meetings on July 12, 19, 21, 28, and 29, August 10, 25, and 28, September 11 and 26, October 15, 22, and 27, 1780, as well as on February 23, April 6, May 15, and June 5, 1781; see Rochambeau Papers, vol. 15 (no pagination). The same preoccupation dominated Rochambeau's correspondence with La Luzerne between June 1780 and June 1782; Rochambeau Papers, vol. 14.
15. Rhode Island, Letters to the Governor, vol. 15, nos. 17 and 18.
16. Robert A. East, *Business Enterprise in the American Revolutionary Era* (New York: Columbia University Press, 1938), pp. 82–100.
17. Kennett, *French Forces*, p. 70; and Jean des Cilleuls, "Le Service de l'intendance à l'armée de Rochambeau," *Revue Historique de l'Armée* 13, no. 2 (1957): 47–48 and 61n.
18. Rochambeau Papers, vol. 2, pp. 50–54; and Kennett, *French Forces*, pp. 66–67.

19. Rochambeau Papers, vol. 8, pp. 115–116, and vol. 7, pp. 169 and 206. Confirmation of French financial difficulties can be found in Mackenzie, *Diary*, vol. 2, p. 473.
20. Kennett, *French Forces*, pp. 67–68.
21. Fersen, *Lettres*, p. 98, as well as pp. 76 and 110.
22. Gilbert Bodinier, *Les officiers de l'armée royale combattants de la guerre d'Indépendance des Etats-Unis de Yorktown à l'an II* (Vincennes: Service Historique de l'Armeé de Terre, 1983), p. 142.
23. Kennett, *French Forces*, p. 71.
24. See the announcement that "A number of Negro Men, Women and Boys, lately captured by his Most Christian Majesty's fleet," were to be sold, in the *Newport Mercury* of June 9, 1781.
25. Rochambeau Papers, vol. 8, pp. 56–57, 68, and 79, vol. 9, p. 30, vol. 14, pp. 13 and 16, vol. 15, meetings of July 29 and October 27, 1780.
26. A.G., YA 514, Ordonnance du Roi, Pour régler le traitement des Troupes destinées à une expédition particulière, du 20 Mars 1780.
27. The source for this and the following information on the troops' supplies is the Livre d'ordre, unless noted otherwise.
28. Kennett, *French Forces*, p. 74; and Rochambeau Papers, vol. 8, p. 87, and vol. 15, meeting of August 28, 1780.
29. Rhode Island, Council of War, meeting of August 9, 1780, and Rhode Island, Letters to the Governor, vol. 15, nos. 28 and 33.
30. Bartlett, *Records of the State of Rhode Island*, vol. 9, p. 379.
31. Leland and Burnett, "Letters From Lafayette to Luzerne," p. 368; Fersen, *Lettres*, pp. 28–31, 80–82, and 91; and Lévis-Mirepoix, "Lettres du Baron de Montesquieu," pp. 199–200.
32. Kennett, *French Forces*, p. 87; and Rochambeau Papers, vol. 7, p. 203.
33. For two examples, see Lafayette to Vergennes, February 1, 1781, in Benjamin Franklin Stevens, ed., *Facsimiles of Manuscripts in European Archives Relating to America, 1773–1783, With Descriptions, Editorial Notes, Collations, References, and Translations* (London: Privately printed, 1889–1898), vol. 17, document no. 1633; and Lafayette to Washington, March 8, 1781, in Gottschalk, *Letters of Lafayette to Washington*, p. 156.
34. Autographed letter from Chastellux to La Luzerne, dated May 28, 1781, in the collection of the Clements Library of the University of Michigan in Ann Arbor.
35. Bernard Faÿ, ed., "L'Armée de Rochambeau jugée par un Français," *Franco-American Review* 2 (1937): 114–120.
36. Bodinier, *Officiers*, pp. 187–191, contains an excellent discussion of these relationships.
37. Ibid., p. 195; Rice and Brown, *American Campaigns*, vol. 1, p. 241; and Thomas Balch, *The French in America During the War of Independence of the United States, 1777–1783*, trans. Edwin S. Balch and Elise W. Balch (Philadelphia: Porter and Coats, 1891 and 1895; reprint Boston: Gregg Press, 1972), vol. 1, p. 134.
38. Fersen, *Lettres*, p. 116.
39. The following details on dueling come from Bodinier, *Officiers*, pp. 193–196, with corroborating information in Rice and Brown, *American Campaigns*, vol. 1, p. 266n.; B.N., N.A.F. 17691, "Journal par Lauberdière," pp. 42–43; and Morris Bishop, "A French Volunteer," *American Heritage* 17 (1966): 106–107.

40. Bodinier recounts an instance in which a lieutenant killed a captain of the Saintonge Infantry in a duel; for his punishment, he was ordered to his uncle's chateau until he was granted a pardon. See *Officiers*, p. 194.
41. The fullest account of this incident can be found in Dawson, "With Rochambeau at Newport," pp. 336–338. As late as January 1782, Rochambeau was still explaining the incident to the minister of war; see Rochambeau Papers, vol. 12, p. 225.
42. See A.G., 1 YC 869, 188, 932, and 966; 10 YC 1; and A.N.,D^2 C 32.
43. Livre d'ordre for November 19, 1780, and January 3 and 9, 1781.
44. See A.G., 10 YC 1 for Cornevin's service record; Bodinier, *Dictionnaire*, p. 381, for La Barollière's career; Blanchard, *Journal*, p. 105, for a brief account of the incident; and *Newport Mercury* of June 2, 1781, for a notice on the execution.
45. B.N., N.A.F. 17691, "Journal par Lauberdière," p. 24.
46. See the stimulating article by James Kirby Martin, "Benedict Arnold's Treason as Political Protest," *Parameters: Journal of the U.S. Army War College* 11 (1981): 63–74.
47. For brief descriptions of the general situation at this time, see Piers Mackesy, *The War for America, 1775–1783* (Cambridge: Harvard University Press, 1964), pp. 384–386; and Kennett, *French Forces*, pp. 89–91.
48. "Letter From De Vergennes to Lafayette, August 7, 1780," *American Historical Review* 8 (1902–1903): 506–508; Rochambeau Papers, vol. 14, pp. 45 and 47; and Doniol, *Histoire*, vol. 4, pp. 584–586, and vol. 5, pp. 467–468.
49. Henry Clinton, *The American Rebellion: Sir Henry Clinton's Narrative of His Campaigns, 1775–1782, With an Appendix of Original Documents*, ed. William B. Willcox (New Haven: Yale University Press, 1954), p. 456. Clinton expressed the same sentiments frequently in his narrative.

4

MARCH TO VICTORY

JUST AS ALLIED FORTUNES were reaching their nadir, the French took their first minor but successful action against the enemy. Within three months of his defection, Benedict Arnold had been given command of a British force of twelve to fifteen hundred men operating in Virginia against local patriots. Shortly afterward, in late January 1781, a violent storm struck the English ships off Rhode Island, damaging some, scattering others, and breaking their blockade. The way was now open for the French to send a naval expedition to the South to relieve struggling American forces there, a course of action Washington had been advocating for weeks.[1] Charles René, chevalier Destouches, who as senior captain had assumed command of the French naval forces at Newport upon Ternay's death in December, dispatched four vessels (one ship of the line, two frigates, and a cutter) under Captain Le Gardeur de Tilly to the Chesapeake on February 9. This tiny fleet—far inferior to what Washington had in mind—arrived in Chesapeake Bay a few days later and began to attack enemy forces under Arnold almost immediately. Arnold withdrew up the Elizabeth River toward his base at Portsmouth. The French ships drew too much water to follow him, and Tilly was afraid of the sudden arrival of a superior British squadron; consequently, the French stopped their pursuit and returned to Newport, arriving on February 24.

The expedition was hardly a major success. Washington was disappointed and angry; Virginians, including Thomas Nelson who had urged Tilly to press on against Arnold, were resentful.[2] Nonetheless, there were some positive results. Before returning to Rhode Island, Tilly had captured the British ship *Romulus* (forty-four guns), eight merchantmen (four of which he had to burn and four of which he kept as prizes), and five hundred enemy prisoners.[3] Above all, even this limited success encouraged the French to plan more ambitious operations against the enemy. Furthermore, the arrival in Boston of the frigate *Astrée* under Captain Jean François de La Pérouse at the end of February brought Rochambeau the first dispatches he had received from France since his departure the previous May; more important, its cargo included 1.5 million livres of desperately needed cash.[4]

Furnished with both means and motivation, Rochambeau made preparations to send a much larger expedition, including the entire French naval squadron under Destouches and eleven hundred select troops, to the Chesapeake to cooperate with U.S. forces under Lafayette in crushing Arnold. This decision set off a new round of squabbles among the French officers about who would go and in what capacity, which Rochambeau had to settle— to no one's complete satisfaction.[5] Since this expedition would seriously deplete his forces, Rochambeau, with Washington's approval, requested and received temporary reinforcements of around twelve hundred militiamen from Rhode Island and Massachusetts.[6] On March 6, Washington visited Newport, which gave him a triumphal reception, and wished the expedition well in person when it sailed two days later.

Expectations, however, exceeded results. On March 16 the French forces encountered a British naval squadron under Admiral Marriot Arbuthnot near the entrance to Chesapeake Bay. A three-hour engagement followed in which both sides suffered similar losses; with the timid caution typical of most French naval commanders of the period, Destouches determined that he could not proceed and turned back to Newport, putting in there on March 26. The French ships had received substantial damage (although apparently somewhat less than that which they had inflicted on the English), but the military casualties were slight: seven soldiers killed and twenty-nine wounded.[7]

Official public reaction was laudatory. Antoine Charles du Houx, baron de Vioménil, who had been in charge of all army personnel, commended a number of his officers for their conduct on March 16, including Colonel Montmorency-Laval of the Regiment of Bourbonnais who had received "a bruise on the thigh" during the fighting.[8] Rochambeau publicly congratulated the grenadiers of Soissonnais Infantry for their role, and the Providence *American Journal and General Advertiser* later quoted one of those gallant grenadiers whose leg had been shot away by cannon fire: "I give Thanks to God that I still have two Hands and a Leg to serve my King."[9] Congress passed a resolution praising the French, especially Destouches, for their "zeal & vigilance," even though they had not achieved their objective.[10]

Major Frederick Mackenzie of the Royal Welsh Fusiliers, an astute observer of and participant in the American Revolution, probably came closer to the truth with his comment, "The disappointment of the French and Rebels in this their first attempt at a conjunct operation, must be very great, and most sensibly felt by them."[11] Indeed, the English attempted to exploit Franco-American discord by publishing in the New York Tory press a letter from George Washington to a relative, Lund Washington, expressing frustration with the slowness and inadequacy of French measures against Arnold in Virginia.[12] The letter, in fact, had been sent at the time of the February expedition, and as Washington explained, it was written in haste and for purely personal reasons. Rochambeau graciously accepted Washington's regrets about the incident and assurances of his "sincere esteem & attachment." Nevertheless, there can be little doubt that the alliance continued to suffer serious strains.

In the weeks after the March expedition to the Chesapeake, a number of other schemes to employ Rochambeau's corps against the enemy were advanced. Even before Destouches had brought the expedition back to Newport, Governor John Hancock of Massachusetts, using La Pérouse as an intermediary, was urging a French operation against Penobscot in Maine (then part of the state of Massachusetts), which the English were using as a base to attack U.S. commerce. Although Destouches favored this plan, Rochambeau was typically cautious, and without wishing to offend important interests in the Northeast, Washington did not want to divert French naval and military elements from what he considered more critical objectives. Rochambeau, in turn, used Washington's reservations to sway Destouches, who exercised a completely independent command over the navy and remained intrigued with the Penobscot project until early May 1781.[13]

In late April, Major Benjamin Tallmadge of Washington's secret service visited Rochambeau in Newport to propose an amphibious attack against a Tory base at Lloyd's Neck on Long Island. Rochambeau felt the enemy post was too well protected and the French naval squadron too ill-prepared for the plan to be practical at the time; Washington concurred.[14]

About the same time, La Pérouse, who had received special orders from Louis XVI to lead an expedition against the British in Hudson Bay, required two hundred and fifty troops from Rochambeau's army for the operation. Although the minister of war, Henri Philippe, marquis de Ségur, had instructed Rochambeau to cooperate with La Pérouse, Rochambeau was reluctant to further weaken his command and managed to delay providing the detachment until early June. A few days later, in light of changed conditions, La Pérouse suspended his plans for the expedition.[15]

FROM YORKTOWN TO VALMY

The fortunes of the French continued to vacillate between encouraging and disillusioning developments. On May 8, 1781, the ship *Concorde* arrived at Boston carrying Louis Jacques, comte de Barras, who was to take command of the French naval forces at Rhode Island, and the vicomte de Rochambeau, the French military commander's son; they brought a number of dispatches filled with good and bad news. On the positive side, the French government had allocated an additional 6 million livres in needed funds for Rochambeau's corps; over six hundred reinforcements were already at sea on their way to Rhode Island; and François Joseph Paul, comte de Grase, who commanded the large convoy from which the reinforcements had been detached, promised to have his fleet in North American waters by late summer to coordinate his efforts with Rochambeau's. On the other hand, the king had decided not to send the additional ten thousand troops the vicomte de Rochambeau had requested; even worse, the long anticipated second division of around twenty-five hundred men was not going to be sent to the United States either. On top of this, Rochambeau was supposed to furnish two hundred and fifty soldiers to serve in La Pérouse's expedition to Hudson Bay and seven hundred more to complement the military contingents in the fleet, of which Barras formally took command on May 15.[16]

By late May 1781, Rochambeau had good reason to be concerned with the deteriorating strength of his corps. Since their arrival he had lost ten officers: Four had died, four had returned to France, and two had resigned their commissions.[17] More serious was the loss of enlisted men. Although the death rate declined during the winter of 1780–1781, three hundred and twenty-five soldiers had died by May 1781 (including those killed in action in March and the two hussars executed in April), and an additional sixty soldiers had deserted.[18] Even after Rochambeau had managed to reduce his troop commitments to the navy to seven hundred men, he was left with barely four thousand men. When allowance was made for soldiers on the sick list, those employed in auxiliary services (such as transport, hospital, and bakery duties), and those required to guard French positions and supplies, Rochambeau claimed he would have fewer than three thousand men (excluding the eagerly awaited reinforcements) fit and available to go on campaign.[19] This was not some academic consideration; by late May preparations were well under way for the most important military action by the French in the war.

On May 22, 1781, Rochambeau had met with Washington at Wethersfield, Connecticut, to plan an offensive against the British. Although Rochambeau favored the Chesapeake, he deferred to Washington, who continued to press for an attack on New York, and agreed to unite his forces with the American army on the east bank of the Hudson. Washington also wanted the French fleet transferred from Newport to Boston. Again, Rochambeau was reluctant, because this would leave French installations and supplies in Rhode Island largely unprotected, but he agreed, knowing his authority did not extend over the navy and Admiral Barras would make the final decision.[20] In fact, the French had begun preliminary preparations for a troop movement (buying horses, renting wagons, gathering hospital supplies) in early April; by mid-month they were moving heavy equipment, stores, and baggage to Providence where they were safer; and by the last week of April Pierre François de Béville, Rochambeau's quartermaster general, had mapped out a route from Rhode Island to the U.S. headquarters at New Windsor.[21] Although committed to joining Washington in New York, Rochambeau had not renounced the possibility of a campaign in the South, as he made clear in a letter to Admiral de Grasse less than a week after the Wethersfield conference.[22]

Back in Newport, Rochambeau faced a busy schedule. One major issue to be resolved was the disposition of the French naval squadron, which Rochambeau had agreed to transfer to Boston. On May 31, however, a "council of war," including the ranking military and naval officers of the French forces, decided unanimously to stay at Newport; a second council of war, composed of the naval officers and called by Barras to meet aboard the *Neptune* on June 8, confirmed the earlier decision.[23] Another problem was the guard detachments that would be left behind in Rhode Island under the orders of Brigadier General Claude Gabriel de Choisy, since Rochambeau could ill afford to weaken further his meager forces. Fortunately, the small convoy carrying 660 reinforcements for Rochambeau's corps arrived in Boston in early June, just in time to resolve this difficulty. Although only about 400 of the men were fit for duty (260 were noted as ill with scurvy), the newcomers were ordered to Rhode Island, where most would be left to serve under Choisy.[24]

And then came the countless tasks that had to be completed to put an army into motion. Staff officers were instructed to compile exact lists of the horses available and their condition. Unit commanders had to provide the numbers of "shoes, shirts, and other clothing" required for the troops. Among other things, "cartridges, balls, cartridge pouches, cooking pots, cloaks, weapons, canteens, picks, tents, axes, [and] shovels" had to be issued to each unit according to need and availability. If all of this were not enough, on the afternoon of June 1 each regiment had to furnish "a captain, a lieutenant, a sub-lieutenant and 8 squads to assist at the execution" of Sergeant Cornevin for the attempted murder of an officer.[25]

Time was pressing, since the French were to leave Newport on June 9 and 10. The French—at least the officers who almost alone have left records—viewed their departure with mixed emotions. Although they would miss the hospitality and sociability they had found amid local families, they were also anxious to broaden their experience in America and to get on with the mission that had brought them there.[26] The citizens of Newport formally acknowledged their gratitude to Rochambeau "for his particular Attentions for the Welfare of this Town during his command here."[27] And although the *Newport Mercury* stopped publishing announcements in French after June 23, it kept its readers informed about the exploits of Rochambeau's corps throughout the rest of the year.[28]

Simultaneously, as the French army prepared to leave Newport, arrangements had to be made for the detachments that would remain in Rhode Island. The protection of the French defensive works and naval squadron at Newport was entrusted to General Choisy, who had four hundred infantrymen and thirty artillerymen assigned to his command, along with a thousand local militiamen. As soon as the reinforcements in Boston could join the main body of French troops, they were to be sent to Choisy, who, in turn, would release an equal number of soldiers under his orders to join Rochambeau's force. This plan would allow the newcomers, who were still recovering from the ocean voyage, to acclimate to their new assignments gradually. The reinforcements, who had departed from France on March 22 as part of Admiral de Grasse's large convoy, had been drawn from seven infantry regiments (Auvergne, Neustrie, Languedoc, Boulonnais, Anhalt, La Marck, and Barrois), as well as from the second battalion of the Auxonne Artillery. More than a third of the men arrived in the United States too ill to perform regular duties.[29] Some, like their comrades before them, did not survive the voyage; for example, Antoine Petitjean, a twenty-five-year-old private from Lorraine who had enlisted in the Auxonne Artillery five years earlier, "died at sea during the crossing from France to America on March 27, 1781."[30] Most of the men resembled Petitjean in that they were relatively young (in their twenties) but had already served five or more years in the army.[31]

Besides Choisy's forces at Newport, additional French troops had to be stationed at Providence under the orders of Choisy's second in command, Louis Aimable de Prez de Crassier, a major in the Royal Deux-Ponts Infantry, to guard the stores that were left there—including most of the siege, or heavy, artillery and magazines. Major de Prez encountered the same difficulty in finding quarters for his contingent that his predecessors had met the previous year in their attempts to establish a hospital in the town.[32] Eventually, however, de Prez succeeded in obtaining quarters for his detachment;

the town authorities turned over a workhouse to be used as a barracks after it had been repaired at the expense of the French.[33]

The main body of French troops, who were transported to Providence by boats, began arriving there on June 10, whereas their heavy baggage was carted overland. Arrangements had been made to store much of their equipment and to lodge French officers in private homes; the soldiers were either quartered in large empty houses or, more commonly, once again in tents.[34] For the eight days they remained in Providence, the French resumed their normal routine while the final preparations for the march to New York were being completed. Duties were assigned, guard posts established, patrols sent out, formations held, times for reveille and retreat set, and warnings made about the protection of civilian property.[35] One Providence newspaper even ran advertisements in French for at least one issue.[36]

For the march, impedimenta were severely restricted: Every regiment was allotted a maximum of twelve wagons with a capacity of fifteen hundred pounds each; captains were limited to three hundred pounds of baggage and lieutenants to one hundred and fifty pounds. Some officers, like First Lieutenant Jean François Louis de Lesquevin de Clermont-Crèvecoeur of the Auxonne Artillery, were "very much annoyed to leave our heavy baggage behind."[37] Meanwhile, Rochambeau ordered the infantry elements of Lauzun's Legion to Lebanon, where they joined the hussars stationed there; together they formed a separate column to cover the left flank of the French army. And as the reinforcements arrived from Boston, they were sent on to Choisy.[38] Perhaps more critical for the ultimate success of the upcoming campaign was the arrival of additional funds on the same convoy as the reinforcements; Benoît Joseph de Tarlé, Rochambeau's chief financial officer, estimated that with this new money the army could support itself until October 20 (one day after Cornwallis's surrender, as it turned out).[39]

On June 17 Rochambeau issued marching orders: Beginning the following day, each of the four infantry regiments—together with some of the artillery, baggage train, and hospital facilities—would leave one day apart. The time of assembly, the order of the march, formations, guard duties, arrangements for food distribution, work details, and the locations of hospitals and camps were all specified in advance. From then until the end of the month, when the entire corps reached Newtown, Connecticut, each contingent occupied the same camp on four consecutive days. Beginning July 1, the army was divided into two brigades for marching, the first consisting of the regiments of Bourbonnais and Deux-Ponts with their attachments and the second including the regiments of Soissonnais and Saintonge and their support forces.[40]

The organization of the march—however complicated—proved to be easier than its execution. Pioneers armed with axes and other tools had to precede each contingent to ensure that the route was cleared. Streams and rivers had to be crossed either where they could be forded or where ferries were available. The sites of encampments, including the location of hospitals and bakeries, had to be prepared. Fresh drinking water was a constant concern; when there were doubts about the quality of the water, the soldiers were issued rum to mix in it, with the admonition never to drink the rum straight (*pur*).[41] Sometimes there was a shortage of certain supplies that had to be purchased on the march. At one point, the daily ration of bread was reduced to only four ounces, although the troops were issued an additional allowance of rice and fresh meat (provided by slaughtering the cattle that accompanied the French columns).[42]

Not surprisingly, the soldiers found marching especially difficult during the first days; they had been cooped up in Newport for eleven months and were unaccustomed to the exertion it required, particularly since each soldier carried around sixty pounds of equipment.[43] In addition, the French army had to contend with roads Lieutenant Crèvecoeur described as "frightful" and with such heat that Rochambeau set reveille at between 2:00 and 3:30 A.M., with a departure time an hour and a half later, to take advantage of the cool of early morning.[44] Under these conditions the lead unit could cover between ten and eighteen miles per day. Inevitably, the artillery and baggage wagons (containing camp tents and cooking utensils) traveled more slowly and broke down more readily, and the units at the rear of the march were continually struggling to keep up with those ahead of them.[45]

In spite of a few unpleasant incidents, such as a fire in the woods outside of Windham, Connecticut, that was caused by the negligence of French soldiers in extinguishing their campfires, contacts between the French forces and local inhabitants along their route were generally cordial.[46] At Bolton, Connecticut, an unusual incident occurred when a minister named Cotton asked to adopt the four-year-old daughter of a grenadier in the regiment of Deux-Ponts (Adam Gabel, thirty years old and a veteran of more than ten years) and offered the soldier's wife, who was accompanying the troops, the equivalent of thirty *louis* in return; the mother refused.[47] More normal relations consisted of Americans furnishing goods and services (usually, but not always, for a fee) and the French providing entertainment (especially banquets and dances, for example, at Plainfield, Marion, and Hartford, Connecticut).[48]

Some contacts, however, were more hostile and even violent. By the end of June and the beginning of July, as Rochambeau's army was leaving

Connecticut and entering New York, the number and belligerence of American Tories increased; using the irregular terrain, they began to snipe at the French columns.[49] Lauzun's Legion, which had followed a separate route about fifteen miles from the main body and closer to the coast, was the only French unit to engage in any real combat. At Washington's behest, Lauzun marched his unit ahead of Rochambeau's army to link up with an American force under General Benjamin Lincoln and launch a joint attack on Fort Knyphausen, one of the keys to the British defense of New York, on the night of July 2. The attack failed, according to Lauzun, because of the premature action of Lincoln who had to be saved by the French.[50] This was not an auspicious omen for Allied cooperation!

Following this failure, Lauzun led his legion toward White Plains, where he was to rendezvous with the main force. Rochambeau's first contingents arrived at North Castle on July 3 and waited for the trailing units; once assembled, the entire French corps moved on to unite with the U.S. army under Washington at Philipsburg, about twenty miles distant. General Washington's orders of the day for July 6 publicly welcomed the French, congratulating them for the zeal and ardor that had enabled them to overcome the obstacles of their long, difficult journey and singling out the rear elements who had enjoyed almost no rest.[51] Indeed, the last day's march was so long and the heat so excessive that more than four hundred soldiers "dropped from fatigue" before completing it.[52]

Despite some distorted claims about the speed of the march—Rochambeau wrote Ségur that they had covered 220 miles in eleven days—and the number of desertions—Rochambeau told Barras that not a man had been left behind "except ten love-sick soldiers of Soissonnais who returned to see their sweethearts [*maîtresses*] at Newport"—the march had indeed been a major achievement.[53] The entire corps, at staggered intervals, had covered approximately 180 miles from Providence to Philipsburg in nineteen days, including five days of rest enjoyed by the leading elements; although hundreds of troops continued to straggle in after the arrival of the main force, by July 8 Rochambeau counted four thousand men present and ready for duty.[54] The French losses were minor: Four or five men died during the march, and nine others deserted (four from Soissonnais, three from Lauzun, and one each from Saintonge and Deux-Ponts).[55] Furthermore, all three deserters from Lauzun's Legion were Germans (from Saxony, Brandenburg, and Prussia) who had been recruited in the United States. Some of the deserters were apprehended and punished severely. Joseph Martel, a twenty-seven-year-old Burgundian who enlisted in the Soissonnais Infantry in February 1773, was condemned to chains for his desertion on June 19.

François Roy had been born in a village in Franche-Comté the same year as Martel, enlisted in the same regiment three months earlier, and deserted the same day; his sentence was even harsher—condemnation to death. The prospect of such a fate could hardly have been encouraging to those contemplating escape into the alien U.S. environment. For the time being at least, it was lack of money and not lack of personnel that most concerned Rochambeau; writing to Ségur on July 8, he pleaded, "In the name of God, Monsieur, do not forget the hard cash and real funds for the month of October."[56]

As the French set up their camp, a new routine was established. Guard posts were assigned at Rochambeau's headquarters, the artillery park, hospital, magazines, and supply depots; foraging expeditions were organized; work details were selected; and arrangements were made for the regular distribution of food. The latter was sometimes a problem because the enemy attempted to block food shipments from going up the Hudson River to the French encampment; at one point in mid-July the daily bread ration again had to be limited to a quarter of a pound. In response, Rochambeau set up an infantry outpost and artillery battery on the river to protect the shipments, and by early August the ration was up to one pound of bread plus eight ounces of corn and a pound and a half of fresh meat for each soldier per day.[57]

What most clearly distinguished this situation from the previous experiences of the French troops was the proximity of their American comrades in arms in the Continental Army, whom they would live alongside for the next six weeks. On the other hand, the same strict segregation that had been observed during the French encampment at Newport was imposed at Philipsburg. No French personnel, including officers, could leave camp without a pass signed by a major general, and anyone who attempted to do so would be punished "as a Marauder"; even sutlers were forbidden to go outside the camp to purchase supplies without written authorization. The commanders of the guard were "to allow no Foreigners, be they Americans or deserters, to enter the precincts [*l'intérieur*] of the army."[58]

Other factors reinforced official restrictions on contacts between the personnel of the two armies. The language barrier and other cultural differences undoubtedly played a major role. So, too, did the greater logistical support enjoyed by the French. Within two days of effecting his juncture with the Americans, Rochambeau noted, "*Our neighbors lack everything.*" One of his staff officers observed that the American regiments were drastically understrength and that their troops were "almost completely naked," although the officers were somewhat better maintained.[59] On at least one occasion French officers had to warn their soldiers not to mock the American troops for their ragged appearance, lack of discipline, or inadequate support services.[60] Some U.S. officers felt humiliated by the financial advantages enjoyed by their French counterparts. Colonel Ebenezer Huntington of Connecticut wrote his elder brother, Andrew, on August 2, 1781, "We are serving with the French Army where the Officers dine in luxury and give us frequent invitations to their tables, we can't go to them, because we can not return the Compliment."[61] Again, Major Mackenzie had some perspicacious—albeit biased—observations about "the animosities and misunderstanding which must naturally arise between troops so totally opposite in language, Character, Sentiments, manners, and Religion"; he claimed that American deserters testified to the resentment they and their comrades felt toward the French and that French deserters affirmed that they and their compatriots held American troops in "the utmost contempt."[62]

Although official attitudes and announcements continued to emphasize Allied friendship and French and U.S. leaders sponsored dinners and balls to foster close relations, strains persisted.[63] Reconnaissance and foraging expeditions became common assignments for some of the French troops during July and early August; these duties, frequently carried out by the dashing but unruly hussars of Lauzun's Legion, allowed those men to display not only their bravery in the face of danger but also their lack of restraint in dealing with foreign civilians, particularly those suspected of being enemy sympathizers. For example, during a scouting mission near Morrisania, New York, on July 21, one such patrol was fired upon by local Tories just a day after Lieutenant Jacques Hartmann of the same unit had been killed by a party of "De Lancey's Tories." After the enemy attack was driven back with only minor casualties, some of Lauzun's troops vented their hostility by pillaging nearby houses. This and all other depredations committed by French soldiers were severely dealt with by their commanders.[64] One can readily speculate that such experiences only added to Allied tensions.

More direct evidence of low morale in the French army is provided by a burst of desertions between late July and mid-August. Around two dozen soldiers deserted; most were from Lauzun's Legion, and half went over to nearby elements of the British army. Punishment of those apprehended was harsh. Corporal Jean Pierre Verdier, thirty-three years of age, was hanged for his crime on August 17, despite more than fifteen years of prior service in the Regiment of Bourbonnais. Only the intervention of his colonel saved a deserter from the Regiment of Royal Deux-Ponts from an identical fate.[65]

The situation was no better for the small French garrison left behind in Rhode Island under the command of General Choisy. In early July Lieutenant Colonel Stephen Kimball of the Rhode Island militia complained to Governor Greene that both Choisy and Barras had reneged on commitments to support his forces in an attempt to capture Block Island from the Tories and that, as a result, it remained in enemy hands.[66] On July 10 Barras did send a small expedition, comprising around 250 troops and four ships, to attack an enemy fort at Lloyd's Neck on Huntington Bay, Long Island. The French failed to achieve the surprise they had hoped for, were repulsed with light casualties, and returned to Newport four days after their departure—yet one more Allied disappointment.[67] Nonetheless, within a month the undaunted Barras was preparing another, more ambitious offensive by his fleet and Choisy's entire Newport garrison against Newfoundland. In fact, by early August his plans had progressed to the stage that he gave a farewell banquet for prominent ladies and gentlemen of Newport aboard his flagship, the *Duc de Bourgogne*.[68] Then, suddenly, the strategic situation of the Franco-American allies—together with the whole course of the war—was dramatically and decisively changed.

As Barras completed arrangements for an expedition to Newfoundland and Rochambeau began intensive, if unenthusiastic, preparations for a siege of New York, developments in the Caribbean—always the primary focus of French interests in the Western Hemisphere—drastically altered their plans.[69] On the evening of August 14, a courier from Rhode Island arrived at the Allied camp in New York; included among the dispatches he carried to Rochambeau were Barras's proposal for an attack against Newfoundland and, most important, a letter from Admiral François Joseph de Grasse in which the admiral outlined his plans for late summer and early autumn 1781. In response to an earlier request for assistance from Rochambeau, de Grasse, who had secured a loan from Spanish sources in Cuba, wrote that he was leaving Haiti (Saint Domingue) in early August with a fleet of nearly thirty ships of the line and over three thousand troops to sail to Chesapeake Bay where he would remain until mid-October. This decision seemed to offer an unprecedented opportunity for a decisive victory over the British in the South. Furthermore, on August 11 General Clinton had received approximately twenty-five hundred Hessian reinforcements in New York, which made him too strong to be attacked with any great expectation of success. Washington, therefore, gave up his long-cherished project for the capture of New York and joined Rochambeau in pleading that Barras renounce his northern plans and instead sail southward with Choisy's troops and the French siege artillery, thereby ensuring Allied naval and military predominance in the Chesapeake. Barras agreed. Washington ordered Lafayette to keep the British forces under General Charles Cornwallis occupied in Virginia. And the Allied commanders started issuing the orders necessary to set their armies in motion.[70]

Thus commenced one of the most remarkable feats of military and naval coordination of the age. Washington's and Rochambeau's forces broke camp and began their march on August 18. A number of American units under the command of General Heath, together with substantial stores and the French bakeries, were left behind to cover the withdrawal and deceive the English in New York. From the beginning the troops had to contend with hot and stormy weather, impassable roads, overloaded wagons, inadequate draft animals, difficult fords, insufficient ferries, and a shortage of cash. The last problem, at least in Rochambeau's opinion, was compounded by the greed of American businessmen, among whom even "the most patriotic" provided loans "only at an excessive interest rate." The arrival in Boston of a shipment of 1.8 million livres from France in late August alleviated the situation and allowed Rochambeau to loan Washington twenty thousand dollars to help pay his desperate soldiers.[71]

Almost simultaneously, back in Rhode Island Barras was finishing his preparations for sailing. The siege train was loaded aboard his ships. Official farewells were again exchanged on August 20. Approximately six hundred soldiers under the orders of General Choisy embarked on Barras's vessels the following day, leaving behind a contingent of only a hundred men, commanded by Major de Prez of the Royal Deux-Ponts, to guard French equipment and supplies at Providence. On August 23 the French naval squadron set sail to rendezvous in the Chesapeake with De Grasse's fleet from the West Indies and with the armies of Washington and Rochambeau now en route from New York to Virginia.[72]

Meanwhile, since February 1781 the marquis de Lafayette had been in command of an American force in Virginia, originally intended to bring Benedict Arnold to bay. Although he failed to achieve that objective, Lafayette was able to occupy Richmond at the end of April and to join forces with General Anthony Wayne's small army of a thousand men on June 10. His opposite number, Lord Cornwallis, had been operating in the Carolinas since the U.S. surrender of Charleston in May 1780. After some inconclusive successes, in late April 1781 Cornwallis decided to move his weary army to Virginia and united with General William Phillips's forces at Petersburg on May 20. Thereafter, Lafayette hounded and harassed the British but because of his inferior strength could not force a decision. Cornwallis, however, was unable to catch "the boy" who continued to elude him. This inconclusive cat-and-mouse activity led Cornwallis to head toward the coast; by June 25 he had reached Williamsburg, which he soon evacuated in favor of Portsmouth. Finally, in early August the British commander established his forces at Yorktown and at Gloucester, just across the York River, an excellent position where he could readily receive reinforcements or, if necessary, easily evacuate as long as England continued to exercise the naval predominance it had enjoyed throughout the war. Shortly afterward, Lafayette received orders from Washington to ensure that the British army remained in just that situation.[73]

The ultimate Allied objective was not generally known until the end of August when the rank and file in Rochambeau's army first became aware that their destination was Virginia. At about the same time, the English in New York realized this, too.[74] On September 3 the French troops halted on the outskirts of Philadelphia to refresh and refurbish themselves from the exertions of their march. Later that same day the Regiments of Bourbonnais and Deux-Ponts and Lauzun's Legion paraded into the city in full dress; the next day the second division, composed of the Soissonnais and Saintonge Regiments, made a similar ceremonial entry; and on September 5 the soldiers of Soissonnais performed a drill on the Commons, where the French army was encamped, before a large and appreciative crowd that was impressed by their fine appearance.[75] That very day news arrived that Admiral de Grasse had anchored in Chesapeake Bay with his fleet, including twenty-eight ships of the line and about thirty-three hundred French troops under the command of Claude Anne, marquis de Saint-Simon. Since Washington was unable to procure enough shipping to transport the entire Franco-American army by sea, after consulting with Rochambeau he decided to send the bulk of the forces overland, and approximately two thousand elite troops embarked on the vessels that were available.[76]

In Virginia, Saint-Simon's units had begun to disembark at James Island on September 2 and effected a junction with the Americans under Lafayette a few days later near Williamsburg. Although some wanted to attack Cornwallis immediately—especially the comte de Grasse who was anxious to return to the West Indies, which he had left virtually defenseless—the Allied commanders agreed to await the combined forces, already well on their way, which would give them an overwhelming advantage over their foe. Meanwhile, Lafayette and Saint-Simon proceeded to cut off Yorktown by land, as Cornwallis, confident of British naval supremacy, refused to take any action beyond the improvement of his fortifications.[77]

Unfortunately for Cornwallis and for British hopes of winning the war, a naval engagement off the Virginia Capes on September 5, 1781, destroyed decisively, albeit temporarily, the control of the seas that determined his fate.[78] Admiral Samuel Hood, who had pursued de Grasse from the Caribbean in vain, joined another English squadron under Admiral Thomas Graves at New York, from where their combined fleet departed on August 31 under Graves's orders. De Grasse, informed of the English presence on the morning of September 5, set sail abruptly and, after maneuvering off the mouth of Chesapeake Bay, engaged the enemy that afternoon. The fighting was suspended two hours later, at sunset. Both sides suffered severe damage, and each sustained over two hundred casualties, although the British losses were somewhat more serious. The two fleets stalked each other during the next four days until a storm dispersed them on September 9. The French commander decided to return to the Chesapeake and continue his blockade of the British army at Yorktown and Gloucester. Upon reaching Cape Henry on September 11, de Grasse encountered Barras who had departed from Newport in late August with his own squadron, the troops under Choisy, Rochambeau's siege train, and much-needed supplies. This fleet, which had arrived the previous day, increased the already significant superior naval strength the French enjoyed over the English. On September 13 Graves decided to sail back to New York to refit. The trap was rapidly closing around Cornwallis; the arrival of Washington's and Rochambeau's armies would complete the process.

By the beginning of the second week of September, the Allied armies had reached the Head of Elk—the northern end of Chesapeake Bay—and began to split up to continue their movement to Virginia as expeditiously as possible.[79] Because of a shortage of boats, only the grenadiers and chasseurs of the French regiments, along with certain select American units—approximately two thousand men in all—embarked on those vessels available between September 9 and 11 and sailed under the command of General Benjamin Lincoln. Although normally travel by sea was much faster than by land, poor weather and inadequate provisions delayed this contingent so that the troops took nearly as long to reach their destination as did their comrades. Meanwhile, Washington and Rochambeau rode on ahead with only a small escort and on September 14 reached Williamsburg, where they set up headquarters. Most of the French and American forces continued their march on foot, reaching Baltimore on September 12. There they received information that Barras had sent ten ships to transport the Allied troops to Virginia. The forces then marched to Annapolis where they embarked on September 19 and 20 and sailed the following day. They arrived at the mouth of a small creek near Williamsburg on September 25 and disembarked over the next two days. Only the French field artillery, wagon train, and draft and riding animals—over two hundred wagons, eight hundred oxen, and fifteen hundred horses—continued to march overland, escorted by Lauzun's mounted troops; they would not reach Yorktown until October 6. Except for these elements, the rest of the Allied forces—American and French, military and naval—were in place to finish off the British army at Yorktown by the last days of September 1781.

Notes

1. For more information about this expedition, see Kennett, *French Forces*, pp. 94–97; Rochambeau Papers, vol. 1, pp. 239–242; and James Thomas Flexner, *George Washington in the American Revolution (1775–1783)* (Boston: Little, Brown, 1967), pp. 410–419.
2. Flexner, *Washington in American Revolution*, pp. 418–419; and Emory G. Evans, *Thomas Nelson of Yorktown: Revolutionary Virginian* (Charlottesville: University Press of Virginia, 1975), p. 97. Nelson became governor four months later, a position he held until November 30, 1781, when he retired because of ill health.
3. Rochambeau Papers, vol. 7, p. 238.
4. Ibid., vol. 1, pp. 241–242.
5. Accounts of this expedition can be found in Kennett, *French Forces*, pp. 98–100; Whitridge, *Rochambeau*, pp. 119–124; and Harold A. Larrabee, *Decision at the Chesapeake* (New York: Clarkson N. Potter, 1964), pp. 130–131.
6. Rochambeau Papers, vol. 7, pp. 240–250.
7. Ibid., vol. 9, pp. 5–6. The rare journal of a simple soldier, a grenadier in the Regiment of Bourbonnais, provides a participant's account of this engagement. The "Journal Militaire" of this anonymous soldier is in the Library of Congress, Manuscript Division, MMC 1907, Milton S. Latham Journal (no pagination), which will henceforth be cited as Latham, "Journal." This journal gives the total French casualties—naval and military—as 69 dead and 129 wounded. The regimental contrôles corroborate the number of army dead.
8. Rochambeau Papers, vol. 7, p. 266.
9. Livre d'ordre for April 1, 1781; and the April 4, 1781, issue of the newspaper.
10. Reprinted in the *Newport Mercury* of April 28, 1781.
11. Mackenzie, *Diary*, vol. 2, p. 495 (entry for March 26, 1781).
12. See the correspondence between Rochambeau and Washington in late April 1781 in Rochambeau Papers, vol. 7, pp. 288–291, reproduced in Doniol, *Histoire*, vol. 5, pp. 452–455.
13. Rochambeau Papers, vol. 1, p. 242; vol. 7, pp. 252, 257, 272–273, 279–281; vol. 9, pp. 54–56.
14. Ibid., vol. 9, pp. 281 and 286–287; and Kennett, *French Forces*, pp. 102–103.
15. Rochambeau Papers, vol. 12, pp. 19, 27–28, 49, and 60–61; and René Georges Pichon, "Contribution à l'étude de la participation militaire de la France à la guerre d'indépendance des Etats-Unis, 1778–1783" (Thèse du troisième cycle, Université de Paris I, 1976), pp. 482–484 and 503.
16. Rochambeau Papers, vol. 12, pp. 19–21, 27–28, and 57–58. Rochambeau managed to reduce the number of troops required by the navy to a total of seven

hundred, many of whom were to be drawn from the coming reinforcements.
17. A.G., YA 513 contains a list of officer losses in Rochambeau's corps from August 1780 through May 1781.
18. Like other statistics on enlisted men, these are drawn from the regimental registers or contrôles: A.G., 1 YC 188, 966, 932, and 869; A.G., 10 YC 1; and A.N., D² C 32.
19. Rochambeau to Ségur, June 1, 1981, in Rochambeau Papers, vol, 9, p. 103.
20. Two somewhat different discussions of the conference can be found in Bonsal, *When the French Were Here*, pp. 82–87; and Flexner, *Washington in the American Revolution*, pp. 428–431.
21. See Rochambeau Papers, vol. 15, meeting of generals and top administrative officers at Newport on April 6, 1781 (no pagination); Livre d'ordre for April 24, 1781; and Heath, *Memoirs*, pp. 260–261.
22. Reproduced in Doniol, *Histoire*, vol. 5, pp. 475–476.
23. Rochambeau Papers, vol. 9, pp. 99 and 112.
24. Ibid., vol. 1, p. 246; Doniol, *Histoire*, vol. 5, p. 494; and Deux-Ponts, *My Campaigns*, pp. 112–113.
25. Livre d'ordre for May 29 and June 1 and 2, 1781. See pp. 41–42 on the attempted murder.
26. Warrington Dawson, ed., "Un garde Suisse de Louis XVI au service de l'Amérique: Le Baron Gaspard de Gallatin," *Le Correspondant* 324 (1931): 673–674; Fersen, *Lettres*, p. 117; Rice and Brown, *American Campaigns*, vol. 1, p. 245; and Allan Forbes and Paul F. Cadman, *France and New England*, vol. 2 (Boston: State Street Trust, 1927), p. 35.
27. Newport Town Proceedings for June 5, 1781.
28. For example, the issues of July 14, September 15, and October 6 and 13, 1781.
29. Rochambeau Papers, vol. 9, pp. 126–131; and Livre d'ordre for June 9 and 13, 1781.
30. A.G., 10 YC 1. Petitjean can be found under no. 59 in Duchaffaut's company.
31. Unfortunately, the regimental registers do not always indicate transfers, but the fifty reinforcements from the Neustrie Infantry seem to be typical. See A.G., X^b 22, "Etat des cinquante volontiares tirés du Régt. de Neustrie pour passer à Rhode Island en Amérique," dated Quimper, March 13, 1781.
32. See p. 17 . French soldiers were still hospitalized in Providence in June 1781.
33. Rhode Island, Letters to the Governor, vol. 17, nos. 9 and 18; and Providence Town Meetings of August 28 and 30, 1781.
34. Stone, *Our French Allies*, pp. 387 and 391; Preston, "Rochambeau and the French Troops in Providence," pp. 10–15; Providence Town Meetings of April 9 and 18, 1781; and Rhode Island Historical Society, Providence Town Papers, vol. 6, nos. 2413 and 2478.
35. Livre d'ordre for June 10, 11, and 13, 1781.
36. See the *American Journal and General Advertiser* for June 13, 1781.
37. Rice and Brown, *American Campaigns*, vol. 1, pp. 246–247 and 26–27.
38. Livre d'ordre for June 13 and 16, 1781; and Acomb, *Journal of Von Closen*, p. 84.
39. Rochambeau Papers, vol. 3, p. 279 (duplicated in vol. 9, p. 106).
40. A handy itinerary of the French army can be found in Bonsal, *When the French Were Here*, p. 252. Livre d'ordre for June 17 through July 6, 1781, contains daily details. Lauzun's Legion followed a different route to the left of the main body.

41. See Rochambeau Papers, vol. 3, pp. 310–314, which can also be found in Rice and Brown, *American Campaigns*, vol. 2, pp. 9–16; and Livre d'ordre for June 25, 1781.
42. Blanchard, *Journal*, p. 107; Jean Baptiste Donatien de Vimeur, comte de Rochambeau, *Memoirs of the Marshal Count de Rochambeau, Relative to the War of Independence of the United States*, trans. M.W.E. Wright (Paris: French, English, and American Library, 1838; reprint New York: New York Times and Arno Press, 1971), pp. 56–57; and Livre d'ordre for June and July 1781.
43. Acomb, *Journal of Von Closen*, p. 84; Rice and Brown, *American Campaigns*, vol. 1, p. 28; "Diary of a French Officer, 1781 (Presumed to be that of Baron Cromot du Bourg, Aid to Rochambeau)," *Magazine of American History* 4 (1880–1881): 293; and Kennett, *French Forces*, p. 24.
44. For Crèvecoeur's description, see Rice and Brown, *American Campaigns*, vol. 1, p. 28 (an evaluation confirmed by Acomb, *Journal of Von Closen*, p. 85). Livre d'ordre for June 24–July 6, 1781, contains the times for first call, assembly, and departure.
45. Rochambeau Papers, vol. 3, pp. 310–314, as well as vol. 12, pp. 70 and 73; and Acomb, *Journal of Von Closen*, p. 89.
46. Kennett, *French Forces*, pp. 113–114; Dawson, "Gallatin," p. 674; and Stone, *Our French Allies*, pp. 393–394.
47. Both Acomb, *Journal of Von Closen*, p. 85, and "Diary of a French Officer," p. 293, recount the episode; A.G., 1 YC 869 provides the data on Gabel. An additional peculiarity of this incident is that it is one of the very rare pieces of evidence that some wives—perhaps a score—accompanied the French troops in America.
48. Rice and Brown, *American Campaigns*, vol. 1, pp. 247–248; Robin, *New Travels*, p. 24; Forbes and Cadman, *France and New England*, vol. 1, p. 149; and Stone, *Our French Allies*, pp. 393–394.
49. Rice and Brown, *American Campaigns*, vol. 1, p. 30; and Dawson, "Gallatin," p. 675.
50. John Austin Stevens, "The Operations of the Allied Armies Before New York, 1781," *Magazine of American History* 4 (1880): 3–9; and Lauzun, Memoirs, pp. 200–201.
51. Stevens, "Allied Armies Before New York," p. 10. Washington's welcome can be found in Livre d'ordre for July 7, 1781, and excerpts in *American Journal and General Advertiser* of July 21, 1781.
52. "Diary of a French Officer," pp. 296–299; and Rice and Brown, *American Campaigns*, vol. 1, pp. 32–33.
53. Doniol, *Histoire*, vol. 5, pp. 510–511. Different estimates on desertions can be found in Acomb, *Journal of Von Closen*, pp. 86 and 90–91; and "Diary of a French Officer," pp. 293 and 295.
54. Rice and Brown, *American Campaigns*, vol. 2, maps 27–39; Kennett, *French Forces*, p. 117; and Rochambeau Papers, vol. 9, p. 152. Latham, "Journal," counts 207 miles in twenty days with seven days of layover.
55. The information on deaths and desertions is from the regimental registers listed in note 18 in this chapter. The number of deaths cannot be exact because it is not always clear whether they occurred on the march or in a hospital back in Rhode Island.

56. Rochambeau Papers, vol. 12, pp. 88–89.
57. Ibid., vol. 1, p. 248, and vol. 12, p. 96; and Livre d'ordre from July 8 to August 17, 1781.
58. Livre d'ordre for July 13 and August 9, 1781.
59. Quoted in Cilleuls, "Service de l'intendance," p. 50; and B.N., N.A.F. 17691, "Journal par Lauberdière," p. 55.
60. Lee Kennett, "Le Bilan d'une rencontre: l'armée française en Amérique, 1780–1782," *Annales historiques de la Révolution français* 48 (October–December 1976): 531; and Kennett, *French Forces*, pp. 118–119.
61. "Letters of Ebenezer Huntington, 1774–1781," *American Historical Review* 5 (1899–1900): 728.
62. Mackenzie, *Diary*, vol. 2, pp. 569, 583, and 589.
63. Stinchcombe, *American Revolution and French Alliance*, pp. 146–148; James Thatcher, *Military Journal of the American Revolution, From the Commencement to the Disbanding of the American Army; Comprising a Detailed Account of the Principal Events and Battles of the Revolution, With Their Exact Dates, and a Biographical Sketch of the Most Prominent Generals* (Hartford, Conn.: Hurlbut, Williams, 1862; reprint New York: New York Times and Arno Press, 1969), pp. 265–266; and Charles A. Campbell, "Rochambeau's Head-Quarters in Westchester County, N.Y., 1781," *Magazine of American History* 4 (1880): 46, all testify to cordial social contacts.
64. Rice and Brown, *American Campaigns*, vol. 1, pp. 248–253; Dawson, "Gallatin," pp. 680–681; "Diary of a French Officer," pp. 302–303; Kennett, "Bilan d'une rencontre," pp. 531–532; B.N., N.A.F. 17691, "Journal par Lauberdière," p. 58 verso; and Livre d'ordre for July 30, 1781.
65. See the contrôles listed in note 18 of this chapter; "Diary of a French Officer," pp. 303–306; Rice and Brown, *American Campaigns*, vol. 1, p. 40; and Mackenzie, *Diary*, vol. 2, pp. 563–589.
66. Rhode Island, Letters to the Governor, vol. 16, no. 94. Another minor example of Franco-American misunderstanding at this time can be found in letter no. 102 in the same volume.
67. Brief accounts of this action are in Stevens, "Allied Armies Before New York," p. 25; Kennett, *French Forces*, p. 120; Rice and Brown, *American Campaigns*, vol. 1, p. 34; and Dawson, "Gallatin," pp. 677–679.
68. Kennett, *French Forces*, p. 130; Pichon, "Participation militaire de la France," p. 532; and Larrabee, *Decision at the Chesapeake*, p. 250.
69. Kennett, *French Forces*, pp. 122–126, describes the situation in New York.
70. Rochambeau Papers, vol. 12, pp. 100–109; Doniol, *Histoire*, vol. 5, pp. 526–528; George Washington, *The Diaries of George Washington 1748–1799*, ed. by John C. Fitzpatrick (Boston: Houghton Mifflin, 1925), vol. 2, pp. 253–254; Clinton, *American Rebellion*, p. 325; Perkins, *France in the American Revolution*, pp. 359–363 and 377–378; Bonsal, *When the French Were Here*, pp. 114–117; Kennett, *French Forces*, pp. 130–131; and Shea, *Operations of the French Fleet*, pp. 61–65 and 148–152.
71. For the preparations and early march, see Heath, *Memoirs*, pp. 275–278; Rice and Brown, *American Campaigns*, vol. 1, pp. 40 and 253–255; Washington, *Diaries*, vol. 2, p. 155; Deux-Ponts, *My Campaigns*, p. 122; and Acomb, *Journal of Von Closen*, p. 106. On Rochambeau's financial situation, see Rochambeau

Papers, vol. 9, p. 183, and vol. 12, p. 119. One testimony on the plight of Washington's troops can be found in "Letters of Ebenezer Huntington," pp. 727–728.
72. Rice and Brown, *American Campaigns*, vol. 1, pp. 134–135; and *Newport Mercury* for September 1, 1781.
73. Henry P. Johnston, *The Yorktown Campaign and the Surrender of Cornwallis, 1781* (New York: Harper and Bros., 1881; reprint New York: Da Capo Press, 1971), pp. 32–69, contains an excellent account of the background of this decisive campaign.
74. Rice and Brown, *American Campaigns*, vol. 2, p. 59.
75. Ibid., vol. 1, p. 46; Robin, *New Travels*, p. 44; and Virginia State Library, Commonwealth of Virginia, Executive Papers, Box 15, letter from J. Jones, J. Madison, and T. Bland to Governor Nelson, dated Philadelphia, September 3, 1781. My special thanks to Ms. Gentry of the Virginia State Library who allowed me to use her invaluable card file as a guide to these documents, which at the time (April 1977) were being prepared for microfilming.
76. Washington, *Diaries*, vol. 2, pp. 258–259; and Bonsal, *When the French Were Here*, pp. 126–132.
77. See Johnston, *Yorktown Campaign*, pp. 96–98; Manceron, *Vent d'Amérique*, pp. 441, 466, and 472–474; Larrabee, *Decision at the Chesapeake*, pp. 142–145; Shea, *Operations of the French Fleet*, pp. 66 and 154; Gottschalk, *Letters of Lafayette to Washington*, p. 225; William Feltman, *The Journal of Lieut. William Feltman, of the First Pennsylvania Regiment, 1781–82, Including the March Into Virginia and the Siege of Yorktown* (Philadelphia: Historical Society of Pennsylvania, 1853; reprint New York: New York Times and Arno Press, 1969), pp. 11–12; and U.S. Congress, *Correspondence of General Washington and Comte de Grasse, 1781, August 17–November 4*. U.S. 71st Congress, 2d session, Senate document 211 (Washington, D.C.: U.S. Government Printing Office, 1931), p. 26.
78. Larrabee, *Decision at the Chesapeake*, pp. 199–223, provides a full description of the combat and its immediate aftermath (to September 13). See also Johnston, *Yorktown Campaign*, pp. 99–101; and Kennett, *French Forces*, p. 136. It is interesting to note that this single two-hour engagement cost nearly as many French casualties (209) as did the entire siege of Yorktown (253).
79. On the various means of transportation and routes to Virginia taken by different Allied elements, see Rochambeau Papers, vol. 2, pp. 250–251; Rice and Brown, *American Campaigns*, vol. 1, pp. 52–55, and vol. 2, pp. 83–84; Robin, *New Travels*, pp. 48–51; Deux-Ponts, *My Campaigns*, pp. 127–134; Rochambeau, *Memoirs*, pp. 63–65; and Dawson, "Gallatin," pp. 683–686.

5
YORKTOWN

THE DIVERSE ARRAY of Allied forces converged on Virginia from various points of departure hundreds of miles distant: Barras's naval squadron, carrying the remnants of the French garrison, from Rhode Island; the armies of Washington and Rochambeau from their positions outside New York City; Lafayette's American forces who had been dogging Cornwallis in the South since spring; and de Grasse's fleet, with Saint-Simon's corps on board, from the Caribbean. Even before this extraordinary juncture—which dramatically highlights France's role in the American Revolution—was effected, the Allied commanders were planning the deployment of their forces. Upon their arrival in Williamsburg on September 14, Washington and Rochambeau immediately contacted Lafayette and Saint-Simon at their separate camps and shortly afterward established their own headquarters one block apart in the town itself. On September 17 Washington and Rochambeau, accompanied by members of their staffs, went to confer with Admiral de Grasse aboard his flagship, the *Ville de Paris*. A few days later, however, their plans were jeopardized when de Grasse received news that an English squadron, commanded by Admiral Robert Digby, was in American waters to reinforce British naval forces already there. Washington and Rochambeau had all they could do to convince the French admiral to remain anchored off Yorktown and not put to sea against the enemy.[1]

Yet, Allied victory would also depend on other, more mundane factors than considerations of North American strategy. In particular, it is virtually impossible to exaggerate the importance of supplies; contemporary military and civil authorities were consistently preoccupied with logistical problems.

In letters to Governor Thomas Nelson on September 4 and 11, Lafayette complained that both the French and his own American troops were without "one grain of flour."[2] Nelson made every effort—including the unauthorized expropriation of goods and services—to fill this and other needs. He appointed special agents to collect supplies and supervise their distribution to the Allied forces. In addition to essential foodstuffs, the armies needed cattle, fodder, horses, wagons, harnesses, halters, and local workers to assist in transporting supplies. The problems such exceptional demands created under any circumstances were further compounded by a dry summer and the ravages of British troops in Virginia. Beyond this, as consistently occurred, French payment in specie made local farmers and merchants reluctant to sell their products to Americans; even Nelson's aide, St. George Tucker, was putting aside supplies to sell privately to the French.[3] Strategic and tactical concerns prevailed, however, and although logistical issues remained unresolved, on September 28 the Allied armies marched a dozen miles from Williamsburg to take up their preliminary positions before Yorktown.

Despite the fact that Cornwallis made no attempt to impede this movement, the rigors of the long journey to Virginia, the continuing shortages of food, and the unaccustomed heat took their toll among the French. When the march to Yorktown began, around three hundred men, including ten officers, were already hospitalized, and according to Lieutenant Clermont-Crèvecoeur of the Auxonne Artillery, the excessively high temperature on September 28 affected another eight hundred, two of whom fell dead at his feet.[4] Compared with their American comrades, however, the French troops were fortunate, for Rochambeau's cash continued to attract the major share of available goods. Indeed, the authorities in Virginia were deeply concerned about the adverse effect this situation was having on American supplies. Throughout late September and early October, Governor Nelson was warned repeatedly that French gold and American greed would cause the U.S. army great suffering "if some other mode [of supply] is not speadily adopted to prevent it."[5]

Thus commenced the decisive battle of the American Revolution, an engagement for which the American army was largely unsuited, since only two of its generals had ever been present at a siege: Baron Friedrick von Steuben, whose experience had occurred in Europe, and Lincoln, whose exposure to such warfare consisted of defending and surrendering Charleston, South Carolina, in spring 1780. On the other hand, most French officers had either formal education in, or practical experience with, the techniques of such an operation. Beyond that, the French had come equipped with the appropriate weapons and tools. Finally, by European standards this

YORKTOWN

was a minor affair; the contemporaneous siege of Gibraltar, for instance, occupied forty thousand besiegers for three and a half years.[6] In light of the circumstances, Washington and his subordinates generally had to follow the French lead.

Meanwhile, the siege began. On the evening of September 29–30, Cornwallis withdrew his troops from outlying posts because he wanted to concentrate his available forces to defend Yorktown while he awaited a relief expedition from New York.[7] The French moved into their positions and began the arduous tasks of digging about three and a half miles of trenches, erecting earthworks, and laying the siege guns. This work involved serious danger, as well as hard physical labor, because the soldiers were exposed to enemy fire, and additional troops had to be detailed to protect the workers.[8]

As the Allied forces made the necessary preparations for a classic eighteenth-century siege outside Yorktown, another—less important and largely ignored—confrontation was taking place at Gloucester Point, across the York River from the main engagement. Cornwallis had established a garrison there to ensure control of the mouth of the river and to secure the area in the event of a retreat. By September 20 General George Weedon, the American commander at Gloucester, had assembled his Virginia militiamen—whose number varied daily but never exceeded twelve hundred. Four days later the cavalrymen of Lauzun's Legion—around three hundred strong—who had ridden overland to Gloucester, joined the Americans, and on September 28 Lauzun's infantry of roughly the same strength arrived with the duke himself.

From the beginning, relations between Lauzun and Weedon were strained. One of Weedon's first communications with Lauzun was to relay a complaint that some of his hussars had engaged in pillage at West Point on their way to Gloucester. More basic than any allegations of misconduct by Lauzun's troops, however, were the striking differences between the two men in almost every personal characteristic. Weedon had been a humble tavern keeper before the war who had risen through his efforts to the command of the local militia; both because of the undependability of his men and his own inclination, he was a cautious officer. Lauzun was an aristocratic court favorite who had raised and owned his own regiment; his reckless courage embodied the archaic virtues of chivalry. To complicate matters further, both Weedon and Lauzun held the rank of brigadier, although Rochambeau had indicated that Lauzun was under the American's orders. Before any question of subordination arose, on October 1 Rochambeau, with Washington's approval, sent General de Choisy, who was senior to both Weedon and Lauzun, to take command of all Allied troops at Gloucester. Simultaneously, the comte de Grasse had been prevailed upon to release approximately eight hundred marines (actually, soldiers from regular infantry regiments who "garrisoned" the ships) to reinforce the Franco-American contingent at Gloucester, although the French admiral warned that this was "the last sacrifice" he could make.

The only significant fighting to occur at Gloucester came on October 3. Lieutenant Colonel Banastre Tarleton, infamous for his vicious behavior in the Carolinas—including the depredation of civilian property and the massacre of prisoners of war (POWs)—led a force of six hundred from the British camp at Gloucester Point on a foraging expedition, only to encounter a Franco-American force whose advance guard consisted of Lauzun and his hussars. In typical fashion, Lauzun immediately led a charge against the enemy and failed to engage Tarleton in hand-to-hand combat only because the latter's horse threw him. Also typically, Weedon missed the skirmish because he was delayed by a lack of transportation, a fact that further intensified Lauzun's disdain. As a result of this affair, the British suffered around fifty casualties, whereas three Frenchmen were killed and a dozen wounded, including two of Lauzun's officers. Thereafter, the Allies moved their lines to within a mile and a half of the enemy position, but combat was restricted to the exchange of fire between hostile patrols. Cornwallis's belated attempt to escape by ferrying troops to Gloucester failed on October 16, and the British garrison there surrendered three days later.[9]

The primary scene of the battle remained Yorktown.[10] After establishing their defensive works, on October 6 the French completed the trenches that brought them to within about five hundred meters of the enemy outposts. By October 10 the Allied siege guns—ninety French and sixty American pieces of heavy artillery—were in place and had begun shelling Yorktown. Within two days a second parallel trench, even closer to the British lines (little more than three hundred meters away), was dug. The bloodiest combat of the battle took place on October 14 at about eight P.M. when simultaneously four hundred elite French troops commanded by the baron de Vioménil and a similar number of Lafayette's Americans under Lieutenant Colonel Alexander Hamilton attacked the British strongholds on the outskirts of Yorktown known as Redoubts nos. 9 and 10. The fighting was brief but bitter; French casualties numbered nearly one hundred men, a quarter of the assault force. The Americans captured their objective more quickly and at only one-third the cost, much to their satisfaction. The British, however, counterattacked shortly afterward. Just before dawn on October 16, Lieutenant Colonel Robert Ambercromby led between three and four hundred hand-picked British troops in storming a French artillery battery; they drove off the defenders and were able to spike four guns before being repulsed by a sortie led by the vicomte de Noailles.

No accounts of gallant military deeds or changing configurations on maps, however, convey the whole story of the siege; this important Allied victory carried a significant human cost. From the beginning of the engagement, the French army had suffered daily casualties, for example, an officer and two soldiers wounded while occupying British outposts on September 30. The losses continued and mounted thereafter: three hussars killed during Lauzun's headlong charge against Tarleton on October 3; fourteen casualties from enemy bombardment on October 7; eight more the next day, including an officer whose arm was shot away; the heavy losses resulting from the capture of Redoubt no. 9 on October 14; and a score of casualties sustained during the defense of the artillery positions on October 16. Losses from combat nevertheless paled in comparison to the ravages of disease and illness—the normal pattern in eighteenth-century warfare. Whereas there were approximately three hundred patients in French hospitals at Williamsburg when Rochambeau's army set out for Yorktown on September 28, by October 11 there were four hundred and over five hundred only four days later; furthermore, there was a growing shortage of medical supplies and personnel.[11] The climate and weather in Virginia contributed to the spread of malaria, and the heavy duties imposed by the siege left many of the French susceptible to fevers and chills. Rochambeau himself suffered from fever in the course of the battle (his fourth such attack).[12]

In spite of their losses, the Allies continued to close the trap on Cornwallis. By mid-October the English commander viewed his situation as desperate. During the night of October 16, he began to send troops across the York River in the hope that they might break through the Franco-American lines at Gloucester and thereby escape imminent defeat. A sudden storm scattered their boats and thwarted this last resort. At 10 A.M. on October 17, Cornwallis sent an envoy to formally request a truce to discuss surrender terms.

Although Cornwallis asked for a twenty-four-hour cease-fire, Washington allotted him only two hours in which to submit his proposals for preliminary terms. These proved acceptable, and commissioners—Lieutenant Colonel John Laurens representing the Americans and the vicomte de Noailles the French—met and discussed the definitive terms with their English counterparts the next day. Washington would only accept the same terms that had been forced on General Lincoln at the capitulation of Charleston the previous year (the defenders were required to case, rather than unfurl, their colors); furthermore, he demanded that the draft agreement be signed before noon October 19. Cornwallis had no choice but to agree. At two o'clock that afternoon the British troops filed out of Yorktown between the French and American armies while a similar ceremony was held at Gloucester. Pleading illness, Cornwallis sent General Charles O'Hara as his deputy; when the latter attempted to surrender Cornwallis's sword to Rochambeau, the French commander referred him to Washington, who had General Lincoln accept the token of submission.[13]

What were the consequences and significance of this momentous victory? At first, there was little opportunity to enjoy the Allied success, for it was believed that General Clinton was sending a relief expedition from New York that might reverse the situation; therefore, American and French troops quickly filled in the trenches and parallels they had recently excavated lest they be available for enemy use. Indeed, an English fleet of thirty-six ships—which, ironically, had cleared New York harbor at almost the very hour of the surrender ceremony—did arrive off the Capes on October 27, but after Cornwallis's fate became clear, it departed within forty-eight hours.[14]

There could be little doubt that the British defeat was critical. The more than eight thousand troops who surrendered at Yorktown constituted about one-quarter of Britain's military strength in North America. And more important, even though the British continued to retain strongholds in New York, Charleston, Halifax, Savannah, and elsewhere, the government had lost confidence that it could defeat the Americans. News of Cornwallis's surrender reached London on November 25. On December 8 the ministers decided no more troops should be sent to America. In late February 1782 the House of Commons voted to petition George III to end the war, and on March 4 it passed a resolution that all those who supported "the further prosecution of offensive war on the continent of North America for the purpose of reducing the revolted colonies to obedience" would be considered "enemies to His Majesty."[15] Shortly afterward, the cabinet of Lord North resigned, and the way was open for peace negotiations.

In contrast, news of Yorktown was greeted with joyous celebration throughout the United States and France. For example, in Boston there were demonstrations, fireworks, and a ball on November 5. Newspapers like the *Newport Mercury* ran special issues, or extras, with reports and documents relating to the capitulation. On November 26 King Louis XVI ordered all the archbishops and bishops of his kingdom to have *Te Deum* celebrations in the churches of their dioceses and instructed Rochambeau to do the same in his army.[16] Official expressions of American gratitude toward the French began with Washington's "After Orders" of October 20.

YORKTOWN

On October 29 a resolution of the Congress thanked Rochambeau "for the cordiality, Zeal, Judgement and fortitude with which he Seconded and advanced the progress of the allied army against the british [sic] garrison in York" and promised to erect a marble column there to commemorate the French alliance.[17]

The French contribution to the victory was crucial. The entire campaign was inconceivable without the intervention of the French navy. And it is very unlikely that Washington's seven to eight thousand Continentals could have successfully besieged a larger enemy force, even with an additional two or three thousand Virginia militiamen; the French regulars from Rhode Island and the West Indies, who together numbered slightly more than the American line troops, were essential to the land operations. Furthermore, although casualty estimates vary widely from source to source, there is a general concurrence that the French losses (between 186 and 389 total casualties) were more numerous and more serious (between 52 and 98 killed) than those of the Americans (a maximum of 299 casualties, including 28 killed).[18]

The French government did not ignore the sacrifices of the officers and men in its armed forces. On October 24 the duc de Lauzun left for France aboard the *Surveillante* to carry the news of Yorktown to France and arrived at Brest after a crossing of only twenty-two days. On November 20 Guillaume de Deux-Ponts departed on the frigate *Andromaque* with captured flags and a complete report on the French operations in Virginia.[19] Both officers also brought requests for official recognition of outstanding performances by the personnel of Rochambeau's army. Eventually, 126 of Rochambeau's officers, including the commanding general, and one sergeant received some sort of award—promotions, decorations, new appointments, pensions, special bonuses; in addition, every officer below the grade of major was authorized to receive a cash bonus ranging from one hundred to four hundred livres, according to rank.[20]

There was nothing unusual about this form of recognition in eighteenth-century France. In fact, a number of Rochambeau's officers felt the rewards were inadequate. Lauzun, who had been led to expect munificent gifts from the king for himself and his comrades, was offended by what he considered shabby treatment by the government. For example, his nomination of Lieutenant Sonnette for promotion to captain contained the notation that a horse had been killed underneath the lieutenant in America; the minister's snide reply was that Sonnette "be paid for his horse, at the most." Lauzun himself felt cheated of his just reward and refused to carry notification of the royal awards back to America.[21] Officers in the United States expressed

73

similar sentiments when informed of the decisions. Claude Blanchard, Rochambeau's commissary, wrote that "the favors were awaited with impatience and received with dissatisfaction."[22] Jean Baptiste Antoine de Verger, a sublieutenant in the Royal Deux-Ponts Infantry, responded sarcastically to the announcement of the bonuses for lieutenants: They "will not bankrupt France!"[23] Even the mild-mannered Rochambeau, although expressing gratitude for the promise of an appointment with an income of thirty thousand livres, noted, "I would be more [grateful] if His Majesty had seen fit to add to this favor the decoration of the Cordon bleu" and requested a more definite commitment from the king to give his son the command of his own regiment.[24]

Frustration at what many considered their government's ingratitude was not the only source of tension in Rochambeau's army after the victory of Yorktown. Another problem was the drastic differences between French and American attitudes toward, and treatment of, British POWs. For the French, the current conflict was but the latest in a long series of conventional wars against a traditional enemy, and the next confrontation might reverse the positions of victor and defeated. The officers of the French and English armies shared a comparable social background, a cosmopolitan culture, and the same professional values. Consequently, the French officers socialized with, entertained, and even loaned funds to their unfortunate brothers in arms from Cornwallis's forces. This treatment, however, appalled Americans, who for six and a half long years had been engaged in a revolutionary and civil war marked by atrocities and reprisals against bitterly hated opponents.[25] The conduct of British forces in the South had been especially vicious. According to Lauberdière, "Theft, rapine, murder, arson have accompanied their steps everywhere in Virginia." As a result, he claimed, "The Americans were very frustrated by the capitulation. They hoped that in an assault they would be able to avenge the Tyranny . . . the cruelties that they had experienced at the hands of the English during the war."[26]

A number of specific incidents highlighted these differences and contributed to growing strains between the Allies. Only a month after the British surrender, Rochambeau was so shocked by American negligence of the sick and wounded prisoners, who had been concentrated at Gloucester, that he asked Governor Nelson to intervene and do something for these men "who lack everything."[27] This kind of complaint contrasted strikingly with the cordiality of Anglo-French relations in the weeks after Yorktown. For example, when Admiral Robert Digby discovered that thirty-eight British prisoners more than the number agreed on had escaped incarceration, he promised to see to it that an equal number of French subjects in British custody would be released.[28] And Rochambeau was guaranteed reimbursement for his loan to Lord Cornwallis "as soon as possible."[29]

The most famous instance of Franco-American disagreement over the treatment of POWs illustrates the fierce nature of the Anglo-American struggle, which the French failed to understand. Joshua Huddy, a captain in the New Jersey militia and a British prisoner, had been released into the custody of Captain Richard Lippincott of the Associated Loyalists, who proceeded to hang Huddy for the alleged murder of a Tory soldier. When the British refused to hand Lippincott over to the Americans for justice, Washington had one of the Yorktown prisoners of equal rank, Captain Charles Asgill, selected at random to be hanged in retaliation. The French were flabbergasted—as much by the fact that Washington, the model of integrity, was involved as by the offense to their code of military honor—and they protested vehemently. It required months of negotiations and the intervention of the French court before Asgill was released.[30]

Disagreement over POW policies reflected a fundamental difference between the French and the Americans over the very nature of the war against England. Other, less basic factors also increased Franco-American tensions. Although such sentiments are difficult to document and impossible to measure, long-suffering Americans must have resented attitudes about the battle of Yorktown like that expressed by Ann Dulany of Baltimore: "It was the French that did everything."[31] On the other hand, some French felt Americans failed to appreciate their decisive contribution to U.S. independence; Théodore de Lameth, whose brother Charles was seriously wounded during the attack on Redoubt no. 9, felt Americans never offered "recognition of the blood that has been shed for them."[32]

Lack of understanding between the Allies had, in fact, been fostered by efforts to keep the American and French armies apart from each other, for, as had been the case in New York, the two forces had occupied entirely separate encampments and had different areas of responsibility during the recent siege. In addition, the rare contacts that did take place were at times unpleasant. For instance, when a Captain Duffy of the 4th Artillery Regiment was court-martialed for conduct unbecoming an officer in the midst of the battle, one of the charges against him was "abusing a French soldier."[33]

The dispersal of Allied forces helped to ease tensions. By November 5 most of American troops had departed, and the previous day Admiral de Grasse had set sail, after embarking Saint-Simon's troops, to return to the Caribbean. At first, Washington hoped to keep the victorious forces together to pursue their advantage, and he suggested to de Grasse that their next objective be Charleston. The French admiral, however, felt he was overdue in the West Indies.[34] The strategic plans of the French court for the coming year remained uncertain, and without this information neither Rochambeau nor Washington could set their own plans for the next campaign.[35] Under the circumstances the only reasonable course of action was for Rochambeau's army to take up winter quarters in Virginia.

Because of the limited facilities available, the French troops were stationed in a number of locations: Rochambeau's headquarters, together with the Regiment of Bourbonnais, seven of the ten companies of Royal Deux-Ponts, and most of the battalion of Auxonne Artillery at Williamsburg; the Regiment of Soissonnais and the grenadier and chasseur companies of Saintonge at Yorktown; the remaining eight companies of the Saintonge Infantry at Halfway House (between Yorktown and Hampton); three companies of the Royal Deux-Ponts Regiment at Jamestown; Lauzun's Legion at Hampton; a small detachment of artillery at Gloucester; and the siege artillery at West Point. At General Greene's urgent request and with Washington's approval, in February 1782 Rochambeau dispatched Lauzun's Legion to the North Carolina border where, under the command of Brigadier de Choisy, it established itself at Charlotte Courthouse; a battalion (five companies) of the Regiment of Saintonge replaced it at Hampton.[36]

As the French settled in, a major concern of the local inhabitants was the same as that of the people of Rhode Island: the conduct of these foreign troops who would be living in their midst for the next few months. Drawing upon his earlier experiences at Newport, Rochambeau attempted to reassure the citizens that all would be well. During the first week of November he informed Governor Nelson that French foraging expeditions would be rigorously supervised and that any claims arising from irregularities by French forces would be settled, although he pointed out that British and American forces had been foraging in the same area. Rochambeau also requested that Nelson encourage inhabitants to sell their goods to the French with the assurance that they would not be molested in any way.[37] Two weeks later, in an address to the General Assembly at Williamsburg, the French commander pointed out that—with the approval of General Washington and Governor Nelson—his army would be quartered "in a way that would entail the least cost to the inhabitants, with orders to repair, at the King's expense, all the houses [damaged by the English or in the siege] that could be promptly refurbished to lodge soldiers." He reminded the representatives that the French troops had been acclaimed for their exemplary discipline in every state through which they had passed by their "good brothers and faithful allies."[38] When the wing of the College of William and Mary that was serving as a hospital for French wounded was seriously damaged by a fire a few days later, Rochambeau displayed his good faith by contributing funds ("12,000 lb.") to repair it.[39]

Virginians also made efforts to foster Franco-American amity. In early December Governor Benjamin Harrison, who had recently replaced Thomas Nelson, wrote Rochambeau of his approval of the way the French were handling charges for forage; he also promised to comply with the latter's request for cooperation in the apprehension of French deserters (many from the group of the sick left behind by de Grasse). On December 20 Harrison issued a proclamation urging his constituents to help in capturing French deserters and guaranteeing that Virginians who furnished provisions "to the army and fleet of our great ally now in this state . . . will be at liberty to vend their commodities in a fair and amicable manner."[40]

On other levels, too, there were indications of goodwill between the Allies during the winter of 1781–1782. There was a steady stream of social and recreational activities: receptions, hunts, dinners, horse races, cockfights, and, in von Closen's words, "endless balls." In mid-December Rochambeau claimed, "I am now on a Regimen of two Fox hunts per week and a ball for the Ladies every Thursday."[41] Public festivities also brought French and Americans together. For example, Rochambeau's celebration of a *Te Deum* (as ordered by Louis XVI) on December 15 was the occasion for a banquet and yet another ball to which the most prominent gentlemen and ladies of Williamsburg were invited. Two weeks later the French provided the spectacle of bonfires in honor of the capture of the island of St. Eustatius from the English. In mid-January news of the birth of an heir to the French throne—although not officially observed until summer 1782—was greeted with ceremonies in Virginia, including an address from "the Corporation of the City of Williamsburg" to Rochambeau that offered congratulations on the dauphin's birth and formally recognized "the discipline and good order that have been so strictly observed by the troops quartered in this city." The same body exchanged mutual congratulations with La Luzerne, the French minister to the United States, when he visited in late March. And in June the College of William and Mary awarded honorary degrees to two French officers—General de Chastellux, the well-known savant and traveler, and Jean François Coste, the chief physician of Rochambeau's army; the only other recipients of such an honor from the college prior to 1790 were Benjamin Franklin and Thomas Jefferson.[42]

Personal relations between the French officers and their hosts sometimes showed signs of strain, however. Despite the fact that French nobles were from a society much more similar to that of the Virginia gentry than to that of the Rhode Island merchants, many seemed to prefer the latter to the

Southern planters whom they found to be pretentious, vain, slothful, and tasteless. The same unfavorable judgments did not, however, always extend to the wives and daughters of the local elite. It was in Virginia that the first marriage between one of Rochambeau's officers and an American took place. In late June 1782 Captain Augustin Rouxelin Denos, who commanded a company in the Saintonge Infantry, married "a rather rich widow from the vicinity of Halfway House." Another officer, the chevalier de Coriolis, a lieutenant in the Regiment of Bourbonnais, was so taken with a daughter of the Blaire family of Williamsburg that he proposed to her no less than four times, all in vain.[43]

A persistent source of friction between Americans and French consisted of allegations by Virginians of damage to or theft of property by men of Rochambeau's command. Even as the siege of Yorktown was commencing, some of Rochambeau's soldiers, who had been suffering from a shortage of supplies since leaving Georgetown, attacked and pillaged a food transport yet managed to escape punishment.[44] Shortly after Cornwallis's surrender, French troops under the orders of Joseph Hyacinthe, comte de Vioménil had appropriated houses in Yorktown to serve as their winter quarters. Several inhabitants protested, claiming the French treated them as Tories, and asked for relief "from this second Tyranny" (the first being the British occupation). Vioménil expressed surprise at such grievances and maintained that the only buildings fit for habitation after the siege were those he had repaired and that he had provided adequate housing for the owners and their families while his own officers were lodged as many as ten to a single room. Nevertheless, complaints continued throughout the winter; for example, in late January it was charged that the courthouse at Yorktown, which was serving as a French hospital, was filled with such a "disagreeable smell" that local magistrates were unable to hold their sessions in it.[45] Rochambeau's response to American complaints was almost always conciliatory. In December, when Americans claimed a cargo of cocoa and coffee purchased by Cornwallis before the surrender and subsequently seized by the French as part of the spoils of victory, Rochambeau was willing to comply because "our court would be disturbed that we had any conflict of interest with the Americans." Similarly, in March 1782, when U.S. authorities wanted to arrest four French sailors for theft, Rochambeau again refused to challenge their claims because "I am certain that nothing would be more disagreeable to our Court and that the enemy Gazettes would not fail to make a big commotion about it."[46]

As had happened before, Lauzun's Legion was the focal point for more than its share of controversy. Within three weeks of the Allied victory, an

YORKTOWN

American citizen charged that the unit held a horse stolen from him. Choisy, who commanded the Legion in Lauzun's absence, showed the man all the mounts belonging to the Legion; the horse the American identified as his property had, in fact, been a gift to Lauzun from General Washington.[47] In late December Mary Harris of Gloucester alleged that some hussars from Lauzun's regiment had robbed her of food, silverware, bedclothes, and kitchen utensils, whose value she estimated at twenty-one pounds, ten shillings, three pence. When offered the opportunity to pick the culprits from a formation of all the hussars, however, she refused, saying she wouldn't be able to recognize them. Upon assurances of Harris's honesty and, once again, to avoid public acrimony, Rochambeau indemnified her for her losses by a payment of seventy dollars.[48] Even after its transfer to the North Carolina border, civilians continued to complain about the conduct of the Legion; for example, in spring 1782 the "harsh methods" Choisy employed in commandeering buildings to lodge his sick were brought to the attention of Governor Harrison, who conveyed the protest to Rochambeau so he might reprimand his subordinate.[49]

No problem plagued Franco-American relations in Virginia more than accusations that the French army was harboring escaped slaves, an issue that arose more and more frequently as rumors about the imminent departure of Rochambeau's forces spread in spring 1782. Again, Lauzun's Legion and Brigadier de Choisy figured prominently. After Rochambeau promised to hand over "any Negroes in the French army belonging to Americans," a "Trusty Sergeant" was sent to Choisy's headquarters at Charlotte Courthouse to supervise the delivery of runaways with this unit. Subsequently, the names and descriptions of seventeen slaves "delivered up by General Choissy, commander of the French legion, to Col. Thomas Reade of Charlotte county" were published in both Richmond newspapers.[50]

Choisy was not the only French officer charged with providing refuge for slaves, nor did Virginians stop protesting when he complied with their demands. In May 1782 William Dandridge wrote Governor Harrison that some of his slaves were with the French forces, including one who was being sheltered by a French major who claimed he was a freeman in his employ; such actions, according to Dandridge, were a threat to all "in this country where they [slaves] compose so large a share of the property of the inhabitants." Complaints multiplied, and the following month Governor Harrison asked Rochambeau to "give immediate orders for the securing of all the Negroes without distinction that are amongst your Troops." This demand was too much, even for the normally compliant Rochambeau who responded that "tho' I owe justice to the Inhabitants of Virginia, the officers of my army have an equal right to it, that several of them have negroes the property of which is founded upon rights as sacred as those of the Virginians." He pointed out that some blacks had been bought from the French navy in Newport, that more had been purchased or hired otherwise, and that some were indeed free; furthermore, Rochambeau reminded the governor, he had given his full cooperation to all who wished to search his army for their alleged slaves. He neglected to mention that one of his own soldiers, Jean Baptiste Pandoua, who had enlisted in the Regiment of Soissonnais as a musician in January 1777, was an African (a native of Madagascar). Nevertheless, Rochambeau continued to cooperate, allowing Virginians to inspect all blacks in his forces and handing over any claimed by these "gentlemen"; when a runaway hid in one of his wagons and made good his escape, the French commander compensated the owner for the loss. Yet, even after the French left Virginia, Governor Harrison wrote ahead to his state's representatives in Congress, warning them that many slaves belonging to owners in Virginia and the Carolinas accompanied these troops and urging the delegates to try to reclaim them as they passed through Philadelphia on their march northward.[51]

Not all dealings between Rochambeau's army and citizens of Virginia were as volatile as those that involved escaped slaves; other claims for reimbursement were settled without hostility. Shortly after Yorktown, procedures for the submission of bills by Americans were established, and an intermediary between the claimants and the French, Dudley Diggs, was appointed. Surviving evidence suggests that, on the whole, this system worked. For example, after some bickering, in February 1782 John Paradise was compensated for trees on his estate that had been cut down by the French for firewood. In March a consolidated charge for more than forty-four thousand livres, covering corn, fodder, oats, and other produce taken by the French between late September and November 19, 1781, was presented for payment. In early May forty-nine individuals who had submitted charges for forage received more than six thousand livres. According to Diggs's carefully maintained receipt book and Governor Harrison's public announcement near the end of the French stay in Virginia, in settling the claims of Virginians against the French, Diggs "finished the business much to the satisfaction of the people."[52]

Although Virginians might generally have been satisfied, one might suspect that the French—particularly Rochambeau—were less pleased, for, as his correspondence with La Luzerne clearly shows, the French commander was continually worried about a lack of funds and supplies. Because of a shortage of cash and "to avoid being at the mercy of usurers" for taking loans, in December Rochambeau resorted to a practice he had abandoned the previous August: He authorized the use of letters of exchange, even though they were being discounted between 18 and 25 percent. His major concern was the arrival of a French frigate, the *Emeraude,* said to be bringing him 2 million livres in specie.[53] Indeed, Major de Prez, who commanded a small detachment (eighty-odd men) still in Providence guarding stores and magazines, was ordered to delay his departure for the South so his contingent could escort the cash safely overland once it had been unloaded in Rhode Island. After months of waiting, the money arrived in late March. By the second week of May, de Prez had reached Philadelphia with it, only to be held up by the French minister there pending new orders for Rochambeau's corps.[54] Meanwhile, the French continued to pay what they considered high prices for what were sometimes inferior goods; for instance, of 151 cattle delivered to the French during the siege of Yorktown, a half dozen died of distemper before they could be slaughtered.[55]

Another, even more pressing aspect of survival was the health of the army under Rochambeau. The exertions of the march and the siege, the inclement weather, the inadequacy of supplies, and the fighting itself had debilitated many French officers and men. Shortly after the British surrender, French military hospitals were crowded, and their patients, according to one American observer, Dr. James Tilton, were allowed to remain "in a languid and putrid condition."[56] During the ten months Rochambeau's forces spent in Virginia, from September 1781 to June 1782, 6 officers died, 3 in combat or as a direct result of wounds received in combat; in the same period, 149 enlisted men perished, 30 to 40 of whom were combat casualties. As usual, sickness and disease—assisted by unsanitary medical and health conditions—were responsible for most of the deaths, but there were other causes as well.[57] For instance, two soldiers, one from the Regiment of Bourbonnais and one from Royal Deux-Ponts, were lost in a shipwreck on February 2, 1782; and Jacques Bergeot, a twenty-five-year-old infantryman in Lauzun's Legion, was executed "for the crime of homicide on October 1, 1781."[58]

Although they were clearly the most unfortunate, the sick and the dying were not the only members of the French army to suffer during their sojourn in Virginia. In addition to inadequate rations, fatigue, and injuries and illnesses too minor to require hospitalization, soldiers were also subjected to the wear and tear of the nearly seven hundred-mile march and the three-week siege, which damaged or destroyed much of their equipment and clothing. Inspections revealed the extent of such losses. General de Vioménil's review of the Regiment of Saintonge on November 12, for example, concluded that the following equipment was needed: 500 uniforms, 690 jackets, 1,030 pairs of breeches, 1,000 hats, 200 cartridge boxes, 151 musket slings, 200 sabers, as well as different kinds of cloth and braid for repairing uniforms. Vioménil's inspection of the battalion of Auxonne Artillery eleven days before resulted in comparable recommendations for replacements: 235 complete uniforms (including jackets and gaiters), 540 hats, 47 cartridge boxes, 150 musket slings, 540 pairs of breeches, along with stockings, cloth of linen and serge, braid, and leather. The regimental quartermaster of Royal Deux-Ponts estimated that the damages incurred by the unit during its march from Providence to Williamsburg amounted to just under sixteen hundred livres. The enemy capture of the French schooner *Charlotte* in Chesapeake Bay in February 1782 intensified the shortages because the ship was carrying many of the goods badly needed by Rochambeau's units.[59]

Physical pain, discomfort, and deprivation were not the only problems affecting the French during their winter in Virginia. As the officers and men resumed the monotonous routine of garrison duty, many also suffered from boredom. Some officers, mostly from the higher ranks, were able to return to France, at least for a time.[60] Others traveled within the United States for pleasure and on business; for example, in February Rochambeau and some of his staff visited former governor Nelson, Thomas Jefferson, Governor Harrison, and the Randolph family; and that spring, while serving as Rochambeau's courier to General Washington in New York and to the Congress at Philadelphia, Captain von Closen rode 980 miles in just nine days.[61] Most officers, however, did not enjoy such opportunities, and a number found themselves increasingly restless, especially after recuperating from the fatigue of the campaign.[62] The dissatisfaction with the rewards granted by the government added to their disgruntlement.

All of this contributed to insubordination and discord among the officers. Less than two weeks after the British surrender, Major Jean Ladislas Pollerescky of Lauzun's Legion, who was suspected of a number of shady financial dealings in America, was put under arrest by his commanding officer the very day Captain Henry Escelent of the same unit was arrested for horse stealing. In April Cadet Girault, also of the Legion, was imprisoned for dueling with his fellow officer Sublieutenant Jacques Joseph L'Halle and subsequently recalled to France. L'Halle was taken into custody a few months later for threatening to beat the cook. Lauzun's lieutenant colonel, Claude Etienne Hugau, was arrested for challenging the authority of Colonel in Second Dillon, and although Rochambeau later accepted Hugau's position as "basically correct," he found his manner of asserting it "reprehensible" and upheld Dillon's action.[63] Such insubordination was not confined to Lauzun's Legion. When Jean Baptiste de Jujardy, a commissary for Rochambeau's army, refused to obey the orders of Jean Baptiste d'Allière, comte de Saint-Maisme, the colonel of the Soissonnais Infantry and temporary commanding officer at Yorktown, the colonel had him arrested, another decision Rochambeau later confirmed.[64]

The soldiers habitually expressed their dissatisfaction in more passive fashion, notably by deserting. Although the desertion rate in Virginia was somewhat higher than that in Rhode Island (seventy-four for the ten months spent in the South compared with sixty-two during the eleven months in New England), this may have been because the troops were dispersed in seven or eight scattered detachments and thus were more difficult to supervise; in any event, the difference was slight. Furthermore, twenty-two of the deserters had been recruited in America, often among deserters from the British forces, and another thirty or so were German-speaking natives of Alsace, Lorraine, or neighboring German states who could easily be assimilated by the German settlers whom they had encountered, especially in Pennsylvania, on their march from New York.[65]

This desertion rate, which was unusually low—particularly for wartime—can be explained in part by the measures taken by the authorities.[66] When apprehended, deserters faced harsh punishments. Pierre Collier, a twenty-one-year-old drummer who had deserted from the Auxonne Artillery, was forced to run a gauntlet composed of one hundred men from his regiment while they beat him with metal ramrods. Four soldiers of the Saintonge Infantry who had gone over to the enemy were caught and condemned to death by hanging. This sentence was later modified so that only one of the soldiers—either the most culpable or one selected by lot, if all were equally guilty—was to be executed, and the other three were to be confined on French vessels for an indefinite period.[67] Those soldiers who, undeterred by the threat of such punishments, still abandoned their units were pursued rigorously. Rochambeau not only sent his own officers, like Sublieutenant Jean Népomucène Rupplin of Royal Deux-Ponts, to bring back deserters, he also commissioned Captain John Miller of the Continental Army to hunt deserters who had sought refuge among the German immigrants in Pennsylvania and Maryland.[68] In addition, announcements were published in local newspapers giving physical descriptions of deserters, urging the inhabitants to cooperate in their apprehension, and offering rewards in "Hard Dollars" for those returned. Governor Harrison gave his full support to these efforts and ordered "all civil and military officers" to do the same, even after Rochambeau's army left the state.[69]

All of these considerations, however, still cannot fully explain why a mere score of French-speaking soldiers made good their escape from the very difficult conditions they faced in Rochambeau's army. One final factor—more difficult to substantiate but perhaps more important than any of the others—was the alien nature of the American environment and society. Native French troops had to cope with a foreign language, different customs, strange food, and often hostile attitudes. Official and unofficial efforts to return deserters only confirmed their sense of alienation. Obviously, a few French soldiers found their situation so intolerable or the promise of a new life in America so attractive that they wanted to leave the army. Besides the deserters, thirty enlisted men received discharges in Virginia, eight of whom decided to take their retirement pensions there; for example, Jean Baptiste Poulnot, an artillery sergeant with twenty-five years of service, retired in Williamsburg with an annual pension of 262 livres.[70]

German and German-speaking soldiers in Rochambeau's army were more likely to desert. Unlike the French, they were not the objects of old and deep national biases. Furthermore, they could readily find a congenial refuge among the many Germans living in the United States—including even friends and relatives on occasion—with whom they shared common customs, language, and often religion. Also, America seemed to offer enormous economic and political advantages over their native country.[71] Nonetheless, the vast majority of Rochambeau's personnel, segregated from the local inhabitants by both official policies and cultural differences, preferred the oppressive but familiar surroundings of French army life.

As Rochambeau was attempting to cope with such immediate problems as relations with his American hosts, inadequate funds and supplies, and the maintenance of discipline in his command, his role—and that of his tiny army—in the general strategy of the war remained uncertain. By June 1782 he had not received a response to his correspondence after Yorktown in which he had not only announced the victory but had also requested reinforcements and orders for the next campaign. And since it took from three weeks to three months for a letter from Rochambeau's headquarters in the United States to reach the ministry at Versailles and the reply might take as long as four and a half months to reach Rochambeau, this constituted an especially agonizing delay.[72]

In striking contrast to U.S. involvement, France's involvement in the war against England was global in character; as a result, developments in one region could and often did have an important impact on French strategy elsewhere. The entry of the Netherlands into the war against England in December 1780, which meant French warships could use Dutch naval bases on the Cape of Good Hope and in Ceylon, had raised French hopes of recovering influence in India that had been lost to the British in the Seven Years' War. Such efforts began in late March 1781 when Admiral Suffren and his small squadron broke away from a large convoy under Admiral de Grasse and sailed eastward. Suffren subsequently enjoyed a series of victories in the Indian Ocean that threatened English dominance in the area and that extended until June 1783, when he received news that a peace treaty had been signed. Dutch participation in the hostilities also led to increased French responsibilities in the Caribbean, always a principal region of French interest; for example, in early 1782 French forces captured Guyana from the British, who had earlier taken it from the Dutch.[73] In light of France's limited resources, the commitments in both the East and West Indies meant restriction of its military efforts in North America.

The most tangible effect of this situation on the French army in Virginia was a lack of reinforcements to fill its ranks, which were being depleted daily by death, desertion, and discharge. Although the French government had planned to send 830 replacements to Rochambeau—together with 600 troops to India and 4,000 to the Caribbean islands—in October 1781 the ministry decided to postpone the departure of the soldiers destined for North America and to increase the size of the expedition to India by 3,900 men.[74] These decisions reflected the government's changing priorities, which ultimately resulted in no substantial reinforcements for Rochambeau. Two dozen cannoneers from the first battalion of the Regiment of Auxonne Artillery—which had remained in France—were dispatched to the second battalion in Virginia, and officer replacements were posted to North America, but after spring 1781 no large contingent of French troops went to the United States.[75]

From time to time, limited detachments from the regimental depots in France were ordered to North America, but conditions prevented their departure. Sublieutenant Michel Giraud de La Chau of the Soissonnais Infantry, who was captured by an English ship on his first attempt to join his regiment in America in 1781, was, after his release, put in charge of two hundred recruits earmarked for Rochambeau's army. After an unsuccessful attempt to sail from Brest, followed by an eight-month stay at Saint-Jean d'Angély, La Chau's command again embarked for the United States—only to be held up for three more months at the Island of Aix, where it received news of the peace. At this point, La Chau led the recruits back to the regimental depot in Valenciennes. Similarly, Joseph Pierre Alexandre de Bertrand and François Joseph de Stack, cadets in the Regiment of Royal Deux-Ponts, were given command of two hundred men who marched from the regimental depot at Neuf Brisach in Alsace to Brest, where they embarked on ships bound for America on May 15, 1782; unable to leave the coast because of poor weather and an English blockade, they put into Rochefort on July 2. After reembarking on January 4, 1783, only to debark again on January 31, they returned to Neuf Brisach in late March.[76] Perhaps it was just as well that Rochambeau received no news from France; it would only have intensified his frustration!

By June 1782, Washington, unable to make plans or take action, was pressing Rochambeau for a decision either to join him in an attack against New York or to turn to South Carolina where the British still held Charleston. Meanwhile, Americans, anxious for an end to their seven-year conflict with England, were beginning to revive their suspicions and distrust of France and its war aims.[77] Rochambeau had still received neither instructions nor reinforcements from Europe and was again short of cash. The weather in Virginia was turning hot—excessively so for French tastes—and with the heat came a variety of bugs and illnesses. In the midst of these difficulties, on June 8 Rochambeau received confirmation of the decisive defeat of Admiral de Grasse at the Battle of the Saints on April 12. This engagement, which cost the French a half dozen ships and approximately three thousand casualties—including de Grasse, who was made a prisoner—reestablished English predominance in American waters and left Rochambeau's army in a precarious position. Under these circumstances, Rochambeau decided to leave Virginia and join Washington's army in New York.[78]

Notes

1. Washington, *Diaries*, vol. 2, pp. 260–261; the Washington-De Grasse correspondence, dated September 22 and 23, 1781, in Shea, *Operations of the French Fleet*, pp. 187–189; and Whitridge, *Rochambeau*, pp. 210–211.
2. Quoted in J. Bennett Nolan, *Lafayette in America, Day by Day* (Baltimore: Johns Hopkins University Press, 1934), pp. 196 and 198.
3. For fuller information on Nelson's role in this important and complicated matter, see Evans, *Thomas Nelson*, pp. 113–122; Virginia Executive Papers, boxes 15, 16, and 17 (for September and early October 1781); and *Official Letters of the Governors of the State of Virginia*, vol. 3: *The Letters of Thomas Nelson and Benjamin Harrison* (Richmond: Virginia State Library, 1929), pp. 43, 48, 72, 80, 83, and 85.
4. Eyewitness testimony can be found in Blanchard, *Journal*, pp. 143–145; and Rice and Brown, *American Campaigns*, vol. 1, pp. 57 (for Clermont-Crèvecoeur) and 138–139.
5. See *Official Letters of the Governors of Virginia*, vol. 3, pp. 64 and 74; and Virginia

Executive Papers, boxes 16 and 17. The quotation is from John Pierce's letter of September 27, 1781, to Nelson (box 16), but the same sentiment can be found throughout this correspondence.
6. Larrabee, *Decision at the Chesapeake*, p. 263; Kennett, *French Forces*, pp. 142–144; and Flexner, *Washington in the American Revolution*, pp. 454–455.
7. Whitridge, *Rochambeau*, pp. 213–214. Clinton wrote Cornwallis that he expected to send ships carrying five thousand troops on October 5.
8. Kennett provides excellent information on the details of preparing the siege in *French Forces*, pp. 145–146, and interesting observations about the early siege are found in Edward M. Riley, ed., "St. George Tucker's Journal of the Siege of Yorktown, 1781," *William and Mary Quarterly*, 3rd ser. 5 (1948): 381–385.
9. For the situation at Gloucester, see Harry M. Ward, *Duty, Honor or Country: General George Weedon and the American Revolution* (Philadelphia: American Philosophical Society, 1979), pp. 216–227; Lauzun, *Memoirs*, pp. 205–208; Blanchard, *Journal*, pp. 145–146; and Rochambeau Papers, vol. 1, pp. 251–252; vol. 9, p. 202; and vol. 12, pp. 140–141 and 171–172.
10. Unless noted otherwise, the following brief description of the battle is based on eyewitness accounts in Chinard, "Journal de Guerre de Brisout de Barneville"; "Diary of a French Officer"; and Riley, "Tucker's Journal of Yorktown"; supplemented by Johnston, *Yorktown Campaign*, pp. 105–150; Bonsal, *When the French Were Here*, pp. 148–165; and John Austin Stevens, "The Allies at Yorktown, 1781," *Magazine of American History* 6 (1881): 1–53.
11. Blanchard, *Journal*, pp. 149–150.
12. Rochambeau Papers, vol. 9, p. 215.
13. Flexner, *Washington in the American Revolution*, p. 464, is but one source among many containing an account of the surrender.
14. Washington, *Diaries*, vol. 2, pp. 271–272.
15. Flexner, *Washington in the American Revolution*, pp. 460, 468, and 477; Mackesy, *War for America*, pp. 435–436 and 474; Richard W. Van Alstyne, *Empire and Independence: The International History of the American Revolution* (New York: John Wiley and Sons, 1965), p. 203; and Léon Chotteau, *La Guerre de l'indépendance (1775–1783): Les Français en Amérique* (Paris: Charpentier, 1876), p. 374. The quotation is from Clinton, *American Rebellion*, pp. 595–596.
16. Akers, *Samuel Cooper*, p. 323; *Newport Mercury* of November 6, 1781; Rochambeau Papers, vol. 9, Louis XVI to Rochambeau, dated Versailles, November 26, 1781 (no pagination).
17. Washington's orders are cited in Rice and Brown, *American Campaigns*, vol. 1, p. 150, and the congressional resolution in Rochambeau Papers, vol. 3, p. 290.
18. A complete list of the estimates of casualties would be long and not particularly useful; most of the primary and secondary accounts of the battle noted in this chapter give some—inevitably different—figures.
19. Chotteau, *Français en Amérique*, pp. 331–332 and 336; and B.N., N.A.F. 17691, "Journal de Lauberdière," p. 100.
20. Individual rewards are listed in Rochambeau Papers, vols. 9 and 10 (unpaginated), letters of Ségur to Rochambeau, dated December 5 and 17, 1781, and January 27, March 19, April 2 and 3, 1782. The bonuses paid to all company grade officers from commanding captain to sublieutenant amounted to between one-fifth and one-fourth of their annual salary.

21. Lauzun, *Memoirs*, pp. 209–210; Maugras, *Lauzun*, pp. 250–251; and Bodinier, *Officiers*, p. 154 (which contains the quotation).
22. Quoted in André Girodie, " 'Soissonnais' et l'Amérique. Lettres inédites," *Franco-American Review* 1 (1936): 237.
23. Rice and Brown, *American Campaigns*, vol. 1, p. 181.
24. Letter from Rochambeau to Ségur, dated April 28, 1782, in Rochambeau Papers, vol. 11, pp. 94–95 (duplicated in vol. 12, pp. 256–257).
25. Kennett, "Bilan d'une rencontre," p. 532. For the testimony of two French officers about this situation, see Rice and Brown, *American Campaigns*, vol. 1, pp. 64 and 151. An earlier example of similar sentiments in Rhode Island is described on p. 17.
26. B.N., N.A.F. 17691, "Journal de Lauberdière," pp. 91 verso and 101.
27. Rochambeau to Nelson, November 21, 1781, Rochambeau Papers, vol. 12, p. 185.
28. Digby to Rochambeau, November 28, 1781, ibid., vol. 3, p. 297.
29. Clinton to Rochambeau, December 31, 1781, ibid., pp. 301–302.
30. For a succinct account of this episode, see Marion Balderston and David Syrett, eds., *The Lost War: Letters From British Officers During the American Revolution* (New York: Horizon Press, 1975), p. 217n.
31. Quoted in Kate M. Rowland, "Maryland Women and French Officers," *Atlantic Monthly* 66 (1890): 654.
32. Théodore de Lameth, *Mémoires, Publiés avec Introduction et Notes par Eugène Welvert* (Paris: Fontemoing, 1913) pp. 26–27.
33. Feltman, *Journal*, pp. 13–26, provides an example of the very limited contact American and French officers had during and after the battle; the Duffy incident is described on p. 19.
34. Washington to De Grasse, October 28, 1781, in Doniol, *Histoire*, vol. 4, p. 695; and Bonsal, *When the French Were Here*, pp. 170–171.
35. In fact, by late 1781 the French government had committed itself to greater efforts in India and the Caribbean rather than North America, and by early 1782 reinforcements were on their way to both theaters of operations. See Dull, *French Navy and American Independence*, pp. 258–263; and Mackesy, *War for America*, pp. 437–451.
36. Information on the location of the French troops' quarters in Virginia has been extracted from Blanchard, *Journal*, p. 155; Robin, *New Travels*, pp. 65–66; Acomb, *Journal of Von Closen*, p. 162; Rice and Brown, *American Campaigns*, vol. 2, pp. 170–171; and Rochambeau Papers, vol. 12, pp. 181, 217–221, and 228–231, and vol. 11, pp. 60–66.
37. Rochambeau Papers, vol. 9, pp. 230–232 (duplicated in vol. 12, pp. 180–182).
38. Ibid., vol. 12, pp. 183–184, reproduced in Doniol, *Histoire*, vol. 5, p. 585.
39. Evelyn M. Acomb, ed., "The Journal of Baron Von Closen," *William and Mary Quarterly*, 3rd series 10 (1953): 211.
40. Rochambeau's request appears in his letter to Governor Nelson of November 21, 1781, Rochambeau Papers, vol. 12, p. 185; Harrison's reply is in *Official Letters of the Governors of Virginia*, vol. 3, p. 105; and the governor's proclamation appeared in the December 29, 1781, issue of the *Virginia Gazette, or, the American Advertiser* (Richmond).
41. Chinard, "Journal de Guerre de Brisout de Barneville," p. 278; Acomb, *Journal of Von Closen*, pp. 166–179; and Rochambeau Papers, vol. 11, p. 12.

YORKTOWN

42. Acomb, "Journal of Von Closen," p. 213; Rice and Brown, *American Campaigns*, vol. 1, p. 152; Rochambeau Papers, vol. 12, pp. 214–226; the *Virginia Gazette, and Weekly Advertiser* (Richmond) for March 30 and April 6, 1782; and John E. Lane, "Jean François Coste, Chief Physician of the French Expeditionary Forces in the American Revolution," *Americana* 22 (1928): 60.
43. Kennett, *French Forces*, p. 157, and Kennett, "Bilan d'une rencontre," p. 539. Kennett views the French officers' negative view of Southern planters as a form of self-criticism. Robert Selig, on the other hand, maintains: "French officers found the more aristocratic lifestyle of Virginia much more to their liking" ("American Campaigns of Flohr," p. 6). On the French officers and Virginian women, see Rice and Brown, *American Campaigns*, vol. 1, p. 66; B.N., N.A.F. 17691, "Journal de Lauberdière," p. 117 verso; and Ludovic de Contenson, ed., "Lettres d'un officier de l'armée de Rochambeau: Le chevalier de Coriolis," *Le Correspondant* 326 (1932): 808–825. It is interesting to observe how Coriolis's ardor cooled as time and distance away from his beloved increased.
44. Selig, "American Campaigns of Flohr," p. 10.
45. For the problems at Yorktown, see *Official Letters of the Governors of Virginia*, vol. 3, p. 105; and the following correspondence in Virginia Executive Papers: William Reynolds to Governor Nelson, November 16, 1781 (box 18); David Ross to William Davies, November 17, 1781 (box 18); Vioménil to Governor Harrison, December [5?], 1781 (box 19); and William Reynolds to Governor Harrison, January 23, 1782 (box 20).
46. Rochambeau to M. de La Villebrune, December 13, 1781, and March 12, 1782, in Rochambeau Papers, vol. 11, pp. 5 and 72–75.
47. Ibid., vol. 3, pp. 292–293.
48. Choisy to Rochambeau, December 31, 1781; Dudley Diggs to Rochambeau, January 2, 1782; Rochambeau to Diggs, January 12, 1782; and Diggs to Governor Harrison, February 8, 1782, all in Virginia Executive Papers, box 20.
49. *Official Letters of the Governors of Virginia*, vol. 3, p. 204.
50. Rochambeau to the Governor, March 10, 1782; Thomas Read to Choisy, March 19, 1782; Choisy to Read, March 20, 1782; and Read to the Governor, March 22, 1782, all in Virginia Executive Papers, box 21. The list of slaves was published in the *Virginia Gazette, and Weekly Advertiser* of March 30 and April 6 and 13, and the *Virginia Gazette or American Advertiser* of April 13, 20, and 27, 1782.
51. *Official Letters of the Governors of Virginia*, vol. 3, pp. 257–263; William Dandridge to the Governor, May [?], 1782, and Rochambeau to Governor Harrison, June 28, 1782, Virginia Executive Papers, box 23; A.G., 1 YC 966 contains information on Pandoua, who, ironically, deserted in the United States two months before his regiment's departure.
52. Most of the documentation can be found in Virginia Executive Papers: Le Pellier to Governor Harrison, February 17, 1782 (box 21); "Procés verbal of the dammages committed by the french army," March 16, 1782 (box 22); "List of forage taken by order of the Quarter Master General," May 3, 1782 (box 22); and "Receipts for Claims Against the French Army," April 29, 1782 (box 22). See also Governor Harrison to the Speaker of the House of Delegates, May 30, 1782, in *Official Letters of the Governors of Virginia*, vol. 3, p. 237.
53. See Rochambeau Papers, vol. 14, pp. 119–181, for the period between Septem-

ber 23, 1781, and June 28, 1782, in particular Rochambeau to La Luzerne, December 10, 1781, on p. 128.
54. Ibid., vol. 9, pp. 234–235; vol. 12, pp. 211 and 240; vol. 11, p. 83; and vol. 14, pp. 159–160.
55. Ibid., vol. 14, pp. 142–144; and Jeremiah Wadsworth to C. Stewart and E. Blaine, November 8, 1781, Virginia Executive Papers, box 18.
56. Rice and Brown, *American Campaigns*, vol. 1, p. 64; and Lane, "Jean François Coste," p. 59.
57. A.G., YA 513 lists officer losses, and the contrôles of the various units provide the data on the soldiers and NCOs; it is not always possible, however, to be certain about the cause of death for the enlisted men.
58. Stone, *Our French Allies*, p. 502n.; and A.N., D^2 C 32, under the company of chasseurs.
59. A.G., X^b 91, X^b 104, and X^d 24.
60. Asa Bird Gardiner, *The Order of the Cincinnati in France* (Providence: Rhode Island State Society of the Cincinnati, 1905), pp. 74–107 and 150–172.
61. Acomb, "Journal of Von Closen," pp. 215–227. Other examples can be found in the *Newport Mercury* for December 19, 1781; Bishop, "A French Volunteer," p. 107; and the *Virginia Gazette, and Weekly Advertiser* for April 27, 1782.
62. See, as an example, the comments of Lieutenant Clermont-Crèvecoeur in Rice and Brown, *American Campaigns*, vol. 1, p. 66.
63. Bodinier, *Officiers*, p. 188.
64. Rochambeau Papers, vol. 11, p. 121 (duplicated in vol. 12, p. 275).
65. See the regimental registers A.G., 1 YC 188, 869, 932, and 966; A.G., 10 YC 1; and A.N., D^2 C 32.
66. For comparable figures on desertions in the French army in the late 1780s and early 1790s, see my article, "The Regeneration of the Line Army During the French Revolution," *Journal of Modern History* 42 (1970): 307–330.
67. On Collier, see A.G., 10 YC 1; for the Saintonge deserters, Rochambeau Papers, vol. 11, pp. 56–57, or vol. 12, p. 227.
68. Acomb, *Journal of Von Closen*, p. 191; and National Archives, Revolutionary War Pension and Bounty-Land-Warrant Application Files, S. 11072 (pointed out to me by John Dann of the University of Michigan).
69. Rochambeau Papers, vol. 11, p. 58; Menonville to Davis, May 3, 1782, in Virginia Executive Papers, box 22; and the *Virginia Gazette, or, the American Advertiser* for December 29, 1781, and February 23, March 2, May 25, June 1 and 8, and November 9, 16, and 23, 1782. As late as 1785, thirteen deserters from the French army in Virginia took advantage of a royal amnesty and turned themselves in to the French vice consul at Richmond; see J. Rives Childs, "French Consul Martin Oster Reports on Virginia, 1784–1796," *Virginia Magazine of History and Biography* 76 (1968): 37.
70. For the overall statistics, see the regimental contrôles; for Poulnot, 10 YC 1.
71. A draft article by Robert A. Selig, "Transatlantic Revolutions? The Case of the Royal Deux-Ponts, 1780–1791," generously provided by the author, contains keen observations on this issue and has led me to modify some of my conclusions.
72. Rochambeau to Washington, June 8, 1782, in Rochambeau Papers, vol. 11, p. 117. The lengths of time indicated here for communication with the French

government are based on a rapid, unscientific sample of a half dozen pieces in Rochambeau Papers, vols. 10 and 12, which indicate dates of reception of correspondence on both sides of the Atlantic. Such lapses in communications may also have contributed to morale problems, at least among officers.
73. For information on these other theaters of operations, often ignored or neglected by American historians, see Mackesy, *War for America*, pp. 446–500; and Duc de Castries, *La France et l'indépendance américaine* (Paris: Perrin, 1975), pp. 330–336.
74. Dull, *French Navy and American Independence*, pp. 258–259.
75. Information on reinforcements, and the lack thereof, for Rochambeau's army can be found in Langeron papers, Ms. f Fr. 160, vol. 2, pieces 143, 144, 215, 218, 221, 253, and 262, as well as Rochambeau Papers, vol. 3, p. 375, and A.G., X^d 24 (for the Auxonne Artillery).
76. For the Soissonnais Infantry, see A.G., X^b 53, and for Deux-Ponts, A.G., X^b 104.
77. One example of Washington's growing impatience is seen in his letter of June 24, 1782, to Rochambeau (in cipher) in Rochambeau Papers, vol. 4, p. 462. On the general atmosphere in America, see Stinchcombe, *American Revolution and French Alliance*, pp. 183–190.
78. Rice and Brown, *American Campaigns*, vol. 1, pp. 71–72; Rochambeau Papers, vol. 11, p. 117; Acomb, "Journal of Von Closen," p. 228; and Rochambeau, *Memoirs*, pp. 85–86. The extent of the French losses in the naval battle of April 12 again highlights the context within which French efforts in the United States must be placed.

6
THE LONG JOURNEY HOME

ALTHOUGH STILL GRAVELY CONCERNED about the situation in which his command found itself and bitterly frustrated by the lack of direction from his government, once Rochambeau made the decision to leave Virginia he pressed forward with his plans. There were the usual logistical problems and complications, but by the end of June 1782 the preparations were complete, and farewells were exchanged during the last week of that month. The General Assembly of Virginia formally noted its gratitude for the good relations between the French troops and the "Citizens of this Commonwealth" and expressed regret at the former's coming departure.[1] The mayor, recorder, aldermen, and Common Council of Williamsburg paid tribute to the military protection, good conduct, and "social, polite, and very friendly intercourse" afforded by the French. The president and professors of the "University of William and Mary" expressed similar sentiments, especially recognizing Rochambeau's generosity in replacing a building destroyed by fire and the contributions of some of his officers to "science as well as liberty."[2]

As had been the case throughout the French stay in the United States, the experience of Lauzun's Legion was somewhat different from that of the rest of the French forces. In February 1782 the unit had been dispatched to Charlotte Courthouse, where it again became a focus of controversy. In addition to civilian complaints (discussed in chapter 5), General Greene frequently complained about the military disposition and inadequate strength of this detachment during spring 1782.[3] Despite these problems, however, when the legion was ready to depart in June, local authorities thanked Colonel Dillon, who had replaced the despised Choisy, for "the polite and Genteel behavior" of his officers and "the orderly behavior of their Troops since he took the Command at this Station."[4] Shortly afterward, the six hundred officers and men of the unit left for Petersburg and assumed the function of vanguard for Rochambeau's army on its march to Georgetown.

Meanwhile, the main body of the force assembled at Williamsburg and on July 1 began to march northward in four separate divisions, each consisting of an infantry regiment with its support elements and baggage train. The divisions left on consecutive days and occupied the same camp on four successive days. Staff officers and a detachment of pioneers went ahead to identify the route, select campsites, and clear and repair roads when necessary. To avoid the worst of the heat, the French restricted their marching to between 2:00 A.M. and shortly after dawn; thus, they were able to travel an average of twelve to thirteen miles per day. By July 20 the last division reached Georgetown.[5]

The departure of Rochambeau's main force from Williamsburg did not terminate relations between the French and Virginians. For one thing, Governor Harrison appointed a special agent, Captain Slaughter, to accompany the French and facilitate procurement of whatever they needed on their march. The French were to pay for everything except quarters and boats, which would be provided by the state by renting or requisitioning them.[6] More important, Rochambeau had left behind at Yorktown and West Point a detachment composed of four hundred infantrymen and three companies of artillerymen to guard the French siege artillery until it could be loaded aboard French ships; their commanding officer was a lieutenant colonel in the Saintonge Regiment, the chevalier de La Valette, who had been recommended for promotion to brigadier general for his distinguished conduct during the siege of Yorktown. Because of its important defensive works and since U.S. siege artillery also remained at Yorktown, Governor Harrison sent a detachment of six hundred men under Colonel Charles Dabney there in late June. To avoid possible dispute about who was in charge, Harrison also appointed General Edward Stevens, who was senior to La Valette, as commander.

Despite these precautions, controversy arose when La Valette received orders to leave for Baltimore with all the French artillery in late July. On Rochambeau's recommendation, La Valette began to raze the fortifications at Yorktown. The governor immediately ordered Dabney to take possession of the works and halt the demolition. After La Valette's departure in mid-August, Harrison continued to complain about his conduct.[7] The unhappy

La Valette reached Baltimore with most of his troops sick only days before the French army left for New York.

The main body of Rochambeau's corps had arrived in Baltimore in stages between July 23 and 27 and remained there for the next month. The French officers and soldiers refreshed themselves, avoided excessive exertion during the hottest period of the year, and entertained and were entertained by the populace. Shortages of certain supplies continued to be a problem; for example, in early August the commanding officer of the Royal Deux-Ponts Regiment claimed his men still needed twenty-four hundred shirts and a thousand hats, since the hats they had received were "ridiculously small, and would not even stay on one's head."[8]

To help relieve such problems and in the absence of hard cash, Rochambeau authorized the use of letters of exchange, even though they brought only 80 percent of their face value.[9] Despite shortages, the French put on a dress parade and review by Rochambeau on August 5 that greatly impressed local spectators.[10] Six days later a joint address from the governor and the Council of Maryland expressed to Rochambeau the state's esteem and gratitude for the French contribution to Yorktown and acknowledged that "the decorum and exemplary discipline observed by your troops on their march through the State have given Entire satisfaction to our citizens."[11] Baltimore merchants publicly stated identical sentiments about "the decorum and order" of the French soldiers and "the great politeness of the officers" and claimed that their presence eradicated any trace of anti-French prejudice "which the English have so pertinaceously attributed to the Americans."[12] The French officers socialized extensively, including attending the inevitable balls, and a Catholic chapel was opened for the French troops during their stay in Baltimore.[13]

Of course, Franco-American relations in Baltimore were not perfect, and, naturally, it was a member of Lauzun's Legion who disrupted things. Shortly after arrival, the comte de Dillon, the unit's commanding officer, was racing through the streets with a hussar whose horse knocked down a child; the child's father abused the soldier, and a crowd beat him and left him for dead in the street while Dillon managed to escape. The colonel subsequently lodged a complaint with the justice of the peace, but the only satisfaction he was able to extract was a decision to fine the father four shillings if the hussar died.[14] This episode provides one more example of the differences between Franco-American relations on a public and a personal level and of the fundamentally bittersweet nature of the relationship.

Before the advanced elements of his army reached Baltimore, Rochambeau rode to Philadelphia where he conferred with Washington on

July 19. The central issue was the use to be made of Rochambeau's army. Washington proposed a joint expedition against Canada, which Rochambeau had to reject since he had verbal orders prohibiting him from engaging in any offensive aimed at Canada (lest the Americans achieve unchecked dominance of the entire Atlantic seaboard). Instead, it was agreed that the French would recuperate in Baltimore until the summer heat had abated; there they would be joined by La Valette's detachment, including the artillery, still in Virginia; and then they would unite with Washington's army on the Hudson River outside New York (which would prevent that major garrison from sending reinforcements against the French in the Caribbean).[15] Although the Allies had not yet received official news of it, the British evacuation of Savannah on July 11 would have confirmed this decision.

On August 19 the troops and artillery that had been left in Virginia began to disembark in Baltimore; more than two-thirds of the men were ill. When the French corps left the city in the order in which they had arrived between August 23 and 27, these men and a few of their disabled comrades from other units—a total of four hundred—were left behind, together with nearly three hundred able-bodied soldiers who stayed to guard the heavy guns. Once again, Lieutenant Colonel La Valette was given the dubious distinction of commanding the detachment, with instructions to send groups of men to the main army as they regained their health.[16]

Rochambeau's army passed through Philadelphia, where the troops were again warmly received, in early September on its way to Trenton where the order of march was changed: The four infantry regiments were grouped into just two divisions, and Lauzun's Legion was given the mission of protecting the right flank.[17] On September 16 the French reached King's Ferry on the Hudson and over the next two days crossed to the east bank to join Washington's army encamped at Peekskill. Following a review of the two armies by their commanding generals—during which the American troops greatly impressed the French officers with how well they were armed, uniformed, and trained—on September 23 the French regiments marched to their separate encampment outside Crampond, where they had more space and better opportunities for foraging.[18] Three days later the duc de Lauzun, who had been dispatched to France with news of Yorktown shortly after the British surrender, rejoined his unit; accompanying him were a number of young court aristocrats from the most illustrious families in France.

Lauzun had attempted to return from Brest on the frigate *Gloire* on May 19, but the English blockade and a severe storm forced the ship back to Paimboeuf to refit. When the repairs were completed, the *Gloire* sailed southward along the French coast to Rochefort where it joined another frigate, *Aigle*, and the two left port on July 15.[19] The American cause had become the rage at Versailles, and among the officers aboard the two vessels were Charles Louis Victor, prince de Broglie, the twenty-six-year-old son of Marshal de Broglie and recently appointed colonel in second of the Saintonge Regiment; the baron de Montesquieu, grandson of the great philosopher, appointed colonel in second of the Bourbonnais Regiment two months after his arrival in America at age thirty-two; the comte de Ségur, son of the minister of war, colonel in second of the Soissonnais Regiment, age twenty-nine; comte Talleyrand-Périgord, an eighteen-year-old sublieutenant who would serve as aide de camp to General Chastellux and whose brother, then bishop of Autun, became one of the most famous characters of the age; and the comte de Vauban, great grandnephew of the famous marshal, a colonel since 1779 (at age twenty-five), and an aide de camp to Rochambeau.

The two ships carrying this noble cargo had an eventful crossing. After stopping at the Azores for three weeks to take on fresh supplies and allow the sick to recover, they were engaged by the British ship *Hector* (seventy-four guns) on September 4–5 and suffered over thirty casualties. A week later, just off the mouth of the Delaware, they were again attacked by British ships. Before the *Aigle* was lost and the *Gloire* managed to escape, the officers and specie (around 2 million livres) they were carrying were landed, with some difficulty, on September 13 and 14. Both men and money made their way to Philadelphia and, subsequently, to Rochambeau's headquarters in New York where they arrived on September 26.

It is highly questionable whether these enthusiastic but largely inexperienced officers added much of military value to Rochambeau's little army, although the funds they brought constituted a substantial contribution. The newly arrived officers also brought news from home, including long overdue instructions from the French government. The most important communication was a letter from the marquis de Ségur, the war minister, to Rochambeau, dated April 30, 1782. The dispatch assured Rochambeau that the king was "perfectly content with your services" and gave him directions for his next movements. If the British were to evacuate either New York or Charleston, Rochambeau was to embark his entire army on ships under the command of Louis Philippe Rigaud, marquis de Vaudreuil, who would rendezvous with him in Chesapeake Bay. They would then sail to Saint-Domingue (Haiti) where Rochambeau was to cooperate with the Spanish commander in the area, Bernardo de Gálvez. Since Rochambeau had requested leave for his health and the Caribbean climate might be bad for him, he was authorized to take his leave after his troops were settled in Saint-Domingue.[20]

Of course, when Ségur composed these instructions Rochambeau's army was still in Virginia, and the minister did not know the whereabouts of Vaudreuil's squadron. In fact, Vaudreuil had succeeded in escaping from the disastrous defeat of the Saints (April 12, 1782) and headed north with thirteen ships of the line to put into Boston for repairs. On July 26 he had anchored briefly in Chesapeake Bay, informed Rochambeau of his destination, offered to transport twelve hundred to fifteen hundred men to New England, and requested about three hundred soldiers, artillerymen, and grenadiers to assist him in a plan to attack the British post at Penobscot. Rochambeau rejected Vaudreuil's proposal, claiming Penobscot was too well defended and that Washington did not regard it as important to the American cause (a decision Washington thoroughly endorsed a week and a half later). Rochambeau did send Brigadier General de Choisy, together with three artillery and two engineer officers, to help Vaudreuil organize the fortifications in Nantasket Roads, near Boston, but when Vaudreuil requested a contingent of six hundred men to guard such works in mid-September Rochambeau again turned him down, arguing that there was no fear of enemy attack on Nantasket and that even if there were, thousands of local militia were readily available to repulse it.[21]

Within three weeks of establishing camp at Crampond, Rochambeau held general inspections of his regiments to evaluate their status. Since leaving Williamsburg on July 1, fifty-eight soldiers had died, sixty-eight had deserted, and ten had been discharged. More than six hundred men were hospitalized, and another three to four hundred were serving in various detachments, most in Baltimore. The articles of clothing that needed to be replaced included nearly twenty-one hundred complete uniforms, around seventeen hundred coats, more than four thousand pairs of breeches, and twenty-eight hundred hats. In addition, knapsacks, canteens, musket straps, bayonets, sabers, and flintlocks had to be replaced, and hundreds of other pieces of clothing and equipment required extensive repairs. And this was for the four infantry regiments only! On top of everything else, these essential items cost twice as much in America as in France.[22]

Some of the officers had exhausted their available means over their long stay and extensive travels in the United States and were feeling the pinch. It is difficult, though, to arouse great sympathy for Louis Philippe de Ségur, who complained of being forced to leave behind in France his kitchen equipment, his "great tent," and other provisions, as well as two servants, including his cook. The poor man was left with only four servants and "twelve or thirteen trunks"![23] Ségur's situation stands in sharp contrast to that of Jeremiah Olmy (or Ohny) who was stationed nearby with the Continental

Army, and who wrote on October 15 that local merchants shunned the American camp "as they Would a Mad Dog" because the Americans had no money while less than a dozen miles away the French camp "abounds in plenty."[24]

After the French had established themselves in their new location, a regular routine quickly developed. Indeed, it was in part to combat boredom—as well as to let the soldiers earn some extra money—that Rochambeau authorized a number of his men to construct a canal for a local miller.[25] Thanks to the garrulous Ségur, who apparently thought his daily activities were of great interest to his wife, we possess an account of what was probably a typical routine for superior officers: It consisted mostly of dining, riding, inspecting various guards, and socializing with fellow officers.[26] Life on the march or in civilian surroundings was undoubtedly more exciting.

By late September Rochambeau was simply waiting for news of events that would determine his next move. Beginning September 23 the French commander received regular reports from an American agent in New York about British activity there, especially rumors about preparations to leave the city; simultaneously, La Luzerne relayed news about Charleston from Philadelphia.[27] Even without definite information, Rochambeau decided to act, and as early as September 25 he told Vaudreuil in Boston to begin making preparations to embark his army. Vaudreuil responded that he would be able to accommodate a maximum of four thousand, and Rochambeau decided he would have to leave his convalescents and Lauzun's Legion (cavalry would be of little use in the West Indies) behind, because the men in his infantry and artillery units together with the officers and their servants numbered over four thousand.[28]

Interestingly, Rochambeau's actions were in line with instructions from the Ministry of War, which were dated August 18 and 26 but did not arrive in the United States until the end of December. Because the government had received information that the English had evacuated Charleston (not true) and Savannah (true) and planned to leave New York (unclear), Rochambeau was instructed to send as much of his army as possible on Vaudreuil's ships to the French islands in the Caribbean, since it was believed that the British forces leaving North America were going to attack there. Rochambeau was to leave his sick and enough healthy troops to protect the French hospitals, heavy artillery, magazines, and supplies in the United States. He was also to assure Washington that if the English returned to North America his army would follow immediately. All of these plans, however, were to be kept secret unless it became necessary to implement them.[29]

Rochambeau had decided to direct the bulk of his forces toward Boston; he even sent carpenters and blacksmiths from his army to hasten the refitting of Vaudreuil's ships there.[30] Formal farewells were exchanged by the Allied comrades in arms, and Washington, whose relations with Rochambeau had been proper, courteous, and cooperative but never warm, remarked that the parting was marked by "sentiments of sincere affection and mutual regret."[31] On October 21 and 22, the French infantry and field artillery units departed, marching as they had since leaving Trenton in two divisions, or brigades, that occupied the same campsites on successive days. At the same time, the duc de Lauzun was ordered to march the hussar and infantry elements of his legion to Wilmington, Delaware, and was given command of all remaining French troops in the United States, including La Valette's detachment and the siege artillery in Baltimore, as well as the men scattered in small hospitals along the route of the march—well over eleven hundred personnel. Most of these men would not return to France until the following May.[32]

As the French marched northeastward there was talk of an imminent departure from the United States, but no definite word was given until they reached Hartford, Connecticut, on October 29. There, Rochambeau announced that he had decided to return to France for reasons of health and intended to turn the command over to the baron de Vioménil; he also disclosed that the troops' immediate destination was Boston where they would board ships for the West Indies.[33] Meanwhile, Vaudreuil had informed Rochambeau that the ships' repairs were going slowly and that some new problems had arisen, notably that lightning had struck and destroyed the mizzen mast of the *Auguste,* which was being refitted in Portsmouth, New Hampshire. He advised Rochambeau to delay his arrival in Boston.[34] The weather was becoming colder; rain had turned to sleet and sleet to snow. Consequently, despite the hospitality extended to the French by Governor Trumbull and the State Council, Rochambeau decided to take his army to Providence, which was closer to Boston (about fifty miles away), where the surroundings were more familiar, and where he was sure to find adequate quarters and firewood for his army while waiting for Vaudreuil's fleet to be ready.[35] After a week's stay in Hartford, the French left for Providence.

Rochambeau and his suite reached Providence on November 8, and two days later the rest of the army began to arrive. Well before their arrival Rochambeau had sent Pierre François Béville, his quartermaster general, to arrange with the state authorities for quartering his men.[36] As had been the situation during their previous stay in Providence, many officers were lodged in private homes, often with the same families who had housed them the previous year. The rest of the officers and the soldiers set up tents, but severe cold and heavy frosts forced them to move into barracks in North Providence within a few days of their arrival; one officer observed, "the tents were frozen so stiff that, after the pegs and poles were removed to take them down, they stood alone."[37]

For many of the French officers the return to Rhode Island was a veritable homecoming. They quickly resumed relations with their former hosts and hostesses in Providence and began a new round of socializing, including—as always—banquets and balls capped off by the "very splendid Ball" given by Rochambeau for "the Ladies and Gentlemen of the Town" on November 18. The officers who had joined the army since mid-1781 were also quickly made comfortable by the warm welcome they received.[38]

Newport, which had been "home" to most of the French officers for nearly a year, surpassed Providence in cordiality. The local press had continued to carry news of the French after their departure in 1781 and had increased its coverage when it appeared that Rochambeau's army was coming north again.[39] Some of the younger officers visited Newport from Providence, and "all faces lighted up when they saw the French returning."[40] Not surprisingly, the French gave a ball for their friends during their brief visit there. To add to the happiness of the Allies, throughout November unconfirmed reports of the British evacuation of Charleston arrived continually at Rochambeau's headquarters.[41]

As with many homecomings, the joy of the occasion was marred by strains. Again, money proved to be a sore spot. The French considered the fees they were charged for cutting wood and for other damages to property near their quarters in North Providence excessive (over forty-six hundred dollars) and apparently complained to state authorities. The General Assembly appointed a committee of three men to investigate and make what they felt to be a just evaluation. Their itemized report concluded that the French had been overcharged by slightly more than a thousand dollars. The assembly ordered this sum—less the committee's expenses—to be refunded to the French and instructed the attorney general to prosecute those responsible if the refund was not paid within twenty days.[42] Not all financial dealings ended so favorably for the French, however. As the time for their departure approached, many French officers attempted to sell their horses, since they could not be transported on the ships available. The result was a buyer's market; some officers complained that they were being paid only a third of the animals' value.[43]

On the whole, however, Franco-American relations in Rhode Island remained friendly, and when the French were preparing to leave for Boston in late November there was another outpouring of gratitude for their services and regret at their departure. On November 27 the governor of Rhode Island, in an address to the General Assembly, cordially acknowledged the services of Rochambeau's army, from the commanding general to the private soldiers. And two and a half weeks later, Washington once again thanked Rochambeau while recognizing the "exact order and discipline of the Corps under your command."[44]

At the end of November Rochambeau transferred his command to Vioménil and, with Chastellux and some of his staff, left for Philadelphia. Shortly afterward the French army began its march to Boston, with each of the four infantry regiments leaving on successive days beginning December 1. Because of the additional problems involved in loading the field artillery, the artillery companies had departed two weeks earlier, arrived in Boston on November 18, and discharged their horses three days later. Meanwhile, Vaudreuil was finishing the complex preparations required for such an operation: refitting his squadron (including thirteen ships of the line and nine frigates), acquiring and storing the supplies necessary for a voyage to the Caribbean, coordinating troop movements for a smooth embarkation, and keeping himself informed of the whereabouts of enemy vessels. The logistical arrangements were further complicated by winter conditions.[45] Despite the weather, the French infantry units were able to complete the march from Providence in two days and even had time to spruce up before parading through the city, where they were greeted enthusiastically. The troops arrived one day apart between December 3 and 6 and after marching into Boston immediately embarked on fifteen of the waiting ships, although most of the officers remained in the much more comfortable quarters provided by local citizens—some until as late as December 21.[46]

In Boston the officers enjoyed the kind of welcome they had often experienced since leaving Virginia: celebrations in their honor, banquets, balls, and public accolades. The *Boston Gazette and Country Journal*, a weekly appearing every Monday, reported the arrival of the French—"A finer Corps of Men never paraded on the Streets of Boston"—on December 9 and commented that the "Behaviour of these Troops, during their long March, sufficiently contradicts the *infamous Falsehoods* and *Misrepresentations* usually imposed on the World by *perfideous Britons*."[47] The *Continental Journal and Weekly Advertiser*, published on Thursdays, printed the same story verbatim in its December 12 issue. On December 11 the selectmen of the city named a committee (including Samuel Adams) to express their gratitude and congratulations to the French; the following day Vioménil thanked them and praised Franco-American friendship.[48] At the same time, financial problems continued to dog the French forces; prices rose rapidly when they arrived and remained high during their stay but fell when they left. For example, within two days of their departure from Boston, French bills of exchange rose from 75 to 90 percent of face value.[49]

The departure—possibly expedited by further reports of the English evacuation of Charleston, which finally did take place on December 14—came on December 24, 1782. Aboard Vaudreuil's ships were approximately four thousand officers and men of the French expeditionary corps, as well as nearly one hundred nonmilitary administrative personnel (for example, the financial and medical staff, civilian workers, the chaplain) and three to four hundred officers' servants.[50] The main squadron was to join other ships (including the *Auguste* whose mast had been cracked by lightning) that had docked at Portsmouth, about sixty miles from Boston. The ships there, however, were unable to sail until December 29 and failed to make the planned rendezvous. When they did depart from Portsmouth, the French left behind a small contingent of sailors and soldiers—including the sick—who remained there until summer 1783 when they took possession of the ship *America* (seventy-four guns), a gift to King Louis XVI from the U.S. Congress.[51]

Most of the men at Portsmouth and in the other detachments left in America would make their way back to France within the coming year. Others from Rochambeau's corps, however, stayed in the United States permanently. In all, including the troops who remained in America under Lauzun's command, slightly more than three hundred had deserted, including eighty men recruited there; and one hundred and forty, including thirty "American" recruits, were discharged for various reasons in the United States.[52] Even without discounting the men who enlisted in America, most of whom were defectors from the British forces, the proportion of deserters is remarkably low (slightly over 5 percent) for a period of two and a half years or more. Likewise, the number discharged in the United States over the same period can perhaps best be appreciated by comparing it with the 830 discharges among the men of Rochambeau's former units during the second half of 1783, after their return to France. The inescapable conclusion is that the vast majority of the French preferred their arduous and dangerous life in the army and the possibility of returning home at some indefinite time in the future to whatever opportunities they might enjoy in the alien environment of America.

It is interesting to investigate—even briefly—those who did stay in the United States. But we must recognize that it is impossible to attribute precise motives for the decisions of men who have not left a single document in their own hand; the best one can do is to uncover the most likely reasons for their actions based on surviving circumstantial evidence.

Officers could resign their commissions whenever and for whatever reason they chose, and when they did resign they were usually dropped from military records with no explanation. Consequently, one cannot determine how many might have taken up residence in the United States, although one gets the distinct impression that very few did so. In all, thirty-one officers voluntarily left active duty while serving in America, a dozen during their last four months in the country.[53] The clearest evidence that some officers stayed in the United States is marriage. For example, Nicolas Anciaux, the quartermaster treasurer of the Regiment of Royal Deux-Ponts, resigned on May 25, 1782, to marry in the United States, and Jean Georges Curien, sublieutenant in the Soissonnais Regiment, did the same on December 9, 1782. Both were *officiers de fortune* who had previous service as enlisted men dating back more than twenty years. Benoît François van Pradelles, a native of the Austrian Netherlands serving as a lieutenant in the Royal Deux-Ponts, resigned his commission on October 28, 1781, when he was twenty-six, to marry a woman in Baltimore, where he lived until his death in 1809. A young nobleman, Arsène Gillaume Joseph Barbier de La Serre, a sublieutenant in the Regiment of Saintonge, did not resign from the army until 1784, when he returned to America where he married a woman of English birth.[54]

Although it is even more difficult to find evidence of the fate of enlisted men when they left military service in America, it is safer to assume that many remained there; they were much less likely to possess the means to return to Europe, although there are unusual instances when the unit register notes "discharged in America to return to France." It is still probable that a majority of the men discharged in the United States stayed there, since they could have been discharged back in France. There can be little doubt that most of the fourteen soldiers who officially retired from the army in 1782 decided to enjoy their pensions in America. For example, Jean Sicard (fifty-one years old, twenty-four years of service), Pierre Fontaine (age forty-three, with same length of service), and Jacques Lavit (forty-three years of age, over twenty-five years of service) of the Regiment of Auxonne Artillery were all "discharged with the military pension of [between 184 and 262 livres] at Boston in North America the 1st of December 1782."[55] By taking their discharge there when they could have received the same benefits in France a few months later, they apparently opted to forfeit free passage home (all were French natives) and to live in the United States.

Desertions are more of a problem to analyze because the range of possible motives is almost as great as the number of deserters. Certain factors did, however, influence desertions. Men tended to desert with comrades. Henrich Messerte and Christophe Estheimer—soldiers in the Royal Deux-

Ponts Infantry, the same age (twenty-two), both Protestants (unusual among the overwhelmingly Catholic soldiers of the French army), both from villages in the Duchy of Deux-Ponts, who had enlisted three days apart in October 1777 in the same company of their regiment—deserted together on April 19, 1782.[56] François Aubry, thirty-nine years old with over sixteen years of service, and Pierre Dapre, thirty years of age with ten years' service, had been transferred from the Regiment of Toul Artillery to the battalion of Auxonne Artillery serving in America on January 14, 1782; the two veteran soldiers deserted in Boston on November 28 of that year.[57]

Such factors as comradeship and alienation had an effect on desertions under any circumstances. What peculiar elements affected the desertion rate in America? As indicated in chapter 5, while stationed in Virginia German troops were more inclined to desert than native Frenchmen. Indeed, it is striking that during their entire sojourn in the United States, two-thirds of all deserters from Rochambeau's army came from the Regiment of Deux-Ponts and Lauzun's Legion, which together contained less than one-third of the total personnel. These units contained nearly all of the foreigners (that is, non-French)—over 97 percent—in Rochambeau's entire force, and nearly all of the men were German or German-speaking (for example, from the German cantons of Switzerland).[58] As discussed previously, these soldiers—and those who defected from German units in the British forces to enlist in the same regiments—were much more likely to desert than their French comrades, largely because they found more compatible conditions in America, particularly among the numerous German immigrant communities. Other evidence tends to support this conclusion. The issues of the *Providence Gazette and Country Journal* for December 7, 14, and 21, 1782, carried an advertisement offering a reward for the apprehension of ten German deserters from the French army; the notice gave the name, age, and physical description of each man and promised twenty dollars plus expenses for every one of the men delivered to "the Gaol at Boston." Almost as an afterthought the announcement simply mentioned, "A like Reward will be given for every French Deserter."

The desertion rate was also increased by the proximity of departure. More than one-fourth of desertions in the units that sailed from Boston on Christmas Eve 1782 came after the men had been informed that they would soon be leaving—that is, during the last two months of their stay in the United States. Similarly, over one-fifth of the desertions from Lauzun's Legion occurred during the unit's final two months (out of thirty-four) in the United States.[59] If the soldiers wished to stay, they had to act quickly and decisively.

These two factors—the predominance of Germans among the deserters and the disproportionately large number of desertions shortly before departure—suggest that many of these men deserted in order to remain in the United States after their units left. One must beware, however, of posing too logical an explanation for desertions. Jean Baptiste Pandoua from Madagascar, who had enlisted in the Soissonnais Infantry on January 17, 1777, at age fifteen and was carried on the regimental roll as "Negro Enlisted as musician," deserted while on march in Connecticut on October 27, 1782, after witnessing the lot of black slaves from New England to the South and back again.[60]

Clearly, America offered certain attractions to some of the soldiers who served there under Rochambeau. The paucity of records for ordinary people in the eighteenth century and problems in following the lives of common soldiers after their separation from military service, however, make any precise statistical analysis impossible. Nevertheless, some suggestive observations can be made thanks to the intensive research of Robert Selig, who has studied the Regiment of Royal Deux-Ponts in detail. Perhaps as many as sixty to eighty veterans of this unit, discharged in France between 1783 and 1791, subsequently returned to the United States. The Catholic chaplain of the regiment (in which more than 60 percent of the soldiers were Catholic), a Carmelite priest named Deratz—or Rignatz—and later known as Paul de St. Pierre, came back to the United States in 1784 and served as a missionary in the Mississippi Valley until his death after the turn of the century. Similarly, Georg Daniel Flohr, a private in the same regiment and a native of Deux-Ponts (that is, the Duchy of Zweibrücken), returned to America after the execution of Louis XVI in January 1793 and became a Lutheran pastor to various congregations in western Virginia until his death at Wytheville in April 1826.[61] Thus, religious vocation might be added to the cultural, social, economic, and political motivations that attracted some of Rochambeau's officers and men to the American way of life.

Although a handful of officers and possibly a few hundred soldiers from Rochambeau's expedition remained in America, most departed with their units, never to return. By far the largest contingent was the force that sailed with Vaudreuil in late December, but other, smaller groups left at various times over the next ten months. After leaving Rhode Island at the end of November, Rochambeau, accompanied by about two dozen of his officers and their attendants, had proceeded to Philadelphia and then on to Annapolis, where—for the last time—he received official recognition of his achievements and of the exemplary discipline of his troops from the Congress and the state legislature of Maryland. At Annapolis on January 8, 1783, he and his entourage boarded the *Emeraude* and sailed for France, arriving off Nantes on February 10.[62]

The duc de Lauzun was left in command of the remaining French personnel in the United States, most of whom were concentrated at Baltimore (about four hundred convalescents and guards for the heavy artillery under La Valette) and Wilmington (the base for the more than five hundred officers and men of his Legion). In April 1783 a French ship, the frigate *Active*, carried Lauzun orders to bring the remaining French troops back to France now that hostilities had ended.[63] A flurry of activity followed in preparation for the embarkation, in addition to last-minute discharges and desertions. Thirty-five men were discharged from Lauzun's Legion in early May, a number of whom—for example, Zachaire Colowsky, Henry Jeriez, and Jean Schwartz, all from Brunswick, all in their twenties, and all recruited in the United States between September 12 and November 1, 1780, together with "Jean" Folmer of Pennsylvania, the only American enlisted by a unit of Rochambeau's—were "discharged in America the 1st of May 1783 having been Enlisted only for [the duration of] the War." The number of desertions from the unit rose dramatically: There were none from November through February and only two in March but sixteen in April and eleven during the first week and a half of May.[64] Similar developments occurred, but on a smaller scale, among the troops at Baltimore; for example, Jean Pierre Bosque, a cannoneer in the Auxonne Artillery, was discharged May 1, the same day Thomas La Forest, a five-year veteran in the Regiment of Soissonnais, deserted while "detached at Baltimore in America."[65]

Lauzun's unit sailed on May 11 and La Valette's detachment four days later; both arrived in France the following month. The last remnants of Rochambeau's expedition, consisting mostly of convalescents, plus a small detachment of the Auxonne Artillery and four officers—eighty-five men in all—left Baltimore on October 5 and reached Brest November 10, 1783.[66]

This turned out to be less than five months after the arrival of the main body that had sailed from Boston and Portsmouth at the end of 1782. These troops had experienced a remarkable voyage. When Vaudreuil's fleet left Boston on December 24, it ran into stormy weather and heavy seas, the effects of which were compounded by seasickness, a poor diet, and close quarters; and as Captain von Closen of the Royal Deux-Ponts remarked, "all these discomforts are only part of the vexatious existence . . . aboard a warship!"[67] Since officers' accommodations were luxurious in comparison, one shudders to imagine the lot of the poor soldiers! For some, the consequences were fatal; for example, Nicolas Bourrot, a forty-year-old native of Lorraine who had enlisted in the Bourbonnais Infantry in June 1761, "died at sea the

25th of December 1782," only a day after they set sail.[68] The foul weather prevented the ships from Portsmouth from joining the main squadron as planned and created the same hazards—high winds, bitter cold, massive waves (the *Amazone* was swamped on the night of January 6–7), and severe seasickness. Storms also scattered thirty merchant ships that were sailing with the convoy; some ran aground and others were captured by the English, including the *Allégeance*, carrying two companies of the Regiment of Saintonge, which were subsequently interned on Jamaica.[69]

The main fleet—battered but essentially intact—paused briefly off Puerto Rico during the third week of January. There it was learned that superior British naval forces prevented the French from going to Saint-Domingue, and it was decided that they would join their Spanish allies at Porto Cabello in Venezuela instead.[70] It was on the way there that the greatest tragedy of the voyage struck Vaudreuil's squadron. About one o'clock on the morning of February 4, the *Bourgogne* struck a rock about a league and a half from shore and began to break up slowly. There are conflicting stories about what happened thereafter, but the following is basically accurate.[71] All of the small boats aboard that could be used as "lifeboats" were quickly occupied (often by officers and crew members) and rowed to shore; rafts were then constructed from pieces of the ship. Even when all of these means had been exhausted—three days after the ship first ran aground—around 250 men remained clinging to the wreckage, although all officers, naval and military, including the ship's captain, had escaped. The last survivors were not picked up until February 7. Estimates of the total number of lives lost vary between 120 and 300. More certain are the casualties among Rochambeau's former units: Four officers and twenty-seven men of the Bourbonnais Infantry and one officer and five men of the Auxonne Artillery were lost.[72]

Another consequence of this disaster was bitter animosity among soldiers in the Regiment of Bourbonnais toward their officers. Not only had the officers abandoned their men, but some of the officers who had secured places on the rafts had used their pistols and swords to drive off soldiers who attempted to climb aboard. When the survivors were subsequently reunited in Porto Cabello, the soldiers of Bourbonnais mutinied against the officers who had deserted them. It required all of General de Vioménil's efforts to restore calm with the promise of an inquest.[73]

The French began arriving at Porto Cabello about a week after the shipwreck. Despite the problems they had experienced in adapting to the United States, they found Venezuela even more different from France in its climate, flora, fauna, customs, and people, and they liked it even less. Shortly after arriving, a number of officers left Porto Cabello for Caracas for their

THE LONG JOURNEY HOME

edification and a healthier climate. Those left behind soon began to suffer from tropical diseases that caused fevers and sores. A score of soldiers died during their brief—six to seven week—stay. One less-natural death further contributed to the general unpleasantness. Charles Louis Jean Berthier, a twenty-four-year-old sublieutenant and younger brother of Louis Alexandre Berthier (then a captain on the general staff, later a marshal and Napoleon's chief of staff), died on February 17 from a wound sustained in a duel the day before. A fellow officer had accused Berthier of stealing from a chest they had shared aboard the *Neptune* on the voyage from New England; the latter defended his honor by challenging his accuser to a duel. After two inconclusive engagements with swords on February 4 and 11, they switched to pistols for the fatal confrontation on the 16th. When news of the preliminary peace treaty with England arrived on March 24 and the French prepared to sail, the pleasure with which Colonel Broglie prepared to leave "this vile Porto Cabello" was obviously shared by others in the expeditionary force.[74]

The French left Venezuela on April 3 and 4 and arrived off Saint-Domingue a week and a half later. They stayed there only a couple of weeks, and few of the troops even disembarked. Some of the officers did go ashore, including the comte de Ségur whose family owned a plantation outside Port-au-Prince.[75] He and Captain Berthier visited his plantation between April 14 and 19, and Ségur remarked that at one point he was surrounded by "a crowd of slaves who knelt when they addressed me, and whose life or death is in my hands." Thirteen months earlier, while impatiently waiting to sail to the United States, he had written, "Liberty, for which I am going to fight, inspires me with strong enthusiasm."[76] Apparently, this noble "freedom fighter" saw no contradiction in these sentiments!

At the end of April and the beginning of May, the French fleet sailed for France. On June 17 most of the ships reached Brest, and the troops landed during the following three days. The vessels carrying the officers and men of the Regiment of Soissonnais had been diverted to the Mediterranean; they arrived at Toulon on July 10.[77] One striking aspect of the voyage home was the very limited loss of life: only a dozen soldiers died in the transatlantic crossing—far fewer than the number who perished on the trip to the United States, during which thirty-one men died. Even more impressive is the fact that whereas around 240 of Rochambeau's troops died in the six months following their arrival in America, only 70 died during the half year after their return to France.[78] Although it is impossible to offer a diagnosis from this distance, a few observations seem in order. For most of the soldiers, the crossing from the Caribbean to Europe lasted three weeks less than the voyage to North America. On the other hand, the Regiment of Soissonnais took exactly the same amount of time to reach Toulon and was none the worse off. Probably more important was the brief stop at Saint-Domingue where the French took on fresh water, fruit, and vegetables—the best available antidotes for the scourge of scurvy. And possibly, the men who sailed back to France in summer 1783 were healthier than they had been in spring 1780.

In any event, the decline in the death rate was only one unusual development—and hardly the most outstanding one—among the extraordinary experiences of these men during the previous three years. The officers and soldiers of Rochambeau's American units now settled in to the established routines of peacetime military service, but not before undergoing still more important changes.

Notes

1. Virginia Executive Papers, box 23; Rochambeau Papers, vol. 4, p. 465 (duplicated in vol. 12, pp. 284–285); and the *Virginia Gazette, or, American Advertiser* of June 29, 1782, contain copies of this address, dated June 25, 1782.
2. Rochambeau Papers, vol. 4, pp. 480–481 (also vol. 12, pp. 286–288).
3. See p. 79 for the civilian complaints; and Rochambeau Papers, vol. 12, pp. 236–237 and 266–267 for the Greene-Rochambeau correspondence.
4. See Virginia State Library, Charlotte County Court Order Book, No. 5 (1780–1784), sessions of June 3 and July 1, 1782. Dillon requested that the section of the address implying dissatisfaction with Choisy be altered.
5. Rice and Brown, *American Campaigns*, vol. 2, pp. 173–174; Kennett, *French Forces*, p. 162; and Rochambeau Papers, vol. 3, pp. 327–335.
6. House of Delegates Resolution dated July 1, 1782, Virginia Executive Papers, box 24; and Governor Harrison to Captain Slaughter, July 2, 1782, in *Official Letters of the Governors of Virginia*, vol. 3, p. 263.
7. For the problems with La Valette's detachment, see *Official Letters of the Governors of Virginia*, vol. 3, pp. 254–255, 257, 265–266, 286, 288, and 303; La Valette's letters to Harrison of July 9 and 28 in Virginia Executive Papers, box 24; and Rochambeau Papers, vol. 12, pp. 283–284, and vol. 13, pp. 6–7.
8. See the letter dated Philadelphia, August 7, 1782, in A.G., X^b 104.
9. Rochambeau Papers, vol. 11, p. 166.
10. Rice and Brown, *American Campaigns*, vol. 1, p. 75.
11. Rochambeau Papers, vol. 4, p. 502, duplicated in vol. 13, pp. 20–21, and published in the *Virginia Gazette, and Weekly Advertiser* of August 31, 1782.
12. Quoted from the *Pennsylvania Packet* of August 31, 1782, in John Austin Stevens, "The Return of the French, 1782–3," *Magazine of American History* 8 (1881): 31.
13. Kathryn Sullivan, *Maryland and France, 1774–1789* (Philadelphia: University

THE LONG JOURNEY HOME

of Pennsylvania Press, 1936), pp. 120 and 135.
14. Rice and Brown, *American Campaigns*, vol. 1, p. 161. The hussar's fate is not certain.
15. Rochambeau Papers, vol. 11, pp. 170–171, and vol. 5, pp. 537–541 and 636; as well as Kennett, *French Forces*, p. 161; and Whitridge, *Rochambeau*, p. 244.
16. Rochambeau Papers, vol. 3, p. 325, and vol. 11, pp. 196 and 198 (duplicated in vol. 13, pp. 19 and 21–22); and Acomb, *Journal of Von Closen*, pp. 225 and 227.
17. Rice and Brown, *American Campaigns*, vol. 1, pp. 162–163, and vol. 2, p. 184.
18. Ibid., vol. 2, pp. 185–187; and Rochambeau Papers, vol. 5, p. 637, duplicated in vol. 13, p. 74.
19. Two contemporary accounts furnish the basis for the following: Prince de Broglie, "Journal du voyage du prince de Broglie, colonel en second du régiment de Saintonge aux Etats-Unis d'Amérique et dans l'Amérique du sud, 1782–1783," *Mélanges publiés par la Société des Bibliophiles françois*, deuxième partie, pièce no. 6 (1903): 15–42; and Louis-Philippe, comte de Ségur, *Mémoires, ou Souvenirs et Anecdotes*, 2d ed. (Paris: Alexis Eymery, 1825), vol. 1, pp. 295–374. Biographical information on the officers is from Bodinier's *Dictionnaire*.
20. Rochambeau Papers, vol. 4, pp. 418–420, duplicated in vol. 13, pp. 30–32.
21. Ibid., vol. 13, pp. 12–14 and 23–28.
22. The inspection reports (dated October 12 and 13, 1782) for the four infantry regiments can be found in ibid., vol. 5, pp. 553, 557–559, 564, 569, and 573. More complete and precise data are furnished by the regimental contrôles.
23. Ségur, *Mémoires*, vol. 1, p. 376, and Ségur, "Extraits de lettres," p. 158.
24. Rhode Island, Letters to the Governor, vol. 18, no. 21.
25. Weelen, *Rochambeau*, p. 259.
26. Ségur, "Extraits de lettres," pp. 174–175.
27. See the correspondence of Benjamin Tallmadge in Rochambeau Papers, vol. 5, pp. 519–520, 531–532, 535–536, 579, 585, 593–594, and 607–609, and La Luzerne's in Rochambeau Papers, vol. 5, pp. 574 and 590.
28. Ibid., vol. 11, pp. 210–213, 257, and 215, duplicated in vol. 13, pp. 41–43, 75, and 44–45.
29. Ibid., vol. 13, pp. 87–91.
30. Ibid., p. 50.
31. Flexner, *Washington in the American Revolution*, pp. 497–498.
32. Rice and Brown, *American Campaigns*, vol. 2, pp. 182, 187–188; and Rochambeau Papers, vol. 11, pp. 224–226 (duplicated in vol. 13, pp. 50–51) and 247, and vol. 5, pp. 599–600.
33. Rice and Brown, *American Campaigns*, vol. 1, p. 169, and vol. 2, p. 190; and Ségur, *Mémoires*, vol. 1, p. 391.
34. See the Rochambeau-Vaudreuil correspondence during the second half of October and early November in Rochambeau Papers, vol. 11, pp. 223, 228, and 239, and vol. 13, pp. 53, 58, and 59.
35. Rice and Brown, *American Campaigns*, vol. 1, p. 168; Ségur, *Mémoires*, vol. p. 392; Stone, *Our French Allies*, p. 511; and Broglie, "Journal du voyage," pp. 61–62.
36. See the proceedings of the General Assembly for the last Monday of October 1782 in Bartlett, *Records of the State of Rhode Island*, vol. 9, p. 603.
37. Preston, "Rochambeau and the French in Providence," p. 19; and Rice and Brown,

American Campaigns, vol. 1, pp. 81 (which contains the quotation) and 169.
38. Forbes and Cadman, France and New England, vol. 1, pp. 170–171; Charles Nicolas Gabriel, Le Maréchal de Camp Desandrouins, 1729–1792 (Verdun: Renvé-Lallemant, 1887), p. 360; and Ségur, Mémoires, vol. 1, pp. 400–402. The quotation is from the Providence Gazette and Country Journal of November 23, 1782.
39. See the Newport Mercury of June 8, August 3, September 28, and November 2, 16, and 23, 1782.
40. Rice and Brown, American Campaigns, vol. 1, p. 81; the quotation is from Lieutenant Clermont-Crèvecoeur. For further information about the visit, see Ségur, Mémoires, vol. 1, pp. 397–398; and Broglie, "Journal du voyage," pp. 65–70.
41. Rochambeau Papers, vol. 5, pp. 603 and 606, and vol. 13, pp. 75 and 76. In fact, the evacuation did not take place until December 14, 1782.
42. Bartlett, Records of the State of Rhode Island, vol. 9, pp. 627, 649–650, and 674.
43. For examples of French officers receiving low prices for their horses, see Contenson, "Lettres d'un officier: Cariolis," p. 819; and Rice and Brown, American Campaigns, vol. 1, p. 170.
44. Rochambeau Papers, vol. 5, pp. 619 and 628. The governor's address can also be found in Bartlett, Records of the State of Rhode Island, vol. 9, pp. 619–620.
45. Rice and Brown, American Campaigns, vol. 1, p. 256, and vol. 2, p. 192; Rochambeau Papers, vol. 5, pp. 598, 602, 611, 612, 614, 616, 621, and 623; and Heath, Memoirs, p. 331.
46. See the anonymous account of the voyage from Boston to Porto Cabello in A.N., M 1036; and Ségur, Mémoires, vol. 1, pp. 418–421.
47. Italics in the original.
48. Copies of both addresses were published in the two Boston newspapers noted here (the issues of December 16 and December 12, respectively), as well as in the Newport Mercury and Providence Gazette and Country Journal (both on December 21).
49. Heath, Memoirs, pp. 332–333; and East, Business Enterprise, p. 67.
50. These numbers have been calculated from data in the Rochambeau Papers, vol. 5, p. 618, and vol. 11, p. 246, and in unit inspection reports and contrôles.
51. For information on the French at Portsmouth, see Rochambeau Papers, vol. 13, pp. 29 and 48; Rice and Brown, American Campaigns, vol. 1, p. 85, and vol. 2, p. 195; and Smith, "French at Boston," p. 66.
52. These and other statistics on Rochambeau's soldiers are drawn from the unit registers.
53. A.G., YA 513. Fourteen died in America.
54. See Bodinier, Officiers, p. 213, and Bodinier, Dictionnaire, pp. 7, 117–118, 470, and 24, respectively.
55. For these specific examples, the records are in A.G., 10 YC 1.
56. A.G., 1 YC 869.
57. A.G., 10 YC 1.
58. Again, the sources for these data are the unit contrôles or registers.
59. Ibid.
60. A.G., 1 YC 966.
61. Again, I thank Bob Selig for this information, contained in his letters to me, dated October 11, 1994, and July 21, 1995, as well as his articles, "Georg Daniel Flohr's Journal: A New Perspective," Colonial Williamsburg 15 (1993): 53, and

"Private Flohr's Other Life," *American Heritage* 45 (1994): 95. See also John M. Lenhart, "German Catholic Soldiers and Their Chaplain in the Revolutionary War," *Central-Blatt and Social Justice* 23 (1931): 17 (also provided to me by Bob Selig).
62. Rochambeau Papers, vol. 13, pp. 100–103; and Lauberdière, "Journal," pp. 172–173.
63. Lauzun, *Memoirs*, p. 221; and Maugras, *Lauzun*, p. 302.
64. A.N., D² C 32.
65. A.G., 10 YC 1, and 1 YC 966.
66. Noailles, *Marins et soldats*, pp. 339–340; Pichon, "Participation militaire de la France," pp. 609–610; Rochambeau Papers, vol. 6, p. 674; and a letter dated February 26, 1784, in A.G., X^d 24. It is possible that some isolated French soldiers remained in America after this but certainly in no significant number.
67. Surviving accounts of the voyage are unanimous about conditions; for example, Verger and Berthier in Rice and Brown, *American Campaigns*, vol. 1, pp. 170–171 and 256–257; the anonymous account in A.N., M 1036; Ségur, *Mémoires*, vol. 1, pp. 425–426; Blanchard, *Journal*, pp. 185–187; and Acomb, *Journal of Von Closen*, p. 279.
68. A.G., 1 YC 188.
69. See Clermont-Crèvecoeur's journal in Rice and Brown, *American Campaigns*, vol. 1, pp. 85–92, for a firsthand description of the voyage of the ships from Portsmouth. For other details, see Broglie, "Journal du voyage," p. 78; Ségur, *Mémoires*, vol. 1, p. 428; and A.G., X^b 91 for the experiences of the companies of Saintonge Infantry.
70. Blanchard, *Journal*, p. 187; and Dumas, *Memoirs*, pp. 73–74.
71. This description is based on Gabriel, *Desandrouins*, pp. 371–389; Broglie, "Journal du voyage," pp. 81–82; Rice and Brown, *American Campaigns*, vol. 1, pp. 87–88; and especially Maurice La Chesnais, ed., "Relation inédite du naufrage de la Bourgogne, vaisseau de 74 canons portant à bord une partie du régiment d'infanterie du Bourbonnais par le chevalier de Coriolis, lieutenant à ce régiment," *Revue Militaire Française* 2 (1870): 262–289.
72. A.G., X^b 25; the number of soldiers lost is confirmed by the regimental contrôle.
73. Latham, "Journal," provides a soldier's account of the officers' conduct, substantiated by an officer's version in Gabriel, *Desandrouins*, p. 383, which also contains the only mention of the mutiny (p. 384n).
74. For more information on the stay in Venezuela, see Rice and Brown, *American Campaigns*, vol. 1, pp. 95 and 261–279; Ségur, *Mémoires*, vol. 1, pp. 434–471; Broglie, "Journal du voyage," pp. 88–124 and 147–148; and Maurice La Chesnais, ed., "Un Officier français au Venezuela (1783)," *La Revue du Mois* 7 (1909): 171–189.
75. See Rice and Brown, *American Campaigns*, vol. 1, pp. 96–99 and 279–281; A.N., M 1036; Ségur, *Mémoires*, vol. 1, pp. 478–487.
76. The quotations are from Ségur, "Extraits de lettres," p. 204, and Ségur, *Mémoires*, vol. 1, p. 301, respectively.
77. Rice and Brown, *American Campaigns*, vol. 1, pp. 99–100 and 180; and Emile Coste, *Historique du 40ᵉ Régiment d'Infanterie de ligne* (Paris: Chamerot, 1887), p. 13.
78. The statistics are drawn from the unit contrôles; also see pp. 18 and 20.

Part Two

THE FRENCH REVOLUTION AND REVOLUTIONARY WAR

7
BETWEEN REVOLUTIONS

IN RETROSPECT, the six years between the return of Rochambeau's special expedition and the advent of the French Revolution represent a period of quiet normality between two great upheavals; yet, they were also years of significant change for those units and the men in them. In the United States Rochambeau's army of five thousand had constituted a substantial military force and been a decisive factor in the course of the war. In France the corps was broken up into its constituent elements and scattered in various garrisons, thereby losing the collective identity it had possessed for more than three years. Furthermore, the regiments, or parts thereof, made up but a small—and not particularly important—portion of the regular military establishment of one hundred and seventy thousand men. Major changes were also made in the units' personnel, as the number of American veterans progressively declined over the years. Because of their extensive military experience and the advancement in rank that often went with it, however, those men enjoyed an influence in their regiments disproportionate to their dwindling numbers.

The units and men that had contributed to the success of the American Revolution played a less prominent role in the larger context of the French Revolution. Consequently, they must be treated differently in this part of the study, as comparatively minor participants in events taking place on a much grander scale.[1] One might question the usefulness of pursuing their story into the era of the French Revolution. The basic reason for doing so is an attempt to evaluate the influence of the American Revolution on the only substantial group of "ordinary" people to have had personal experience with both revolutions. In addition, such a study affords an unusual opportunity to follow the same group of soldiers over a long span of time. Finally, since Rochambeau's former units continued to reflect accurately the development of the French army as a whole during the Revolution, such an investigation provides a history of that institution in microcosm during the most critical transformation it experienced.

Within only a few weeks after disembarking in mid-1783, the units witnessed important personnel changes. The officers were ordered to begin their "semester" leave immediately; this biennial leave, to which half the officers in each regiment were entitled every year, would last until September 25. In addition, hundreds of soldiers were eligible for discharge because their enlistments had expired, they had become disabled, or their prior service qualified them for retirement. Indeed, so many soldiers were entitled to leave their regiments that the minister of war ordered that they not all be released at once "so that there is not, at the same time, too large a number of them on the same route."[2] Even though the minister's concerns may have been exaggerated, 832 soldiers who had served in the American war would be discharged before 1783 was over, most within two or three months of disembarkation.[3]

The returning regiments were assigned to new garrisons as quickly as possible: On July 10 the Regiment of Bourbonnais departed for Metz, on July 20 Deux-Ponts left for Landau, on July 22 the Saintonge Infantry began its march to Sarrelouis, and three days later the second battalion of Auxonne Artillery set out to join the rest of the regiment in the city of Auxonne.[4] Typically, the assignments were in regions of the country where most of the line army was traditionally stationed. The Regiment of Soissonnais, which had sailed to southern France, would man various garrisons in Languedoc, beginning with Montpellier where it arrived in early September.[5] Besides occupying new quarters, each unit had to absorb hundreds of recruits who had been raised by the regimental depot in France during the unit's overseas tour of duty. Within a year of arriving in their new garrisons, the Regiment of Bourbonnais incorporated 567 recent enlistees, Saintonge 432, Deux-Ponts 507, and Soissonnais between 450 and 500.[6] The second battalion of Auxonne Artillery received the reinforcements needed to bring it up to strength from the first battalion, which had remained in France.

The most drastic changes in Rochambeau's old units occurred in Lauzun's Legion. As a reward for contributions to the victory at Yorktown, Lauzun was promised that his legion would be converted into a regiment, the Lauzun Hussars—a more permanent part of the regular army—and that he would be its proprietary commander.[7] The reorganization took place at Hennebont,

Brittany, in early October 1783. Over 140 men who had served in the American Revolution were discharged; others were transferred; and 149 recruits raised by the "auxiliary company," which had stayed in France as a depot, were inducted into the regiment. The reorganization resulted in a light cavalry regiment of four squadrons composed of 413 enlisted men and 25 officers (with 13 vacancies, mostly for junior officers). Shortly afterward, the new unit was ordered to Lauterbourg in Alsace, where it arrived in December.[8]

As the officers and soldiers of Rochambeau's old command resumed the routine of peacetime military service, what can be said about the general impact of the American Revolution on France and about the specific role of these American veterans? Before responding to these questions, a few observations are necessary. First, this inquiry will be restricted to the years before 1789, for once the French Revolution began to unfold it tended to subsume the experiences and ideas of its American predecessor. Second, because direct testimony about the influence of the American Revolution is scarce— indeed, almost totally absent in the case of Rochambeau's enlisted men— one has to rely heavily on circumstantial evidence. Third, at this point we shall examine three major areas that have been most often identified as links between the two revolutions: the financial effects of French participation in the war against Britain, the influence of American political ideas in France, and the impact of North American warfare on French military reforms. In each case the procedure will be to evaluate first the overall effects of French participation in the American Revolution and then the particular contribution of Rochambeau's veterans. Finally, the responses of the individual regiments to specific developments in the course of the French Revolution will be treated in later chapters.

Historians of various persuasions have long maintained that France's intervention in the War of American Independence broke the French treasury and led to Louis XVI's calling of the Estates General, thereby letting loose a wave of revolution in that country.[9] Recent works have demonstrated that the cost of the war to France was considerably less (by approximately half) than has been traditionally estimated: a total of somewhat more than 1 billion livres beyond ordinary expenditures, most of which was for naval rather than military expenses.[10] One study, in fact, convincingly argues that the true origins of France's financial catastrophe are to be found in the Seven Years' War and the ill-advised measures taken to cope with the debt arising from that contest.[11] All now agree that the fundamental problem was the institutional defects of the Old Regime, which made significant financial reform impossible within the existing structure. At most, the American Revolution aggravated a preexisting condition or hastened the inevitable crisis in state finances. In any event, the cost of Rochambeau's army was of little consequence.[12]

The ideological influence of the American Revolution is more controversial than the war's financial toll. The number of publications about the United States grew significantly during the course of the war—sometimes with subsidization from the French government—and continued to do so after hostilities ceased. The number of books on American topics published in France averaged only two per year prior to 1775; during the Revolution this figure rose to seven and from the peace to 1789 reached an average of nine. In addition, periodicals and newspapers, such as *Les Affaires de l'Angleterre et de l'Amérique* and *Le Courier de l'Europe*, carried news from North America that presented the Americans and their cause in a favorable light.[13] These publications described the American people as naturally virtuous citizens who enjoyed a simple, tolerant, free, and egalitarian society. Their political institutions—often known only through various states' written constitutions—guaranteed popular sovereignty, individual liberties, and a balance of powers. Such descriptions, embodying the principles of the Enlightenment, often reflected the ideals of European writers more accurately than the realities of American life. Indeed, it was the American myth—which Europeans were predisposed to embrace—that encouraged them in their belief that political, social, and economic change could be achieved on their side of the Atlantic.[14]

What role did French veterans of the American Revolution play in spreading this political ideology, regardless of its basis in reality? About forty-five officers and only two soldiers who served under Rochambeau left writings of some sort (journals, memoirs, collections of letters), most still in manuscript. Of those works that have been published, only five appeared prior to 1789. Rochambeau's official report on the Yorktown campaign was published by the *Gazette de France* and *Gazette de Leyde* on November 20 and 30, 1781. Jean François Coste, the chief physician of the expeditionary force, published a pharmacopoeia for the use of his subordinates in North America, and, subsequently, his discourse on the adaptation of the medical philosophy of the ancients to the New World (originally delivered in acceptance of an honorary degree from the College of William and Mary) appeared in Europe in 1783; both were in Latin. Abbé Robin, who joined the French army as a chaplain just as it was about to leave Providence in mid-1781, wrote a fairly typical eighteenth-century travel account with wide-ranging comments about the flora and fauna, the people and customs he had encountered in the United States; the work was published in Paris in 1782 and in Philadelphia (in English) the following year. In 1786 the marquis de

Chastellux, the most inveterate traveler of the officers, published a narrative of his journeys that resembled Robin's in its approach and in many of its observations. Both men presented an essentially favorable portrait of America and Americans that conformed to enlightened preconceptions about the natural qualities of the country and its inhabitants.[15] None of these publications was concerned with politics except peripherally, and none could be seriously considered revolutionary.

The press, then, did not serve as a vehicle for Rochambeau's veterans to spread ideas borrowed from the American Revolution. An organization formed shortly after their return to France, however, might have served to disseminate such an ideology—namely, the Society of the Cincinnati. This group was established by American officers in New York in May 1783, and a French branch was approved by Louis XVI seven months later. The latter quickly became the rage in France, and many army officers who lacked the necessary credentials—originally, service at the grade of colonel or above in Rochambeau's forces—applied for membership. For instance, the marquis du Bouchet, who had served as an aide de camp to Rochambeau with the rank of major, was refused admission to the French order; undaunted, he sailed to America, petitioned the American society meeting in Philadelphia, and was admitted. In mid-July 1784, after his return to France, he explained his motivation: "Honour is the God of Frenchmen, and Glory is their Sweetheart." The correspondence of French President-General Rochambeau with other would-be members indicates that many officers shared du Bouchet's sentiments; their letters exhibit intense competition to join the Cincinnati and bitter resentment over rejection. Conspicuous by its absence is an expression of commitment to any of the principles of the American Revolution. Indeed, in 1784 Gabriel Honoré de Riquetti, comte de Mirabeau, who became a leader in the early stages of the French Revolution, wrote a pamphlet denouncing the society as antiegalitarian and antirepublican.[16] The Society of the Cincinnati served the purpose of traditional aristocratic exclusiveness more than the cause of revolutionary liberalism.

Although those who had served under Rochambeau in the United States did not use any public forum—neither publication nor organization—to propagate ideas from America, they may have helped to spread such principles by word of mouth, particularly since oral communication was so common and important in the eighteenth century. It is, of course, impossible to trace or evaluate such a phenomenon. Nevertheless, based on what these men recorded, regardless of whether their comments appeared in print, one can determine the impressions made by the American experiences and suggest what they might have conveyed to others.

After the war Lafayette became the focus of an informal circle, including other veterans of the American Revolution, that intentionally propagated American ideals such as liberty and equality.[17] Some officers who had served under Rochambeau shared those views. Perhaps the most outspoken was the comte de Ségur. Although he had spent only about three months on American soil and had never actually fought for the American cause and although his family's West Indian plantation kept a large number of slaves, this court aristocrat claimed he and other officers brought back to France "a lively passion for freedom and for independence."[18] Yet, what seems to have impressed most of Rochambeau's veterans, who had lived in the United States for about two and a half years, were not abstract political principles but more mundane practices, notably religious toleration and social equality rooted in widespread economic prosperity.[19]

Even those impressions were not free of criticism. Some maintained that because of the great diversity of religious sects in the United States, what appeared to be religious tolerance was merely an unavoidable acceptance of reality and that, in fact, all of the sects felt "ill will and scorn for each other." Even the Quakers, the favorites of Enlightenment literature in Europe, were accused of rigid sectarianism and shameless profiteering from the war. Furthermore, when one religious group constituted a majority, it attempted to intimidate those in the minority. Despite their rivalries, however, all Protestant denominations continued to harbor hostile prejudices against Catholics, including their French allies.[20] As for U.S. prosperity, some argued that one cause was the cupidity of merchants, a characteristic the French had experienced firsthand on more than one occasion when they were stationed in America.[21] And some officers believed one consequence of mercantile wealth was a growing social stratification based on money that threatened the egalitarian nature of American society and created hierarchical distinctions less justified than those in France.[22] Finally, even American enthusiasts had difficulty explaining the fact that the land of liberty and equality was also the home of seven hundred thousand black slaves.[23]

Evidence of the financial and ideological effects of the American Revolution on France is, at best, equivocal, and the role that might be attributed to Rochambeau's army in these areas is negligible or contradictory. The pertinent question of the military influence of the American war remains. Commonly, three military developments in France have been ascribed to American influence: the creation of a citizens' militia, the establishment of the principle and practice of "careers open to talent," and the introduction of new, more open tactics, especially the increased employment of light troops.

BETWEEN REVOLUTIONS

Perhaps no aspect of American warfare received wider or more favorable attention from contemporaries than the militia. From the beginning of the fighting, French observers in the United States sent back enthusiastic reports about the huge numbers of men (hundreds of thousands!) the militia was capable of enrolling, its ability to be self-sustaining, its military effectiveness, and how naturally American farmers and frontiersmen adapted to such service. Despite the military setbacks that typified the first years of fighting, this image persisted, and the American victory at Saratoga merely confirmed and spread faith in the militia's invincibility.[24] Not only the French were deluded about the qualities of American militiamen. Many Americans ridiculed the automatons of European armies and were convinced that their own citizen-soldiers were more than a match for any enemy. Furthermore, Americans commonly viewed a standing army as an "engine of oppression" and felt the use of professional soldiers reflected a lack of civic virtue in society.[25]

No amount of idealization, however, could compensate for military defeats. Consequently, as the *rage militaire* of the first year of the war gave way to disillusionment and discouragement, Congress reluctantly began to raise a regular force, the Continental Army. Gradually, soldiers were recruited and even more gradually armed, equipped, and trained as professionals; indeed, the process approached completion only in the last year of the war. In similar fashion, despite both a general hostility toward the use of foreign "mercenaries" and unpleasant experiences with French adventurers who volunteered their services early in the war, Congress eventually found it useful or necessary to employ foreign professionals, such as Louis Le Begue Duportail, Friedrich von Steuben, François Louis Teissedre de Fleury, and others.[26]

Whatever reservations might have existed regarding the Continental Army, virtually all American military leaders far preferred it to any militia forces. Many openly disparaged the militia—for example, Nathanael Greene, Alexander Hamilton, John Lacey, and Daniel Morgan—and there were few more convinced or consistent critics than George Washington.[27] These men had been victimized too often by untrained, undisciplined, and undependable militia units. French officers who had firsthand experience with the American militia, such as Lauzun in his attempt to cooperate with General Weedon at Gloucester, quickly disabused themselves of the romantic notions prevalent in Europe and arrived at identical conclusions regarding the military inadequacies of militiamen. At best, the French had some grudging respect for the long-suffering fortitude the militia occasionally exhibited.[28]

Besides the professional disdain French officers felt for the fighting qualities of American militiamen, from Rochambeau down they also had a very different conception of the nature of the U.S. conflict than did their allies. As discussed previously, the overwhelming majority of Rochambeau's officers had not volunteered to serve the cause of liberty but, like the soldiers under their orders, served in the American war simply because their units had been assigned that duty. Indeed, the cheering that greeted the announcement of their destination in mid-June 1780 had not been caused by enthusiasm for the American cause but rather reflected the relief the men felt at not being sent to the Caribbean, notorious for its deadly climate.[29] For the French, this was a traditional war, and they did not appreciate the fact that Americans were fighting a revolutionary and civil war; hence the French horror at the atrocities militiamen were especially prone to perpetrate.[30] In addition, for the French the War of American Independence was a colonial conflict, and the great geographic differences—the huge territory involved, the peculiar terrain, the sparse population, the lack of crucial political centers (like the capitals of European states), and the remoteness from Europe—made it difficult to conceive of adapting such a distinctively American institution as the militia to a European setting.[31]

Their attitudes toward warfare and their exposure to the defects of the American militia system, therefore, led few of Rochambeau's officers to favor the adoption of a similar institution in their own country. Besides, a militia of sorts already existed in France, the *milice* or *troupes provinciales*. This was a force that trained irregularly in peacetime and was called to active service in wartime to take over garrison duties and allow regular army units to go to the front. Because of the gross inequities in its selection process, the burden of serving in the *milice* fell almost exclusively on the poorer peasantry; according to the *cahiers* of 1789, it was one of the most detested institutions in France on the eve of the Revolution.[32] Despite all this, the image of the indomitable militiaman remained intact among certain circles in Europe.[33] And, as we shall see, this myth would have some, albeit limited effect on the establishment of the National Guard in France at the beginning of the French Revolution.[34]

Social relationships in the American army elicited a more ambivalent response from French officers who were astonished to see American officers fraternizing with their troops, since they had such little contact with their own men. They also found it remarkable that a shoemaker or a butcher could not only enter the army as a commissioned officer but could rise as high as his abilities took him, to the rank of colonel or even general. Yet, they could not deny that some of those merchants, farmers, and artisans made competent military leaders.[35] After all, even Washington, universally admired by Rochambeau's officers, was neither a professional soldier nor an aristocrat. Whatever the advantages of a more open military society, however, it remained contrary to most French officers' sense of social order. One strongly suspects that the comte d'Estaing made explicit what others felt about American officers when he scornfully described "captains who are not good enough company to be permitted to eat with their general officers" and "colonels who are innkeepers at the same time."[36]

This ambivalence about the relative merits of talent and birth faithfully mirrored the atmosphere that had been developing among French noble officers since mid-century. On one hand, there was a growing appreciation of more rational, professional standards, yet there was also a firm refusal by nobles to surrender domination of the officer corps, which was both the historical justification of their privileges and, for many by the late eighteenth century, the only honorable occupation and source of income readily available.[37] The Revolution finally ended this ambivalence. As early as August 26, 1789, the Declaration of the Rights of Man and Citizen announced the abolition of all privileges based on birth and the establishment of ability as the criterion for admission to, and advancement in, public service. Later in the Revolution the elimination of most of the officer corps of the Old Regime through emigration and purges led to the thorough implementation of the principle of careers open to talent in the army.[38] Very few of Rochambeau's former officers had any part in early revolutionary legislation, and none had the slightest control over the circumstances that resulted in the massive turnover in officers between 1791 and 1794.

It is hardly surprising that neither an American-style militia nor military advancement on the basis of merit alone was introduced in France before 1789. The ramifications of both such innovations extended far beyond the army to the very foundations of the existing political and social structure and in themselves would have constituted a revolution. The composition of the army and battlefield tactics, in contrast, were more strictly military affairs, and the 1780s saw significant reforms in those areas. The question is, to what extent were these changes affected by American examples?[39]

To answer this question, it is necessary first to identify the tactical innovations associated with the American Revolution. Essentially, they fall into two categories, both involving light troops, especially light infantry: the deployment of skirmishers or sharpshooters in open formations using individually aimed fire (in contrast to massed or closed formations firing in volleys) and their employment in functions associated with the *petite guerre*, or *guerilla*, such as reconnaissance, patrols, raids, ambushes, outposts, and screening the main body of troops. Examples of these activities can indeed be found in the American war; however, two crucial qualifications are necessary. First, Washington explicitly rejected Charles Lee's proposals to wage large-scale partisan warfare and, like other American military leaders, used traditional formations and linear tactics whenever he could.[40] Second, when light infantry units were initiated in the Continental Army, they were modeled on the *jäger* or *chasseur* units of European armies.[41] Not even Lafayette, who emphasized U.S. contributions of any sort, alluded later to his American experiences when writing about the value of skirmishers. And Rochambeau's officers were equally silent about being impressed by the originality of American tactics.

Since the mid-eighteenth century there had been a growing emphasis on light troops in Europe, a tendency that accelerated during the Seven Years' War. Influential military figures, such as Maurice de Saxe, advocated substantial increases in the number of light units in the regular army, part of an ongoing process of substituting them for irregular levies. It was not by chance that in the infantry regiments Rochambeau took to America one of ten companies was composed of *chasseurs*, the result of a general reorganization in 1776. These policies continued after the American Revolution, as exemplified by the conversion of Lauzun's Legion into an hussar regiment. In 1788 twelve infantry battalions of *chasseurs à pied* and twelve cavalry regiments of *chasseurs à cheval* were created.[42] At the most, therefore, the experiences of the American Revolution reinforced a long-established and continuing trend in Europe, and no unequivocal evidence exists even for this.

It appears, then, that the military impact of the American Revolution in France was, like its financial and ideological influence, very limited. The developments taking place there—such as the idealization of the citizen-soldier, the growing emphasis on officer professionalism, and the expansion of the role of light troops—were part of a general intellectual ferment that found a sympathetic response in certain military circles and had clear native roots. This indigenous movement was evidenced in other military reforms of the period.

The second half of the eighteenth century in France was marked by increasing pressures for change, including military reform. The debacle of the Seven Years' War—for French officers, a "strange defeat"—greatly intensified those pressures. By the 1780s one group above all was pushing for military change: the provincial nobility who felt their future was as intimately linked to military service as their past had been. From a modern perspective, their objectives seem strange, a kind of premodern professionalization. They aimed at the elimination of wealth as a consideration for entrance into or promotion within the army; instead, they wanted equal opportunities for advancement by merit but only for those of indisputably noble background (preferably with a family history of military service). Their successes included legislation that phased out the purchase system beginning in 1776 and demanded four generations of nobility for a direct commission after 1781 while retaining the practice of commissioning rankers with exemplary service but restricting them to the grade of lieutenant. Simultaneously, longer experience was required of noble officers for promotion to major (twenty years) and lieutenant colonel (twenty-five years). A committee of twenty-five lieutenant generals under the chairmanship of Marshal de Contades, meeting between 1780 and 1784, endorsed these and other changes along similar lines.[43] Although some reforms of this nature may have been influenced by the general atmosphere of the Enlightenment, which spanned the Atlantic Ocean, these measures were totally independent of—as well as largely contradictory to—requirements demanded of officers in the American army, and none of Rochambeau's officers had anything to do with these decisions.

With rare exceptions (to be discussed later), the officers who had fought in America under Rochambeau were passive elements in the events of the middle and late 1780s. This was even more true of the simple soldiers and NCOs (various grades of sergeants and corporals), whether they stayed in the army or returned to civilian life. Of the slightly more than 6,000 enlisted men commanded by Rochambeau (and Vioménil) in America, including those recruited there and reinforcements from France, between 4,800 and 4,900 returned to France in 1783; approximately 680 men had died, 350 had deserted, and 150 had been discharged since the original departure from Brest in May 1780.[44] Disembarkation was followed by the mass discharges, assignment to new garrisons, and incorporation of recent recruits into the veteran units described earlier.

Even after these adjustments had been completed by the end of 1783, Rochambeau's former units continued to undergo change, albeit at a slackening rate. Although the number fell far short of the huge figures of the previous year, around five hundred veterans were discharged in 1784. Most of the discharges were allotted because the soldiers had fulfilled the term of their original enlistments, but nearly eighty were because of retirement, and a number of men were discharged as no longer fit for active duty. In the Regiment of Soissonnais, for example, Pierre Gourbil, forty-one years old, was discharged because of wounds sustained in his leg and foot; Jean Baptiste Chandelier, only twenty-four, had also been debilitated by a gunshot wound in his right arm received at Yorktown; and Nicolas Bertrand, age twenty-seven, was discharged because he had lost one eye and "sees poorly with the other, due to wounds."[45] Thereafter, the total number of discharges continued to drop each year: slightly more than 350 in 1785, just over 300 in 1786, less than 240 in 1787, and only 110 in 1788. The decline from year to year was primarily the result of the decreasing number of American veterans whose original eight-year enlistment had not yet expired.

Although discharges were responsible for by far the largest number of separations from the army, two other categories accounted for substantial losses—death and desertion. Between their arrival back in France and the end of 1788, 360 of the troops who had served in America died of natural causes—a clear decline in the death rate, possibly because of the better medical facilities available to military personnel in France.[46] Yet, soldiers' continuing vulnerability to disease is evidenced by the large number of men in the Saintonge Infantry who died while the regiment was stationed in the province of Saintonge; fifty-nine veterans perished in what appears to have been an epidemic that struck their unit between August 1786 and July 1787. The desertion rate in the regiment also rose in the same period, possibly because of fear the deadly disease engendered.

After their return to France, Rochambeau's regiments usually experienced a more normal pattern of desertion. One group of chronic deserters, the soldiers who had enlisted in the United States, had shrunk to a handful; only 28 of 161 were left by mid-1783. Most of the American recruits had previously deserted from the British army, and over half deserted from the French service before their units sailed from America. The desertion rate dropped significantly in Lauzun's Hussars and the Deux-Ponts Infantry, which together had accounted for more than two-thirds of desertions in America, mostly by German soldiers who found compatriots there. It is interesting that the only mass desertion from either unit between 1783 and 1789 occurred when a score of American veterans in Deux-Ponts failed to return to the regiment in June 1788 after leaves they had been granted to return home expired. The desertion rate in French regiments, however, rose to levels customary for peacetime service as the soldiers found themselves once again in familiar surroundings. In all, nearly 370 veterans of the American war deserted between their return to France and the beginning of 1789.

The overwhelming majority of losses in the "American" regiments—close to 98 percent of the total—were the result of discharge, death, or desertion. A tiny number of soldiers, fifty-eight in all, were transferred to other regiments, including forty-five veterans of the second battalion of Auxonne Artillery who went to the Colonial Artillery in February 1785.

An even smaller number of men were lost to these regiments by their promotion to officer. Ten experienced NCOs were commissioned during the three years Rochambeau's corps spent in America and only fifteen more between their return to France and the end of 1788. Given the average strength of these units during those years, the odds that a soldier from the ranks would be made an officer were slightly better than one in two thousand. Without remarkable talent or extraordinary luck, most veteran soldiers during the Old Regime were destined to very restricted careers until the events of the French Revolution established new, more equitable standards for advancement. To take just one example among scores of possibilities, Jacques Mitier, a native of the city of Nîmes in Languedoc, enlisted in the Regiment of Saintonge on April 17, 1768, at age twenty. It took seven years for him to be promoted to corporal, and he did not reach the rank of sergeant major until he had nineteen years of service. He would probably have ended his career in that grade had it not been for the Revolution; as it was, Mitier was appointed sublieutenant in September 1791, lieutenant the following April, and captain in late October 1792—three promotions in the course of thirteen months![47]

As a consequence of these various changes in strength, by the beginning of 1789 approximately 1,700 of Rochambeau's former soldiers were still in the regular army. By the same date, about 320 of the officers who had commanded them in America remained on active service.[48] Compared with the adventures these men had experienced between 1780 and 1783, their peacetime routine seemed rather dull and depressing. The soldiers usually lived in crowded, unsanitary quarters grudgingly provided by the local populace. Their food and other necessities, such as firewood, clothing, bedding, and candles, were often inadequate in quantity and quality; furthermore, the soldiers had to purchase food, as well as other goods and services, from their meager pay. As a consequence, many enlisted men took additional jobs to supplement their income. Leaves were much more restricted for soldiers than for officers, both in their length and in the number authorized; in addition, any time spent on leave was added to the term of enlistment. For those who could not find outside work or take a leave, drill and training, together with regular guard duties, took up most of their working hours. In these duties the soldiers were supervised primarily by NCOs and *officiers de fortune*, whereas their noble officers mostly kept to themselves.[49] The monotony of this routine was broken up by changes of garrison (a move that occurred every two years or so, on average) and occasional maneuvers (notably those held near Metz in September 1788, which involved three of these regiments).[50]

Another common activity of the regular army, often very unpopular with both soldiers and officers, was the maintenance or restoration of law and order.[51] In spring 1789 such missions began to increase dramatically in frequency, as economic and political crises converged and popular disturbances multiplied. A small detachment of the Soissonnais Infantry was called on to deal with a typical incident. During Holy Week of 1789, a crowd attacked the home of a local *seigneur* named Barrot near the village of Villefort in Languedoc; Barrot was killed, his house looted, and his records burned. The district constabulary arrested and imprisoned seven suspects, but a mob of two hundred attacked the jail and forced their release. On April 20, at the request of local authorities, thirty soldiers and an officer from the Regiment of Soissonnais were dispatched to Villefort to help reestablish order.[52] Although no one at the time could have suspected it, the French Revolution was under way, and the French army—including the men and units that had served in the American Revolution—would play a prominent role in it.

Notes

1. Even the types of sources used in this part are different, as will be evident.
2. Langeron Papers, Ms. f Fr. 160, nos. 405 and 410.
3. As throughout this study, the regimental contrôles furnish the statistical data unless other sources are indicated.
4. Langeron Papers, Ms. f. Fr. 160, no. 413.
5. Ibid., no. 405; and Girodie, "Soissonnais et l'Amérique," pp. 233–234.
6. See A.G., X^b 25 for Bourbonnais, X^b 91 for Saintonge, 1 YC 869 for Deux-Ponts, and X^b 53 and Rochambeau Papers, vol. 5, p. 564, for Soissonnais.
7. Letter from Ségur to Rochambeau, dated Versailles, December 5, 1781, in Rochambeau Papers, vol. 10 (no pagination).
8. See the relevant documents in A.G., X^c 83, and A.N., D^2 C 32.
9. A few examples suggest the range of historians who have held such a view: M. Marion, "De la participation financière de la France à la guerre de l'indépendance américaine," *Revue du dix-huitième siècle* 3 (1916): 6; Louis Gottschalk, *The Place of the American Revolution in the Causal Pattern of the French Revolution* (Easton, Pa.: American Friends of Lafayette, 1948), p. 9; and A. A. Fursenko, "The American and French Revolutions of the Eighteenth Century (An Attempt at a Comparative Characterization)," *Soviet Review* 16 (1975): 77.
10. See Robert D. Harris, "French Finances and the American War, 1777–1783," *Journal of Modern History* 48 (1976): 236 and 257–258; Jonathan R. Dull, "France and the American Revolution: Questioning the Myths," *Proceedings of the First Annual Meeting of the Western Society for French History* (Las Cruces: New Mexico State University Press, 1974), p. 118, and Dull, "France and the American Revolution Seen as Tragedy," in Ronald Hoffman and Peter J. Albert, eds.,

Diplomacy and Revolution: The Franco-American Alliance of 1778 (Charlottesville: University Press of Virginia, 1981), pp. 86, 101, and 104; and Orville T. Murphy, *Charles Gravier, Comte de Vergennes: French Diplomacy in the Age of Revolution, 1719–1787* (Albany: State University of New York Press, 1982), p. 399.

11. James C. Riley, *The Seven Years War and the Old Regime in France: The Economic and Financial Toll* (Princeton: Princeton University Press, 1986).
12. See p. 33.
13. For more information, see Claude Fohlen, "The Impact of the American Revolution on France," in Library of Congress Symposia on the American Revolution, *The Impact of the American Revolution Abroad* (Washington, D.C.: Library of Congress, 1976), pp. 28–30; Hélène Maspero-Clerc, "Une 'gazette anglo-française' pendant la guerre d'Amérique: le 'Courier de l'Europe' (1776–1788)," *Annales historiques de la Révolution française* 48 (1976): 585–588 and 593–594; and Jacques Godechot, "Revolutionary Contagion, 1770–1825," *Proceedings of the Annual Meeting of the Western Society for French History*, vol. 4 (Santa Barbara: Western Society for French History, 1977), pp. 245–255.
14. For an excellent brief summary of the American "image," see Robert R. Palmer, "The Impact of the American Revolution Abroad," in Library of Congress Symposia on the American Revolution, *The Impact of the American Revolution Abroad* (Washington, D.C.: Library of Congress, 1976), pp. 11–13. Much fuller development of these themes can be found in Echeverria, *Mirage in the West*, especially pp. 1–174; Otto Vossler, *Jefferson and the American Revolutionary Ideal*, trans. Catherine Philippon and Bernard Wishy (Washington, D.C.: University Press of America, 1980); and Gérard Defamie, "Le mythe américain à la veille de la Révolution française," *L'Information Historique* 36 (1974): 59–64.
15. Rice and Brown, *American Campaigns*, vol. 1, pp. 285–348, contains a "Checklist of Journals, Memoirs, and Letters of French Officers Serving in the American Revolution" that is the most complete compilation available and provides the basis for the previous conclusions. The following are the titles of the works by Coste: *Compenduim pharmaceuticum, Militaribus Gallorum Nosocomiis, in Orbe Novo Boreali adscriptum* (Newport: Henry Barber, 1780), and *De Antiqua Medico-philosophia orbi novo adaptanda: Oratio habita in capitolio Gulielmopolitano in comitiis Universitatis Virginiae* (Leyden: n.p., 1783). Robin's account is entitled *Nouveau Voyage dans l'Amérique Septentrionale, en année 1781; et Campagne de l'Armée de M. le comte de Rochambeau* (Paris: Montard, 1782) and its translation by Philip Freneau, *New Travels Through North America: In a Series of Letters; Exhibiting, the History of the Victorious Campaign of the Allied Armies, Under his Excellency General Washington, and the Count de Rochambeau, in the Year 1781* (Philadelphia: Robert Bell, 1783). The title of Chastellux's book is *Voyages de M. le Marquis de Chastellux dans l'Amérique Septentrionale dans les années 1780, 1781, and 1782*, 2 vols. (Paris: Prault, 1786).
16. See Gardiner, *The Order of the Cincinnati*; Minor Myers Jr., *Liberty Without Anarchy: A History of the Society of the Cincinnati* (Charlottesville: University Press of Virginia, 1983), chapter 7; and Rochambeau Papers, vol. 13, p. 105, and vol. 6. Du Bouchet's quotation is in Myers, p. 153.
17. See Louis Gottschalk, *Lafayette and the Close of the American Revolution* (Chicago: University of Chicago Press, 1965), pp. 420–421; Lloyd S. Kramer, "America's Lafayette and Lafayette's America: A European and the American

Revolution," *William and Mary Quarterly,* 3rd ser. 38 (1981): 233–236; and Michel Devèze, *L'Europe et le Monde à la fin du XVIIIe siècle* (Paris: Michel, 1970), pp. 385–386.
18. Ségur, *Mémoires,* vol. 1, p. 300.
19. For a general treatment, see Echeverria, *Mirage in the West,* pp. 98–100; Bodinier, *Officiers,* p. 350; and Lee W. Ryan, *French Travelers in the Southeastern United States, 1775–1800* (Bloomington: Principia Press, 1939), pp. 30–31 and 72–73. Specific examples can be found in E. W. Balch, ed. and trans., "Narrative of the Prince de Broglie, 1782," *Magazine of American History* 1 (1877): 231, 234, and 306; Blanchard, *Journal,* pp. 52 and 112; Chinard, "Journal de Guerre de Brisout de Barneville," p. 241; Robin, *New Travels,* pp. 42, 50, and 84; and Fersen, *Lettres,* p. 74. Interestingly, the only available observations on American society by an enlisted man fundamentally agree with the officers' views; see Robert A. Selig, "A German Soldier in New England During the Revolutionary War: The Account of Georg Daniel Flohr," *Newport History* 65 (1993): 53 and 58–59, and Selig, "A German Soldier in America," pp. 579–581.
20. Durand Echeverria, ed. and trans., "The American Character: A Frenchman Views the New Republic from Philadelphia, 1777," *William and Mary Quarterly,* 3rd ser. 16 (1959): 391–395; and Rice and Brown, *American Campaigns,* vol. 1, pp. 47–48, 82–83, and 153. The quotation is from Echeverria, p. 391.
21. For example, see pp. 33, 37, 80–81, 101, and 102–103.
22. Rice and Brown, *American Campaigns,* vol. 1, pp. 82–83; Broglie, "Journal du voyage," p. 47; and Ryan, *French Travelers,* pp. 31–32.
23. Echeverria, *Mirage in the West,* p. 129. Some French officers offered rationalizations for slavery, and most accepted the institution, but Private Flohr of the Royal Deux-Ponts was appalled by what he considered an unnatural system; see Selig, "A German Soldier in New England," pp. 55–56, Selig, "A German Soldier in America," pp. 582–584, and Selig, "Georg Daniel Flohr's Journal," pp. 51–52.
24. See the very useful discussion in Orville T. Murphy, "The American Revolutionary Army and the Concept of the Levée en Masse," *Military Affairs* 23 (1959): 13–20; and Jacques Godechot, "L'Influence de la tactique et de la stratégie de la guerre d'indépendance américaine sur la tactique et la stratégie française de l'armée de terre," *Revue internationale d'Histoire militaire,* no. 41 (1979): 141.
25. Marcus Cunliffe, *Soldiers and Civilians: The Martial Spirit in America, 1775–1865* (Boston: Little, Brown, 1968), p. 42. These ideas are more fully developed in Charles Royster, *A Revolutionary People at War: The Continental Army and American Character, 1775–1783* (Chapel Hill: University of North Carolina Press, 1979), e.g., pp. 35–37.
26. For an excellent summary, see Robert K. Wright Jr., " 'Nor Is Their Standing Army to Be Despised': The Emergence of the Continental Army as a Military Institution," in Ronald Hoffman and Peter J. Albert, eds., *Arms and Independence: The Military Character of the American Revolution* (Charlottesville: University Press of Virginia, 1984), pp. 50–74, and for a more complete treatment, Wright, *The Continental Army* (Washington, D.C.: U.S. Army Center of Military History, 1983); as well as Royster, *Revolutionary People,* pp. 43, 46–47, 58, 66–67, and 228.

BETWEEN REVOLUTIONS

27. John Shy, *A People Numerous and Armed: Reflections on the Military Struggle for American Independence* (New York: Oxford University Press, 1976), pp. 151, 173, and 217; Don Higginbotham, "The American Militia: A Traditional Institution With Revolutionary Responsibilities," in Don Higginbotham, ed., *Reconsiderations on the Revolutionary War: Selected Essays* (Westport, Conn.: Greenwood Press, 1978), pp. 84–85; and Robert Middlekauff, *The Glorious Cause: The American Revolution, 1763–1789* (New York: Oxford University Press, 1982), pp. 300–301 and 335–336.
28. On these attitudes generally, see Orville T. Murphy, "The French Professional Soldier's Opinion of the American Militia in the War of the Revolution," *Military Affairs* 32 (1969): 191–198. For Rochambeau's officers, see pp. 69–70; Rice and Brown, *American Campaigns*, vol. 1, p. 152; and Faÿ, "Armée de Rochambeau jugée," p. 120.
29. Fiechter, "L'Aventure américaine," pp. 67–68; Selig, "A German Soldier in New England," p. 53; and Selig, "A German Soldier in America," p. 579.
30. Kramer, "America's Lafayette," p. 237; Higginbotham, "American Militia," pp. 100–101; and Middlekauff, *Glorious Cause*, pp. 392 and 467. Also, see p. 74.
31. Peter Paret, "The Relationship Between the Revolutionary War and European Military Thought and Practice in the Second Half of the Eighteenth Century," in Don Higginbotham, ed., *Reconsiderations on the Revolutionary War: Selected Essays* (Westport, Conn.: Greenwood Press, 1978), pp. 155–156.
32. On the French militia, see León Hennet, *Les milices et les troupes provinciales* (Paris: L. Baudoin, 1884), pp. 221–273; and Albert Depréaux, "Les régiments provinciaux et l'ordonnance du 19 octobre 1773," *Revue d'histoire moderne et contemporaine* 13 (1938): 267–286.
33. Cunliffe, *Soldiers and Civilians*, p. 215; Defamie, "Mythe américain," p. 62; and Robert R. Palmer, *The Age of the Democratic Revolution: A Political History of Europe and America, 1760–1800*, vol. 1: *The Challenge* (Princeton: Princeton University Press, 1959), pp. 241 and 332.
34. See pp. 139–140 and 141.
35. Bodinier, *Officiers*, pp. 340 and 350; Rice and Brown, *American Campaigns*, vol. 1, p. 48; and Durand Echeverria and Orville T. Murphy, eds. and trans., "The American Revolutionary Army: A French Estimate in 1777," *Military Affairs* 27 (1963): 155–158.
36. Quoted in Stanley J. Idzerda et al., eds., *Lafayette in the Age of the American Revolution: Selected Letters and Papers, 1776–1790*, vol. 2 (Ithaca: Cornell University Press, 1979), p. 203.
37. See p. 129, for an example of the exclusion of commoners.
38. See my article " 'Careers Open to Talent' in the Armies of the Revolution," in Warren F. Spencer, ed., *The Consortium on Revolutionary Europe, Proceedings, 1982* (Athens, Ga.: Consortium on Revolutionary Europe, 1983), pp. 60–74.
39. On this issue the acknowledged master is Peter Paret; see his *Yorck and the Era of Prussian Reform, 1807–1815* (Princeton: Princeton University Press, 1966), pp. 21–25 and 39–43; "Colonial Experience and European Military Reform at the End of the Eighteenth Century," *Bulletin of the Institute of Historical Research* 37 (1964): 47–59; and "Relationship Between Revolutionary War and European Military Thought," an updated version. The following discussion is based on these sources, unless noted otherwise.

40. Piers Mackesy, "What the British Army Learned," in Ronald Hoffman and Peter J. Albert, eds., *Arms and Independence: The Military Character of the American Revolution* (Charlottesville: University Press of Virginia, 1984), pp. 203–204.
41. Wright, *Continental Army*, pp. 133–134 and 149.
42. Samuel F. Scott, "Military Nationalism in Europe in the Aftermath of the American Revolution," in Ronald Hoffman and Peter J. Albert, eds., *Peace and the Peacemakers: The Treaty of 1783* (Charlottesville: University Press of Virginia, 1986), pp. 175–176.
43. The best general discussion of this topic is David D. Bien, "The Army in the French Enlightenment: Reform, Reaction and Revolution," *Past and Present*, no. 85 (November 1979): 68–98. One particular aspect of this topic is described in Marc Martin, *Les Origines de la presse militaire en France à la fin de l'ancien régime et sous la Révolution (1770–1799)* (Vincennes: Ministère de la Défense, 1975), pp. 51 and 80–82.
44. These and subsequent statistics come from the regimental registers.
45. For these and other examples, see "Etat des Hommes Estropiés en Amérique," in A.G., X^b 53.
46. On the status of French military medicine, see Isser Woloch, *The French Veteran From the Revolution to the Restoration* (Chapel Hill: University of North Carolina Press, 1979), pp. 195 and 200–203.
47. Average strength has been calculated from available inspection reports for the years 1784 through 1788 in A.G., X^b 25, 53, 91, and 104; X^c 83; and X^d 24. For Mitier, see A.G., 1 YC 932, 14 YC 119, and Classement Général, Officiers, under his name.
48. Bodinier, "Officiers de Rochambeau," p. 143.
49. See Scott, *Response of the Royal Army*, pp. 32–45, for a general discussion of life in the French regular army in the middle and late 1780s.
50. Information on garrisons and maneuvers can found in regimental histories in the series A.G., Historiques, cartons 10, 31, 55, 66, 125, and 138.
51. The extent of this practice is described in Geoffrey Best, *War and Society in Revolutionary Europe, 1770–1870* (New York: St. Martin's Press, 1982), pp. 16–17.
52. See the letter of the comte de Périgord, dated April 22, 1789, in A.N., H 1453.

8
THE ROYAL ARMY CONFRONTS THE FRENCH REVOLUTION

AS POPULAR VIOLENCE MOUNTED in the early months of 1789, political activity reached unprecedented proportions as the French people prepared for the first meeting of their national representative body, the Estates General, in 175 years. The election of deputies and the preparation of lists of grievances, *cahiers de doléances*, to guide these deputies, together with a massive outpouring of political pamphlets and propaganda, affected every region of the country and precipitated all kinds of expectations—many unrealistic and some contradictory. Confronted with these unanticipated developments, the vacillating Louis XVI began to take measures to halt and, if possible, reverse the movement his earlier policies had unleashed. To enforce such a decision, he needed armed backing; the only force capable of coping with such a situation was the regular army. Consequently, beginning in late June the king ordered a massive military buildup in and around the capital that would reach its peak in mid-July.[1] Even a political moderate like Camusat de Belombre, a merchant from Troyes and deputy of the Third Estate for that *bailliage*, was convinced that an aristocratic plot was afoot to occupy Paris and Versailles, with a force of around fifty thousand soldiers, and crush all hope of reform.[2]

The Troyes deputy was essentially correct about the objective, although he exaggerated the means for achieving it. In fact, Louis XVI had summoned more than 20,000 line troops to the capital where they were to join the elite regiments of French and Swiss Guards, approximately 3,600 and 2,300 men, respectively. Among the units that were to participate in the planned coup were the Bourbonnais and Saintonge Regiments, each about 1,100 strong, and a 300-man detachment of Lauzun Hussars; altogether, these three units included more than 700 men who had fought under Rochambeau in the United States.[3] Fortuitously, this constitutes a "made-to-order" test case to measure the influence of the American Revolution on the response of French veterans of that struggle to the first great crisis of the French Revolution. The troops in the Paris area constituted a kind of random sample, since they had been chosen primarily on the basis of their garrisons' proximity to the capital. And by chance, they included nearly half of the American veterans still on active duty in the French army.

The consequences of these circumstances are striking, largely because they are unexpected. Among the 17,000 regular troops who had reached Paris by July 14, 760 deserted during the month of July (nearly 45 men per thousand), and more than 1,600 deserted in the last six months of the year (just over 94 men per thousand). In the units that had served under Rochambeau in America, in contrast, only twenty soldiers deserted in July (8 men per thousand), of whom three were veterans of the American war, and thirty-three deserted during the second half of 1789, including seven American veterans (just about thirteen men per thousand in all). Therefore, if one were to argue that the American Revolution had an effect on these soldiers, it would seem to have been to strengthen discipline, since their comrades in other regiments were much more likely to display at least passive support for revolution by deserting.

It should be emphasized that determining motivation for desertion is tricky at best, especially in the absence of direct testimony and with only limited circumstantial evidence. With these reservations in mind, however, one can still suggest that the situation is perhaps not as paradoxical as it first appears. The peculiar character of military service in the American Revolution—stricter discipline, frequent encampments, long marches, combat conditions—in a largely alien environment may have created tighter bonds between the officers and men of these regiments than did normal garrison duty at home. In addition, by July 1789 the remaining American veterans had accumulated at least nine years of service, and many had a much greater personal investment in their military careers; consequently, they were less likely to desert than soldiers who had enlisted more recently. Furthermore, although the American veterans constituted only slightly more than one-quarter of the enlisted personnel in their regiments, because of their lengthy experience and the noncommissioned rank that frequently went with it, they enjoyed disproportionate influence over their younger, less experienced comrades. Ironically, then, service in the American Revolution may have made these veteran units better defenders of the Old Regime against the French Revolution—at least at first.

THE ROYAL ARMY CONFRONTS THE FRENCH REVOLUTION

This is not to claim that the American Revolution turned these soldiers into counterrevolutionaries. Not only did some of Rochambeau's veterans desert, but a number also joined the paid companies of the Parisian National Guard, a decision that at the time represented a clear commitment to the cause of the Revolution. More than a dozen men who had served in Rochambeau's corps in America enlisted in the National Guard of the capital.[4] For example, Armand Hyvert, a native of Chinon in Touraine, born in 1758, enlisted in the Regiment of Saintonge in 1776 and served with it in America. Upon his discharge in early November 1784, he joined the French Guards for a bounty of 120 livres and served with that regiment until his enlistment in the 3rd Division of the National Guard of Paris on September 1, 1789.[5] Jean Beuzelin (or Beuselin), who had been born in the Norman village of Colleville in 1757, joined the French Guards (for 100 livres) in 1786 following his discharge from the same regiment, where he had also served for eight years. He was enrolled in the 5th Division of the National Guard on the same day as Hyvert.[6] Ignace Joseph Dette, from the countryside of French Flanders, served twenty-four years in the Bourbonnais Infantry—including the American campaigns—before being honorably discharged on April 14, 1788. Twenty months later, when he was between forty-seven and fifty-three years of age (he gives his birth date variously as 1736 and 1742), he joined the Parisian National Guard, where he remained until December 31, 1791, when he was discharged with an annual pension of 273 livres for all his years of military service.[7] Although a cynic might note that these men may have been motivated at least in part by self-interest, other American veterans—for example, Pierre Thiriat and François Lahogue of Saintonge and Jean Pierre Garnier of Soissonnais—gained neither bonuses nor pensions by volunteering to serve in the National Guard.[8]

At least one of Rochambeau's veterans, who had fought in America as an artilleryman, risked his life in the famous attack on the Bastille. In December 1776 Claude Marneur, a native of Franche-Comté, had joined one of the companies of Auxonne Artillery that accompanied Rochambeau to America. Ten months after completing his eight-year enlistment, he enrolled in the French Guards where he served as a cannoneer. It was in this capacity that he helped Parisian crowds capture the fortress-prison-armory. For his role in the crucial events of July 14, 1789, Marneur was formally recognized as a *vainqueur de la Bastille*.[9]

The response of American veterans and their units to the political crisis in the capital in July 1789, then, was mixed; one can hardly claim that the American Revolution had radicalized these soldiers. But what of those who had returned to civilian life before this? What, if anything, did they contribute to the revolutionary events of 1789? It has been claimed that French veterans of the war in America, where they had been exposed to unfettered private property, played an important role in the agrarian violence that led to the destruction of feudalism in France during the summer of 1789.[10] This claim has some serious problems, including its conceptualization, its methodology, and the data that serve as its basis. The following comments summarize why it is highly unlikely that American veterans had any significant impact on French peasant uprisings during this period.[11]

Of the French expeditions to America, only Rochambeau's corps spent enough time in the United States to be influenced by its sojourn there. By mid-1789 there were at most twenty-five hundred of these surviving veterans in civilian society—that is, less than one American veteran for every ten thousand inhabitants—nationally. Of the soldiers who had been discharged or who had deserted in France, twice as many were originally from urban centers as the population generally (approximately 37 percent compared with 18 percent, respectively). Furthermore, veterans from rural areas tended to settle in more urban localities after their discharge.[12] Given the suspicion, even hostility, between town and countryside in the eighteenth century, it is unlikely that local peasants would accept the leadership of many of the former soldiers. In addition, the highest regional concentrations of discharged American veterans often bore no relation to the course of the Great Fear of summer 1789, as mapped by Georges Lefebvre. For instance, the largest numbers of veterans came from the provinces of Lorraine and Alsace, but the former was almost untouched and only the southern third of the latter was affected by this peasant violence.[13] Some of the provinces that were the scene of widespread antifeudal disturbances and also home to a comparatively large number of American veterans, such as Normandy, were simply the largest and most populous provinces in the kingdom. Finally, one in eight of the American veterans was non-French; these men either had returned home after being discharged or, if they remained in France, were unlikely to have great influence over the native peasantry.

Thus, without attempting the virtually impossible task of tracing the lives of over two thousand individuals after they had left army service, one can reasonably conclude that as a group Rochambeau's former soldiers could not have been responsible for the attack on feudal institutions in France. Indeed, even if one could find some evidence for this, the task of proving that such action was a consequence of their exposure to landholding practices in the United States is impossible.

THE ROYAL ARMY CONFRONTS THE FRENCH REVOLUTION

If, on the whole, the enlisted men who had served under Rochambeau during the American Revolution did not contribute to major developments during the early French Revolution, what of the officer veterans? In fact, some were associated with Lafayette and other leaders of the first stages of the Revolution; for example, Lauzun, Noailles, and Alexandre and Charles de Lameth were members of the Society of Thirty, which is commonly credited with providing early direction to the liberal movement.[14] When the Estates General began to meet in early May, among the 278 deputies representing the Second Estate were eight noble officers who had served under Rochambeau in the United States: Lauzun (now duc de Biron), Broglie, Custine, the two Lameth brothers, Noailles, François Louis Thibault de Menonville, and Charlus (now duc de Castries). All but the last have been identified among the liberal nobility.[15]

It is certain that some of the leading proponents of change in 1789 were officers who had fought in the American Revolution. Much of their activity centered around Lafayette, who was generally supported by Rochambeau's veterans, notably the vicomte de Noailles. When the Paris National Guard, which had been formed spontaneously at the height of the July crisis to cope with the dangers of both counterrevolution and anarchy, was being organized, these men held up the commonly accepted image of the American militia as a model.[16] Furthermore, some of the veterans provided early leadership for other National Guard formations. Louis Alexandre Berthier, who had served on Rochambeau's staff and eventually became Napoleon Bonaparte's chief of staff, served in the latter capacity in the Versailles National Guard from summer 1789 to spring 1791.[17] Claude Etienne Hugau, whose father was a domestic servant in Paris, had joined the army in 1757 at age sixteen and worked his way up the ranks, receiving his commission as sublieutenant nine years later. He served as lieutenant colonel of Lauzun's Legion throughout its stay in America and in the hussar regiment that succeeded it until his retirement in March 1789. Four months later he was selected commander of the National Guard of the city of Evreux, the beginning of a second career—in politics—that lasted until early 1815.[18] François Bernard Sinéty and Jean François Le Bret, who had been captains in the Soissonnais Infantry while it was stationed in the United States, held the same rank in their local National Guard units (at Apt in the Vaucluse and Gisors in the Eure) during the early Revolution.[19]

Other of Rochambeau's former officers played a prominent role in revolutionary developments during this time. Dominique Louis Ethis de Corny, the commissary officer in charge of the preparations for Rochambeau's corps in America, who had retired from military service at the beginning of 1789, not only participated in the establishment of the Parisian National Guard but was also a member of the delegation that tried to convince the commander of the Bastille—Bernard René, marquis de Launay—to avoid bloodshed on July 14 by cooperating with popular demands.[20] During the famous session of the self-proclaimed National Assembly on the night of August 4, 1789, the vicomte de Noailles and duc de Biron took the lead in endorsing the abolition of feudal privileges.[21] Noailles also played a major role on the assembly's Military Committee, where he advocated equal opportunities for promotion for all officers and was frequently supported by the prince de Broglie and Alexandre de Lameth—comrades from Rochambeau's corps.[22]

American veterans also contributed in more general ways to the creation of the new regime in France. The French branch of the Society of the Cincinnati favored the early changes.[23] Most of Rochambeau's former officers in the assembly voted for the Declaration of the Rights of Man and Citizen—clearly inspired by American precedents—and for subsequent legislation that established new constitutional principles similar to those of the United States. Just how much this activity owed to the American example and how much it reflected a common source of ideas for both revolutions—the Enlightenment—is controversial.[24] The reactions of some of Rochambeau's veterans to developments in France, however, indicate that the U.S. influence was limited, even contradictory at times.

In 1789 Charles César Robin, who served as a chaplain in Rochambeau's corps during 1781, published a historical analysis of the Estates General, with recommendations for subsequent policies and institutional reforms. In two volumes he made only passing reference to the United States and based his position entirely on French history and traditions.[25] Furthermore, as early reforms went beyond vague generalities and especially as they began to challenge monarchical authority and noble privilege, the officers' original support began to deteriorate, although open hostility remained negligible during the first year of the Revolution; for instance, only one of Rochambeau's veterans, Jean Louis de Rigaud, vicomte de Vaudreuil, emigrated in 1789.[26] The comte de Ségur, who had been lyrical in his praise of American liberty in 1782 when he served briefly in the United States, came back from Russia, where he had been the French ambassador from 1784 to 1789, and heaped the same kind of panegyrics on the empire of Catherine the Great as he had on the republic of George Washington. He supported an absolute veto for the king, a declaration of duties to balance the rights of citizens, and a restoration of some of the seigneurial privileges abolished in August 1789.[27] The growing intensity of political disagreement was strikingly evidenced by duels fought between revolutionary supporters and opponents, one of which pitted Charles de Lameth against the duc de Castries—each of whom had served in Rochambeau's command in the United States.[28]

There was, therefore, no necessary direct link between the American and French Revolutions—at least as far as Rochambeau's veterans were concerned. Even in a more general way, most connections appear tenuous. The relation French contemporaries saw between the American Revolution and their own was often based on their impressions—often highly romanticized—of American conditions rather than American realities. Certainly, the National Guard in France bore little resemblance to actual American militia forces, although it did conform in many respects to what the French imagined the latter to be.[29] Likewise, political leaders and the public in France found other institutional and individual models they wanted in the American Revolution, often with little concern for historical accuracy.[30]

More real and immediate were the political disorders that spread through France in the aftermath of July 14 and the deterioration of military discipline that frequently accompanied them. The old system was collapsing and the new struggling to establish itself. In these conditions the only agencies capable of maintaining public order were the National Guard, still in the early stages of formation, and the regular army, which had traditionally functioned as a police force during peacetime. Now, however, in summer and early autumn 1789, line troops, fortified by the example of their comrades in Paris, refused to repress popular disturbances either by deserting—a passive form of insubordination—or, less often, by defying their superiors and actively supporting revolutionary activities by civilians. Incidents of this nature occurred at Rennes, Auxonne, Strasbourg, Nancy, Thionville, Bordeaux, Caen, and elsewhere. The most famous and consequential such incident took place at Versailles in early October when the soldiers of the Regiment of Flandre refused to take action against the crowd of women who forced the royal family and the government to move to Paris.[31] These developments alarmed many officers, some of whom were also concerned by the pace and extent of changes introduced by the new authorities. For example, after the comte de Rochambeau arrived in Strasbourg in July 1789 to take command of the province of Alsace, he quickly became disgusted with the breakdown of civil order and the disintegration of discipline among units under his orders; he asked to be relieved of command, pleading ill health, and left Alsace within six months to retire to his estate near Vendôme.[32]

Rochambeau would have been less disillusioned if his command had consisted of the same units that had served under him in America. In 1789 those six regiments maintained markedly better discipline than the army as a whole; their desertion rate was only half the average of the other regular units. This achievement was especially impressive for the three regiments (Bourbonnais, Saintonge, and Lauzun) that had been part of the military buildup in and around Paris in mid-July, because most of those units had suffered substantial—sometimes drastic—increases in the number of deserters.[33] Purges of potential troublemakers may have helped to preserve discipline in those units during late 1789, as other regiments were racked by desertions. At the end of August thirty-nine soldiers, including seven American veterans, were abruptly dismissed (*chassé*) from service in the Regiment of Bourbonnais. Fifty-six men, among them twenty-two American veterans, in the Regiment of Saintonge experienced the same fate during the last week in October. The officers of the Regiment of Soissonnais chased off thirty-two of their men, five of whom had fought in America, during 1789, most in September. Yet, by themselves these dismissals cannot explain the conduct of the "American" units. For one thing, the regiments of Royal Deux-Ponts Infantry, Lauzun Hussars, and Auxonne Artillery had only twenty-one such discharges among them, yet discipline in those units did not noticeably suffer. On the other hand, the implementation of similar policies throughout the army resulted in four to five times as many men being dismissed for disciplinary reasons as in previous years; nonetheless, the general tide of insubordination continued to swell.[34]

No single factor or group of factors conclusively determined the way Rochambeau's veterans responded to revolutionary developments in France; the most one can do is identify certain tendencies. As discussed previously, the discipline maintained in the regiments that had participated in the American expedition apparently owed something to the peculiar conditions there that had created greater unit cohesion. In addition, the American veterans had a greater personal stake in their military careers than did their less experienced comrades; not only did they have more time invested in the army, but the years between 1780 and 1783 when they were "on campaign" in America counted doubly (that is, as eight, not four, years of service) toward their retirement. Also, they usually exercised more authority and responsibility than other soldiers in their units. Finally, the Royal Deux-Ponts Infantry and Lauzun Hussars, largely composed of Germans and French subjects from Alsace and Lorraine, were, in fact, German units. Like other foreign regiments of the Royal Army, they were presumed to be better disciplined than their French counterparts, particularly in dealing with civil disturbances; this presumption often proved correct.[35] All of these considerations help to explain why Rochambeau's "American" units generally exhibited better discipline than the rest of the regular army during the early

Revolution. They do not, however, account for individual conduct, which varied widely and unpredictably.

While it was garrisoned in the small town (population just over two thousand) of Neuf-Brisach in upper Alsace, the Royal Deux-Ponts Infantry suffered slightly more desertions during 1789 than the Bourbonnais or Saintonge Regiments, although those two regiments had been exposed to the intense political propaganda and turmoil in Paris in mid-July.[36] Furthermore, no obvious bonds existed among the deserters from Deux-Ponts. For example, German-born Jean Stoertz, a Calvinist who had enlisted in the Regiment of La Marck in 1777 at age twenty-two and been transferred to Deux-Ponts while it was in America, deserted on August 3, 1789; later the same month Jacob Sugg, a Catholic from Weissembourg, Alsace, who had joined the regiment in 1778 when he was eighteen and been promoted to corporal earlier in 1789, also deserted. Since the two were not even in the same company, there seems to be no common element in the desertions.[37] Two men who deserted from the Regiment of Saintonge at the same time did have more in common, but, unfortunately, this only makes their desertions less explicable. Jean Perrucheau and Louis Thomas were in the same company (the elite grenadiers); both were in their early thirties and were from small villages in France (in the Nivernais and Lorraine, respectively). In addition, both had been promoted to corporal in 1786, and both had around twenty years of service (counting their campaigns in America).[38] These last two characteristics, rank and long service, usually tended to discourage desertion. Nevertheless, on July 24, a week after leaving the tumultuous capital, the two men deserted.

All things considered, Rochambeau's former units survived the first six months of the French Revolution better than most regiments of the French army. The following year, 1790, witnessed the near collapse of the army. In some respects, the "American" regiments followed the same pattern as other regular units.[39] In spite of the ominous and obvious trouble signs exhibited by troops during the second half of 1789, about half of the officers in those regiments—as throughout the army—took their customary annual leave from October 15, 1789, to June 1, 1790, thereby reducing supervision over increasingly discontented soldiers.

Meanwhile, the policy of discharging soldiers whose conduct was—or was suspected of being—seditious continued in all regiments. In 1790 ninety-one soldiers, including nineteen American veterans, were summarily dismissed from the Regiment of Bourbonnais. Possibly, the large number of discharges, especially of veterans of the American war, reflected lingering tensions between those soldiers and some of their officers who had administered particularly brutal punishments in America and had abandoned their men when the *Bourgogne* was shipwrecked in February 1783.[40] Although fewer such discharges occurred in the other "American" regiments, there were some in all of them: forty in Saintonge, thirty-eight in Deux-Ponts, eighteen in Soissonnais, eight in Lauzun, and two in Auxonne. During the same year more than a third of all regiments in the Royal Army experienced some form of mass insubordination, ranging from excessive desertions to outright mutiny. One of Rochambeau's old units—the Regiment of Royal Deux-Ponts—reflected the general turmoil. Of Rochambeau's entire expeditionary corps the men of this German unit had probably enjoyed the closest relationship with Americans and perhaps had been the most affected by their American experiences.[41] Ironically, this regiment had received the most glowing praise of any regiment in the annual reports of inspectors general over the previous five years. In spite of these evaluations and contrary to foreign units' reputation for reliability, in May 1790 the men of this regiment mutinied against their officers, and in the course of the year 129 of them—a third of whom were American veterans—deserted.[42]

Even more unusual than the collapse of discipline in the Regiment of Deux-Ponts is the fact that the other five units that had served in Rochambeau's expeditionary force continued to exhibit markedly more cohesion than the army as a whole. Every one of the units had a desertion rate well below the army average; indeed, except for the Bourbonnais Infantry (again, possibly a residue of American experiences), the desertion rate was only half as high as that in the army as a whole. Yet, the men in these units were exposed to the same kinds of situations as the soldiers in other regiments. For example, in early August 1790 a deputation of enlisted men of the Auxonne Artillery presented their officers with a list of demands for financial reimbursement, including three months' back pay for those who had fought in America. Similar complaints about the use and misuse of unit funds figured prominently in about a third of the confrontations between officers and men in the army as a whole during 1790. In this case, a compromise solution was worked out since the soldiers presented their demands, in the words of Lieutenant Colonel du Teil, "with all possible propriety."[43]

Similarly, the Soissonnais Infantry managed to maintain discipline in 1790 under the most trying conditions—conditions that led to the disintegration of other units. By fall 1789 this regiment was dispersed in eight separate detachments, charged with the unpopular duty of policing disturbances over grain. In late 1790 the regiment was sent into the papal enclave around Avignon to restore law and order in the face of civilian unrest.[44] Throughout those months there were no incidents of insubordination and only a score of desertions, in striking contrast to much of the rest of the army.

Lauzun's regiment of hussars displayed the most remarkable conduct during the period. In this unit the enlisted men followed their officers beyond the boundaries of discipline and into the realm of counterrevolution. In July 1789 the regiment furnished a detachment of three hundred men to the military buildup in and around Paris; it arrived at Marly on July 11 and left to return to the regimental garrison at Verdun on July 18.[45] Like the other two "American" regiments in the Paris area, Bourbonnais and Saintonge, the Lauzun Hussars had comparatively few deserters: only two in July and eight for the year, none of whom had served in America. Over the next thirteen months the regiment, consisting of around six hundred men— more than five hundred of whom were from Alsace and German-speaking areas of Lorraine—continued its exemplary behavior, losing only three deserters in 1790. For both this reason and the general reputation for trustworthiness foreign regiments enjoyed, François Claude Amour, marquis de Bouillé, selected two of the regiment's squadrons (about a hundred hussars each) to assist in repressing the great soldiers' mutiny at Nancy in late August 1790. In the course of this action, fifteen men from the detachment were killed and twenty-five wounded; three officers were also killed, including Captain Georges Uzdowsky and Lieutenant Jean Baptiste Dubet, who had survived the American war unscathed.[46]

The regiment's continual performance of repressive missions confirmed popular suspicions of and animosity toward these "foreign" troops. In turn, civilian attitudes seem to have strengthened unit cohesion and increased antirevolutionary sentiment among both officers and soldiers. Less than two months after Nancy, they paraded through the streets of Belfort, where the regiment had been transferred, shouting "to the devil with the Nation" and "long live aristocrats" while simultaneously threatening and abusing townspeople.[47]

During 1790 the regiments that had participated in the 1780–1783 American expedition, on the whole, continued to exhibit more disciplined conduct than the rest of the Royal Army. At the same time, individual units reflected the full range of responses to the Revolution evidenced throughout the regular army, from mutiny and mass desertion to apparent indifference to violent hostility. What, then, can be concluded? The shared American experiences and their effects generally tended to contribute to greater morale and discipline, but exposure to the revolutionary atmosphere in France could undermine or destroy these intangible elements as the memories of those experiences faded further into the past.

More than the passage of time weakened the impact of service in the American Revolution. Events during the first year and a half of the French Revolution helped to reduce further the already dwindling number of American veterans on active duty. Whereas "normal" departures from the army—such as discharges, deaths, and retirements—continued at the prerevolutionary pace, dramatic increases occurred in some types of separation from certain units. From July 1789 to December 1790, twenty-seven American veterans received disciplinary discharges from the Regiment of Bourbonnais and twenty-six from Saintonge; in the six years between their return to France in June 1783 and July 1789, the two regiments together had lost only ten American veterans for this reason. Similarly, from 1787 through 1789 the Regiment of Deux-Ponts averaged 29 desertions per year, a third by men who had served in America; in 1790 the number of deserters swelled to 129, 33 of them American veterans.

Although numbers such as these are needed to understand the course of large and complex phenomena, they also blur the human, individual aspects of historical developments. What did it mean to be *chassé*? Unlike courts-martial, no transcripts of these proceedings were kept. The charges could be vague; it was sufficient simply to be identified as a "bad subject" (*mauvais sujet*).[48] Apparently, no formal hearing took place; certainly, no appeal of the decision was allowed. Nevertheless, the consequences for the soldier could be immensely important. For instance, Sergeant Jean Ferrier of the Saintonge Infantry, a native of Angoulême who had enlisted in 1769 at age twenty-three, was dismissed on October 30, 1789, after more than twenty-four years of service (counting his wartime campaigns). Jean Baptiste Lehetre from rural Normandy had never risen above the rank of private but had the same length of service in the same regiment as Ferrier when he was *chassé* earlier that week; he had known no life outside the army since age sixteen. Joseph Guillet from Grenoble was only one year older than Lehetre when he joined the Bourbonnais Infantry on November 20, 1773; he was summarily discharged in August 1789. Guillet's comrade in the same regiment, Fidel Dussart from Lille, was also seventeen when he enlisted at the end of 1764. Eleven years later he was promoted to corporal, the rank he held when he was "sent away by order of the commander" on August 7, 1790, after having spent well over half his life in uniform.[49]

The consequences of desertion could be equally grave, although the deserter rather than his superiors made the decision. Sometimes, as in Paris in July 1789, deserters were encouraged by support from civilians or emboldened by comrades in their unit—especially their company—who joined them in this hazardous venture.[50] No evidence exists, however, of civilian influence on the breakdown of discipline in the Regiment of Deux-Ponts in 1790, although circumstances suggest possible collusion among some of the deserters. During May, twenty-eight soldiers deserted the regiment, among them seven veterans of the American war.[51] One of the veterans deserted on May 30 and the other six the following day. They had much in common. They ranged between twenty-nine and thirty-four years of age and had been in the army for twelve to fifteen years. None held noncommissioned rank, although one, Johannes Fischer from Alsace, had been a corporal briefly before being demoted in 1789. Three of the deserters were from the same company, Captain Claude Théodore du Hainaut's, and two others were in Captain Charles Guillaume Rühl's company. To take such a drastic step and risk the harsh punishments for this military crime (including possible prolongation of service, imprisonment, physical beating, or condemnation to the galleys) was almost certainly easier for a group than for a single individual.[52]

The case of Sergeant Phillip Wenger defies ready explanation and once more highlights the complexity of this issue. Wenger, a native of Bischviller, Alsace, enlisted in the grenadier company of Deux-Ponts in November 1772 at age twenty-two. Shortly after returning from America he was promoted to corporal; two years later he became a sergeant. Counting his wartime campaigns, he had slightly less than twenty-two years of service when he deserted on October 9, 1790. He gave up a successful career and expectations of further advancement because, as Wenger was undoubtedly aware, the opportunities for additional promotion—even the possibility of a commission as an *officier de fortune*—were the best in this elite company. The considerations that prompted this momentous decision on his part we shall never know.

In contrast, the overall situation in the Royal Army at the end of 1790 is clear.[53] Insubordination by the troops had mounted in frequency and intensity, reaching a climax at Nancy, which became a veritable pitched battle between the mutineers and Bouillé's army of forty-five hundred; indeed, the latter were credited with a military "campaign" for their participation in the repression of the garrison. All of this seriously undermined the officers' confidence in their troops and in their ability to command them. Simultaneously, the wholesale dismissals, at least some of which appeared arbitrary, together with accusations of pecuniary malfeasance were destroying the soldiers' faith in their officers and their willingness to follow the latter's orders. In addition, the revolutionary atmosphere was adding a political cast to the growing divisions. For example, six soldiers who were dishonorably discharged from the Regiment of Saintonge on April 26 and 27 complained that this treatment by their officers was politically motivated, that they were staunch "patriots" who had become "victims of their love for the Fatherland." Civilian authorities in the department of the Meuse gave credence to their claims but could do little else.54 The coming year, 1791, would bring even greater crises for the French army, including the "American" regiments.

Notes

1. For further details, see Scott, *Response of the Royal Army*, pp. 51–57.
2. Lynn Avery Hunt, *Revolution and Urban Politics in Provincial France: Troyes and Reims, 1786–1790* (Stanford: Stanford University Press, 1978), p. 70; and Hunt, *Politics, Culture, and Class in the French Revolution* (Berkeley: University of California Press, 1984), pp. 40–41.
3. See Scott, *Response of the Royal Army*, pp. 57–69, for the general situation in Paris, and the regimental registers, A.G., 14 YC 17 (Bourbonnais), 14 YC 119 (Saintonge), and the uncoded contrôle for the Lauzun Hussars, vol. 1 (1786–August 23, 1792) for the "American" units.
4. The registers for only three of the six divisions of the *Garde nationale soldée* (the 3rd, 4th, and 5th) are available in A.G., 20 YC 645, 646, and 647. Consequently, these are minimum figures. A discussion of the composition and role of the Paris National Guard can be found in Dale L. Clifford, "The Real National Guard: Local Culture in Paris, 1789–90," paper presented at the International Congress on the History of the French Revolution, Washington, D.C., May 5, 1989.
5. See A.G., 1 YC 932 (for Saintonge), 11 YC 141 (French Guards), and 20 YC 645 (Paris National Guard).
6. A.G., 1 YC 932, 11 YC 167, and 20 YC 647.
7. A.G., 1 YC 188, 14 YC 17, and 20 YC 647.
8. A.G., 1 YC 932, 14 YC 119, and 20 YC 646 for Thiriat; the same, except 20 YC 647 for Lahogue; and 1 YC 966 and 20 YC 645 for Garnier.
9. A.G., 10 YC 1; and cited in Joseph Durieux, *Les Vainqueurs de la Bastille* (Paris: H. Champion, 1911), p. 228.
10. The provocative article that expounded this hypothesis is Forrest McDonald, "The Relation of the French Peasant Veterans of the American Revolution to the Fall of Feudalism in France, 1789–1792," *Agricultural History* 25 (1951): 151–161.
11. For a fuller discussion of these problems and an elucidation of the brief discussion that follows, see my article, "The Soldiers of Rochambeau's Expeditionary Corps: From the American Revolution to the French Revolution," in *La Révolution américaine et l'Europe (Colloque international du Centre National de la Recherche Scientifique, 21–25 février 1978, Paris-Toulouse)*, Claude Fohlen and Jacques Godechot, eds. (Paris: Editions du C.N.R.S., 1979), pp. 567–573.
12. Corvisier, *Armeé française*, vol. 2, p. 914.
13. Georges Lefebvre, *The Great Fear of 1789: Rural Panic in Revolutionary France*,

THE ROYAL ARMY CONFRONTS THE FRENCH REVOLUTION

trans. Joan White (New York: Vintage Books, 1973), map on p. 4.
14. Daniel L. Wick, "The Court Nobility and the French Revolution: The Example of the Society of Thirty," *Eighteenth-Century Studies* 13 (1980): 263–284, contains interesting observations on this group.
15. Bodinier, *Officiers*, pp. 383 and 387–388.
16. Fohlen, "Impact of the American Revolution on France," pp. 35–36; Godechot, "Revolutionary Contagion," p. 6; Bernard Faÿ, *The Revolutionary Spirit in France and America: A Study of Moral and Intellectual Relations Between France and the United States at the End of the Eighteenth Century*, trans. Ramon Guthrie (New York: Harcourt, Brace, 1927), pp. 269–271; Gilbert Bodinier, "Etude du comportement des officiers qui on combattu en Amérique pendant la Révolution," in *Actes du 102e Congrès National des Sociétés Savantes. Limoges, 1977*, vol. 2 (Paris: Bibliothèque Nationale, 1978), p. 109.
17. Rice and Brown, *American Campaigns*, vol. 1, pp. 196–197.
18. A.N., D² C 32; A.G., Xᶜ 83; and Bodinier, *Dictionnaire*, p. 248.
19. Bodinier, *Dictionnaire*, pp. 440 and 296.
20. Ibid., pp. 188–189; Lasseray, *Français sous treize étoiles*, vol. 1, pp. 206–211; and Gardiner, *Cincinnati in France*, p. 166.
21. Bodinier, *Dictionnaire*, pp. 362 and 226–227.
22. Bodinier, *Officiers*, p. 391.
23. Gardiner, *Cincinnati in France*, pp. 45–48.
24. For a limited sampling of thoughts on this issue, see Faÿ, *Revolutionary Spirit*, pp. 265–267; Fohlen, "Impact of the American Revolution on France," pp. 35–36; Godechot, "Revolutionary Contagion," pp. 3–4; Fursenko, "American and French Revolutions," p. 92; Palmer, "Impact of American Revolution Abroad," pp. 13–15; and Joyce Appleby, "America as a Model for the Radical French Reformers of 1789," *William and Mary Quarterly*, 3rd ser. 28 (1971): 269–286.
25. Charles César Robin, *Histoire de la constitution de l'empire françois, ou Histoire des Etats-généraux, pour servir d'introduction à notre droit public*, 2 vols. (London: Godefroy, 1789).
26. Bodinier, *Officiers*, p. 438, and Bodinier, *Dictionnaire*, p. 405.
27. See p. 109; and Leon Apt, *Louis-Philippe de Ségur: An Intellectual in a Revolutionary Age* (The Hague: Nijhoff, 1969), pp. 65 and 70.
28. Bodinier, *Officiers*, pp. 196–197; Lameth was wounded, and the next day a crowd destroyed the Castries's townhouse in Paris.
29. For a fuller discussion, see Scott, "Military Nationalism," pp. 177–182.
30. Echeverria, *Mirage in the West*, pp. 161–167; James A. Leith, "Le culte de Franklin en France avant et pendant la Révolution française," *Annales historiques de la Révolution française* 48 (1976): 560–566; and Kenneth N. McKee, "The Popularity of the 'American' on the French Stage During the Revolution," *Proceedings of the American Philosophical Society* 83 (1940): 480–487.
31. For a fuller discussion, see Scott, *Response of the Royal Army*, pp. 70–80.
32. Whitridge, *Rochambeau*, pp. 266–272.
33. Desertion statistics for the "American" units have been drawn from the regimental contrôles. For the army as a whole, see Scott, "Regeneration of the Line Army," pp. 311–313.
34. Again, the sources for data on discharges are the unit contrôles. The general policy is described in Scott, *Response of the Royal Army*, pp. 81–82.

35. Samuel F. Scott, "Foreign Mercenaries, Revolutionary War, and Citizen-Soldiers in the Late Eighteenth Century," *War and Society* 2 (1984): 48–54.
36. The differences in the number of deserters were admittedly not great: twenty-one in Deux Ponts, fifteen in Bourbonnais, and seventeen in Saintonge. What makes the desertion rates remarkable is the difference in environments.
37. See A.G., 14 YC 144.
38. A.G., 14 YC 119.
39. Unless otherwise noted, the data on Rochambeau's units are drawn from inspection reports and regimental registers as follows: A.G., X^b 25 and 14 YC 17 for Bourbonnais; X^b 53 and 14 YC 58 for Soissonnais; X^b 91 and 14 YC 119 for Saintonge; X^b 104 and 14 YC 144 for Deux-Ponts; X^c 83 and uncoded contrôle, 2 vols (1786-An IX) for Lauzun; and X^d 24 and uncoded contrôle (1786-An II) for Auxonne. The situation in the army as a whole is described in Scott, *Response of the Royal Army*, pp. 81–97.
40. See pp. 42 and 108.
41. See pp. 105–106.
42. On the mutiny, see Bodinier, "Officiers de Rochambeau," p. 158.
43. See the report dated August 4, 1790, in A.G., X^d 24.
44. On the police activities of Soissonnais, see A.N., $D^{xxix\,bis}$ 2, dossier 22, pièce 17; and the letter of the Commissaires du Roi, dated April 21, 1791, in A.N., F^7 3659^1; as well as the inspection report of October 1, 1789, in A.G., X^b 53.
45. A.N., BB^{30} 161, and A.G., YA 420.
46. Bodinier, *Officiers*, p. 438; and Lucien de Chilly, *Le Premier Ministre constitutionnel de la querre, La Tour du Pin: Les Origines de l'armée nouvelle sous la Constituente* (Paris: Perrin, 1909), pp. 240–244.
47. See *Rapport fait à l'Assemblée Nationale dans la séance du samedi 30 octobre, au nom des Comités militaires et des rapports, sur les événemens arrivés le 21 octobre à Béfort* in the University of Pennsylvania's Maclure Collection of French Revolutionary Materials, vol. 832.
48. Scott, *Response of the Royal Army*, pp. 81–82.
49. These soldiers are recorded in their regimental contrôles, A.G., 14 YC 119 and 14 YC 17, respectively.
50. For examples, see Scott, *Response of the Royal Army*, pp. 57–58 and 65–66.
51. See the regimental contrôle for Josef Zimmerman, Joseph Vetter, Michel Trautmann, Johannes Fischer, Lorentz Schmitt, Michel Massard, and Jacques Weinsheimer, as well as Sergeant Wenger who deserted in October. The names and spellings are given as they appear in the register entries.
52. On the punishment of deserters, see Scott, *Response of the Royal Army*, pp. 36–38.
53. Ibid., pp. 80–97.
54. A.N., $D^{xxix\,bis}$ 5, dossier 71, pièces 10 and 11.

9
DISINTEGRATION AND PARTIAL RECOVERY IN 1791

DURING 1791 THE DISINTEGRATION of the Royal Army reached its peak: Mass insubordination by the soldiers resumed in the spring following a relatively calm hiatus in the wake of the Nancy mutiny; the politicization of conflicts between officers and men intensified, as counterrevolutionary émigrés pressured noble officers and radical clubs propagandized their military subordinates; and thousands of officers left their posts in reaction to the attempted flight of Louis XVI and his subsequent arrest and suspension. The gravity of the situation was exacerbated by the increasing likelihood of war and growing domestic unrest. In the course of the same year, however, and in response to these dangers the French army began a process of recovery that eventually enabled it to surmount these difficulties and that definitively changed its character.[1]

Some of the regiments that had served in America from 1780 to 1783 continued to display remarkable discipline and cohesion in the midst of mounting tensions; others reflected the general turmoil in the army. The infantry regiments of Bourbonnais and Saintonge and the Auxonne Artillery suffered only half as many desertions as the average of all regiments in the same branch during 1791; and although desertions in the Lauzun Hussars increased, they were still proportionately fewer than in the cavalry as a whole. On the other hand, the desertion rate in the Regiment of Royal Deux-Ponts was nearly double that of the infantry and the rate in the Regiment of Soissonnais nearly two and a half times the average.[2] Even in units in which the soldiers maintained discipline, as in the Saintonge Infantry, the political consequences of the king's flight included the large-scale defection of officers. And this same incident created strains in the solid cohesion the Regiment of Lauzun had consistently displayed until that time.

The troops of the Regiment of Soissonnais had been engaged in police functions in southern France since spring 1789. These onerous duties, which were always unpopular, were made all the more difficult because they were often performed in small, isolated detachments. In November 1790 the regiment was ordered into the papal possessions of Avignon and the Comtat Venaissin, scenes of bitter conflicts between supporters of the Revolution who endorsed annexation by France and conservative elements who favored continuing papal rule. Prorevolutionary factions attempted to win the regulars over, encouraging them to desert and join armed bands in the region; simultaneously, these *patriotes* accused the officers—including Colonel Marie Charles de la Tour Maubourg, the commanding officer of the Soissonnais Infantry—of antirevolutionary activity.[3] Under these pressures the exemplary discipline heretofore exhibited by this regiment collapsed. During 1791, 160 men deserted, 90 (including 7 American veterans) in January and 75 on January 9 alone; subsequently, 89 deserters from the regiment joined the armed band of Mathieu Jouve Jourdan, part revolutionary and part brigand, known as *Coupe-tête*, or "Head-cutter."[4]

The abnormally high desertion rate in the Regiment of Royal Deux-Ponts—114 deserters in 1791, among them 9 American veterans—was the result of peculiar conditions. For one thing, this unit had displayed a tendency toward mass desertions during the previous year when 129 men deserted. In addition, the situation in which the regiment found itself in early 1791 was different from that of Soissonnais or any French regiment. Since the beginning of the Revolution, foreign units had been the focus of popular suspicion and animosity because they were frequently employed in repressive activities. This expectation often became self-fulfilling: Treated as oppressors, foreign troops acted as oppressors, thereby justifying and reinforcing their reputation as such. The Deux-Ponts Infantry, however, had not been engaged in police activities to the degree many foreign units had; furthermore, its soldiers had been more immediately influenced by the events of the early Revolution than any of the "American" regiments. In spite of these considerations, the personnel of the regiment were distrusted simply because they were foreigners.[5] This antipathy, together with the widening split between soldiers and officers, contributed to the large number of deserters; for example, more than a score of men from the regiment (among them four American veterans) became deserters in March 1791 when they failed to return from authorized leave. A month later, on April 16, eighty soldiers (of whom seven had served in the United States) were discharged "as subjects of [the duke of] Deux Ponts," although a dozen returned to the regiment over the next two months.

The actions of regimental authorities contributed to the problem. Starting in early November 1790 Charles II, the duke of Deux-Ponts, had prohibited recruitment for the unit in his territory; the following March and April he ordered all of his subjects to leave the service of France or suffer confiscation of their property. Meanwhile, the colonel of the regiment, Christian de Deux-Ponts, left the regiment on March 16 and officially resigned his command on April 6. When the regiment was selected to assist the king's flight in June, the soldiers revolted against the officers.[6] Similar circumstances affecting other foreign units led to the abolition of all distinctions between foreign and French regiments in the regular army on July 21, 1791; only the Swiss, whose service was regulated by special agreements, *capitulations*, were exempted.[7] The cessation of foreign enlistments and increased efforts to recruit Frenchmen resulted in a rapid and substantial change in the former Regiment of Deux-Ponts; by December, 805 of 1,099 enlisted men (73 percent) were French natives, although still overwhelmingly from Alsace (470 soldiers) and Lorraine (311 soldiers).[8]

The actions of the Lauzun Hussars much more obviously justified the general mistrust of foreign troops. A detachment of the regiment had been summoned to Paris in July 1789 as part of the abortive royal coup. Two squadrons had helped to suppress the mutiny of the garrison at Nancy in late August 1790. In October, soldiers of the regiment had joined their officers in a violent demonstration of royalist sympathies in the streets of Belfort. And throughout this difficult period, discipline within the unit had been virtually perfect. It is not surprising, then, that the Regiment of Lauzun Hussars was one of the units picked by the marquis de Bouillé to assist in the attempted flight of the royal family in June 1791. Detachments were stationed along the route projected by Bouillé and the king, including one at the town of Varennes, where Louis XVI was recognized and taken into custody late on the evening of June 21. When their officers attempted to rally the hussars (over 80 percent of whom were Alsatians and Lorrainers) to rescue the king from the National Guardsmen holding him, the soldiers turned on the officers and joined the populace, shouting "Vive la Nation!"[9] Discipline in the regiment was severely shaken but not destroyed. The consequences for the army as a whole were much more serious.

The reactions of the prerevolutionary officer corps to the first two years of the French Revolution were diverse and generally slow to develop. The bulk of Old Regime officers were provincial nobles committed to a military career. Although some of the early changes made them uneasy, they found other reforms unobjectionable, even beneficial. Few officers responded quickly or decisively to revolutionary developments, and most of those were from the upper aristocracy.[10] The abolition of aristocratic privilege, the erosion of royal power, the reorganization of the Catholic Church, and other general revolutionary measures drastically changed the world nobles had known. Mounting desertions and mutinies threatened the hierarchical structure of the army and directly challenged the officers' authority. The *Journal Militaire* of August 16, 1790, undoubtedly reflected the attitude of its subscribers—largely captains and lieutenants—when it bemoaned the passing of order and discipline: "Honor! Honor! What has become of you?"[11]

The highly charged political atmosphere in France further escalated military problems. In mid-February 1791 the duc de Lauzun—now the duc de Biron and a major general—wrote to his former commander in the United States, Rochambeau, who had returned to active duty as commanding general of the Army of the North, complaining that large numbers of soldiers in his command were participating in local Jacobin clubs in violation of the official prohibition of such activity.[12] By 1791 officers who had responded to the Revolution by emigrating were trying to convince relatives and friends still in France to join their cause.[13]

In spite of these pressures, most officers remained at their posts. A mere handful of officers emigrated at the beginning of the Revolution—for example, the vicomte de Vaudreuil, a young court aristocrat who had served on the staff of General Chastellux in America and emigrated with the king's brother, Artois, in August 1789.[14] Even more peculiar was the behavior of Thomas Antoine, chevalier de Mauduit du Plessis, who in 1777 had volunteered as an artillery officer in the American army, where he served with distinction for two years, and subsequently became a member of Rochambeau's staff between 1780 and 1782. As a result of his experiences, he became enamored with the American ideal of equality and wanted to drop all indications of nobility from his name and become simply Thomas Duplessis-Mauduit. He continued his military career after the American Revolution and in 1788 became colonel of the colonial infantry regiment of Port-au-Prince in Haiti. Apparently, his political views had changed, or perhaps he did not find American principles applicable to French conditions. In any event, he staunchly opposed revolutionary changes in France, particularly any suggestion of black emancipation; he refused to publish orders from the home government; and he disarmed the local National Guard and arrested the members of the Colonial Committee. These antirevolutionary activities alienated many, including some in his own command. On

DISINTEGRATION AND PARTIAL RECOVERY

March 4, 1791, he was attacked and killed by a crowd that included men from his own regiment.[15]

The fate of the chevalier de Mauduit du Plessis was highly unusual—as well as ironic. Other officers became disillusioned with revolution in France more gradually. Pierre Marie Félicité Dezouteux (baron de Comartin since 1784), an aide de camp to General Antoine Charles Vioménil in America, at first embraced the French Revolution; he was closely associated with the Lameth brothers and participated in the women's march on Versailles on October 5, 1789. His attitude subsequently changed; he served with Bouillé in suppressing the Nancy mutiny in August 1790 and supported Louis XVI's unsuccessful flight the following June. Shortly afterward he emigrated, but he returned to Brittany in 1794 to take command of the counterrevolutionary forces of the Chouans.[16] Other officers who had been part of Rochambeau's American expedition also became sufficiently hostile toward conditions in France that they assisted the flight to Varennes.[17] Charles Georges Calixte Deslon de Momeril served as a captain in Lauzun's Legion and in the hussar regiment that replaced it after the American Revolution. In June 1791 he was in charge of a detachment of Lauzun Hussars (then officially designated the 6th Hussars) that failed to rescue the king following his arrest. Shortly afterward he left the country and joined émigré forces gathering for an invasion of France.[18] Similarly, Joseph Louis César, comte de Damas, former aide de camp of Rochambeau and commanding officer of the Monsieur (13th) Dragoons, who helped to arrange the flight, could do nothing to extricate the king and subsequently joined the émigré army of the princes.[19]

Obviously, the changes introduced during the first two years of the French Revolution aroused strong reactions among some officers. A large majority of Royal Army officers, including most American veterans, however, refrained from committing themselves to any particular position; instead, they awaited developments, albeit with a growing sense of anxiety. The flight to Varennes dramatically changed this situation. When Louis XVI secretly left Paris early on June 21, he headed for Montmédy, near the border with Luxembourg; there he would rally loyal forces to crush the Revolution, which he unequivocally denounced in a document left behind in the Tuileries. The closeness of the frontier would, if necessary, facilitate foreign assistance or, in the last resort, provide a handy refuge. This move was a veritable declaration of war against the Revolution by the king. The subsequent arrest and suspension of Louis XVI, together with the requirement of a new oath of allegiance that made no mention of the king, put army officers' loyalty to the ultimate test.

The significance of the flight to Varennes for the French officer corps was paramount. Of 13,875 officers serving in the line army in 1789 and early 1790, 2,879 left the service prior to June 21, 1791, and most of those departures (2,007) were the result of death, retirement, and especially the reorganization of the army in early 1791.[20] Only 872 departures since mid-July 1789—by officers who resigned, failed to return from leave, or simply decamped—could possibly be attributed to political motives; this figure accounted for less than 6.5 percent of all officers. During the ten months between the flight to Varennes and the declaration of war on April 20, 1792, more than 3,800 additional officers (over and above the "normal" departures because of death or retirement) would abandon their posts. The enforcement of the new oath of loyalty, omitting the king's name, caused hundreds of officers to leave the service; around 1,500 officers refused to take the new oath in the weeks following the king's attempted flight. For some regiments this meant the loss of a third, half, or even more of their complement of officers, often within the space of a few days.

Again, the overall impact of the crisis was somewhat less severe in the units that had served under Rochambeau in America than in the army generally, and it varied considerably from regiment to regiment. No evidence exists of any significant reaction to these developments in the Auxonne (6th) Artillery, which continued unshaken in the midst of revolution. More remarkable is the response of the Royal Deux-Ponts (99th) Infantry. Despite its previous disciplinary problems, the regiment survived the crisis precipitated by the king's flight without serious difficulty.[21] Although the Lauzun (6th) Hussars had been deeply involved in the events of June 21–22 and discipline had broken down in those contingents at Varennes, the officers quickly restored their authority. Three officers were chased off by the hussars, and at least two others emigrated in the immediate aftermath of Varennes, but there were no lingering effects.[22] In the Regiment of Bourbonnais (13th) Infantry, the reaction was, on the whole, moderate: Five officers resigned between July 1 and August 6, and four officers did not return when their authorized leaves expired.[23] In the Soissonnais (40th) Infantry, six of the remaining thirty officers who had served in America emigrated shortly after the Varennes incident, and a number of others refused to take the new oath.[24] The officers of the Saintonge (82nd) Infantry reacted the most strongly to the events of June 1791: Twenty-one officers—more than a third of the sixty authorized officers—resigned or deserted their posts between June 29 and July 8; thirteen officer-veterans of the American war emigrated.[25]

Some American veterans were outspoken in their outrage over the treatment of their sovereign and commander in chief. Lieutenant Jean Marie Le

DISINTEGRATION AND PARTIAL RECOVERY

Météier de Kerdaniel, who had been a nineteen-year-old cadet in the Regiment of Saintonge when it sailed for the United States in 1780, resigned his commission in early July 1791, refusing to swear an oath "that made no mention of the king." Denis Jean Florimond de Langlois, marquis du Bouchet, served in the American army in 1777 and 1778, distinguishing himself at the Battle of Saratoga, and was on Rochambeau's staff from 1780 to 1782. On August 7, 1791, just four months after his promotion to colonel, he sent his resignation to the minister of war, saying he would resume his functions only when the king was free. Joseph de Bonnefon, who had been a sublieutenant in the Regiment of Soissonnais during its service in America, published a letter in the *Gazette de Paris* on July 26, 1791, offering himself as a hostage in place of the king. All three officers soon joined the émigré army of Louis Joseph Henri, prince de Condé.[26]

The most extreme response by army officers to the Varennes episode came in December 1791 and involved American veterans. Joseph Hyacinthe, comte de Vioménil, a major general on Rochambeau's staff in the United States, had emigrated the week before Louis XVI's ill-fated flight and subsequently planned to have the citadel of Strasbourg handed over to the émigrés. Toward this end, an agent of his contacted officers in units stationed in that important frontier garrison, among them Captain Zacharie Jean de Corn du Peyroux and Lieutenant Hyacinthe Joseph de Silly of the Bourbonnais (13th) Infantry. Both had served in America from 1780 to 1783; both had older brothers who were officers in the same regiment and who had recently emigrated (in August and November 1791); both were implicated in the émigré plot and were arrested in mid-December. Corn du Peyroux was released for lack of evidence and soon thereafter emigrated and joined his brother in Condé's army. Silly was jailed and was later among the prisoners massacred at Versailles on September 9, 1792.[27]

Such conduct by officers, which ranged from resigning one's commission to plotting the overthrow of the existing government, justified and increased popular hostility toward the officer corps as a whole. For the soldiers in many regiments, this was the final proof that their aristocratic officers were unfit to command, and insubordination spread and intensified. Some units drove off all or nearly all of the officers, and the enlisted men—especially the noncommissioned officers—assumed command. Nearly a third of the regiments in the line army experienced some form of insubordination in 1791, particularly during the second half of the year, and 90 percent of such incidents involved direct confrontations between officers and men. The further collapse of discipline motivated more officers to leave their units and emigrate, thus perpetuating the cycle of mistrust and alienation.[28]

157

As these examples demonstrate, the "American" regiments did not escape the turmoil unscathed; yet, they were less severely disorganized by the problems than much of the Royal Army. In part, this resulted from the fact that until 1792, officers who had served under Rochambeau in America were less likely to abandon their posts than were their fellow officers. Young officers and members of the court aristocracy left the army more quickly and in greater numbers than other groups. Most of the American veterans were from the provincial "nobility of the sword." By 1791 the majority were middle-aged or older and had been in the army for their entire adult life. They had a substantial stake in their military careers, as well as family responsibilities and economic interests in France. In addition, these officers sometimes felt a genuine attachment to their regiments and their men.[29]

Some of the resignations and departures by officers in the second half of 1791 were not politically motivated. For example, the chevalier de La Valette, who had gone to America as the lieutenant colonel of the Regiment of Saintonge and been promoted to brigadier for his conduct at Yorktown, resigned his position (major general in the 14th military division) in late November 1791 at age sixty and after forty-five years of service. He began to draw his pension fourteen months later and was still living in retirement in 1799.[30] Similarly, Claude Bernard Loppin, marquis de Montmort, an aide de camp to the baron de Vioménil in the United States, also left the army at about the same time as La Valette without emigrating.[31] The number of retirements and applications for retirement increased substantially during this period, probably the consequence of the more generous regulations that went into effect in August 1790; indeed, military pensions may have enticed some officers to retire but discouraged them from emigrating.[32]

Furthermore, whereas the defection of so many officers in so short a time is impressive, one must remember that more than half of the officer corps of the Old Regime was still serving at the end of 1791. Almost all of the deputies of the National Assembly who had served in Rochambeau's expedition—for example, Custine, Noailles, and Charles and Alexandre Lameth—took the new oath without difficulty, as did Rochambeau himself.[33] Some officers who had been early and enthusiastic supporters of the Revolution welcomed the new state of affairs. In 1789 Captain Charles Edward Jennings Kilmaine, who had made the American campaigns in Lauzun's Legion and later served in the hussar regiment that succeeded it, told the men in his command that it was their duty to fight foreign enemies "but never to draw their sabers against their fellow citizens in order to serve the schemes of despotism." He denounced Bouillé's role in the flight to Varennes and was the first in his regiment to swear the new oath of allegiance.[34]

DISINTEGRATION AND PARTIAL RECOVERY

The severity of the problems experienced by the French army in 1791 should be neither minimized nor exaggerated. Just as the military establishment in France was reaching its nadir, the first indications of revival appeared. The king's attempted flight clearly posed the danger of war, both internal and foreign. An immediate response of the National Assembly had been to prepare for such an eventuality; within a month of the king's apprehension the deputies had voted to raise an army of a hundred thousand volunteers from local National Guard units throughout the country to be organized, equipped, and supported completely apart from the line army. About a third of the captains and lieutenants and half of the higher-ranking officers had previously served as regulars.[35]

The battalions of "national volunteers" offered some American veterans the opportunity for a second military career, one in which their chances for advancement were much better than those in the regiments of the Old Regime. Bernard La Fage was born on January 6, 1734, in the village of Saint-Ybars in the region that became the department of the Ariège. Less than two weeks before his eighteenth birthday he enlisted in the Regiment of Saintonge. In May 1768 he was appointed regimental quartermaster and eight years later received the rank of lieutenant; in this capacity he made the campaigns of 1780–1783 in America. He retired with the rank of captain in February 1785 after thirty-four years of service. When the 2nd Battalion of the Ariège was formed at the beginning of 1792, La Fage was named its lieutenant colonel in second. A comrade in the same regiment and a native of Les Bordes-sur-Arize, less than twenty kilometers from Saint-Ybars, Jacques Gardel, served as a noncommissioned officer in the United States and was wounded at Yorktown. He was not commissioned as a sublieutenant until three years before his retirement in spring 1789. Gardel commanded the National Guard contingent of his village from August 1789 until he became a captain in the 1st Battalion of the Ariège in January 1792. He was promoted to commanding officer of the unit in May 1793 and was wounded in combat four months later.[36]

It was not only officers of fortune like La Fage and Gardel, who had been commissioned only after long service in the enlisted ranks, who joined the volunteers in 1791. Jacques François Sibaud, who was a sublieutenant in Lauzun's Legion during its stay in the United States and was discharged when the unit was reorganized in 1783, was chosen captain in the 1st Battalion of the Jura in August 1791 and was promoted to lieutenant colonel two months later. Marie Athanase Riffault Duplessis, an aristocrat from the province of Maine, served more than twenty-five years as an officer in the Regiment of Bourbonnais before his retirement as a captain in April 1787.

When the 1st Battalion of the Sarthe was formed during summer 1791, he became its commanding officer. Another noble, Sextius Alexandre François Miollis, from Aix-en-Provence, joined the Soissonnais Infantry at age nineteen in 1778 and made the American campaigns with that unit as a sublieutenant and lieutenant, sustaining a serious wound at the battle of Yorktown. He was discharged with the rank of captain during the reorganization of the army in early 1791. When the 3rd Battalion of the Bouches-du-Rhône was raised a year later, Miollis became its lieutenant colonel. He continued his military service throughout the Revolution, rising to the grade of general of division in 1799, and did not retire from active duty until after the fall of Napoleon in 1815.[37]

Led by such experienced military men, the enthusiastic volunteers of 1791 were rapidly transformed into a reliable fighting force. At the same time, an attempt was begun to reverse the deteriorating situation that had been developing in the regular army during the prior two years. The assembly had viewed the line army as the nation's primary defense against foreign enemies; the national volunteers were never considered a replacement for the army but only a supplement to it. As a result of government efforts—for example, improving the conditions of military service, increasing pay, reforming recruitment practices, and raising the authorized complement of all regiments—more than 50,000 men enlisted in the regular army during 1791, thereby compensating for the huge losses from desertions, discharges, and mutinies since 1789.[38] The regiments that had constituted Rochambeau's corps a decade earlier reflected those gains.[39] The four infantry regiments recruited between 376 men (Saintonge) and 518 men (Soissonnais) and averaged more than 450 new recruits for the year. Even when the substantial losses during the period are taken into consideration, the net gains amounted to over 220 men per regiment. The gains in the cavalry and artillery units were less impressive only because they were smaller regiments to begin with. By the end of 1791, five of those regiments enjoyed greater strength than at any time since 1788; only the Deux-Ponts (99th) Infantry had fewer enlisted men—a mere twenty-three fewer.

To be sure, the true strength of the line army and the regiments that composed it depended on more than just the number of soldiers in the ranks. Indeed, the most striking military phenomenon of 1791 was the wholesale departure of much of the existing leadership. Unless the officer vacancies were filled quickly and competently, the army would soon lose its effectiveness. In September 1790 the assembly had established new regulations regarding the commissioning and promotion of officers that established more rational criteria, primarily examinations and seniority. In November 1791 the mass exodus of hundreds of officers during the previous five months forced the government to abandon examinations and to rely on prior military experience as the basis for selecting new officers. Even before this latest policy could be fully implemented, the number of officers drawn from the ranks of the NCOs had increased substantially—around eight hundred during 1791 alone. Like the officers of fortune under the Old Regime, these men had accumulated a large store of military experience and skill during years, often decades, of service; they had made a commitment to a military career; they were thoroughly familiar with the soldiers under their orders; and they owed their current position and hopes of future advancement to the changes introduced by the Revolution.[40]

During 1791 a score of NCOs in the "American" regiments were commissioned as officers—nearly three times as many as in the previous five years combined.[41] For example, Jacques Mitier, a native of Nîmes, enlisted in the Regiment of Saintonge at age twenty in March 1768; he was promoted to corporal in 1775, sergeant the following year, and sergeant major in 1787 after his return from the American war. He became a sublieutenant on September 19, 1791. That same day Etienne Ferrier of the same regiment was also commissioned. His career closely paralleled Mitier's. He was the same age when he enlisted in 1770 and became a corporal in 1777, sergeant in 1778, and sergeant major only months before his promotion to sublieutenant. Pierre Lauliot from rural Picardy was somewhat older than Mitier and Ferrier—fifty-five—when he was promoted from the ranks in August 1791, and he had risen through the same grades during his twenty-seven years of service.[42] Henry Scherrer from the duchy of Deux-Ponts had even more seniority when he was commissioned on September 5, 1791; he had enlisted thirty years earlier when he was twenty-two and had reached the rank of sergeant major while serving with the Regiment of Deux-Ponts in the United States. It took another decade of service and a revolution before he became an officer. Although he was twenty years younger and had served only half as long, Philippe Wolff was commissioned just ten days after Scherrer. Wolff was a seventeen-year-old from rural Alsace when he joined the same regiment in May 1776. He was promoted to corporal eight years later, possibly as a reward for reenlisting, and within six years had become a sergeant major.[43]

These men were fairly representative of the hundreds of their comrades in the line army who helped to fill the huge gaps in the officer corps created by the resignations and emigration of so many prerevolutionary officers. They had proven their ability through many years of service, including the rigors of combat, yet most were still young enough to provide vigorous leadership. In short, they were professional soldiers. In contrast to most of the aristocratic officers whom they replaced, they enjoyed the confidence—if not the affection—of their subordinates, alongside whom they had so recently served. The promotion of such men to positions of authority, together with the influx of tens of thousands of fresh recruits, provided striking evidence that in spite of its immense difficulties, the line army possessed considerable vitality in 1791.

Fortunately for the survival of the new regime, these vital signs continued to grow in 1792. The flight to Varennes had markedly increased the danger of war. Opponents of the Revolution within and outside France came to see war as the only hope of preserving the monarchy and overthrowing its enemies. Supporters of the Revolution concluded that war was inevitable if revolutionary France were to survive in the midst of a hostile Europe. A number of French leaders, including Louis XVI, began to view war as the means of resolving their political problems.[44] If—or, more likely, when—hostilities commenced, the line army would play a critical role.

Notes

1. On the overall situation see Scott, *Response of the Royal Army*, pp. 97–114 and 136–161.
2. Statistics for the whole army in 1791 are from Scott, "Regeneration of the Line Army," p. 311, and for the "American" regiments from the regimental contrôles.
3. See the report of the royal commissioners, dated Aix, April 21, 1791, in A.N., F^7 3659^1, and the January 23, 1791, issue of the *Journal Militaire*, cited in Martin, *Origines de la presse militaire*, p. 141.
4. A.G., 14 YC 58; and Bodinier, *Officiers*, p. 474.
5. Actually, according to the inspection report of September 12, 1789, only a bare majority—562 of 1,123 men—were foreigners, whereas 458 soldiers were from Alsace and 103 were from "German" Lorraine. See A.G., X^b 104.
6. A.G. 14 YC 144; and information provided by Robert Selig.
7. Scott, *Response of the Royal Army*, pp. 154–155.
8. Inspection report of December 14, 1791, in A.G., X^b 196.
9. On Varennes and especially the role of Lauzun's Hussars, see Michel de Lombarès, "Varennes ou la fin d'un régime (21 juin 1791)," *Revue historique de l'armée*, nos. 3 and 4 (1960): 33–56 and 45–62, and no. 1 (1961): 23–36; François Claude Amour, marquis de Bouillé, *Mémoires du Marquis de Bouillé* (Paris: Baudouin, 1821), pp. 410–412 and 243–244; and the letter of Colonel de Pestalozzi to commissioners of the National Assembly, dated July 3, 1791, in A.G., X^c 245.
10. The general situation of the officer corps before and after the flight to Varennes is summarized briefly in my *Response of the Royal Army*, pp. 103 and 106; also see Capitaine Gilbert Bodinier, "Les Officiers de l'armée royal et la Révolution,"

DISINTEGRATION AND PARTIAL RECOVERY

in *Le Métier militaire en France aux époques de grandes transformations sociales* (Vincennes: Service Historique de l'Armée de Terre, 1980), p. 63.
11. Cited in Martin, *Origines de la presse militaire*, pp. 118–119 and 130; the quotation is on p. 119.
12. See his letter, dated Amiens, February 16, 1791, in A.G., B^{1*} 208. The more general hostility of officers toward soldiers' attendance at political clubs is described in Bodinier, *Officiers*, p. 438.
13. Jacques Godechot, *The Counter-Revolution: Doctrine and Action, 1789–1804*, trans. Salvator Attanasio (Princeton: Princeton University Press, 1981), p. 143.
14. Bodinier, *Dictionnaire*, p. 405.
15. Ibid., p. 339; Lasseray, *Français sous treize étoiles*, vol. 1, pp. 304–307; Balch, *French in America*, vol. 2, pp. 176–178; Gardiner, *Cincinnati in France*, p. 163; and Ségur, *Mémoires*, vol. 1, pp. 378–379.
16. Bodinier, *Dictionnaire*, p. 141, and Bodinier, "Comportement des officiers," p. 111.
17. For a brief account of this episode and its significance for the army, see Scott, *Response of the Royal Army*, pp. 103–108.
18. Bodinier, *Dictionnaire*, pp. 136–137. The names of regular army regiments, reflections of the Old Regime, were officially changed to numerical designations in January 1791.
19. Ibid., p. 121; Gardiner, *Cincinnati in France*, pp. 86–87; Balch, *French in America*, vol. 2, pp. 92–93; and Jean Pinasseau, *L'Emigration militaire. Campagne de 1792. Armée royale. Composition. Ordres de Bataille*, vol. 2 (Paris: Picard, 1964), pp. 9–10.
20. These and subsequent data on the officer corps of the Old Regime are from Bodinier's remarkably comprehensive study, "Officiers de l'armée royale et la Revolution," pp. 59–77.
21. See Bodinier, "Officiers de Rochambeau," p. 147.
22. See the reports dated Saint-Avold, August 10, 1791, and January 7, 1792, in A.G., X^c 245.
23. Report dated September 15, 1791, in A.G., X^b 166.
24. Bodinier, "Officiers de Rochambeau," p. 147. It is not clear exactly how many rejected the loyalty oath.
25. Ibid.; and A.G., X^b 190.
26. Bodinier, *Officiers*, p. 441; for individual biographies, see the same author's *Dictionnaire*, pp. 306, 284–285, and 59.
27. Bodinier, *Officiers*, p. 434, and Bodinier, *Dictionnaire*, pp. 108–109 and 438–439.
28. Scott, *Response of the Royal Army*, pp. 106–111.
29. Bodinier, *Officiers*, pp. 494–496 and 502.
30. Gardiner, *Cincinnati in France*, pp. 94–95; and Bodinier, *Dictionnaire*, p. 92.
31. Gardiner, *Cincinnati in France*, pp. 102–103; and Bodinier, *Dictionnaire*, p. 321.
32. See Woloch, *French Veteran*, p. 88, on this point.
33. Bodinier, "Comportement des officiers," p. 115.
34. Bodinier, *Officiers*, p. 408.
35. A handy summary of the "national volunteers" of 1791 can be found in Jean-Paul Bertaud, *The Army of the French Revolution: From Citizen-Soldiers to Instrument of Power*, trans. R. R. Palmer (Princeton: Princeton University Press, 1988), pp. 49–58.

36. See the proposals for promotion for these two men (September 1783) in A.G., X^b 91, and the entries in Bodinier, *Dictionnaire*, pp. 272 and 212.
37. See Bodinier, *Dictionnaire*, pp. 436–437, 405, and 346.
38. For the general situation in the army, see my "Regeneration of the Line Army," pp. 319–323, and *Response of the Royal Army*, pp. 151–159.
39. The following statistics are based on an examination of the individual entries in the regimental registers.
40. Scott, *Response of the Royal Army*, pp. 153–154, 161, and 113–114.
41. Based on notations in their unit contrôles.
42. See the entries for these men in A.G., 14 YC 119.
43. See A.G., 14 YC 144.
44. This issue is far too complex to discuss adequately here. A recent useful approach to the subject is T.C.W. Blanning, *The Origins of the French Revolutionary Wars* (New York: Longman, 1986).

10
WAR AND THE
TRANSFORMATION OF THE ARMY

THE ISSUE OF WAR became a major preoccupation of the Legislative Assembly when it replaced the National Assembly at the beginning of October 1791. This body, elected the previous month under the terms of the new constitution, included five representatives who had served as officers under Rochambeau in the United States: Mathieu Dumas, an aide de camp with the rank of captain in 1780 and a major general in 1791; Claude Blanchard, a commissary officer who had also been on Rochambeau's staff; Captain Jean Baptiste Aubert du Bayet, a second lieutenant in the Regiment of Bourbonnais during the American campaigns; Henry Crubilier d'Opterre who had been a captain of engineers since 1770 and was finally promoted two months after his election as a deputy; and Claude Etienne Hugau, an officer of fortune who had been a lieutenant colonel in Lauzun's Legion and retired from the army at the same rank in March 1789.

In most respects these men little resembled their illustrious predecessors in the National Assembly. Hugau was the son of a domestic servant, Crubilier d'Opterre came from a bourgeois background, Dumas and Blanchard were nobles of recent vintage, and Aubert du Bayet was from an undistinguished family of the nobility of the sword. None could boast the lineage of a Noailles, Biron, Castries, Broglie, or Custine. Nor did they play a prominent role in the new legislature. They were political moderates and, for the most part, limited their official concerns to military affairs.[1]

As the likelihood of war grew in late 1791 and early 1792, issues affecting the army were of paramount importance to the new government. Essentially, the Legislative Assembly continued and expanded policies initiated by the National Assembly. In January 1792 it took measures to bring line units up to full wartime strength by extending the age limit for recruits to fifty, lowering the minimum height requirements, reducing the length of enlistment to three years, and guaranteeing bonuses to recruits. After declaring war on Austria on April 20, 1792, the assembly made even greater efforts. On July 22 it passed legislation calling for an additional fifty thousand recruits for the regular army and, for the first time, imposed a quota on each department for a minimum number of men. Meanwhile, other measures in May and early July were aimed at raising more than one hundred thousand new national volunteers in 1792.[2]

The results in the line army were impressive: More than seventy thousand men were enrolled during the year. Rochambeau's "American" regiments reflected this influx of recruits: The Bourbonnais (13th) Infantry enlisted 540 men in 1792, the Auxonne (6th) Artillery 477, and the Saintonge (82nd) Infantry 459. The Soissonnais (40th) Infantry recruited 383 men between the beginning of the year and mid-May. Even the regiments with fewer enlistments gained a substantial number of recruits: 310 in the Deux-Ponts (99th) Infantry and 79 in the Lauzun (6th) Hussars. Because of peculiar circumstances, however, only two regiments—Bourbonnais and Auxonne—enjoyed net gains for the year, more than 300 men in each case.[3]

The 82nd Infantry (formerly Saintonge) was the most immediately and dramatically affected by the war. On December 2, 1792, the personnel of the second battalion, consisting of 563 enlisted men (59 of whom were American veterans) and two dozen officers, were killed or made prisoners of war when the French garrison of Frankfurt surrendered to the enemy. A few officers and about 40 soldiers were exchanged in 1793 and another score or so in late October 1794. Most of those who returned to France on parole expressed a willingness to resume their duties, despite their oath.[4] For example, Gilles François Dupont, who had served as a noncommissioned officer in America and was a captain at the time of his capture, returned to France in May 1793 and shortly afterward joined his assigned unit. Another officer of fortune who served in the regimental depot during the American war, Captain Pierre des Vignes, was not repatriated but died in captivity in June 1794. Two brothers, Lieutenant Colonel Gilles du Rosel and Captain Louis du Rosel, who had gone to America in 1780 as lieutenants in the Regiment of Saintonge, were not released until July 1795 after nearly thirty-two months as prisoners of war.[5]

The fate of the former Regiment of Saintonge in 1792 was unique among the units that had formed Rochambeau's expeditionary corps. The problems that ravaged the other five regiments that year were primarily caused by conditions within the units rather than the war. For in 1792, somewhat belatedly, all of these regiments felt the full effects of divisions that had split apart most of the line army earlier.

Tensions between soldiers and officers had been building in the Soissonnais (40th) Infantry for a year or more when the situation reached a crisis in early 1792. During that February nearly all the remaining officers in the regiment left their posts; by the end of the month only five were left— a captain, two lieutenants, and two sublieutenants. The ostensible reason for the officers' exodus was the insubordination of their men, who refused to obey orders and forced the release of one of their comrades imprisoned for military offenses. The soldiers were supported by the local Jacobin club and the populace of Grenoble where the regiment was stationed.[6]

Yet, political motives also appear to have influenced the officers' decision. Most, including thirty-two American veterans, immediately emigrated. Within six weeks of abandoning his regiment, Captain Joseph de Bonnefon, who had served as a sublieutenant in America, published a letter in a royalist newspaper in Paris appealing to other officers to join him in Condé's army "to annihilate this hundred-headed hydra that has been devouring France for three years."[7] Soon, the regiment was in chaos. Desertions, which totaled fifty-five in January and February, continued and probably increased. Exactly what went on during the following months cannot be fully determined because on May 13, 1792, all entries in the regimental register ceased for nearly a year. There is perhaps no more convincing evidence of the plight of the unit than that unprecedented development![8]

Similar tensions were festering in other units, and the outbreak of war released them. Between April 21 and August 10, 1792, nearly eleven hundred officers left the army. By the latter date, close to three-fourths of the prerevolutionary officer corps was gone, a majority for political reasons.[9] Even the most disciplined regiments, such as the Auxonne (6th) Artillery, were affected as the war forced officers to choose sides. Between April 26 and May 6, fifteen officers of the unit "quit their colors," and by May 24 the regiment had thirty-one officer vacancies.[10] Otherwise, the unit kept good discipline. Only fourteen men deserted in the course of the year. When one of the officers, Captain Nicolas Barthélémy, attempted to convince his men to desert with him, they shot him.[11]

In the Bourbonnais (13th) Infantry, which had also remained orderly since massive discharges for disciplinary reasons in 1789–1790, serious problems arose in spring 1792 while the regiment was garrisoned at Neuf-Brisach, Alsace. Within two weeks of the declaration of war, a number of officers abandoned their posts, and by May 8 a dozen, including the colonel in command of the regiment, had emigrated.[12] This exodus contributed to growing suspicions about the remaining officers. On June 4 soldiers of the 13th Infantry halted two wagons on their way from Strasbourg to Basel and began to search them. Captain Louis François d'Arlande de Salton, who had served as an officer in the American war and had managed to escape from the wreck of the *Bourgogne*, and the mayor of Neuf-Brisach ordered the men to stop the search and release the drivers. Meanwhile, the soldiers discovered that the wagons contained weapons, which they believed were being shipped to émigré forces; they arrested Captain d'Arlande and the mayor as accomplices and later threatened their lives. General Victor de Broglie—who had also served in the American expedition and had commanded the Regiment of Bourbonnais from 1783 to 1788—accompanied by a departmental official, arrived within forty-eight hours and ordered the soldiers to release the prisoners and wagons. At first the soldiers—most from the grenadier company—resisted, but through persuasion and the threat of force the general, who had called out a detachment of *chasseurs*, managed to impose his will.

As was typical of such incidents, the repercussions continued. Broglie immediately ordered the transfer of the grenadier company to Strasbourg, away from the scene of the confrontation. On June 9 seven soldiers (six of them grenadiers) were arrested as ringleaders and quickly tried by court-martial in Strasbourg.[13] On June 17, 1792, all seven were sentenced to a year in irons for disobedience; among them was Corporal Jacques Remy, a native of Franche-Comté who had spent more than half of his thirty-four years in the regiment, including two and a half years in the United States.[14] Such disciplinary measures were insufficient to prevent the resignations of Lieutenant Colonels Jean Jacques de Hiton and Jacques Joseph de La Brue, both of whom had been captains in Rochambeau's American corps and both of whom soon joined the army of Louis Joseph Henri, prince de Condé.[15] The cycle of distrust, emigration, and yet more distrust persisted, as it did throughout the army.

The outbreak of war against Austria and Prussia, which involved most of the other German states as well, also affected conditions in the Deux-Ponts (99th) Infantry. On May 27 the officers of the unit emigrated en masse; as a result, only five of the seventy officers who had fought in the American war were left in the regiment.[16] Although replacements were gradually made, discipline continued to deteriorate. Of Rochambeau's "American" units, this one suffered the most heavily from desertions during 1792, losing 222 men—more than a third in December.[17] Although most of the last desertions coincided with an imperial decree of December 19, 1792, ordering all subjects of the Holy Roman Emperor in the service of France to return home or be considered traitors to the Empire, it is unlikely that this order was solely or even primarily responsible for the exodus. First, one must consider the serious difficulty of communicating such a document to troops in an enemy army at the time. In addition, elements of the regiment were continually involved in fighting from autumn 1792 to spring 1793, including the battles of Valmy (September 20), Jemappes (November 6), and Neerwinden (March 18).[18] This situation also helps to explain the high desertion rate, since combat and its aftermath often provided both the occasion and the motivation for increased desertions.

It should probably come as no surprise that of the units that had made the American campaigns under Rochambeau, the Lauzun (6th) Hussars exhibited the most extreme response to the crisis created by the war in 1792. In June a dozen officers resigned and emigrated; an equal number of enlisted men, including three American veterans, "deserted to the enemy" at the same time.[19] Three other officers abandoned their posts in July and nine more in August (five on August 4 and four on August 21). During August seventy hussars (seven of them veterans of the American war) joined their officers in defecting to the enemy. The regiment was completely disorganized; it had lost its colonel, two lieutenant colonels, all but one of its captains, half of its lieutenants and sublieutenants, the regimental surgeon and chaplain, and the quartermaster-treasurer within less than three months. The emigration of this last officer, who had the primary administrative duties in the regiment, was especially striking. Henry Sirjacques, the son of a butcher from Lorraine, had worked his way through the ranks, had received his commission shortly before departing for America in 1780, and was promoted to captain eight years later. Captured with the regimental depot when Longwy surrendered on August 23, 1792, Sirjacques handed his regiment's funds, supplies, and records over to the enemy before he joined the émigré army of the princes.[20] The 6th (Lauzun) Hussars had to be reconstituted.

Events of 1792 had devastating results for the "American" regiments. On the whole, the effects were similar to developments that had occurred elsewhere in the regular army; they simply came somewhat later. The war and the revolutionary response to it were transforming the French army.

The most important political consequence of the war was the overthrow of the monarchy on August 10, 1792. Although domestic conditions undoubtedly contributed, the war precipitated the action. Within the army the general reaction was moderate, since by that late date most personnel who felt continued military service compromised their principles had already left the army.[21] For instance, the 40th (Soissonnais) Infantry—so recently the scene of the most bitter divisions—received the news of this event with "perfect calm," as did the rest of the Army of the Midi of which it was a part.[22]

There were, of course, examples of opposition to the violent dethronement of Louis XVI. Some American veterans risked their lives defending the king during the attack on the Tuileries Palace. Rochambeau's second in command of the American expedition, the baron de Vioménil, was mortally wounded in the fighting and died October 31. One of Vioménil's aides de camp in the United States, Louis Pierre de Quentin de Richebourg de Champcenetz, a major general and governor of the Tuileries in 1792, was also wounded, although he managed to escape. Captain Joseph François Dalmas de Pracontel, who had served in the Auxonne Artillery in America, and Captain Jean Baptiste Coriolis d'Epinousse, a noble of the robe from Aix-en-Provence who had been a lieutenant in the Regiment of Bourbonnais during its tour of duty in the United States, also participated in the defense of the Tuileries; both survived unscathed.[23]

The most famous opponent of the August 10 revolution was the marquis de Lafayette who, after failing to rouse his army against Paris, emigrated with most of his staff, including Generals Alexandre de Lameth and Gabriel de Riccé—both of whom had been captains on Rochambeau's general staff in America. Other officers resigned their commissions in the aftermath of August 10: Among them were Lieutenant Colonel Jean Aymard Josserand du Fort, formerly of the Auxonne Artillery; Colonel Louis Henry de Beffroy, who had been a captain in Lauzun's Legion; and Lieutenant Colonel François Xavier de Hell from the same unit. Aside from the officers who accompanied Lafayette, however, only a score of officers voluntarily left their posts between August 10 and the end of the year; from that time on it became more common for officers to be removed from their positions. General Mathieu Dumas, former aide de camp of Rochambeau and deputy to the Legislative Assembly, was proscribed soon after August 10; General Charles de Lameth was arrested on August 16 for his condemnation of the uprising; and General Louis Alexandre Berthier was dismissed on August 21, although nine months later he enlisted in the army as a volunteer. Lieutenant Colonel Gabriel de Queyssat, who had served in both the American army and Rochambeau's expeditionary corps, was suspended from his functions before August 10 because of his connections with Lafayette.[24] Political reliability became essential for military commanders.

On November 19, 1792, agents of the National Convention, which had replaced the Legislative Assembly and declared France a republic in September, dismissed Captain Charles Marie Bessonies de Saint-Hilaire, although he was one of the handful of officers in the 40th (Soissonnais)

Infantry who had not emigrated. This veteran of the American Revolution was subsequently arrested and spent eighteen months in prison. Nearly three years later, the men of his regiment opposed his reinstatement, alleging his commitment to royalism. This case, however, was unusual. Few company-grade officers (captains or lieutenants) were purged in 1792,[25] in part because the government was much more concerned with the loyalty of higher-ranking officers and in part because most of the unreliable officers had already departed. Of the nearly five hundred officers who had served in Rochambeau's American command, only eighty to ninety remained on active duty by the end of 1792.[26]

As the importance of this group of officers was declining, the role of another group was increasing: the so-called officers of fortune, rankers for whom the French Revolution opened unprecedented opportunities for promotion. In the decade before 1789, the six regiments that had constituted Rochambeau's army in America averaged three promotions from the ranks each year, or one every two years in each regiment.[27] For the first twenty-four months of the French Revolution, this figure did not change substantially. The mass departure of officers set off by Louis XVI's attempted flight was what created hundreds and then thousands of vacancies after June 1791, and the policies of the revolutionary government ensured the promotion of former enlisted men to fill most of them. During 1792 at least twenty-two hundred experienced soldiers—mostly NCOs—were commissioned as officers.[28] Meanwhile, officers who had already been promoted from the ranks were rapidly advancing to higher grades.

During 1792 more than 140 men were commissioned from the ranks of the six "American" regiments, about two-thirds of whom had been participants in the American war.[29] Three of the infantry regiments and the 6th (Lauzun) Hussars averaged twenty-two new officers that year. In the 6th (Auxonne) Artillery, which increased its enlisted strength by more than one-third during the period, fifty-one soldiers were promoted to officer. These new officers varied in age between twenty-nine and sixty and had from twelve to thirty-four years of service when they were commissioned; on average, they were slightly more than forty years of age and had just over twenty-one years of service. By most practical measures they were professional soldiers. For some, military service was as much their heritage as it was for any noble of the sword. Antoine Guichard, for example, was an *enfant du corps* admitted to pay at age thirteen in the Regiment of Soissonnais. He served in America alongside his father, who was also a soldier's son. Antoine was promoted to lieutenant in April 1791 and to captain the following March, just six months after his father had been promoted to the same rank. On

December 26, 1793, the thirty-five-year-old captain was killed in combat—a month after his father's retirement.[30]

Although a few rankers like Captain Sirjacques and Lieutenant Martin Pichon, both veterans of Lauzun's Legion, emigrated, most officers of fortune—or "officers of talent," as they became known after 1789—supported the Revolution, which offered them previously unthinkable career advancement.[31] A few went beyond their professional commitment and became ardent partisans of the revolutionary cause. Charles Martraire, a second-generation soldier, was commissioned a lieutenant in third in the Auxonne Artillery two years before his battalion went to the United States. It had taken him nearly twenty-one years of service to reach that rank; between September 1792 and April 1794 he was promoted three times, the last to chef de brigade, or colonel. Is it any wonder that in the year IV (1795–1796) he was described as "sometimes excessive in his revolutionary principles"?[32] René Nicolas Le Monier had over seventeen years of service when he was commissioned a sublieutenant in the Regiment of Saintonge in 1776. While most of his regiment was in America, Le Monier recruited and trained replacements in France. He received only one more promotion before 1789. The Revolution, however, brought him rapid advancement; by January 1794 he was a general of division. Gunshot and saber wounds, together with other disabilities, soon forced him to retire, and he was admitted to the Invalides in late 1795. There he continued to give evidence of "republican zeal" in his political activity; in 1798 he was denounced as an agitator by the police and forced to leave the Invalides.[33]

These officers and others like them in all regiments were responsible for the survival of the line army during this critical period. Their long experience allowed them to assume the functions of their former superiors with a minimum of disruption. They were familiar with their subordinates, who, in turn, trusted them. They were devoted to the new regime by personal ambition if not political principles. Finally, these men, whose primary functions as NCOs had been to train and discipline soldiers in their regiments, were well equipped to deal with the large influx of raw recruits into their units in 1792 and 1793.

On February 24, 1793, to strengthen its armed forces, the National Convention decreed a levy of three hundred thousand men, including quotas for the departments based on population and previous contributions of manpower.[34] Local authorities were responsible for raising the required number of recruits by whatever means they thought most appropriate. The levy was met with popular resistance in a number of regions, touching off the most bitter uprising in the department of the Vendée, where opposition to the revolutionary government had long been building. That spring and summer French armies suffered a series of setbacks at the hands of foreign enemies that once again opened the frontiers to invasion. In early April General Charles François Dumouriez attempted unsuccessfully to turn his army against Paris and overthrow the government. Beginning in June federalist revolts against the central government swept large areas of the country and were especially dangerous in the southeast. In response to foreign and domestic threats, the Jacobin government took the unprecedented step of mobilizing all national resources, human and material, and establishing military conscription in the declaration of the *levée en masse* on August 23, 1793.[35]

Earlier, on February 21, the Convention had ordered the amalgamation of line regiments and volunteer battalions, which until then had maintained entirely distinct, even rival, organizations. The keystone of the new organization was to be a new tactical unit, the demi-brigade, composed of two volunteer battalions and one battalion of regulars, around thirty-two hundred men in all. Pressing conditions made it impossible to begin this reorganization until the campaign of 1793 was completed. In fact, it would take from the fall of that year until early 1796 to complete the process, and even then some battalions were never amalgamated, including the first battalion of the 82nd (Saintonge) Infantry. At the same time, the revolutionary government established seniority and election as the bases for most military promotions. Both criteria favored experienced soldiers of the line army, since those who voted were often concerned most with professional expertise.[36]

These massive changes transformed the French army. In the regiments that had fought under Rochambeau in America, the veterans of those campaigns were submerged in a mass of more recent soldiers. The 6th (Auxonne) Artillery reflected this trend. At the end of 1792, only about 80 of the 1,262 men in the regiment were American veterans.[37] Hundreds more recruits continued to pour into the regiment, nine-hundred in the next twelve months. More than a hundred of those who joined the unit in late 1792 and early 1793 had previously served in infantry regiments. They were transferred into the artillery where they could receive the technical training required without having to learn the rudiments of soldiering. A number of other newcomers to the regiment had been soldiers in the Swiss regiments of the French army, which were disbanded shortly after the overthrow of the monarchy on August 10, 1792.[38] To cope with such growth, 35 more enlisted men—16 of whom were American veterans—were commissioned in 1793. By the end of that year, of a total enlisted strength of 1,968, fewer than 60 men had served in the American Revolution. A similar situation prevailed in the 6th (Lauzun) Hussars. By the end of 1792 about 35 American veterans remained among the 532 troops in the regiment. A year later the total strength had grown to 894 men, of whom only a score had served in the United States. During 1794, 3 more American veterans left the ranks (one discharged, one commissioned, and one missing in action), and the regiment swelled to over 1,200 men.

Although this pattern was apparently repeated in the infantry regiments of Rochambeau's American expedition, it is impossible to be precise about this because of a breakdown of record keeping that affected each unit in 1792 and 1793. A number of conditions were responsible for the problem, all of which were related to the war. The large numbers of recruits to be enrolled within a short time caused administrative difficulties. The personnel in charge of the paperwork changed frequently, as men were transferred, promoted, discharged, captured, or killed—a situation that often resulted in a decline in the quality of the records. All four regiments served on the front lines and were frequently engaged in combat. Commonly, the two battalions constituting each line regiment operated independently, were assigned to different field armies, were separated by a hundred kilometers or more, and occasionally were broken down into even smaller detachments. As has been noted, the register of 40th (Soissonnais) Infantry halted abruptly in mid-May 1792. The last new entry in the contrôle of the 13th (Bourbonnais) Infantry was on Christmas Eve the same year. In the register of the 99th (Deux-Ponts) Infantry, no entries were made after April 30, 1793; that of the 82nd (Saintonge) Infantry stopped on September 8, 1793.

Despite lacunae, it is possible to reconstruct the history of those units during these difficult times from other sources.[39] Although new legislation brought large numbers of fresh recruits into the line regiments, the new men were not always acceptable. Between April 5 and May 2, sixty-five men who enrolled in the 6th (Auxonne) Artillery under the terms of the law of January 25, 1792, were discharged as unfit for service: one because he was a foreigner, two who had served sentences as convicts, three who were over sixty years of age, nine who had various infirmities, and the rest because they were too small for the arduous task of handling large artillery pieces.[40] Other regular troops deserted their regiments to enlist in the battalions of volunteers where the conditions of service were more attractive.[41] One such young man, the son of a stonecutter from Poitiers, who enlisted in the 30th (Perche) Infantry in March 1791 at age sixteen, was Philippe René Girault, one of the few line soldiers to record his memoirs. In late 1792, while his regiment was stationed in Lorraine, Girault and some of his comrades enlisted in a volunteer unit, the 6th Battalion of the Haute-Saône, to get higher pay. He well knew what he was doing: "It was a kind of desertion, but such disorder then existed in the army that we were sure of impunity. Besides, we had the officers of this battalion as accomplices."[42]

Less than three months before Girault's unauthorized departure from the 30th Infantry, he had participated in the decisive battle of Valmy on September 20, 1792. This engagement, which saved Paris and the newly elected revolutionary government from imminent capture and possible destruction, brought together elements from three of the six units commanded by Rochambeau in the United States: the first battalion of the 99th (Deux-Ponts) Infantry, the 6th (Lauzun) Hussars, and four companies of the 6th (Auxonne) Artillery. They had last served together under combat conditions eleven years earlier—at Yorktown. Although Private Girault was not a member of any of these units, his account of the battle from the point of view of an ordinary line soldier provides a convincing description of the experience for all troops.[43] He went looking for food before the fighting began, got lost, was stopped by a suspicious officer, and was directed to his unit, which was stationed near "a windmill." He claims to have been inspired by a young general who would become King Louis Philippe in 1830, to have had "my uniform plastered by the brains of an officer who was shot a few steps in front of me," and to have lost his shoes in the deep mud that covered the battlefield. There is a ring of truth about this account of various events, which are recorded as having about equal importance for the young soldier.

The war was obviously responsible for mounting losses, as well as the considerable gains, in combat units' strength. Lauzun's old regiment (redesignated the 5th Hussars in June 1793) had been gradually rejuvenated under the command of Colonels Emmanuel de Grouchy (July–October 1792), Charles Edouard Jennings de Kilmaine (January–March 1793), and Adélaide Blaise de Lagrange (October 1792–October 1793), whereas losses from combat increased. During the first two and a half years of the war, the regiment counted thirty-six men killed in combat, forty-two made prisoners of war, forty-six missing in action, and a dozen or so discharged as unfit for duty because of wounds and other disabilities; among these were a half dozen American veterans.[44] The Auxonne Artillery was continually employed in detachments. For example, at the end of 1793 companies of that regiment were serving with four different field armies (the Moselle, Belgium, the North, and the Rhine); others occupied three separate garrisons in France; and another detachment had just participated in the siege of Lyon, a center of the federalist rebellions. Elements of the unit took part in the battles of Valmy, Jemappes, Neerwinden, Wattignies, and Fleurus, as well as in lesser engagements. Yet, because artillery units were seldom exposed to direct enemy fire, combat casualties were relatively light—a total of thirty-five by the end of 1794, five of whom had fought in the American Revolution.[45]

Although gaps in the records allow a less thorough account of the activities of the four infantry regiments that formed Rochambeau's American expeditionary corps, the general pattern is clear. Like their counterparts in the cavalry and artillery, those units played a role in some of the most important military developments of the period, developments that, in turn, helped to determine the course of the Revolution: the victories, such as Valmy and Jemappes, in the last months of 1792 that saved the Revolution and allowed French armies to occupy foreign territory temporarily; the defeats of spring and summer 1793 that led to the creation of the nation in arms; the hard-won successes that had once more delivered France from foreign invasion by spring 1794; and the emergence of a new kind of army that would allow subsequent regimes to subject much of Europe to French control. The history of those regiments and the men who composed them provides an understanding of these momentous events in concrete, human terms.

The 82nd (Saintonge) Infantry began to reconstruct an entire battalion in 1793, following the surrender of its second battalion at Frankfurt in early December 1792. By July 1793 the regimental depot at Besançon had reached 890 soldiers and 22 officers; thirteen and a half months later the second battalion, then stationed at Landau, had mustered 1,113 officers and men.[46] Meanwhile, the first battalion fought in the Rhineland during the winter of 1792–1793 and in the spring retreated from Germany along with the rest of the French forces of General Custine, who had commanded the regiment in the United States. In August 1793 the first battalion was posted to the Army of the West to combat the rebels of the Vendée. It served in this intense struggle for the next fifteen months and remained a separate unit until it was amalgamated into the 81st Demi-Brigade in 1796.[47]

Both battalions of the 13th (Bourbonnais) Infantry also participated in the French offensive into the Rhineland in the last quarter of 1792 and in the retreat into Alsace that followed in early 1793. In January, at the battle of Hocheim, where the first battalion of the 82nd Infantry also fought, fifty-eight men (one an American veteran) of the 13th Infantry were captured by the enemy.[48] In June 1793, thanks to reinforcements, the regiment comprised more than sixteen hundred men. By early 1794 it was once more part of a French advance into the Rhineland. Just before being amalgamated, in spring 1794 the first battalion was assigned to the Army of the Rhine and the second battalion to the Army of the Ardennes.[49]

WAR AND THE TRANSFORMATION OF THE ARMY

The 40th (Soissonnais) Infantry, which had virtually disintegrated in early 1792, began to recover over the following months; by the end of 1792 and early 1793 it reached a total strength of between 1,400 and 1,500 men. It, too, was employed on the northeastern frontier during that time and in the defense of France that followed. Between April and June 1793, 275 recruits were enrolled in the regiment; they came from fifteen different departments, ranging from the Bas-Rhin in the north to the Bouches-du-Rhône in the south and from the Deux-Sèvres west to the Côte-d'Or in the east. Within a little more than a year, nearly half (129 men) had been lost for various reasons. A half dozen of that group were among the 52 soldiers of the second battalion of the regiment killed in combat between August 20 and December 26, 1793. The first battalion suffered more severe losses; it was part of the garrison of Fort Louis that surrendered to the Austrians in mid-November 1793. Although some of its officers and men escaped, the bulk of the battalion was marched to prison camps in Hungary where the men remained until the end of 1796.[50] Among those captured was Jean Le Brun, a thirty-nine-year-old native of Saint-Lô in Normandy with twenty years of service (including his tour of duty in America from 1780 to 1783). Corporal Le Brun escaped the rigors of a long imprisonment; he died—probably of wounds inflicted during the fighting—within two days of his capture.[51]

Unlike the other three infantry regiments that had served in the United States under Rochambeau, the 99th (Deux-Ponts) Infantry was employed on the northwestern, or Belgian, front in 1792 and 1793. After participating in the battle of Valmy, the second battalion contributed to the French victory at Jemappes on November 6, 1792. At the end of January it was joined by the first battalion in the Army of Belgium, and both were involved in the defeat of General Dumouriez's army at Neerwinden in mid-March 1793 and in the subsequent French withdrawal to the frontier. In the course of this action, a number of men were captured by the enemy; among them were four veterans of the American war—Sergeants Anton Dietz and Pierre Erpelding, Corporal Michel Ganiard, and Private Laurent Thirre. All were from German-speaking areas of Alsace or Lorraine; they were between thirty-five and forty-six years old and had between fifteen and twenty-three years of service. Their ultimate fate is unknown. In late 1793 and early 1794 the two battalions were again separated, the first going to Germany and the second to Belgium where it participated in the decisive French victory of Fleurus in late June 1794.[52]

All of Rochambeau's regiments maintained their identity as distinct units until 1794. Between May and December of that year, six of the eight infantry battalions were amalgamated into new demi-brigades.[53] The first and second battalions of the 13th Infantry were incorporated into the 25th and 26th Demi-Brigades on June 17 and May 20, respectively. The two battalions of the 99th Infantry formed parts of the 177th and 178th Demi-Brigades, organized on May 4 and December 19, respectively. The second battalions of the 40th Infantry and the 82nd Infantry were amalgamated into the 80th and 152nd Demi-Brigades on May 2 and July 22, respectively. The first battalions of the last two regiments continued to operate as separate units until "the second Amalgam" in early 1796. No comparable reorganization of cavalry or artillery regiments took place.

By late 1794 the number of Rochambeau's American veterans in the ranks of the French army had shrunk to fewer than three hundred soldiers. They constituted an insignificant portion of the vast armies the French Republic had managed to raise, around three-quarters of a million men. Even in their regiments and demi-brigades they amounted to a mere 2 percent or less of the enlisted personnel.

The number of men who had served as officers under Rochambeau from 1780 to 1783 also continued to dwindle. By late April 1793, of the fifty-six officers in the 40th (Soissonnais) Infantry only three had served in that capacity in America; eighteen other officers had fought the American campaigns as enlisted men.[54] More than half (thirty-two of fifty-eight) of the officers of the 99th (Deux-Ponts) Infantry were American veterans, but only two, Lieutenant Colonel Claude Théodore du Hainaut and Captain François André de Schauenbourg, had gone to the United States as officers; the other thirty had risen through the ranks.[55] In summer 1793 the 13th (Bourbonnais) Infantry included five officers—of a total of fifty-seven—who had served as officers in America: Colonel d'Arlande, Lieutenant Colonel Aubert du Bayet, and Captains Pierre Louis Binet de Marcognet, André Narbonne, and Guillaume Pierre Lemière. The last two were officers of fortune, commissioned in 1776 and 1781, respectively.[56]

Although by 1793 most officers who were not committed to the new regime had left the army, some still departed—voluntarily and involuntarily—after that time. Between two hundred and fifty and three hundred army officers abandoned their posts in 1793 and early 1794, eight of whom had served under Rochambeau in the United States.[57] Lieutenant Colonel du Hainaut of the 99th Infantry left his unit in spring 1793 because the Holy Roman Emperor had threatened to confiscate the possessions of those who continued to serve in the forces of the French Republic.[58] General d'Arlande de Salton, who had been at odds with soldiers under his command in the 13th Infantry in June 1792, deserted his post as commandant of the camp at

Northweiler on August 24, 1793, and joined nearby Prussian forces. On September 11 he was killed by men of his old regiment.[59]

In 1793 and 1794, as the revolutionary government fought desperately against its enemies at home and abroad, it became much more common for officers whose service dated to the Old Regime to be suspended or dismissed, primarily because they were politically suspect. From January 1793 to April 1794, more than six hundred officers were removed.[60] Captain de Schauenbourg, the only man remaining in the 99th Infantry who had served as an officer in the United States, was suspended "as a noble" on September 30, 1793, but was reinstated the following June. General Aubert du Bayet, who had made the American campaigns as a lieutenant in the Regiment of Bourbonnais, was arrested and imprisoned in Paris in early November 1793. He was released and restored to his functions in August 1794 and was promoted to general of division the following February. General Jennings de Kilmaine, formerly of Lauzun's Legion and the 6th Hussars, was suspended on August 4, 1793. Despite his warm support for the Revolution, he was arrested at the end of December 1793 and spent the next fifteen months in prison; he was not reinstated until June 13, 1795.

Others were less fortunate. General Custine, who at various times in 1792 and 1793 had commanded five different field armies and had always disdained what he considered to be political interference in military matters, was recalled to Paris on July 12, 1793. He was subsequently suspended, arrested, tried, condemned to death, and executed on August 28. General Biron (the former duc de Lauzun) was recalled to the capital at about the same time to answer for his conduct in the Vendée; he, too, was imprisoned, tried, and convicted of political crimes. Flamboyant to the end, he was guillotined on the last day of 1793.[61]

Such treatment of high-ranking officers by the Jacobin government might appear to be an example of paranoia at the highest levels. Two considerations must be borne in mind, however, if one wishes to understand this period. First, what was at stake was nothing less than the survival of the republic; the participants on both sides of the struggle appreciated this fact and exhausted all available resources to achieve their goals. Second, there was abundant reason to distrust the officer corps of the Old Regime. The actions of Lafayette and Dumouriez were the most spectacular examples of attempts by officers to change the course of the Revolution, but they were not alone. Captain Jean Baptiste Dartus, a commoner who had served under Rochambeau in America as a sublieutenant in the Regiment of Soissonnais, was suspended from his duties in the 40th Infantry for three months in spring 1793 but was reinstated in June. He was later detained as a political suspect but was released after a few months. Many years later, during the Restoration, he admitted that he had, in fact, been a royalist, as his soldiers suspected, but had remained at his post to be more useful to the émigrés with whom he was in contact. Other officers did the same.[62] Lieutenant Jean Philippe Desprez de la Gralière made no effort to disguise his sympathies. This aristocrat from Poitou had served as a sublieutenant in the Regiment of Saintonge during the American Revolution. In 1793 he was suspended from the army and shortly afterward joined the rebel forces in the Vendée; he was later captured and executed by a firing squad at Angers in January 1794.[63]

Most officers who wanted to oppose the Revolution actively avoided the path of either Dartus or Desprez; rather, they joined one of the émigré armies that assembled beyond the French frontiers in the expectation of a successful invasion of their homeland and the destruction of the revolutionary regime.[64] At the time of Louis XVI's flight to Varennes—the event that initiated the mass defection of the prerevolutionary officer corps—about 300 officers who had served in that capacity in Rochambeau's expedition were still in the line army. Of those, nearly 60 percent (between 175 and 180) emigrated, most in the fourteen months following the arrest and suspension of the king. More than 80 percent of those who emigrated (148 officers) bore arms against France at some point. Those émigrés who fell into the hands of republican forces were treated as traitors. Louis François Philippe de Mosny, who had been a captain in the Bourbonnais (13th) Infantry since 1779, joined the army of Condé shortly after abandoning his regiment in January 1792. He was captured on September 12 during the enemy invasion of France and was shot the next day. Captain Louis Gabriel François de Jousselin, another American veteran, suffered a similar fate. He failed to report back to his regiment, the 82nd Infantry, when his leave expired on July 25, 1792. He later joined the army of Louis Henri Joseph, duc de Bourbon, and was serving in an émigré regiment when he was captured and shot by republican troops in July 1794.[65]

Of the officers who never emigrated, including 120 or so of Rochambeau's veterans, most left the army between June 1791 and April 1794. They were discharged or resigned and returned to their homes, they took their pensions and retired, or they were dismissed. For example, Pierre François Gabriel, comte d'Olonne, who had been an aide de camp to his uncle, the comte de Vioménil, in the United States, held the rank of colonel when he left the army in July 1792. Although other members of his family, including a younger brother who had served with him in America, emigrated and joined antirevolutionary forces, he simply retired to his chateau and subsequently became the mayor of the small town in which it was located, Fauconcourt, in the department of the Vosges.[66]

Some officers whom the revolutionary government decided to remove were defended by their men and even by government officials. Georges Cyr Antoine de Bellemare de Saint-Cyr, whose family's aristocratic lineage dated back nearly six centuries, had been a captain in the Regiment of Saintonge when it served in America; in September 1792 he was dismissed as lieutenant colonel of the 50th Infantry by order of the Convention despite the protests of the soldiers of the regiment.[67] Similarly, on January 25, 1794, Captain François Joseph Donatien de Grivel de Villey, who traced his nobility to mid-fourteenth-century Franche-Comté, was suspended from the 6th (Auxonne) Artillery—where he had served for twenty-two years—because he was a noble, although the officers and men of his company swore that he was "a good citizen and excellent republican, who concerned himself only with his profession and our instruction."[68] Jean Christophe, baron de Wisch, a Danish noble, had become a lieutenant in the Regiment of Royal Deux-Ponts at age eighteen in 1758, was a captain when he was injured at the siege of Yorktown, and became the commanding officer of the 99th Infantry in October 1792. In March 1793 Wisch was promoted to major general and two months later to general of division. On September 27, 1793, he was ordered to cease his functions in conformity with a decree passed by the Convention nine days earlier that ordered the dismissal of all former nobles from service in the armies of the republic. Wisch was doubly suspect as both a foreigner and an aristocrat. Nevertheless, the representatives on mission who were to enforce the decisions of the Convention kept him at his post. More than ten months later, on August 3, 1794, he retired honorably from the French army and returned to his homeland.[69]

Wisch was an unusual case in many respects, not the least of which was the fact that he survived so long as an officer. Of almost 13,900 officers at the beginning of the French Revolution, only about 2,000 remained in April 1794, less than five years later. Even more striking is the difference between those who were gone and those who stayed. By spring 1794 fewer than 1,100 officers were left in the army who had been directly commissioned (compared with around 12,200 in 1789). On the other hand, about half of the nearly 1,700 officers of fortune of 1789 remained on duty five years later.[70] The toll of the Revolution on those who had been officers in Rochambeau's American expedition was even greater; by the beginning of 1794 only 38 of the nearly 500 officers who had served in America from 1780 to 1783 were still in the army (between 7 and 8 percent). The proportion of officers promoted from the ranks was about the same as that for the army as a whole;

half of the 36 officers of fortune of 1789 were still present in early 1794. In comparison, only a score of officers who had been directly commissioned remained on January 1, 1794, and half of them would leave the army over the next three months.[71]

Perhaps the most striking and most enduring change in the composition of the French army brought about by the Revolution was the commissioning of thousands of new officers from the ranks. Those men would form the nucleus of the new officer corps well into the Napoleonic period. By mid-1794 more than three hundred former enlisted men were officers in the units that had served under Rochambeau in the United States, and nearly two-thirds of these officers had participated in those campaigns.[72] Together with officers drawn from the volunteers of 1791 and 1792 and directly commissioned from civilian life, they constituted 90 percent or more of all officers. The men had extensive military experience, and many were combat veterans; they were, in short, professional soldiers. At the same time, they owed their present rank and any hope of future advancement to the revolutionary principle of "careers open to talent."[73] Much of the French military success over the next two decades can be attributed to their contributions.

By 1794, then, the French army was fundamentally different from what it had been less than five years earlier. The army of the Old Regime, the army that had fought the American War of Independence, was composed of soldiers who were mostly long-term professionals and officers whose primary claim to command was their noble birth. Although substantial by contemporary measures, the army numbered only about 170,000 officers and troops in 1789. By 1794 the French army comprised four to five times as many men. Its ranks were overwhelmingly composed of citizen-soldiers, recently enrolled and commanded by the most thoroughly professional officer corps in Europe, perhaps in the world.

Whatever role the veterans of Rochambeau's American expedition might have played as a group in the Royal Army of 1789 had largely disappeared in the republican armies of 1794. Their experiences during those tumultuous years offer insights about the impact of the French Revolution and, at the same time, provide an essentially accurate reflection of the process that transformed the entire army. Furthermore, although the significance of those men as a group was negligible by 1794, some of them continued to have an influence on the French army as individuals. Finally, a brief examination of their careers after the Year II indicates the continuity between this generation of soldiers and their successors (see chapter 11).

WAR AND THE TRANSFORMATION OF THE ARMY

Notes

1. Bodinier, *Officiers*, p. 397, Bodinier, "Comportement des officers," p. 110, and Bodinier, *Dictionnaire*, pp. 164, 17–18, 248, 117, and 52–53.
2. On these policies and their results, see Scott, *Response of the Royal Army*, pp. 162–167.
3. These and other statistical data are from the regimental registers unless otherwise indicated.
4. Besides the unit register, see documents dated July 6, 1793, and 18 fructidor an II (September 4, 1794) in A.G., X^b 190.
5. On Dupont, des Vignes, and the du Rosel brothers, see Bodinier, *Dictionnaire*, pp. 170, 140, and 177–178. Documents in A.G., X^b 91 make it clear that des Vignes was in the unit depot while the rest of the regiment was in America, although Bodinier was unaware of this.
6. Information on the officers' departure is provided by documents dated January 3 and February 3, 6, 9, 10 and 28, 1792, in A.G., X^b 176. See also Bertaud, *Army of the French Revolution*, p. 37.
7. See Bodinier, "Officiers de Rochambeau," p. 147; and Jean Paul Bertaud, *Les Amis du Roi: Journaux et journalistes royalistes en France de 1789 à 1792* (Paris: Perrin, 1984), p. 211, for the quotation.
8. This is the only such example I have found while examining scores of registers for this period. Most personnel had a stake in preserving accurate service records, and maintaining the unit contrôle was taken very seriously.
9. Bodinier, "Officiers de l'armeé royale et la Révolution," p. 65.
10. See the reports on officers, dated May 9 and 24, 1792, in A.G., X^d 24.
11. Jean Paul Bertaud, *Valmy: La Démocratie en armes* (Paris: Julliard, 1970), p. 171.
12. See the correspondence of Lieutenant Colonel Bordenave between May 7 and 16, 1792, in A.G., X^b 166.
13. This incident is described in documents in the Archives departementales du Bas-Rhin, 1L 1439.
14. See A.G., 14 YC 17, no. 196 for the data on Remy.
15. A.G., X^b 166; and Bodinier, *Dictionnaire*, pp. 244 and 266.
16. Bodinier, "Officiers de Rochambeau," p. 149.
17. A.G., 14 YC 144. Because of the lacuna in its records, the Soissonnais (40th) Infantry may have lost more deserters.
18. See the anonymous "Historique du 99ᵉ Régiment de Ligne," pp. 12–16, a handwritten history received at the Archives de la Guerre on May 28, 1889, in A.G., Historiques, Régiments d'Infanterie, carton 66.
19. Data on the soldiers' desertions are from the uncoded regimental contrôle; those on the officers are from "Liste des officiers dudit Régiment qui ont donnés leurs démissions, passés à d'autres Corps, et émigrés," in A.G., X^c 245, and *Etat des officiers de tous grades déserteurs ou émigrés classés par régiment* (Paris: Imprimerie Executive du Louvre, 1793), pp. 5 and 45.
20. Bodinier, *Dictionnaire*, p. 440
21. Scott, *Response of the Royal Army*, pp. 119–120; and Bodinier, "Comportement des officiers," p. 115.

22. Letter of the general council of the department, dated August 17, 1792, in Archives départementales de l'Isère, L 56.
23. Bodinier, *Officiers*, pp. 442–443 and 447, and Bodinier, *Dictionnaire*, pp. 160–161, 392, 120–121, and 108.
24. Bodinier, *Officiers*, pp. 447–450, and the relevant entries in his *Dictionnaire*, pp. 279–280, 403–404, 257, 35, 53–54, 164, 280, 43–44, and 394. On Queyssat, also see p. xi.
25. Bodinier, *Officiers*, p. 450.
26. Ibid., pp. 429, 468, 478, and 492, and Bodinier, "Officiers de Rochambeau," p. 9. This figure is an extrapolation based on the percentage of all army officers who had served in the American war and were still serving on January 1, 1793, and the number of Rochambeau's officers present for duty in 1789. Because of the uncertainty about some officers (for example, those on leave, those on special assignments, prisoners of war) any figure constitutes something of an estimate.
27. Information on officers of fortune is from the unit contrôles unless otherwise indicated. The situation in the Old Regime is described on pp. 11 and 129.
28. Scott, *Response of the Royal Army*, p. 114.
29. The lacuna in the contrôle of the 40th (Soissonnais) Infantry prohibits greater precision and makes this a minimal figure.
30. Bodinier, *Dictionnaire*, p. 235.
31. Bodinier, "Comportement des officiers," p. 108, and Bodinier, "Officiers de Rochambeau," p. 145. Wrong, "Officiers de Fortune," p. 430, confirms this.
32. Bodinier, *Dictionnaire*, p. 336.
33. Ibid., pp. 306–307. Documents in A.G., X^b 91 show that Le Monier did not go to America, as Bodinier claims. For his activities in the Invalides, see Woloch, *French Veteran*, pp. 178–180.
34. See Bertaud, *Army of the French Revolution*, pp. 90–96, for the implementation and results of this legislation.
35. Ibid., pp. 102–132.
36. Ibid., pp. 86–90, 150–153, and 159–171; and Scott, *Response of the Royal Army*, pp. 179–181 and 217–222.
37. Because the date of separation was not always recorded, one cannot be precise about the number of American veterans remaining, but the figures given here and subsequently are close approximations.
38. Besides the unit register, see the document about the Swiss troops, dated March 27, 1793, in A.G., X^d 25. These practices in the army as a whole are briefly described in Scott, *Response of the Royal Army*, pp. 166–167.
39. These sources include the series A.G., Historiques, cartons 10 (for Bourbonnais), 31 (Soissonnais), 55 (Saintonge), 66 (Deux-Ponts), 125 (Lauzun), and 138 (Auxonne). Most of this material consists of manuscript histories of the regiments in question, prepared from the War Archives by French officers in the last quarter of the nineteenth century. In addition, the series of contrôles for the demi-brigades of the "first formation," A.G., 21 YC, and "second formation," A.G., 22 YC, and uncoded contrôles for the Napoleonic period were used to follow the later careers of Rochambeau's veterans. The registers in 14 YC continued to provide some information on soldiers enrolled before the last entry, including the American veterans, even when they stopped recording data on new recruits.

WAR AND THE TRANSFORMATION OF THE ARMY

40. See the lists of these men, dated April 5 and May 2, 1792, in A.G., X^d 24.
41. Scott, *Response of the Royal Army*, p. 158.
42. Philippe René Girault, *Mes campagnes sous la Révolution et l'Empire* (Paris: Le Sycomore, 1983), pp. 21–22.
43. A.G., Historiques, carton 66, Anonymous, "Historique du 99ᵉ Régiment de Ligne" (received at the Archives de la Guerre on May 28, 1889), p. 12; C. Voisin, *Historique du 6ᵉ Hussards* (Libourne: Maleville, 1888), p. 16; A.G., Historiques, carton 138, Anonymous, "Historique du 6ᵉ Régiment d'Artillerie," pp. 3–4; Henri Libermann, *La défense nationale à la fin de 1792: Servan et Pache (10 août 1792–2 février 1793)* (Paris: Perrin, 1927), p. 106n; and Girault, *Mes campagnes*, pp. 16–18.
44. Besides the regimental register, see A.G., X^c 245; and Voisin, *Historique du 6ᵉ Hussards*, pp. 21 and 251–254. Grouchy was the last of the Napoleonic marshals. Jennings de Kilmaine and Lagrange served simultaneously as colonel, since General Dumouriez appointed the former after the minister of war had named the latter to the same position. When Kilmaine was promoted to general, the situation was normalized.
45. See documents during this time in A.G., X^d 24 and 25, the regimental contrôle, and the "Historique du 6ᵉ Regimént d'Artillerie," pp. 3–4.
46. Inspection reports dated July 6, 1793, and 3 fructidor an II (August 20, 1794) in A.G., X^b 190.
47. A.G., Historiques, carton 55, Capitaine Arvers, "1684–1875: Historique des 82ᵉ Régiment d'Infanterie de Ligne et 7ᵉ Régiment d'Infanterie Légère" (received at the Archives de la Guerre on November 19, 1875), pp. 45ff.
48. Ibid., p. 45; and the document dated June 7, 1794, in A.G., X^b 166.
49. A.G., Historiques, carton 10, Anonymous, "Sans Tache: Bourbonnais et le 13ᵉ d'Infanterie, 1597–1892" (received at the Archives de la Guerre on October 17, 1892), pp. 106–133.
50. This information was compiled from documents in A.G., X^b 176; three separate lists (recruits from April to June 1793, combat deaths between August 20 and December 26, 1793, and prisoners of war captured on November 16, 1793) bound with the regimental contrôle in A.G., 14 YC 58; and Coste, *Historique du 40ᵉ Régiment d'infanterie*, pp. 16–25. Ladislas Palásti, "Soldats de la Révolution française en captivité à Szeged," *Annales historiques de la Révolution française* 57 (1985): 353–364, gives some idea of conditions in a Hungarian POW camp of the period.
51. A.G., 14 YC 58.
52. A.G., Historiques, carton 66, "Historique du 99ᵉ," pp. 12–18; A.G., 14 YC 144 and 21 YC for the 177th and 178th Demi-Brigades.
53. Information on the dates of amalgamation and the total strength of the demi-brigades at their formation was furnished by my dear friend and colleague, Jean Paul Bertaud. For this—and much, much more assistance and encouragement— I thank him warmly.
54. See the printed list entitled *Services des officiers du quarantième régiment d'infanterie* in A.G., X^b 176.
55. See the list of officers, dated Phillipeville, April 25, 1793, in A.G., X^b 196.
56. See A.G., Historiques, carton 10, "Bourbonnais et le 13ᵉ d'Infanterie," pp. 94–95.

57. Bodinier, "Officiers de l'armée royale et la Révolution," p. 65, and Bodinier, "Officiers de Rochambeau," p. 149.
58. Bodinier, *Dictionnaire*, p. 159.
59. See p. 168; and Bodinier, *Officiers*, p. 454.
60. Bodinier, "Officiers de l'armée royale et la Révolution," p. 66.
61. See Bodinier, *Dictionnaire*, pp. 427–428, 17–18, 255, 118–119, and 226–227, for succinct biographies of these officers. On Custine, also see Bertaud, *Army of the French Revolution*, pp. 144–147; on Biron, see Bonsal, *When the French Were Here*, p. 209.
62. Bodinier, *Officiers*, p. 453.
63. Bodinier, *Dictionnaire*, p. 139.
64. The following figures have been calculated from a variety of sources, mostly the work of Gilbert Bodinier, especially his *Dictionnaire*.
65. Ibid., pp. 355 and 258.
66. Ibid., p. 368.
67. Ibid., p. 37.
68. Ibid., p. 233, and Bodinier, *Officiers*, p. 426.
69. Bodinier, *Dictionnaire*, p. 485.
70. Bodinier, "Officiers de l'armée royale et la Révolution," pp. 66–67.
71. Bodinier, "Officiers de Rochambeau," pp. 143–145, and Bodinier, *Officers*, p. 489.
72. These figures are drawn from the unit contrôles; lacunae, especially in the records of the infantry regiments, make precise statistics impossible.
73. See my brief article "Careers Open to Talent" for a general view of this subject.

11

IN THE AFTERMATH OF
REVOLUTION, 1794–1815

BY THE YEAR II (1794), Rochambeau's veterans of the American Revolutionary War—slightly more than five hundred officers and men—had become a statistically insignificant component of the French army. Their subsequent careers and exploits, however, continued to exemplify and elucidate the fate of the army during the following years, even through the Napoleonic epoch.[1]

By spring 1794 a dozen nobles who had been officers in Rochambeau's American expedition continued to serve in that capacity. In fact, such a tiny number of survivors was fairly typical in the army generally. In mid-September 1793 the National Convention, under mounting pressure, had declared, "all former nobles who hold posts in the armies of the Republic are dismissed." As the case of General Wisch (discussed in chapter 10) shows, this measure was never fully implemented. Even such an ardent revolutionary as Louis Antoine Saint-Just of the Committee of Public Safety made exceptions to its terms. On January 13, 1794, four months after the decree had been enacted, Lazare Carnot, another member of the same powerful committee and a former captain in the Royal Corps of Engineers, secured the passage of legislation providing for the reinstatement of artillery and engineer officers who had been discharged on the grounds of their noble status; such highly trained and skilled men were too difficult to replace. Military exigency also led the Convention on April 16, 1794, to authorize the Committee of Public Safety to retain as officers any former nobles "whose abilities it believed were of use to the Republic." By this time seven to eight hundred noble officers at most

187

were left in the entire French army, compared with eleven to twelve thousand five years earlier.[2]

Some officers who had been suspended or dismissed from military service later returned to duty, especially after the overthrow of Robespierre on 9 Thermidor, Year II (July 27, 1794). Pierre Louis Binet de Marcognet, for example, had joined Rochambeau's corps in the United States as a cadet in 1781 and continued to serve in the same regiment, the Bourbonnais (13th) Infantry, until he was discharged as a noble in December 1793. He was reinstated as a captain in July 1795, promoted to lieutenant colonel a year later, and by 1811 had reached the rank of general of division. His last military engagement was the battle of Waterloo in June 1815. He retired from the army less than three months later but survived into the reign of Napoleon III.[3]

Philippe François Roch de Wasservas came from a family of German origin that, like Binet de Marcognet's, dated its nobility to the sixteenth century. He entered the Ecole Militaire in 1764, when he was eleven, and spent two years at artillery school before being commissioned in the Auxonne Artillery Regiment in June 1770. After returning from service in America, he was promoted to captain in 1785 but was suspended from his functions in February or March 1794. He returned to duty in May 1795, was promoted to lieutenant colonel in 1799, and retired on June 4, 1809.[4]

Denis Félix Devrigny, whose father (possibly an impoverished noble) was an officer of fortune in the cavalry, followed in his father's footsteps and, after a decade of enlisted service, was commissioned in 1782 while a member of Lauzun's Legion in America. Like a number of his comrades, he enjoyed rapid promotion after 1791. He was a captain in spring 1792 and had become a lieutenant colonel by that autumn; on January 16, 1793, he was promoted provisionally to the grade of colonel; on June 13, 1793, he received another provisional appointment to general of brigade. Only two and a half weeks later, however, he was suspended because of charges that he had gained his promotion to general "by intrigue," had brutalized his troops, and was, in fact, a noble. In early March 1795 he was restored to duty as a colonel, and three months later his promotion to general was confirmed. While serving on Martinique, he died of yellow fever on July 28, 1803.[5]

A few noble officers escaped suspension, dismissal, arrest, or worse by mere chance. The vicomte de Rochambeau, son of the commander of the American expedition, was appointed lieutenant general and given an important command in the French West Indies in summer 1792. In March 1794 he was forced to surrender Martinique to the English and was made their prisoner. Almost certainly, his isolated post and capture by the enemy saved him from the fate of his father, who was imprisoned from early April to late October 1794 and barely escaped execution. Released after a prisoner exchange, the younger Rochambeau returned to France toward the end of 1795. In November 1803 he was the commanding officer responsible for the capitulation of Haiti (Saint-Domingue), after which he spent an additional eight years as an English prisoner of war. In October 1813 he died of wounds sustained during the French defeat of Leipzig.[6]

Louis François Bertrand Dupont d'Aubervoye de Lauberdière, a distant relative of Rochambeau who had been detached from the Saintonge Infantry to serve on the general staff during the American war, also had an unusual experience that saved his military career—and perhaps more. While in Ireland for his wedding to Caroline MacNamara-Hussey, he carried out *une mission de reconnaissance*. He was arrested as a spy by the British authorities in April 1793 and remained in custody until June 1800. He resumed military as well as political duties upon his return to France and served Napoleon faithfully through the Hundred Days.[7]

Some officers who had emigrated subsequently returned to France and were reintegrated into public service. One of the most striking of these cases was Mathieu Dumas. An aide de camp to Rochambeau during the American Revolution and an inveterate soldier-politician, Dumas was proscribed after the overthrow of the monarchy in August 1792 and escaped to Switzerland. In May 1795 he returned to France, was elected to the Council of the Ancients where he supported a monarchical restoration, was again proscribed after the Directorial coup d'état of 18 Fructidor (September 4, 1797), and once more had to flee the country. Undaunted, Dumas returned to France shortly after General Napoleon Bonaparte's successful coup and resumed his military duties on March 28, 1800. He served his new master in a variety of civil and military functions—including fighting in Spain, Germany, and Russia—and was made a prisoner of war in December 1813. His political career lasted into the 1830s.[8]

Other officers who emigrated, either on their own initiative or in response to pressure, had less spectacular, although still rather successful, careers after returning home. The Lameth brothers had also been prominent in political and military affairs; like most émigrés they did not come back to France until after the fall of the Directory. Both Charles de Lameth, who had been seriously wounded during the siege of Yorktown, and his brother Alexandre, who had replaced him on Rochambeau's staff in 1782, fled France shortly after the overthrow of the monarchy on August 10, 1792. Their emigration followed the common pattern of relatives reacting similarly to the Revolution. Also, as did many others, both Lameths returned to France and resumed public functions, including military duties, early in the Consulate. Charles served in Spain from 1812 to 1814, and both were named honorary lieutenant generals in 1814.[9]

Some émigré officers refused to compromise their commitment to the Old Regime and pursued military careers abroad. One of the most successful of these was Louis Alexandre Andrault, comte de Langeron. His family traced its noble origins to the fourteenth century, and his father and grandfather had been lieutenant generals. After a brief tour of duty in the United States as a sublieutenant in the Bourbonnais Infantry, Langeron, like other court aristocrats, enjoyed rapid promotion, reaching the grade of colonel in 1786 when he was only twenty-three. As did other members of the upper nobility, he emigrated early in the French Revolution and served in the Prussian, Austrian, and Russian armies, eventually making his career in the last of these. He fought in numerous conflicts against Russia's enemies, particularly the Turks, and also served in campaigns against Napoleon—including Austerlitz in 1805, the French retreat from Moscow in 1812, in Germany in 1813, and in France in early 1814. Following Napoleon's defeat, Langeron returned to Russia and served in various high military and civil posts until 1831, when he died during the cholera epidemic.[10]

Most surviving émigré officers eventually returned to France, although only a minority reentered the army. Those who left France between 1791 and 1794 and subsequently came back to resume military service—together with the handful of noble officers who managed to retain their posts during the Terror—enjoyed successful careers. As the examples here suggest, virtually all of those who had served as officers during the American campaigns attained at least field grade (major, lieutenant colonel, colonel), and a substantial number eventually became general officers. Such men, however, constituted a clear minority of Rochambeau's veterans in the officer corps of the French army after the Year II. A much larger group consisted of officers who had risen through the ranks, mostly after 1789, and owed their advancement to the Revolution.

By spring 1794 around two hundred officers on active duty had served under Rochambeau's orders in America and had been promoted from the ranks. Some saw only brief service in the Revolution, usually because of their age or physical condition. For example, Guillaume Pierre Lemière, the son of a day laborer in Rouen, enlisted in the Regiment of Bourbonnais in February 1751, two weeks after his seventeenth birthday. Thirty years later he was commissioned a sublieutenant while his regiment was engaged in the siege of Yorktown. He survived the wreck of the *Bourgogne* in February 1783 but lost an eye as a result. Subsequent promotion came only with the Revolution: to lieutenant in July 1790, to captain in November 1791, and to lieutenant colonel in September 1793. He retired on July 16, 1794, at age sixty after forty-three years of service—including campaigns in Germany in the early 1760s, in America in the early 1780s, and those of the Revolution from 1792 to 1794.[11]

Two of Lemière's comrades in the same regiment, Claude Chabanier, a native of Tarascon in Provence, and Claude Flet from rural Picardy, joined the Regiment of Bourbonnais at age twenty in 1761 and 1760, respectively. Both served as sergeants in the United States and enjoyed rapid promotions during the French Revolution. Chabanier was named sublieutenant in January 1792, lieutenant two months later, and captain in January 1793; Flet became a sublieutenant in May 1792, a lieutenant one week later, and a captain in August 1793. Both retired in 1795, Chabanier in January and Flet in October.[12] Jean Stenger, a Lutheran from a small village in Alsace, had a similar career in the Royal Deux-Ponts Infantry, which he joined in July 1768 when he was twenty-four. He, too, had been a noncommissioned officer during the American war. He was promoted to sublieutenant on September 15, 1791, and became a captain within a year. On June 19, 1795, Stenger retired from the army with a pension.[13]

Many "rankers" stayed in the army much longer. Nicolas Tribout, from the village of Bistroff in Lorraine, was thirty-four years old and had served for sixteen years in the Royal Deux-Ponts (99th) Infantry when he was commissioned on April 1, 1791. He had served in all of the American campaigns of Rochambeau's corps and received a gunshot wound in the left leg during the siege of Yorktown, an injury that later contributed to rheumatism in that limb (or so he claimed). By December 1794 he had become a colonel. He saw an additional decade of combat during the National Convention, Directory, and Consulate. He later served two years in Spain and died in early 1813 after experiencing the horrors of the Russian campaign.[14] Nicolas Lenoir, also a native of Lorraine (born in the city of Thionville), enrolled in the Auxonne Artillery in April 1759 when he was eighteen. He had been a sergeant major for five years before going to America with his battalion in 1780. He was not commissioned until February 1792, but within fourteen months had reached the rank of lieutenant colonel. In June 1814 he retired as a colonel after fifty-five years of service, including sixteen campaigns.[15]

The military career of Louis André, from Carcassone in Languedoc, exemplified some of the hazards these long-serving soldiers endured. André joined the Regiment of Saintonge at the beginning of 1770, shortly before his sixteenth birthday; was promoted to corporal after he signed up for his second eight-year enlistment; and served as a sergeant in the American war, sustaining a wound in his left leg during the fighting at Yorktown. He was promoted to sublieutenant in September 1791 and to lieutenant the following April. He was wounded again during the defense of Frankfurt and was made a prisoner when his battalion, together with the rest of the French garrison there, surrendered in December 1792. In June 1794, after his release, he was named a captain. Two years later, in April 1796, he was again captured by the enemy and spent four months in a prisoner-of-war camp. Following his release, André was discharged from active duty, although he served as the commanding officer of a "company of veterans" from September 1798 to November 1810. The following August he took command of a reserve company of the department of the Rhin-et-Moselle, a position he held until the unit was disbanded on July 1, 1814. In November 1820 André petitioned the government of Louis XVIII to be awarded the Cross of Saint Louis.[16]

Although the typical NCO commissioned from the ranks after 1790 enjoyed rapid promotion, usually reaching the grade of captain or higher by 1794, some did not advance as rapidly or as high as the men described earlier. Paul Hoffmann, born at Niederhaussen in the Duchy of Deux-Ponts in 1744, enlisted in his ruler's proprietary regiment in September 1766, served in the United States as a sergeant, and was commissioned a sublieutenant on March 10, 1792. Although he was promoted to lieutenant only eleven weeks later, he was serving in the same capacity when he was killed in combat in 1804.[17] Joseph Steil, from a small village near Colmar in Alsace, enrolled in Lauzun's Legion the year before its departure for the United States, where he served as a hussar. Steil remained a private until 1792 when he was promoted to corporal and then sergeant. He was named sublieutenant in July 1793 but still held that rank in March 1805 (the last date for which there are records on him).[18] Conrad Beltz, another Alsatian who enlisted in the Auxonne Artillery in December 1777 and served as a cannoneer in America, took even longer to gain an officer's epaulets but eventually went further than Steil. Beltz was not commissioned until August 1797. He was promoted to first lieutenant (lieutenant en premier) in June 1802 and to captain in second in March 1806. Although he remained on duty until August 1815, served a total of more than thirty-seven years, participated in twenty-two campaigns, and was wounded twice, he was not promoted again.[19]

Advancement for officers promoted from the ranks was usually more limited than that for those who began their military careers with a commission, even after the French Revolution. Of the officers of fortune, or rankers, who had served under Rochambeau in America, only two reached the grade of general, even during the period when such promotions were most common. One of these was Denis Devrigny, discussed previously; the other was Pierre Laprun.[20] Laprun, whose father was a baker, had begun his military service in the militia of Châlons-sur-Marne in early 1756 when he was eighteen. Like Devrigny, he was already an officer of fortune during the participation of his unit—the second battalion of the Auxonne Artillery—in the American war, from which he emerged a captain. Subsequent promotions took more than a decade but then came rapidly: to lieutenant colonel in August 1793, colonel the next month, general of brigade in February 1794, and general of division in May of the same year. Although cleared of political charges emerging from the government's antiroyalist coup d'état in September 1797, Laprun was discharged from the service and retired in 1799.

Another officer of fortune in a unit that had served under Rochambeau in America who eventually became a general was René Nicolas Le Monier (or Le Monnier). The son of a hat merchant from Maine, Le Monier was a thirty-nine-year-old lieutenant with over twenty-one years of service when his regiment, the Saintonge Infantry, sailed for America in May 1780. He, however, stayed behind in the regimental depot where he and a few other officers and NCOs enlisted and trained recruits while the bulk of the regiment was overseas.[21] Promoted to captain on the eve of the Revolution in May 1789, Le Monier had become a general of division by the end of January 1794 but was unable to assume his duties because of a serious wound received three months earlier. He retired in December 1795 and entered the Invalides.

Not only did just two American veterans from the ranks become general officers, but few rose above the grade of captain—about one in twelve.[22] Those figures, however, do not suggest that the Revolution brought little or no change for army officers. First, the abolition of the criterion of noble birth for a direct commission meant that thousands of men who could never have aspired to become officers before 1789—regardless of their abilities—did become officers during, and as a consequence of, the French Revolution. Second, the fact that many of the rankers were considerably older and more battle worn by the time they were commissioned than officers who had been directly commissioned significantly shortened their subsequent careers and restricted their advancement. Third, even in the vastly expanded armies of the Year II, only a certain number of posts were available for colonels and generals. Furthermore, although nearly 90 percent of the prerevolutionary officer corps had left the army by 1794, most of the vacancies their departures created had been quickly filled, and future openings depended primarily on the much slower process of attrition among officers who were professionally and politically committed to the new status quo. The days of wholesale replacements were over. Finally, more professional standards were being demanded of army officers. In mid-February 1794 the government required that all officers, as well as NCOs, be able to read and write; and clearly, if one hoped to advance, the abilities to "calculate," draw, read a map, and exhibit other qualities of military leadership were becoming indispensable.[23] Such criteria created obvious restrictions for men whose civilian education or military training was deficient—that is, soldiers from the lower classes and civilians who had answered the call to arms during the crises of 1792–1794.

Indeed, the most pervasive characteristic of the French officer corps from before the overthrow of Robespierre in July 1794 to the seizure of power by Bonaparte in November 1799 was its growing professionalism. In the Year II half of the officers in the French army, including all of Rochambeau's American veterans, had service dating to 1789 or before and were essentially professional soldiers. Furthermore, the higher the rank, the greater the proportion of professionals: Seven of eight generals, 85 percent of the colonels, nearly 75 percent of the lieutenant colonels, 60 percent of the captains, and about 45 percent of the lieutenants and sublieutenants had served in the armed forces for a minimum of five years; and the proportion of such officers in the cavalry, artillery, and engineers—branches that required more technical background than the infantry—was even higher.[24] This development subsequently intensified. A law passed by the Convention in April 1795 abolished the practice of electing officers and restricted the role of subordinates to nominating candidates for promotion, leaving the final decision to superior officers. Seven months later, the nomination process was eliminated; henceforth, military authorities made promotions, subject only to the ratification of the Directory.[25] Legislation passed on October 21, 1795, required graduation from the Ecole Polytechnique for admission to both the Artillery and Military Engineer Schools.[26] The army less and less represented "the nation in arms." A distinct military hierarchy was being restored, albeit on bases very different from the Old Regime.

This increasing professionalism did not isolate the army from civilian politics. In fact, every political change during this unstable period had military repercussions. In the Thermidorian reaction following the overthrow of Robespierre and his supporters, the Convention dismissed numerous officers who were suspected of harboring radical sympathies, of being "anarchists" or "extreme republicans" in the political jargon of the day. In autumn 1794 military commanders were instructed to select "an officer of probity and intelligence" from their units to investigate "the conduct and morality of every officer"—in other words, to be a kind of political commissar. Meanwhile, hundreds of officers who had been suspended, dismissed, and imprisoned between 1792 and 1794 were reinstated. A number of those officers made up the cadre of the improvised army that crushed the last popular Parisian uprising of 1 Prairial, Year III (May 20, 1795). Included in this group was Antoine Louis Choin de Montgay, baron de Montchoisy, who commanded a contingent of dragoons that helped to repress this final revolutionary journée.[27] Montchoisy had been a major in Lauzun's Legion from its arrival at Newport until after the Allied victory at Yorktown, when he went on leave (and apparently returned to France). He was promoted to major general in March 1793, suspended and imprisoned six months later, and released after 9 Thermidor. Following the Prairial uprising, he served throughout the Napoleonic period but rallied to Louis XVIII during the first restoration.[28]

In the aftermath of Prairial, many officers were denounced as "Jacobins" and "terrorists" and relieved of command for the very same attitudes and conduct that had won them praise and advancement as "patriots" before Thermidor.[29] The political pendulum swung in the opposite direction following the monarchist uprising of 13 Vendémiaire Year IV (October 5, 1795), which General Bonaparte helped to repress, and then reversed itself yet again when Babeuf's "Conspiracy of Equals" was uncovered in May 1796. Even when one's political opinions did not result in obvious retribution, remarks in officers' dossiers, such as a comment about the excessive revolutionary zeal of Charles Martraire, likely harmed their careers. One might speculate that a subsequent notation that Martraire (who had risen through every rank from simple soldier to colonel) was totally incompetent was based more on his politics than on his ability.[30]

The most severe purge since the Terror came after the government's coup d'état against royalists on 18 Fructidor, Year V (September 4, 1797); indeed, that action subsequently led to the neologism *fructidorisé* for someone who was "eliminated" during this period. For instance, although he escaped prosecution by fleeing to Hamburg, General Mathieu Dumas had to remain in exile until Bonaparte's coup more than two years later.[31] Similarly, Joseph François Gau de Voves—a commissary officer for Rochambeau's artillery in America—was imprisoned during the Terror, returned to duty in late 1794, and then worked in the war ministry to eliminate "terrorist" officers; he escaped deportation with other royalists by going into hiding until the Consulate.[32] General Pierre Laprun was dismissed in early December

1797 on the basis of accusations that he was a royalist sympathizer. Although he denied the charges and they were never substantiated, he was still forced to retire.[33]

Although the later political crises of the Directory had more limited impact, they continued to have ramifications for some army officers. General René Nicolas Le Monier was involved in politics after his admission to the Invalides in 1795; he was one of four representatives elected by his comrades to that institution's administrative council and was simultaneously an active member of the Constitutional Circle of the Rue de Bacq, the most prominent neo-Jacobin organization in Paris. At the time of the coup d'état of 22 Floréal, Year VI (May 11, 1798), when the Directory invalidated the election of nearly a hundred deputies identified as "Jacobins," Le Monier was denounced as an agitator by the police and was forced to leave the Invalides despite the gunshot and saber wounds he had incurred over nearly forty years in the army, during which he had served in every capacity from simple soldier to general of division.[34] Such treatment was hardly appropriate recognition by a grateful nation!

These purges undoubtedly created instability and insecurity within the officer corps; with each shift in the political climate, however, some officers who had been removed during prior crises were returned to duty. Of all of the French generals serving in 1799, one-third had been relieved of command, dismissed, or imprisoned during the previous six years.[35]

Not all officers dismissed between 1794 and 1799 were discharged because of political considerations; some were dismissed for unauthorized absence, abuse of authority, insubordination, negligence, drunkenness, financial peculation, and incompetence. In addition, the reorganization of all infantry units in 1796, the "second amalgam," resulted in the discharge of additional officers, particularly older ones—like those whose service dated to the American Revolution.[36] Finally, there were more routine separations. For example, Henry Crublier d'Opterre, the son of a bourgeois family and a graduate of the school for military engineers at Mézières who had served as a captain of engineers in Rochambeau's American expedition, retired for "reasons of health" with the rank of general of brigade in July 1795.[37] Jacob Bauer—an Alsatian who had enlisted in the Regiment of Royal Deux-Ponts in November 1768, had become a sergeant thirteen years later while serving in America, and was commissioned in May 1792—retired in September 1795. His retirement may have been motivated by resentment, since on April 30, 1794, he had complained to the minister of war that he was kept from receiving command of a company because his primary language was German, even though he claimed he could read and write French "well enough."[38] Claude Dôle, a peasant from a small village in Franche-Comté who had joined the Auxonne Artillery as a private in 1757 when he was twenty, was a lieutenant colonel in the 5th Artillery when he retired in February 1796 after nearly forty years of arduous service.[39]

These losses had nothing to do with political conditions and continued after the Directory had gone the way of previous regimes. Similarly, the death toll among officers who had served with Rochambeau in America mounted with the years. Jean Kreps, a native of rural Lorraine, enlisted in the Regiment of Bourbonnais when he was sixteen in May 1777. Promoted to corporal in 1784 and sergeant in 1791, he remained with the same battalion through every organizational change—to the 13th Infantry Regiment in 1791, the 25th Demi-Brigade in 1794, and the 50th Demi-Brigade in 1796. Kreps was promoted to sublieutenant twenty years after his original enlistment in June 1797 and died of wounds sustained in combat two years later.[40] Hubert Brandmayer, also from Lorraine, had joined Lauzun's Legion in December 1778, served with that unit in America, and remained in the hussar regiment that evolved from it through the wars of the Revolution. He was commissioned in June 1793 and promoted to lieutenant in November 1798. He was killed at the battle of Hohenlinden on December 3, 1800.[41] Like many other young men from Franche-Comté, Jean Pichon joined an artillery regiment—the Auxonne Artillery—when he was nineteen. He was promoted to sergeant when his battalion returned from America in 1783. The Revolution brought rapid but limited advancement: He was commissioned in 1792 and became a lieutenant in 1793 and a captain in 1794, a rank he still held when he died on July 14, 1802, on Saint Domingue (Haiti) during Bonaparte's ill-fated attempt to regain control of the former colony.[42]

The soldiers who had fought under Rochambeau in America and who continued to serve as enlisted men during the French Revolution and the Napoleonic era were affected more by military than by political developments. At the beginning of 1794 three hundred or so veterans of Rochambeau's American expedition were still serving as soldiers in the French army.[43] A few served briefly as officers but later returned to the enlisted ranks. For example, Pierre Tuo, a native of Nîmes in Languedoc, was enrolled in the second battalion of the Bourbonnais Infantry in 1773 at age seventeen. He served as a sergeant in the United States and was promoted to sublieutenant in November 1793. When his battalion was incorporated into the 26th Demi-Brigade in May 1794, it was discovered that the promotion was the result of some "error," and Tuo was reduced to sergeant. In December of that year his name was deleted from the unit register (*rayé*) for reasons unrecorded. François Guidez, from Valenciennes near the Belgian border, enlisted in the first battalion of the same regiment in November 1778 and, as did Tuo, served in combat in both North America and Europe. In October 1794, shortly after the amalgamation of his battalion, he was commissioned in the 25th Demi-Brigade. Thirteen months later, however, Guidez was demoted to sergeant.[44]

By the end of 1794, promotions from the ranks were much less common because most vacancies had been filled. Besides, the huge forces under arms that spring had begun to dwindle and would continue to decrease until after the passage of new legislation on conscription (the Jourdan Law) in September 1798.[45] Thus, fewer officers were required. By 1794 the most talented—or fortunate—soldiers had already been commissioned. After that, only a score of Rochambeau's American veterans would be promoted from the ranks, and most of the promotions came in 1795.[46] The majority of these veterans remained enlisted men as long as they stayed in the army.

The life of these soldiers was difficult and dangerous but not without compensations. The army was, after all, the ultimate defense of the nation and the Revolution, and especially during the Year II the soldiers' contributions were publicly and officially recognized. Indeed, praise for the army was reserved almost exclusively for the troops; the Cordeliers Club of Paris even claimed that "the virtue of the soldier always surpasses that of the officers." Newspapers, songs, poems, civic festivities, government agents, and political clubs all attempted to spread revolutionary patriotism and tighten bonds between the people and the army. Although such propaganda was never totally effective, ample evidence exists of patriotic devotion among the men in the ranks of the armies of the republic.[47]

The soldiers derived support not only from civilian sources but also within their own military society. The most basic unit in the French army of the period was the *ordinaire*, or mess,[48] a group composed of fourteen to sixteen soldiers (sometimes fewer, depending on circumstances) with a corporal in charge. Although the mess usually coincided with a squad, the smallest tactical or combat unit, its primary importance was its logistical and social role. The members of the *ordinaire* pooled their daily rations, consisting of meat, fresh or dried vegetables, rice, salt, and whatever else imagination suggested or necessity dictated. Shortly after dawn all of the ingredients went into a large iron pot, the *marmite*, together with water to make a stew; an hour or two before noon half the broth and most of the vegetables were served with bread as *soupe*, and the meat and remaining ingredients provided the evening meal (around 5 P.M.). The *ordinaire* also provided sustenance of a less obvious but also important nature. It was there that the bonds that would maintain discipline in combat were formed; it was there that revolutionary principles and values were exchanged, including discussions of the political ideals presented in government propaganda; it was there that the interdependence of comrades was formed, sometimes in spite of personal differences.

Corporals supervised the *ordinaire*, including the assignment of duties, the distribution of food, and the maintenance of accounts. The sergeants—including a large proportion of the veterans of the American Revolution—occupied a distinct position between enlisted men and officers, sharing certain characteristics of both but belonging to neither group. By 1794 they were well educated by contemporary standards; over 85 percent were literate, and more than half could "calculate." Even the illiterates had extensive practical experience in the army (often a more fundamental consideration than literacy in combat). They were relatively young—nearly two-thirds were under thirty, and less than a tenth were older than forty—but a substantial minority (nearly 45 percent) had service that dated to the Old Regime.[49] The sergeants, like most of the officers, were professional soldiers, although to a somewhat less degree.

Indeed, from 1794 virtually all men serving in the ranks were becoming more and more militarized. As time and distance from their civilian background increased, army life assumed greater importance. By 1798 five of every six French soldiers—the vast majority of whom had joined the army when they were in their late teens and early twenties—had served for more than four years. Furthermore, after 1794, campaigns were waged almost exclusively on foreign soil, at increasingly further distances from home. The fact that correspondence with families and friends took inordinate lengths of time to reach its destination and sometimes never did arrive intensified the soldiers' sense of isolation and increased their dependence on military society.[50]

Although increasingly the army became a "home" for many, military life was often harsh. Some new recruits suffered so severely from homesickness, or *nostalgie*, that they failed to respond to incentives or threats, refused to eat, and died as a result.[51] Even veterans fully acclimated to army life were exposed to severe deprivations. Necessities, including food, fodder, clothing, and fuel, were frequently inadequate and sometimes totally lacking. Even when provisions were available, other problems, particularly the breakdown of transportation facilities and the reluctance of the local populace to furnish supplies, prevented distribution to the troops. Sometimes weather conditions created difficulties. For example, during the winter of 1794–1795 when the temperature reached –17° C (1° F) at Antwerp, which was occupied by the Army of the Sambre and Meuse, soldiers were unable to eat because their food was frozen solid.[52] Occasionally, the pressures of combat interfered with eating. While defending the forest of Hochstenbach against the Austrians in September 1796, Private Girault complained, "For three days we have not had time to boil water in the marmite. We could only gather a few potatoes, a piece of suet and a tiny onion."[53]

Such hardships, coupled with the demanding and debilitating conditions normally faced by soldiers on campaign, frequently led to illness, which, in turn, was compounded by an appalling lack of hygiene. Vermin, particularly lice, abounded, but when officers ordered infected soldiers to have their heads shaved, the men objected to the treatment as dishonorable. Skin diseases such as scabies were also common. Indeed, dietary deficiencies, harsh weather, inadequate clothing and lodging, along with poor hygiene made soldiers ready prey to an almost limitless variety of diseases and illnesses. In addition, the constant plague of contemporary armies, venereal disease, was widespread, accounting for as many as 20 to 30 percent of hospitalizations.[54] Far fewer soldiers were wounded in combat, and many of them survived, as evidenced by the experience of American veterans like Nicolas Tribout, Louis André, Conrad Beltz, and Antoine Tricot, among others.[55] Those most seriously wounded could only hope the wound was to a limb, for despite the absence of antiseptics and anesthesia (except alcohol), amputation enjoyed a fair rate of success. Wounds to the abdomen, in contrast, were almost always fatal, although a few did survive them—inexplicably.[56]

Perhaps the most frightening prospect for ill or injured soldiers was to be sent to a hospital. Even though health care and medicine had improved among the armies of the republic, especially between 1792 and 1794, most military hospitals were as understaffed, crowded, poorly ventilated, inadequately supplied, and unsanitary as they had been at the time of Yorktown. Furthermore, conditions deteriorated during the Directory and under Napoleon.[57] Once more, Girault offers vivid firsthand testimony about the situation in army hospitals. In December 1794 he was confined in the Hospital of Saint Laurent in Liège, where he said he "could pick out the lice by the fistful" from his bed. Transferred to another hospital at Namur, he could not find even "a bunch of straw" to sleep on. Taking pity on him, two soldiers allowed him to sleep in the bed they already shared. When one of them died, Girault confessed, "I had no scruples about taking over the dead man's straw mattress, despite the fact that it was full of nameless vile things." When the first thaw came in early 1795, "the poor sick died like flies"; he estimated that of the nearly three thousand patients there, fifty or more died each day. Understandably, Girault left without being officially released and simply returned to his unit.[58]

It is not surprising that many of the battle-worn veterans of Rochambeau's American expedition succumbed to the harsh conditions imposed by war. For example, Mathieu Duffraine, who had joined the Regiment of Saintonge in April 1769 when he was nineteen and served as a corporal in the United States, was a sergeant in the 152nd Demi-Brigade at the time of his death on November 27, 1794, "from the hardships [*fatigues*] of war." The same cause of death was listed for Sergeant Sulpice Bret of the same unit when he died at age thirty-seven in Prairial, Year IV (May 20–June 18, 1796).[59] A native of Hesdin in Artois, Ambroise Lagache had served with the same regiment in America when he was in his early twenties. He stayed with his battalion through the wars of the Revolution, was made a POW in December 1792, and was incorporated into the 152nd Demi-Brigade in 1794 and the 75th Demi-Brigade in 1796. Corporal Lagache died "of the plague" in Messidor, Year VII (June–July 1799) during the Egyptian campaign.[60]

Sergeant Jean Leblanc was a veteran of nearly twenty-four years of service, including two terms as a prisoner of war (November 1793–February 1796 and September 1796–April 1797) and thirteen campaigns in North America and Europe with the Soissonnais (40th) Infantry and the 79th Demi-Brigade, when he "died at Saint-Domingue on 28 Brumaire Year XI" (November 19, 1802).[61] Ignace Milliard, an Alsatian who served in his first campaign with the Regiment of Royal Deux-Ponts in America, had just completed his sixteenth campaign, as regimental cobbler in the 17th Regiment of Line Infantry, when he "died of the fever, in camp on September 7, 1806," at age fifty-two.[62] Antoine Tricot, a peasant from the region of Ile-de-France that became the department of the Oise, joined the Bourbonnais (13th) Infantry in December 1777 and fought with that regiment in America. He was promoted to corporal in June 1791 and to sergeant two years later. He was shot in the left arm during the battle of Reichhoffen on November 20, 1793; received three saber blows to the head at the battle of Kaiserslautern on September 20, 1794; and was shot in the left side at the battle of Engen on May 13, 1800. He "died at the military hospital of Boulogne on July 23, 1807" at age fifty-five.[63]

Besides these deaths from "natural" causes, there were also accidental deaths. When he was nineteen, Jean Gilbert had enlisted in the Regiment of Saintonge, the year before its departure for the United States. He continued to serve in the same unit after returning to France, became a corporal in 1791, was captured along with the rest of the second battalion in December 1792, was repatriated, was incorporated into the 152nd Demi-Brigade in

July 1794, and was promoted to sergeant in November 1795. He continued his career in the 75th Demi-Brigade after the 1796 reorganization and sailed for Egypt with that unit in May 1798. On October 11, 1800, after more than twenty-one years of military service on five continents, Gilbert "drowned in the Nile."[64] Even more ironic was the fate of Alexis Morge, described earlier. In January 1809, two months before his fiftieth birthday, this veteran of more than twenty-nine years in the same regiment, the Auxonne (6th) Artillery, was accidentally shot to death—apparently by one of his comrades.[65]

Typically, far fewer American veterans were killed in combat than died of other causes. As time went on, this became even more the case, since these senior soldiers were assigned to less hazardous duties. Nevertheless, combat still took its toll. Georges Richard from Bar-le-Duc, Lorraine, who had joined the Soissonnais Infantry in November 1779 at age seventeen, was a sergeant major in the 79th Demi-Brigade when he was killed in battle on October 21, 1798. François Pelletier from the small Burgundian village of Sermoye had joined the same regiment within three weeks of Richard and was a corporal in the same demi-brigade when he died on March 9, 1799, as a result of recent wounds.[66] General Bonaparte's Egyptian expedition was particularly costly for American veterans of the old Regiment of Saintonge, the second battalion of which had been amalgamated into the 75th Demi-Brigade in 1796. For example, Léonard Duchesne, a native of Rochefoucault in Angoumois, had enlisted in the Saintonge Infantry in July 1778. Promoted to corporal in 1792, he was killed during the fighting at Acre, Syria, in May 1799. Following the failure of the siege, Bonaparte led his army back to Egypt and attacked a Turkish army at Aboukir. In the course of the French victory there in July, Louis Joseph Blou, still a simple soldier after nearly twenty-two years in the army, was killed in the ranks of the 75th Demi-Brigade. Blou, from rural Picardy, had joined the Regiment of Saintonge nine months before Duchesne at age eighteen and like him had spent his entire military career with the same unit.[67]

Another group of combat casualties whose lot may have been the most wretched of all were the prisoners of war.[68] After the demoralizing experience of defeat and capture, these men were commonly marched or otherwise transported long distances from their place of capture (and even further from their homes). For instance, most of the French troops who were captured by Austrian forces—including the first battalion of the 40th (Soissonnais) Infantry, which surrendered in November 1793—were incarcerated in Hungary. Many prisoners suffered from dysentery, diarrhea, other infectious diseases, and, in the case of the wounded, gangrene before they reached the internment camps; others contracted illnesses while there. Since hospitals in POW camps were even worse than those in the French army, the death rate among prisoners was high—10 percent or more each year. For example, Georges Schwartz and Jacob Klein, both of whom were born near Sarrelouis in Lorraine and served in the first battalion of the Regiment of Royal Deux-Ponts in America and, after 1796, as sergeants in the 92nd Demi-Brigade, died as prisoners of war—Schwartz in October or November 1799 and Klein in January 1800.[69] For other soldiers, like Pierre François and Jacques Pericot who served in the Regiment of Bourbonnais in the United States and later in the 26th and 108th Demi-Brigades, all records ceased after their capture (on December 8, 1795, and September 29, 1799, respectively); presumably, these men died in captivity.[70] Prisoners who managed to survive the physical ordeal often suffered psychologically. They were not only cut off from relatives and friends at home but were also isolated from local civilians and segregated from their officers, who were confined in separate facilities.

Although POWs felt it most poignantly, other soldiers also felt they had been abandoned by their government. In addition to the deprivations they suffered—for example, insufficient supplies, pay that was in arrears or in useless paper *assignats,* loss of contact with family—many soldiers were convinced that their wives, children, and parents were not being properly cared for as corruption and counterrevolution flourished among the high and mighty at home. Resentment grew against the civilian authorities, the "mandarins" (*pékins*) who knew little about the soldiers' lot and cared less, as the troops looked increasingly to their generals for support and leadership.[71] Substantial reductions in government efforts to foster political awareness in the army only reinforced feelings of isolation and alienation among the troops.[72]

Although it remains impossible to identify precisely the motives for desertion, this alienation likely played a part in some soldiers' decisions to desert—along with the dreadful conditions of life in the army, the risks of combat, their families' needs, and a sense that they had fulfilled their obligation while others were shirking theirs.[73] Desertions by long-term veterans, accustomed to isolation from civilian society and inured to the dangers and discomforts of a military career, seem especially to fit such an explanation. At least one might speculate that this consideration had some role in the desertions of men like Jean Roussy, Etienne Bailly, and Jean Schumacher. Roussy, born in rural Languedoc in 1761, enlisted in the Regiment of Bourbonnais in February 1777, was promoted to corporal in 1786, and held the rank of sergeant when he deserted from the 25th Demi-Brigade on June 28, 1795. Bailly, a Burgundian, was only a private first class (*appointé*) when he deserted from the 50th Demi-Brigade on September 9, 1797, but he had been in the army since he enlisted in the same regiment as Roussy in February 1774. Schumacher, a native of Baden, had joined the Royal Deux-Ponts Infantry in April 1776 at age twenty-two. He served with that regiment in the American Revolution and, subsequently, served in the 177th, 59th, and 102nd Demi-Brigades. He was a sergeant in the 102nd when he deserted on January 20, 1798.[74]

Desertions by such "old-timers," however, were rare. Much more commonly, men who had spent virtually their entire adult lives in the ranks and managed to survive left the army with honorable discharges and, typically, with retirement benefits.[75] A special category of soldiers who were not—to be entirely accurate—discharged or even officially retired were the veterans admitted to the Hôtel des Invalides in Paris or to one of its "detached" companies outside the capital. Those men continued to wear their uniforms, to be organized in military units, to keep their rank and even be promoted, to take their meals in their assigned "mess," and—on rare occasions—to perform limited military service.[76]

The Invalides, inaugurated by Louis XIV to recognize and recompense military men who were unable to support themselves because of their sacrifices in the service of their country, was something other than an "old soldiers' home." Although a clear majority of the invalides were indeed worn out by age and arduous service, a substantial minority were not superannuated veterans but soldiers who had been debilitated by wounds or disease incurred in the performance of their military duties. For example, a number of relatively young men from Rochambeau's expeditionary corps were admitted to this institution shortly after their return from America. Jean Lindel, a German who had served in the Royal Deux-Ponts since January 1779, was admitted to the Invalides in August 1783 at age twenty-four because he had been "crippled in his right hand by a gunshot wound received in Rochambeau's army in 1781." Pierre Le Breton, from the village of Saint-Saveur in Normandy, entered the Invalides the same month after serving eight years in the Soissonnais Infantry. Le Breton, who was twenty-seven at the time, had "three fingers blown off by a cannon shot aboard the vessel *Ardent* in the Chesapeake." Sebastien Cuisinier, a seven-year veteran of the Regiment of Bourbonnais from Nancy, was thirty-two when admitted to the Invalides in February 1784 for a wound "to his right leg by a bomb explosion at the siege of York in 1781." Louis François Delmard, a native of Lille from the same regiment, was only twenty-two years old when he entered the Invalides with Cuisinier because of a wound in his right thigh suffered during the same engagement.[77]

Nevertheless, most of the veterans who became invalides were older and had served longer than these soldiers. Marin Gerard (Girard in the Invalides register) was forty-seven or forty-eight years old when he was discharged from active duty because of an injury to his left leg and entered the Invalides in spring 1788 after more than twenty-one years of service in the Regiment of Bourbonnais. He died just seven months later, on November 10, 1788.[78] Charles Fauvel, who had served for over thirty years in the Saintonge (82nd) Infantry, also died within less than a year of admission to the Invalides in 1792.[79] Joseph Mariscaille (or Mariscal) from Douai was first admitted to the Invalides in December 1783 after his return from the United States where he had served with Lauzun's Legion. Despite serious injuries to his left leg, he returned to active duty during the French Revolution and became a captain in the 16th Battalion of Light Infantry. In August 1796, when he was in his fifties, Mariscaille was readmitted to the Invalides and remained there until his death on April 30, 1810.[80] Paul Masieu, who was born in 1745 or 1746 in a Norman village and served in America with the Regiment of Saintonge, entered the Invalides in March 1792 following twenty-six years of service after his "wrist had been crippled and [he had suffered] a hernia in America." In 1802 he was transferred to facilities at Louvain, returned to Paris in 1804, and eventually died at Avignon on January 6, 1820.[81] The last of Rochambeau's soldiers in the Invalides, Jean Baptiste Guinez, died October 25, 1831, at age seventy-one. A former wig maker from French Flanders, Guinez had entered the Invalides in April 1784 after five and a half years in the Bourbonnais Infantry, debilitated by a broken left leg incurred "in the service of the King at Providence in America." He married on February 28, 1789, was provisionally promoted to lieutenant in July 1794, left the Invalides in April 1801, and was readmitted on April 20, 1817.[82]

Most of the veterans of the American campaigns of the early 1780s who left active duty after 1794 did not enter the Invalides. Some were simply discharged. For example, André Clairet from Franche-Comté had enlisted in the Regiment of Neustrie in November 1776 at age seventeen. In 1781 he was among the few hundred reinforcements Rochambeau received in America, where he was assigned to the first battalion of the Bourbonnais (13th) Infantry. With the rest of that unit, Clairet was incorporated into the 25th Demi-Brigade, where he remained until his discharge in early May 1795 "for infirmities not acquired in the army." Presumably, he received no compensation for all his years of military service.[83]

A few long-term soldiers resigned from their duties. Sergeant Pierre Lefebvre resigned on October 17, 1796, after seventeen years of service in the Bourbonnais (13th) Infantry and the 26th and 108th Demi-Brigades.[84] Sergeant major Joseph Zabe, who had begun his career with the Regiment of Royal Deux-Ponts in November 1779, resigned from his post in the 17th Demi-Brigade on October 16, 1798.[85] One of the most unusual cases was Chrétien Rossel, an Alsatian who enlisted in Deux-Ponts in December 1768, two months before his nineteenth birthday. After serving in the American campaigns, he was discharged in March 1790. Fourteen months later he joined the Royal Liégeois (101st) Infantry and served with that unit until it was disbanded in August 1792. Rossel then enlisted in the 3rd Battalion of the Bas-Rhin, where he was quickly promoted to sergeant. Ironically, this battalion of national volunteers was amalgamated with the first battalion of the former Deux-Ponts regiment in May 1794. Sometime within the next two years (no date is given), Rossel's long and varied military career ended ignominiously; he was "expunged from the register after being condemned to ten years in irons" for an unspecified but serious offense.[86]

Most veterans enjoyed a more honorable and rewarding separation from the army; about half of the enlisted men who had fought under Rochambeau in America and were discharged after 1793 received army pensions. The amount of the pensions varied according to length of service, rank, and the extent of any disabilities arising from military service, as well as changing government policies. In general, military personnel could draw a pension amounting to one-quarter of their annual pay after thirty years of service (combat service or campaigns counted double); each further year of service, up to a total of fifty years, would add an additional 5 percent of the remaining three-quarters of the yearly salary. Disabilities also increased pensions, with the most serious bringing maximum benefits. Most veterans, especially enlisted men, found it extremely difficult to live decently on their military pensions alone.[87]

As the years—and the virtually endless wars—went on, more and more American survivors left active duty and took their retirement pensions. For example, François Limousin was still a boy—fourteen years old—when he enlisted as a hussar in Lauzun's Legion on March 6, 1779. He spent much of his adolescence in the United States. After returning to France, he remained in the same unit and was promoted to corporal in 1793 and to sergeant a year later. When General Michel Ney, who had also begun his military career as a simple hussar, inspected Limousin's regiment, the 5th Hussars, in February 1802, he ordered that Limousin be discharged because he "is of a worn-out and feeble constitution, has had a leg broken in a fall from his horse during the campaigns in America, and is also suffering from a serious loss of sight in his left eye, all the results of the hardships of war." When he

AFTERMATH OF REVOLUTION

began to draw his pension later that year, Limousin was thirty-seven years old![88] Jean Grellé (or Grelay), who was born in a small village in Berry in July 1763 and enlisted in the Regiment of Soissonnais in March 1779, was nine years older when he retired with a pension on May 1, 1809. Because he had thirty years of service and had participated in twenty campaigns, ranging from the American Revolution to service in Napoleon's Grande Armée in 1806 and 1807, Grellé drew the maximum retirement pay; his pay grade, however, was only that of corporal—a rank he had achieved a mere three years earlier, in February 1806.[89]

Although a handful of officers who had served in Rochambeau's American expedition remained on duty longer, the last remaining enlisted man was Mathias Wervy who had enrolled in Lauzun's Legion in February 1779 at age twenty-five. In February 1787 he was discharged after completing his eight-year enlistment, but nineteen months later Wervy reenlisted in the Lauzun Hussars (designated the 6th Hussars in 1791 and the 5th Hussars in 1793). For the next quarter century he remained with the same regiment, serving as its "chief bootmaker" (a noncommissioned specialist rank), and he participated in all of the regiment's campaigns between 1792 and 1806. At age sixty, after nearly thirty-four years in the ranks—including nineteen campaigns—Wervy was "discharged to enjoy his retirement pension on August 11, 1814, at the disbanding of the unit."[90] An era had ended.

Notes

1. In this chapter no attempt will be made to provide precise statistics or percentages. The relatively small numbers of individuals, the length of the period under discussion, and the dispersal of the men in many different units—and many different records—would make this an extremely formidable task for very limited results. In any event, gaps in the records prohibit absolute accuracy. The specific examples presented here constitute typical cases but are by no means exhaustive.
2. Bodinier, *Officiers*, pp. 412 and 426–427, and Bodinier, "Officiers de l'armée royale et la Révolution," pp. 66–67; Jean-Paul Bertaud, *La Révolution Armée: Les soldats citoyens et la Révolution française* (Paris: Robert Laffont, 1979), pp. 152–153, 156, 177, and 187 (pp. 143–144, 147–148, 172, and 184 in the English translation). On Wisch, see p. 181.
3. Bodinier, *Dictionnaire*, p. 51.
4. Ibid., pp. 483–484.
5. Ibid., p. 140
6. Besides ibid., pp. 479–480, see Weelen, *Rochambeau*, pp. 284–285; and Gardiner, *Cincinnati in France*, p. 80.
7. Bodinier, *Dictionnaire*, p. 171.

FROM YORKTOWN TO VALMY

8. Ibid., p. 164, provides a useful summary of Dumas's career; his memoirs were published in 1839, two years after his death.
9. Bodinier, *Officiers*, pp. 459 and 484. Details on the Lameths are summarized in the same author's *Dictionnaire*, pp. 279–280.
10. Gardiner, *Cincinnati in France*, pp. 193–197; and Bodinier, *Dictionnaire*, pp. 7–8.
11. Rochambeau Papers, vol. 5, p. 563 (October 12, 1782); a proposal for a *gratification* (1787) in A.G., X^b 25; and Bodinier, *Dictionnaire*, p. 306.
12. The careers of these two "rankers" can be followed in A.G., 1 YC 188, 14 YC 17, and the appropriate cartons in Classement Général, Officiers (arranged in alphabetical order).
13. See A.G., 1 YC 869, 14 YC 144, and the relevant carton in Classement Général, Officiers.
14. See p. xii.
15. A.G., 10 YC 1, the uncoded contrôles of 6me Régiment d'Artillerie à pied (1786–4 Ventôse, An II) and (7 Ventôse, An II–28 messidor An XI), and carton 2302 in Classement Général, Officiers.
16. A.G., 1 YC 932, 14 YC 119, and carton 42bis in Classement Général, Officiers. On companies of veterans see following, p. 204.
17. A.G., 1 YC 869, 14 YC 144, and the appropriate carton in Classement Général, Officiers.
18. A.N., D^2 C 32; A.G., 8 YC 17, the uncoded contrôles of the 5e Hussards (Lauzun 1786, 6e Hussards 1791, 5e Hussards, 1793) for 1786 to August 23, 1792, and from August 25, 1792, to Fructidor, An IX (August–September 1801), and Classement Général, Officiers.
19. See A.G., Classement Général, Officiers, carton 238, as well as 10 YC 1 and the uncoded registers cited in note 15 in this chapter.
20. On Devrigny, see p. 188. For Laprun, see Bodinier, *Dictionnaire*, p. 287.
21. Documents in A.G., X^b 91 clearly indicate that Le Monier was "employed in the recruiting depot," although Bodinier lists him as having "gone to America with Rochambeau's corps" (*Dictionnaire*, pp. 306–307); also see p. 172. Similarly, Bodinier claims that Jean Baptiste Eblé, who became a general in 1793, served as a sergeant major with the Auxonne Artillery in the United States; but, in fact, he is not carried in the contrôle of the second battalion that did serve there, and Georges Six indicates that he was at Geneva in 1782. See the latter's *Dictionnaire biographique des généraux at amiraux français de la Révolution et de l' Empire (1792–1814)*, vol. 1 (Paris: Saffroy, 1934), p. 420.
22. This estimate is based on incomplete data for 86 officers promoted from the ranks whose careers could be traced to 1794 and beyond in A.G., Classement Général, Officiers. No information could be found in this huge but uneven series for an additional 136 rankers who were also veterans of Rochambeau's American expedition.
23. Bertaud, *Révolution Armée*, p. 179. On the larger issue, see my " 'Careers Open to Talent,'" especially pp. 65–71.
24. Bertaud, *Révolution Armée*, pp. 182–183.
25. Ibid., pp. 277–278; and Jean-Claude Devos and Denise Devos, "Opinions et carrière des officiers sous le Directoire et le Consulat," in *Le Métier militaire en France aux époques des grandes transformations sociales* (Vincennes: Service Historique de l'Armée de Terre, 1980), p. 89.

26. J. P. Carrez, "L'Ecole d'Artillerie sous la Convention: 20 Septembre 1792–26 Octobre 1795," *Revue Historique des Armées*, nos. 1–2 (1975, special issue): 40 and 42.
27. On these developments, see Bertaud, *Révolution Armée*, pp. 278 and 301; and Devos and Devos, "Opinions et carrière des officiers," p. 89.
28. Documents on Montchoisy, dated October 1781, in A.N., D^2 C 32; and Bodinier, *Dictionnaire*, pp. 99–100.
29. For a more thorough analysis, see Devos and Devos, "Opinions et carrière des officiers," pp. 93–101, which provides the basis for the following brief discussion of political purges, except where otherwise noted.
30. See p. 172; and Bodinier, *Dictionnaire*, p. 336.
31. See p. 189.
32. Cilleuls, "Service de l'intendance," p. 61; and Bodinier, *Dictionnaire*, p. 213.
33. See p. 193.
34. See pp. 172 and 193; as well as Woloch, *French Veteran*, pp. 178–180.
35. This proportion is based on a sample of one-third of all those who served as general officers during that year (159 generals), drawn from Six, *Dictionnaire des généraux*, vols. 1 and 2.
36. Devos and Devos, "Opinions et carrière des officiers," pp. 91–92; and Bertaud, *Révolution Armée*, pp. 280–281.
37. Bodinier, *Dictionnaire*, p. 117.
38. A.G., 1 YC 869, 14 YC 144, and Classement Général, Officiers, carton 190.
39. A.G., 10 YC 1, the uncoded contrôle for the 6me Régiment d'Artillerie à pied (1786–4 Ventôse Year II), and the appropriate carton in Classement Général, Officiers.
40. Kreps's career can be followed through four "generations" of contrôles: A.G., 1 YC 188, 14 YC 17, and the registers for the 25th Demi-Brigade in 21 YC (1ère Formation) and for the 50th Demi-Brigade in 22 YC (2me Formation). The coding of individual volumes in the last two series was incomplete when they were consulted.
41. A.N., D^2 C 32; A.G., 8 YC 17, and the uncoded contrôles for this regiment from 1786 to 26 Fructidor Year IX, as well as the relevant carton in Classement Général, Officiers.
42. A.G., 10 YC 1, and the uncoded register for the 6me Régiment d'Artillerie à pied (1786–4 Ventôse Year II), and Classement Général, Officiers.
43. Because there are no indications in the unit contrôles of the date and type of separation for 431 enlisted men who had served in America from 1780 to 1783 and were still serving between 1786 and 1794, this number could be larger. The evidence strongly suggests, however, that most, possibly all, had left their units by 1794.
44. For both men, see A.G., 1 YC 188 and 14 YC 17; for Tuo, the volume for the 26th Demi Brigade in 21 YC; and for Guidez, the volume for the 25th Demi-Brigade in the same series. The last entry for Guidez is the notation of his demotion, dated 21 Brumaire Year IV (November 12, 1795).
45. Jean-Paul Bertaud, *La Vie quotidienne des soldats de la Révolution, 1789–1799* (Paris: Hachette, 1985), pp. 53–54, and Bertaud, *Révolution Armée*, pp. 337–338.
46. I have identified twenty-two such cases, fourteen in 1795 and none after 1803.

It must be borne in mind, however, that lacunae in the records prevent absolute precision.
47. Bertaud, Révolution Armée, pp. 144–152 and 195–222, and Bertaud, Vie quotidienne des soldats, pp. 198–199, 205, 215–217, and 267–269; as well as John A. Lynn, The Bayonets of the Republic: Motivation and Tactics in the Army of Revolutionary France, 1791–94 (Urbana: University of Illinois Press, 1984), pp. 77, 85, 94–96, and 173–182; the quotation is on p. 77.
48. The best available sources on this important institution are Bertaud, Vie quotidienne des soldats, pp. 134–137 and 142–147; Lynn, Bayonets of the Republic, pp. 164–168, and Lynn, "Structures Versus Standards: Small Unit Cohesion in the Armies of Revolutionary France, 1792–1794," unpublished paper delivered at the 96th annual meeting of the American Historical Association in Los Angeles, December 29, 1981 (kindly furnished by the author).
49. Bertaud, Révolution Armée, pp. 190–191.
50. See ibid., pp. 175 and 275, and Bertaud, Vie quotidienne des soldats, pp. 123–124.
51. Bertaud, Vie quotidienne des soldats, p. 105; and the classic article by Marcel Reinhard, "Nostalgie et service militaire pendant la Révolution," Annales historiques de la Révolution française 30 (1958): 1–15.
52. The best study of the supply problem is Peter Wetzler, War and Subsistence: The Sambre and Meuse Army in 1794 (New York: Peter Lang, 1985); see especially pp. 134–136 and 197–201.
53. Girault, Mes campagnes, p. 57.
54. See Bertaud, Vie quotidienne des soldats, pp. 113 and 166–167; and Wetzler, War and Subsistence, p. 133.
55. See pp. 191–192, and p. 201.
56. Bertaud, Vie quotidienne des soldats, pp. 250–251 and 254; and Woloch, French Veteran, pp. 197–198.
57. See p. 81. For military hospitals during and after the French Revolution, see Bertaud, Vie quotidienne des soldats, pp. 251–255; Woloch, French Veteran, pp. 196–198; and Colin Jones, "The Welfare of the French Foot-Soldier," History 65 (1980): 206–209.
58. Girault, Mes campagnes, pp. 39 and 42–43.
59. For both Duffraine and Bret, see A.G., 1 YC 932, 14 YC 119, and 21 YC, the volume for the 152nd Demi-Brigade.
60. On Lagache, see the same contrôles as in note 59, plus 22 YC for the 75th Demi-Brigade.
61. His career in summarized in A.G., 22 YC, the second volume for the 79th Demi-Brigade.
62. Milliard's service is recorded in the uncoded register of this regiment, which was begun on 1 Vendémiaire, Year XII (September 24, 1803).
63. Tricot's record can be found in the same uncoded series as that in note 62, begun on 1 Vendémiaire, Year XII, the volume for the 50th Regiment of Line Infantry.
64. A.G., 1 YC 932, 14 YC 119, 21 YC, the volume for 152nd Demi-Brigade, and 22 YC, the volume for the 75th Demi-Brigade.
65. See pp. xi–xii.
66. Richard's and Pelletier's careers can be followed in A.G, 1 YC 966, 14 YC 58, and the volumes for the 79th Demi-Brigade in 21 YC and 22 YC.

AFTERMATH OF REVOLUTION

67. On Duchesne and Blou, see A.G., 1 YC 932, 14 YC 119, the volume for the 152nd Demi-Brigade in 21 YC, and the volume for the 75th Demi-Brigade in 22 YC.
68. On POWs in general, see Bertaud, *Révolution Armée*, pp. 251–254, and Bertaud, *Vie quotidienne des soldats*, p. 262. An excellent study of the treatment of French prisoners by the Austrians, the most persistent of France's enemies from 1792 to 1815, is Palásti, "Soldats français en captivité."
69. A.G., 1 YC 869, 14 YC 144, the volume for the 177th Demi-Brigade in 21 YC and for the 92nd Demi-Brigade in 22 YC.
70. A.G., 1 YC 188, 14 YC 17, the volume for the 26th Demi-Brigade in 21 YC and for the 108th Demi-Brigade in 22 YC.
71. Bertaud, *Révolution Armée*, pp. 289–312, and Bertaud, "Napoléon, l'armée et la dictature," *L'Histoire*, no. 30 (January 1981): 48–49.
72. Martin, *Origines de la presse militaire*, pp. 257–261 and 280.
73. On the problem of desertion in general, see Bertaud, *Vie quotidienne des soldats*, pp. 265–267, and Bertaud, *Révolution Armée*, pp. 254–258; as well as Lynn, *Bayonets of the Republic*, pp. 111–112.
74. A.G., 1 YC 188, 14 YC 17, and the volume for the 25th Demi-Brigade in 21 YC for Roussy; the same three registers plus that for the 50th Demi-Brigade in 22 YC for Bailly; and 1 YC 869, 14 YC 144, and the volumes for the 177th Demi-Brigade in 21 YC and for the 59th and 102nd Demi-Brigades in 22 YC for Schumacher.
75. Of the eighty-four enlisted veterans of Rochambeau's expedition discharged between 1794 and 1814, at least thirty-eight retired with pensions, and twenty-three entered the Hôtel des Invalides or joined one of its "detached" companies. These are minimum figures that include only those cases with explicit indications that the soldiers either received a pension or were admitted to the Invalides.
76. Anyone interested in this fascinating topic must read Woloch's *French Veteran*; it is the best work on the subject. After 1791 the "detached" companies were also referred to as companies of "veterans" or "national veterans."
77. These soldiers are recorded in the following contrôles: A.G., 1 YC 869 for Lindel, 966 for Le Breton, and 188 for Cuisinier and Delmard (or Delmare). They are "picked up" in A.G., Invalides, Registre matricule no. 45 under numbers 106.199, 106.220, 106.408, and 106.409, respectively.
78. See A.G. 1 YC 188, and 14 YC 17, as well as Invalides, registre matricule no. 46, number 109.228.
79. A.G., 1 YC 932, 14 YC 119, and Invalides, registre matricule no. 47, number 111.004. According to these military records, Fauvel, a native of Rouen, was somewhere between fifty-two and sixty years of age when he died on Christmas Day 1792.
80. A.N., D^2 C 32; and A.G., Invalides, registre matricule no. 45. Mariscaille's birth date is indicated as being in both 1748 and 1739.
81. A.G., 1 YC 932, 14 YC 119, and Invalides, registre matricule no. 47, number 111.002.
82. A.G., 1 YC 188, and Invalides, registre matricule no. 46, number 106.581.
83. On the reinforcements sent to America, see p. 52. On Clairet, see A.G., 1 YC 188, 14 YC 17, and the register for the 25th Demi-Brigade in 21 YC. Although

the year of Clairet's discharge is not recorded, circumstantial evidence makes it almost certainly 1795.
84. A.G., 1 YC 188, 14 YC 17, and the registers for the 26th Demi-Brigade in 21 YC and for the 108th Demi-Brigade in 22 YC.
85. A.G., 1 YC 869, 14 YC 144, and the registers for the 178th Demi-Brigade in 21 YC and for the 17th Demi-Brigade in 22 YC.
86. A.G., 1 YC 869, 14 YC 144, and the volume for the 177th Demi-Brigade in 21 YC.
87. See Woloch, *French Veteran*, pp. 61, 92–94, 98–102, 105–107, and 230.
88. A.N., D^2 C 32; A.G., 8 YC 17, and the uncoded register for the 6th Hussars, for the period from 1786 to August 23, 1792 (see no. 129).
89. Grellé's military career is summarized in A.G., the uncoded registers for the 3rd Regiment of Line Infantry, vol. 1 (1 Vendémiaire, An XII–13 Messidor, An XIII), and for the 39th Regiment of Line Infantry (3 mai 1808–14 mars 1812). For his earlier service, see A.G., 1 YC 966, 14 YC 58, and the volumes for the 80th Demi-Brigade in 21 YC and for the 83rd Demi-Brigade in 22 YC.
90. For a summary of Wervy's military service, see the uncoded contrôle for the 5th Hussars, vol. 4 (1er Floréal, An XII–18 avril 1809). His prior service is recorded in the earlier registers of the same regiment, where his name is also spelled Wervet.

CONCLUSION

THE OFFICERS AND MEN who served under Rochambeau in America between 1780 and 1783 and continued to serve in the French army during the French Revolution underwent a remarkable historical experience—direct participation in two of the most consequential developments of modern times. The fact that most were rather ordinary men, representative of tens of thousands of their comrades in the French army of the time, makes them attractive subjects of a study to measure, in human terms, the influence of the American Revolution on the French Revolution, which began a mere half dozen years after the troops returned to France.

Certain factors, however, severely limited the effect of the men's American experiences on their later reactions to revolution in their own country. For one thing, from the French point of view the American conflict was a classic kind of warfare waged against a traditional enemy. Service in the United States was a form of overseas duty common in such wars. Only a handful of officers perceived of themselves as fighting for a "cause." In short, for the French this was *not* a revolutionary war. Furthermore, there were major cultural differences between the Americans and French that had been strengthened by prior generations of hostility. Finally, contacts between the French soldiers and the American people, civilians and military alike, were intentionally kept to a minimum. The German troops in Rochambeau's corps, especially in the Deux-Ponts Regiment, constituted something of an exception to this generalization because they shared a number of traits with German settlers in certain regions and thus enjoyed closer relations with those American inhabitants than did most of the French forces. Even those sol-

CONCLUSION

diers, however, remained isolated from civil society during most of their stay in the United States. Although relations between Rochambeau's officers and Americans were less restricted, most officers maintained a distinct social and professional distance between themselves and their hosts and allies throughout their American sojourn.

Between the two revolutions some developments occurred in France that might possibly be traced to the American Revolution. Some, notably mounting financial problems and military reforms, clearly had deeper indigenous roots; at most, the American war reinforced firmly established trends. The growth of a liberal political ideology in France is more difficult to analyze, since similar ideas on both sides of the Atlantic often shared common intellectual sources. Beyond this, images of or myths about America and Americans generally had a greater impact than did actual contact with them. In any event, the veterans of Rochambeau's expedition had ambivalent and conflicting attitudes about the American political and social system, and they played little or no discernible part in propagating American ideals.

The role of the American Revolution in bringing about the French Revolution is, at best, highly speculative. The response of French veterans to events in France once revolution began is somewhat less so. In the Estates General and the National Assembly that succeeded it, a number of aristocrats who had served under Rochambeau became leaders of the liberal cause; they endorsed a reform program that ranged from the Declaration of the Rights of Man and Citizen to the creation of a National Guard. The latter, indeed, may be the clearest example of U.S. influence in the French Revolution; its conception bore a striking resemblance to the *ideal* of the American militia, and American veterans were prominent in organizing it. The basic question, nevertheless, cannot be answered unequivocally: How much did these changes reflect American precedents, and how much did they arise from conditions in France?

The importance of veterans of the American Revolution in the destruction of feudalism during the summer of 1789 is less debatable. Too few ex-soldiers who had been exposed to American practices of landholding were spread too thinly throughout the French countryside (often in regions unaffected by agrarian violence) to have had a decisive impact on the widespread peasant uprisings. Although there may have been instances of individual participation, French veterans can bear no collective responsibility for this rural mass movement.

Perhaps the most striking example of Rochambeau's American veterans' response to the French Revolution came during and immediately following the crisis in Paris in July 1789. Like all the troops summoned to the

CONCLUSION

area, they were weary after the long and rapid march from their garrisons when they entered the divisive political atmosphere of the capital. Like their comrades in other units, they found that preparations to receive them were completely inadequate, and they were subjected to intensive propaganda efforts to destroy or undermine their military discipline. Unlike most of the forces, however, the "American" units maintained nearly perfect order not only during the immediate crisis but also in the following weeks and months. The key to explaining this unusual conduct seems to have been the ties developed between officers and men during their participation in the American war. Although this cohesion eroded more quickly in the Deux-Ponts Infantry, Rochambeau's old regiments generally remained among the best disciplined in the French army until 1792.

A central issue, then, is resolved: The impact of the American experiences of Rochambeau's veterans on their response to the French Revolution was largely negligible; again with the exception of the Deux-Ponts Regiment, the most common—if unanticipated—result was greater cohesion between soldiers and officers. The men did not serve as a vital link in transmitting the principles and practices of the American Revolution to France. On the other hand, the history of those units and their personnel from the American Revolution through the French Revolution provides a vivid, detailed description of the major changes experienced by the entire French army during those momentous times. The officers and men who served under Rochambeau in America constituted a typical cross-section of the army in the late eighteenth century, despite certain inevitable peculiarities. Even their service in the United States was "normal" within the context of the long colonial conflict with England in North America that included King William's War (1689–1697), Queen Anne's War (1702–1713), King George's War (1743–1748), and the French and Indian War (1755–1763).

The truly extraordinary changes for these men came with the French Revolution. Although the number of American veterans left in the army had declined, their importance in their units had increased, and the experiences of their regiments graphically exemplified the fate of the army as a whole. Either as individuals or as members of their units, Rochambeau's former officers and men were involved in most of the key political and military events of the Revolution: the crisis of July 14, 1789; the mutiny at Nancy; the king's flight to Varennes; the overthrow of the monarchy; the crucial victories during autumn 1792 (for example, Valmy and Jemappes); the defeats of the following winter (for example, Frankfurt and Neerwinden); counterrevolution both at home and abroad; the transformation of the army and the military victories of the Year II; the Egyptian expedition; and the

CONCLUSION

coups d'état of the Directory. Tracing the role of these individuals and units in these important developments helps us to appreciate the role of rather ordinary people in the exceptional events of the time and the impact of those events on their lives and careers.

BIBLIOGRAPHY

ARCHIVAL SOURCES

Archives de la Guerre (Vincennes)(A.G.)
B^{1*} 208. Correspondence of General Biron (December 1790–September 1791).
B^{13} 43–49. Justice Militaire. Ancién Régime (1780–1783).
Classement Général Alphabétique. Officiers, 1791–1847. Various cartons, 10-3993.
Historiques. Cartons 10 (for Bourbonnais Regiment), 31 (Soissonnais), 55 (Saintonge), 66 (Royal Deux-Ponts), 125 (Lauzun), 138 (Auxonne).
Invalides. Registres matricules 45, 46, 47, 55, 60, 95, and 96.
K^7 55 (ninety-six folders containing Jean Pinsasseau's research on émigré armies).
X^b 22 (Neustrie).
X^b 25 and 166 (Bourbonnais), 53 and 176 (Soissonnais), 91 and 190 (Saintonge), 104 and 196 (Deux-Ponts).
X^c 83 and 245 (Lauzun).
X^d 24 and 25 (Auxonne).
X^i 1 and 2. Troupes maritimes et coloniales. Documents généraux.
YA 420. Documents d'interêt collectif ou général.
YA 513. Officiers. Décisions, 1780–1782.
YA 514. Expédition d'Amérique. Ordre de Cinncinnatus. Ancien Régime.
1 YC 188 and 14 YC 17. Contrôles de Troupe (Bourbonnais).
1 YC 966 and 14 YC 58. Contrôles de Troupe (Soissonnais).
1 YC 932 and 14 YC 119 and 120. Contrôles de Troupe (Saintonge).
1 YC 869 and 14 YC 144 and 145. Contrôles de Troupe (Deux-Ponts).
8 YC 17. Contrôles de Troupe (Lauzun).
10 YC 1. Contrôles de Troupe (Auxonne).
11 YC 141, 167, and 170. Contrôles de Troupe (French Guards).
20 YC 645, 646, and 647. Contrôles de Troupe (paid divisions of the Paris National Guard).
21 YC. Contrôles de Troupe. Demi-Brigades d'Infanterie. 1re Formation.
22 YC. Contrôles de Troupe. Demi-Brigades d'Infanterie. 2me Formation.

BIBLIOGRAPHY

Uncoded Contrôle de Troupe. 3ᵉ Régiment d'Infanterie de Ligne, vol. 1 (1 Vendémiaire, An XII–13 Messidor, An XIII).
Uncoded Contrôle de Troupe. 39ᵉ Regiment d'Infanterie de Ligne (3 mai 1808–14 mars 1812).
Uncoded Contrôles de Troupe. 5ᵉ Hussards—Lauzun 1786; 6ᵉ Hussards 1791; 5ᵉ Hussards 1793, vol. 1 (1786–23 août 1792), vol. 2 (25 août 1792–26 Fructidor, an IX), and vol. 4 (1 Floréal, An XII–18 avril 1809).
Uncoded Contrôles de Troupe. 6ᵉ Régiment d'Artillerie à pied, vol. 1 (1786–4 Ventôse, An II), vol. 2 (7 Ventôse, An II–28 Messidor An XI), and vol. 3 (26 août 1811–1 septembre 1813).

Archives Nationales (Paris) (A.N.)
BB³⁰ 161. Enquêtes et poursuites contre le baron de Besenval pour sa conduite lors de la prise de la Bastille.
D² C 32. Troupes des Colonies. Volontaires Etrangers de Lauzun. Matricule, Mutations, Situations, 1778–1785.
Dxxix bis. Comité des Recherches. Carton 2, dossier 22, pièce 17 (Soissonnais Regiment in November 1789); carton 5, dossier 71, pièces 9–11 (Saintonge Regiment in April 1790); and carton 18, dossier 198, pièce 23 (Nancy mutiny).
F⁷3659¹. Police générale (Bouches-du-Rhône.)
H 1453. Pièces et correspondances relatives aux troubles et émeutes. Correspondances diverses addressées à Necker, 1789–1790.
M 1036 (documents relating to the American Revolution).

Bibliothèque Nationale (Paris)(B.N.). Département des Manuscrits
N.A.F. 17691. "Journal de l'Armée aux ordres de Monsieur le Comte de Rochambeau pendant les campagnes de 1780, 1781, 1782, 1783 dans l'amérique septentrionale par le général Lauberdière."

Archives départementals du Bas-Rhin (Strasbourg)
1L 1439. Police et discipline militaire, troubles, insurrections, désordres, vols dans les régions, espions.

Archives départmentales de l'Isère (Grenoble)
L56. Administration de 1789 à l'an VIII.

Archives départmentales de la Meurthe-et-Moselle (Nancy)
E 235. Armée de Rochambeau. Livre d'ordre contenant ceux donnés depuis le débarquement des Troupes à Newport en Amérique Septentrionale, 1780.

Library of Congress (Washington, D.C.). Manuscript Division
The Papers of Jean-Baptiste Donatien de Vimeur, Comte de Rochambeau, 1777–1794. Fifteen Vols.
MMC 1907. Milton S. Latham Journal.

National Archives (Washington, D.C.)
Revolutionary War Pension and Bounty-Land-Warrant Application Files, S. 11072.

BIBLIOGRAPHY

Rhode Island State Archives (Providence)
L1. Letters to the Governor. Vols. 14–18.
L2. Letters From the Governor. Vol. 4.
Petitions to the Rhode Island General Assembly. Vols. 18–20.
Records of the Council of War, 1779–1781. 4 Vols.

Rhode Island Historical Society Library (Providence)
Providence Town Papers. Vols. 5–7 and Vol. 4 of 2nd series (March 1780–April 1783).

Providence Public Library
Providence Town Meetings. Vol. 6 (1772–1783).

Newport Historical Society
Inferior Court of Common Pleas. Court Records, 1767–1783. Vols. H–I.
Town Proceedings. Vol. 1 (1779–1816).

Virginia State Library (Richmond). Archives Division
Executive Department. Governor's Office. Letters Received, Boxes 15–25 (August 20, 1781–August 31, 1782).
Charlotte County. Court Order Book, No. 5 (1780–1784).
Prince Edward County. Court Order Book, Nos. 6 and 7 (1773–1784).
York County. Court Order Book, No. 4 (1774–1784).

Colonial Williamsburg Foundation Research Library
Lafayette-Leclerc Papers, 1780–1786.

Boston Public Library Manuscripts
Ms. f Fr. 160. French Expedition to America, 1782. Langeron Papers, 1778–1785. 4 Vols.
G. 380.38.1.60. Letter to Colonel Stephens, Camp before Savannah, Sept. 30, 1779.
R.1.1. 91–94. Letter of James Jarvis to Messers. John D. Neufville and Son, Merchants in Amsterdam, Boston, February 5, 1781.

Clements Library (University of Michigan)
Autographed letter from Chastellux to La Luzerne, dated May 28, 1781.

Houghton Library (Harvard University). Autograph File
Chevalier de Chastellux. Instruction pour le service de l'armée pendant le Quartier d'hyver.

Maclure Collection of French Revolutionary Materials (University of Pennsylvania), vol. 832
Rapport fait à l'Assemblée Nationale dans le séance du samedi 30 octobre, au nom des Comités militaire et des rapports, sur les événemens arrivés le 21 octobre à Béfort.

NEWSPAPERS

American Journal and General Advertiser (Providence). July 5, 1780–August 29, 1781.

219

BIBLIOGRAPHY

Boston Gazette and Country Journal. September 7–November 16, 1778 and December 2, 1782–January 6, 1783.
Continental Journal and Weekly Advertiser (Boston). September 3–November 19, 1778; July 13–August 24, 1780; and December 2, 1782–January 9, 1783.
Gazette françoise (Newport). November 17, 1780–January 2, 1781.
Newport Mercury. January 5, 1780–January 4, 1783.
Providence Gazette and County Journal. July 8, 1780–January 4, 1783.
Virginia Gazette, and Weekly Advertiser (Richmond). January 5–December 28, 1782.
Virginia Gazette, or, the American Advertiser (Richmond). December 22, 1781–December 14, 1782.

PUBLISHED DOCUMENTS

Arnold, James N., ed. *Vital Records of Rhode Island, 1636–1850*. First Series: Births, Marriages and Deaths. Vol. 4, Newport County. Providence: Naragansett Historical Publishing Company, 1893.
Bartlett, John Russell, ed. *Records of the State of Rhode Island and Providence Plantations in New England*. Vol. 9, 1780–1783. Providence: Alfred Anthony, 1864.
Dann, John C., ed. *The Revolution Remembered: Eyewitness Accounts of the War for Independence*. Chicago: University of Chicago Press, 1980.
Dawson, Warrington. *Les 2112 français morts aux Etats-Unis de 1777 à 1783 en combattant pour l'indépendance*. Paris: Société des Américainistes, 1936.
Doniol, Henri. *Histoire de la participation de la France à l'établissement des Etats-Unis d'Amérique: Correspondance diplomatique et documents*. 5 Vols. Paris: Imprimerie Nationale, 1886–1892.
Etat des officiers de tous grades déserteurs ou émigrés classés par régiment. Paris: Imprimerie Executive du Louvre, 1793.
France. Ministère des Affaires Etrangères. *Les Combattants français de la guerre américaine, 1778–1783: Listes établies d'après les documents authentiques déposés aux Archives Nationales et aux Archives du Ministère de la Guerre*. Washington, D.C.: Imprimerie Nationale, 1905.
Moore, Frank. *The Diary of the American Revolution, 1775–1781*. New York: Washington Square Press, 1967.
Official Letters of the Governors of the State of Virginia. Vol. 5, *The Letters of Thomas Nelson and Benjamin Harrison*. Richmond: Virginia State Library, 1929.
Stevens, Benjamin Franklin, ed. *Facsimiles of Manuscripts in European Archives Relating to America, 1773–1783, With Descriptions, Editorial Notes, Collations, References, and Translations*. 25 Vols. London: Privately printed, 1889–1898.

PUBLISHED DIARIES, JOURNALS, LETTERS, MEMOIRS, NARRATIVES, AND TRAVEL ACCOUNTS

Acomb, Evelyn M., ed. "The Journal of Baron Von Closen." *William and Mary Quarterly*, 3rd Ser. 10 (1953): 196–236.
———, ed. and trans. *The Revolutionary Journal of Baron Ludwig von Closen, 1780–1783*. Chapel Hill: University of North Carolina Press, 1958.
Armand, Charles Teffin, Marquis de la Rouerie. "The Letters of Col. Armand (Mar-

BIBLIOGRAPHY

quis de la Rouerie), 1777–1791." *New York Historical Society Collections* 11 (1878): 289–396.

Balch, E. W., ed. and trans. "Narrative of the Prince de Broglie, 1782." *Magazine of American History* 1 (1877): 180–186, 231–235, 306–309, and 374–380.

Balderston, Marion, and David Syrett, eds. *The Lost War: Letters From British Officers During the American Revolution.* New York: Horizon Press, 1975.

Berthier, Alexandre. "Journal de la Campagne d'Amérique, 10 Mai 1780–26 Août 1781." *Bulletin de l'Institut Français de Washington* 1 (December 1951): 43–120.

Blanchard, Claude. *The Journal of Claude Blanchard, Commissary of the French Auxiliary Army Sent to the United States During the American Revolution, 1780–1783.* Translated by William Duane. Albany: J. Munsell, 1876; reprint, New York: New York Times and Arno Press, 1969.

Bouillé, François Claude Amour, marquis de. *Mémoires du Marquis de Bouillé.* Paris: Baudouin, 1821.

Bray, Robert C., and Paul E. Bushnell, eds. *Diary of a Common Soldier in the American Revolution, 1775–1783: An Annotated Edition of the Military Journal of Jeremiah Greenman.* De Kalb: Northern Illinois University Press, 1978.

Broglie, Prince de. "Journal du voyage du prince de Broglie, colonel en second du régiment de Saintonge, aux Etats-Unis d'Amérique et dans l'Amérique du sud, 1782–1783." *Mélanges publiés par la Société des Bibliophiles françois.* Deuxième partie. Pièce 6 (1903): 13–148.

Castries, Armand Charles. "Dans l'armée de La Fayette, souvenirs inédits du comte de Charlus." *Revue de Paris* 64 (1957): 94–110.

Chase, Eugene Parker, ed. and trans. *Our Revolutionary Forefathers: The Letters of François, Marquis de Barbé-Marbois During His Residence in the United States as Secretary of the French Legation, 1779–1785.* New York: Duffield, 1929.

Chastellux, Marquis de. *Travels in North America in the Years 1780, 1781 and 1782.* 2 Vols. Edited and translated by Howard C. Rice Jr. Chapel Hill: University of North Carolina Press, 1963.

Chinard, Gilbert, ed. "Journal de Guerre de Brissot de Barneville, Mai 1780–Octobre 1781." *French American Review* 3 (1950): 217–278.

Clinton, Henry. *The American Rebellion: Sir Henry Clinton's Narrative of His Campaigns, 1775–1782, With an Appendix of Original Documents.* Edited by William B. Willcox. New Haven: Yale University Press, 1954.

Contenson, Ludovic de, ed. "Lettres d'un Officier de l'armée de Rochambeau: Le Chevalier de Cariolis." *Le Correspondant* 326 (March 25, 1932): 807–828.

Dawson, Warrington, ed. "Un garde Suisse de Louis XVI au service de l'Amérique: Le Baron Gaspard de Gallatin." *Le Correspondant* 324 (August 10, 1931): 321–338, and (September 10, 1931): 672–692.

———, ed. "With Rochambeau at Newport: The Narrative of Baron Gaspard de Gallatin." *Franco-American Review* 1 (1936–1937): 330–340.

Deux-Ponts, William de. *My Campaigns in America: A Journal Kept by Count William de Deux-Ponts, 1780–1781.* Translated by Samuel Abbott Green. Boston: J. K. Wiggin and W. Parsons Lunt, 1868.

"Diary of a French Officer, 1781 (Presumed to Be That of Baron Cromot du Bourg, Aide to Rochambeau)." *Magazine of American History* 4 (1880–1881): 205–214, 293–308, 376–385, 441–449, and 7 (1881): 283–295.

BIBLIOGRAPHY

Dumas, Mathieu. *Memoirs of His Own Time, Including the Revolution, the Empire, and the Restoration.* 2 Vols. Philadelphia: Lea and Blanchard, 1839.

Durousseau de Fayolle, Pierre. "Journal d'une campagne en Amérique (1777–1779)." *Bulletin et Mémoires de la Société des Antiquaires de l'Quest* 25 (1901): 1–48.

Echeverria, Durand, ed. and trans. "The American Character: A Frenchman Views the New Republic From Philadelphia, 1777." *William and Mary Quarterly*, 3rd Ser. 16 (1959): 376–413.

———, ed. and trans. "The Iroquois Visit Rochambeau at Newport in 1780: Excerpts From the Unpublished Journal of the Comte de Charlus." *Rhode Island History* 11 (July 1952): 73–81.

Echeverria, Durand, and Orville T. Murphy, eds. and trans. "The American Revolutionary Army: A French Estimate in 1777." *Military Affairs* 27 (1963): 1–7 and 153–162.

Faÿ, Bernard, ed. "L'Armeé de Rochambeau jugée par un Français." *Franco-American Review* 2 (1937): 114–120.

Feltman, William. *The Journal of Lieut. William Feltman, of the First Pennsylvania Regiment, 1781–82, Including the March Into Virginia and the Siege of Yorktown.* Philadelphia: Historical Society of Pennsylvania, 1853; reprint, New York: New York Times and Arno Press, 1969.

Fersen, Axel de. *Lettres d'Axel de Fersen à son père pendant la guerre de l'indépendance d'Amérique.* Paris: Firmin-Didot, 1929.

Girault, Philippe René. *Mes campagnes sous la Révolution et l'Empire.* Paris: Le Sycomore, 1983.

Gottschalk, Louis, ed. *The Letters of Lafayette to Washington, 1777–1799.* New York: Privately printed, 1944.

Heath, William. "The Heath Papers." Part 3. *Collections of the Massachusetts Historical Society.* 7th Ser. 5 (1905): 1–408.

———. *Memoirs of Major-General William Heath.* New York: William Abbott, 1901; reprint, New York: New York Times and Arno Press, 1969.

Idzerda, Stanley, and others, eds. *Lafayette in the Age of the American Revolution: Selected Letters and Papers 1776–1790.* 5 Vols. Ithaca: Cornell University Press, 1979–1983.

Jameson, J. Franklin, ed., and Albert J. Edmunds, trans. "Letters of a French Officer, Written at Easton, Penna., in 1777–1778." *Pennsylvania Magazine of History and Biography* 35 (1911): 90–102.

Jones, Charles C., ed. *The Siege of Savannah in 1779, As Described in Two Contemporaneous Journals of French Officers in the Fleet of Count D'Estaing.* Albany: Joel Munsell, 1874; reprint, New York: New York Times and Arno Press, 1968.

Kennett, Lee, ed. and trans. "Charleston in 1778: A French Intelligence Report." *South Carolina Historical Magazine* 66 (April 1965): 109–111.

La Chenais, Maurice, ed. "Un Officier français au Venezuela (1783)." *La Revue du Mois* 7 (February 1909): 171–189.

———, ed. "Relation inédite du naufrage de la Bourgogne, vaisseau de 74 canons portant à bord une partie du régiment d'infanterie de Bourbonnais par le chevalier de Cariolis, lieutenant à ce régiment." *Revue Militaire Française* 2 (1870): 262–289.

Lameth, Théodore de. *Mémoires, Publiés avec Introduction et Notes par Eugène Welvert.* Paris: Fontemoing, 1913.

BIBLIOGRAPHY

Lauzun, Armand Louis de Gontaut Biron, Duc de. *Memoirs of the Duc de Lauzun*. Translated by C. K. Scott Moncrieff. London: George Routledge and Sons, 1928; reprint, New York: New York Times and Arno Press, 1969.

Leland, Waldo G., and Edmund C. Burnett. "Letters From Lafayette to Luzerne, 1780–1782." *American Historical Review* 20 (1914–1915): 341–376 and 577–612.

"Letter From DeVergennes to Lafayette, August 7, 1780." *American Historical Review* 8 (1902–1903): 506–508.

"Letter From the Marquis de Lafayette to Dr. Samuel Cooper, 1780." *American Historical Review* 8 (1902–1903): 89–91.

"Letters of Ebenezer Huntington, 1774–1781." *American Historical Review* 5 (1899–1900): 702–729.

Lévis-Mirepoix, Emmanuel de, ed. "Quelques Lettres du Baron de Montesquieu sur la Guerre d'Indépendance Américaine." *Franco-American Review* 2 (1938): 192–204.

Mackenzie, Frederick. *Diary of Frederick Mackenzie, Giving a Daily Narrative of His Military Service as an Officer of the Regiment of Royal Welch Fusiliers During the Years 1775–1781 in Massachusetts, Rhode Island, and New York*. 2 Vols. Cambridge: Harvard University Press, 1930; reprint, New York: New York Times and Arno Press, 1968.

Massey, Edouard R., trans. "Rhode Island in 1780, By Lieutenant L.J.B.S. Robertnier." *Rhode Island Historical Society Collections* 16 (July 1923): 65–78.

Morgan, Marshall, trans. "Alexandre Bethier's Journal of the American Campaign: The Rhode Island Sections." *Rhode Island History* 24 (July 1965): 77–88.

Moultrie, William. *Memoirs of the American Revolution, So Far as It Related to the States of North and South Carolina, and Georgia, Compiled From the Most Authentic Materials, the Author's Personal Knowledge of the Various Events, and Including an Epistolary Correspondence on Public Affairs, With Civil and Military Officers, at That Period*. 2 Vols. New York: David Longworth, 1802; reprint, New York: New York Times and Arno Press, 1968.

Murdoch, Richard K., trans. "A French Account of the Siege of Charleston, 1780." *South Carolina Historical Magazine* 67 (July 1966): 138–154.

Pontgibaud, Charles Albert de Moré, Chevalier de. *A French Volunteer of the War of Independence (The Chevalier de Pontgibaud)*. Edited and Translated by Robert B. Douglas. New York: D. Appleton, 1898.

Rice, Howard C., Jr., and Anne S.K. Brown, eds. and trans. *The American Campaigns of Rochambeau's Army, 1780, 1781, 1782, 1783*. 2 Vols. Princeton and Providence: Princeton University Press and Brown University Press, 1972.

Riley, Edward M., ed. "St. George Tucker's Journal of the Siege of Yorktown, 1781." *William and Mary Quarterly*, 3rd Ser. 5 (1948): 375–395.

Robin, Abbé. *New Travels Through North America: In a Series of Letters; Exhibiting the History of the Victorious Campaign of the Allied Armies, Under His Excellency General Washington and the Count de Rochambeau, in the Year 1781. Interspersed With Political and Philosophical Observations, Upon the Genius, Temper, and Customs of the Americans; Also Narrations of the Capture of General Burgogne, and Lord Cornwallis, With Their Armies; and a Variety of Interesting Particulars, Which Occurred, in the Course of the War in America*. Translated by Philip Freneau. Philadelphia: Robert Bell, 1783; reprint, New York: New York Times and Arno Press, 1969.

BIBLIOGRAPHY

Robin, Charles César. *Histoire de la constitution de l'empire françois, ou Histoire des Etats-Généraux, pour servir d'introduction à nôtre droit public.* 2 Vols. Paris: Godefroy, 1789.

Rochambeau, Jean Baptiste Donatien Vimeur, Comte de. *Memoirs of the Marshal Count de Rochambeau, Relative to the War of Independence of the United States.* Edited and translated by M.W.E. Wright. Paris: French, English, and American Library, 1838; reprint, New York: New York Times and Arno Press, 1971.

Seeber, Edward D., trans. *On the Threshold of Liberty: Journal of a Frenchman's Tour of the American Colonies in 1777.* Bloomington: Indiana University Press, 1959.

Ségur, Louis Philippe, Comte de. "Extraits de lettres écrites d'Amérique par le comte de Ségur, colonel en second du régiment de Soissonnais, à la comtesse de Ségur, dame de Madame Victoire, 1782–1783." *Mélanges publiés par la Société des Bibliophiles françois.* Deuxième partie. Pièce 6 (1903): 149–205.

———. *Mémoires, ou Souvenirs et Anecdotes.* 2d ed. 3 Vols. Paris: Alexis Eymery, 1825.

Shea, J. G., ed. *The Operations of the French Fleet Under the Count de Grasse in 1781–1782, as Described in Two Contemporaneous Journals.* New York: Bradford Club, 1864; reprint, New York: Da Capo Press, 1971.

Shy, Arlene Phillips, ed. "Puritan Revolutionary: Selected Letters of Edmund Quincy." In *Sources of American Independence: Selected Manuscripts From the Collections of the William L. Clements Library,* Vol. 2, edited by Howard H. Peckham, 428–498. Chicago: University of Chicago Press, 1978.

Sifton, Paul G., ed. "La Caroline Méridionale: Some French Sources of South Carolina Revolutionary History, With Two Unpublished Letters of Baron de Kalb." *South Carolina Historical Magazine* 66 (April 1965): 102–108.

Stiles, Ezra. *Literary Diary of Ezra Stiles.* Vol. 2. Edited by Franklin B. Dexter. New York: Charles Scribner's Sons, 1901.

Sturgill, Claude C., ed. "Rochambeau's Mémoire de la Guerre en Amérique." *Virginia Magazine of History and Biography* 78 (January 1970): 34–64.

Thatcher, James. *Military Journal of the American Revolution, From the Commencement to the Disbanding of the American Army; Comprising a Detailed Account of the Principal Events and Battles of the Revolution, With Their Exact Dates, and a Biographical Sketch of the Most Prominent Generals.* Hartford: Hurlbut, Williams, 1862; reprint, New York: New York Times and Arno Press, 1969.

U.S. Congress. *Correspondence of General Washington and Comte de Grasse. 1781. August 17–November 4.* 71st Congress, 2nd session. Senate Doc. 211. Washington, D.C.: U.S. Government Printing Office, 1931.

Washington, George. *The Diaries of George Washington, 1748–1799.* 4 Vols. Edited by John C. Fitzpatrick. Boston: Houghton Mifflin, 1925.

Willcox, William B., ed. "The Clinton-Parker Controversy Over British Failure at Charleston and Rhode Island." In *Sources of American Independence: Selected Manuscripts From the Collections of the William L. Clements Library,* Vol. 1, edited by Howard H. Peckham, 188–225. Chicago: University of Chicago Press, 1978.

Yeager, Henry J., ed. and trans. "The French Fleet at Newport, 1780–1781." *Rhode Island History* 30 (August 1971): 86–93.

SECONDARY SOURCES: BOOKS

Adelman, Jonathan R. *Revolution, Armies, and War: A Political History.* Boulder:

BIBLIOGRAPHY

Lynne Reinner Publishers, 1985.
Akers, Charles W. *The Divine Politician: Samuel Cooper and the American Revolution in Boston.* Boston: Northeastern University Press, 1982.
Anderson, Matthew Smith. *War and Society in Europe of the Old Regime, 1618–1789.* Leicester: Leicester University Press, 1988.
Apt, Leon. *Louis-Philippe de Ségur: An Intellectual in a Revolutionary Age.* The Hague: Nijhoff, 1969.
Balch, Thomas. *The French in America During the War of Independence of the United States, 1777–1783.* 2 Vols. Translated by Edwin S. Balch and Elise W. Balch. Philadelphia: Porter and Coats, 1891 and 1895; reprint, Boston: Gregg Press, 1972.
Bertaud, Jean Paul. *Les Amis du Roi: Journaux et journalistes royalistes en France de 1789 à 1792.* Paris: Perrin, 1984.
———. *The Army of the French Revolution: From Citizen-Soldiers to Instrument of Power.* Translated by R. R. Palmer. Princeton: Princeton University Press, 1988.
———. *La Révolution Armée: Les soldats-citoyens et la Révolution française.* Paris: Robert Laffont, 1979.
———. *Valmy: La Démocratie en armes.* Paris: Julliard, 1970.
———. *La Vie quotidienne des soldats de la Révolution, 1789–1799.* Paris: Hachette, 1985.
———. *La Vie quotidienne en France au temps de la Révolution.* Paris: Hachette, 1983.
Best, Geoffrey. *War and Society in Revolutionary Europe, 1770–1870.* New York: St. Martin's Press, 1982.
Blanning, T.C.W. *The Origins of the French Revolutionary Wars.* New York: Longman, 1986.
Bodinier, Gilbert. *Dictionnaire des officiers de l'armée royale qui ont combattu aux Etats-Unis pendant la guerre d'Indépendance, 1776–1783, suivi d'un Supplément à Les Français sous les treize étoiles du commandant André Lasseray.* Vincennes: Service Historique de l'Armée de Terre, 1982.
———. *Les officiers de l'armée royale combattants de la guerre d'Indépendance des Etats-Unis de Yorktown à l'an II.* Vincennes: Service Historique de l'Armée de Terre, 1983.
Bonsal, Stephen. *When the French Were Here: A Narrative of the Sojourn of the French Forces in America, and Their Contribution to the Yorktown Campaign, Drawn From Unpublished Reports and Letters of Participants in the National Archives of France and the MS Division of the Library of Congress.* Garden City, N.J.: Doubleday, Doran, 1945.
Castries, Duc de. *La France et l'indépendance américaine: Le Livre du bicentenaire de l'Indépendance.* Paris: Perrin, 1975.
Chilly, Lucien de. *Le Premier Ministre constitutionnel de la guerre. La Tour de Pin: Les Origines de l'armée nouvelle sous la Constituente.* Paris: Perrin, 1909.
Chotteau, Léon. *La Guerre de l'indépendance (1775–1783): Les Français en Amérique.* Paris: Charpentier, 1876.
Corvisier, André. *L'Armée française de la fin du XVIIe siècle au ministère de Choiseul: Le Soldat.* 2 Vols. Paris: Presses Universitaires de France, 1964.
———. *Armées et sociétés en Europe de 1494 à 1789.* Paris: Presses Universitaires de France, 1976.
Coste, Emile. *Historique du 40e Régiment d'Infanterie de ligne.* Paris: Chamerot, 1887.

BIBLIOGRAPHY

Cunliffe, Marcus. *Soliders and Civilians: The Martial Spirit in America, 1775–1865.* Boston: Little Brown, 1968.

Devéze, Michel. *L'Europe et le Monde à la fin du XVIIIe siècle.* Paris: Michel, 1970.

Dull, Jonathan. *The French Navy and American Independence: A Study of Arms and Diplomacy, 1774–1783.* Princeton: Princeton University Press, 1975.

Durieux, Joseph. *Combattants périgourdins de la guerre américaine (1778–1783).* Périgueux: Imprimerie de la Dordogne, 1907.

———. *Les Vainqueurs de la Bastille.* Paris: H. Champion, 1911.

East, Robert A. *Business Enterprise in the American Revolutionary Era.* New York: Columbia University Press, 1938.

Echeverria, Durand. *Mirage in the West: A History of the French Image of American Society to 1815.* Princeton: Princeton University Press, 1957.

Evans, Emory G. *Thomas Nelson of Yorktown: Revolutionary Virginian.* Charlottesville: University Press of Virginia, 1975.

Faÿ, Bernard. *The Revolutionary Spirit in France and America: A Study of Moral and Intellectual Relations Between France and the United States at the End of the Eighteenth Century.* Translated by Ramon Guthrie. New York: Harcourt, Brace, 1927.

Flexner, James Thomas. *George Washington in the American Revolution (1775–1783).* Boston: Little Brown, 1967.

Forbes, Allan, and Paul F. Cadman. *France and New England.* Vols. 1 and 2. Boston: State Street Trust, 1925 and 1927.

———. *The Soldiers of the French Revolution.* Durham: Duke University Press, 1990.

Forrest, Alan. *The French Revolution and the Poor.* Oxford: Basil Blackwood, 1981.

Gabriel, Charles Nicolas. *Le Maréchal de camp Desandrouins, 1729–1792: Guerre du Canada (1751–1760), Guerre de l'Indépendance Américaine (1780–1782).* Verdun: Renvé-Lallemant, 1887.

Gardiner, Asa Bird. *The Order of the Cincinnati in France: Its Organization and History: With the Military or Naval Records of the French Members Who Became Such by Reason of Qualifying Service in the Army or Navy of France or of the United States in the War of the Revolution for American Independence.* Providence: Rhode Island State Society of the Cincinnati, 1905.

Godechot, Jacques. *The Counter-Revolution: Doctrine and Action, 1789–1804.* Translated by Salvator Attanasio. Princeton: Princeton University Press, 1981.

Gottschalk, Louis. *Lafayette and the Close of the American Revolution.* Chicago: University of Chicago Press, 1965.

———. *The Place of the American Revolution in the Causal Pattern of the French Revolution.* Easton, Pa.: American Friends of Lafayette, 1948.

Hennet, Léon. *Les milices et les troupes provinciales.* Paris: L. Baudoin, 1884.

Herbert, Sidney. *The Fall of Feudalism in France.* New York: Barnes and Noble, 1969.

Histoire militaire de la France. Vol. 2, *De 1715 à 1871.* Paris: Presses Universitaires de France, 1992.

Hunt, Lynn Avery. *Revolution and Urban Politics in Provincial France: Troyes and Reims, 1786–1790.* Stanford: Stanford University Press, 1978.

Idzerda, Stanley J., and Roger E. Smith. *France and the American War for Independence.* N.p.: Scott Limited Editions, n.d.

Johnson, Hubert C. *The Midi in Revolution: A Study of Regional Political Diversity, 1789–1793.* Princeton: Princeton University Press, 1986.

Johnston, Henry P. *The Yorktown Campaign and the Surrender of Cornwallis, 1781.*

BIBLIOGRAPHY

New York: Harper and Bros., 1881; reprint, News York: Da Capo Press, 1971.
Jusserand, Jean Jules. *With Americans of Past and Present*. New York: Charles Scribner's Sons, 1916.
Kaplan, Lawrence S. *Colonies Into Nation: American Diplomacy, 1763–1801*. New York: Macmillan, 1972.
Kennett, Lee. *The French Forces in America, 1780–1783*. Westport, Conn.: Greenwood Press, 1977.
Kite, Elizabeth S. *Brigadier-General Louis Lebègue Duportail, Commandant of Engineers in the Continental Army, 1777–1783*. Baltimore, Philadelphia, and London: Johns Hopkins Press, Dolphin Press, and Oxford University Press, 1933.
Larrabee, Harold A. *Decision at the Chesapeake*. New York: Clarkson N. Potter, 1964.
Lasseray, André. *Les Français sous les treize étoiles (1775–1783)*. 2 Vols. Paris: Protat, 1935.
Lawrence, Alexander A. *Storm Over Savannah: The Story of Count d'Estaing and the Siege of the Town in 1779*. Athens: University of Georgia Press, 1951.
Lefebvre, Georges. *The Coming of the French Revolution*. Translated by R. R. Palmer. New York: Vintage Press, 1957.
———. *The Great Fear of 1789: Rural Panic in Revolutionary France*. Translated by Joan White. New York: Vintage Books, 1973.
Lewis, Charles Lee. *Admiral De Grasse and American Independence*. Annapolis: U.S. Naval Institute, 1945.
Libermann, Henri. *La défense nationale à la fin de 1792: Servan et Pache (10 août 1792–2 février 1793)*. Paris: Perrin, 1927.
Library of Congress, Symposia on the American Revolution. *The Impact of the American Revolution Abroad: Papers Presented at the Fourth Symposium, May 8 and 9, 1975*. Washington, D.C.: Library of Congress, 1976.
Loughrey, Mary Ellen. *France and Rhode Island, 1686–1800*. New York: King's Crown Press, 1944.
Lynn, John A. *The Bayonets of the Republic: Motivation and Tactics in the Army of Revolutionary France, 1791–1794*. Urbana: University of Illinois Press, 1984.
Mackesy, Piers. *The War for America, 1775–1783*. Cambridge: Harvard University Press, 1964.
Manceron, Claude. *Les Hommes de la Liberté*. Vol. 2, *Le Vent d'Amérique: L'Echec de Necker et la Victoire de Yorktown, 1778–1782*. Paris: Robert Laffont, 1974.
Martin, Marc. *Les Origines de la presse militaire en France à la fin de l'ancien régime et sous la Révolution (1770–1799)*. Vincennes: Ministère de la Défense, 1975.
Maugras, Gaston. *Le Duc de Lauzun et la cour de Marie-Antoinette*. Paris: Plon, 1913.
Merlant, Joachim. *Soldiers and Sailors of France in the American War for Independence (1776–1783)*. Translated by Mary Bushnell Coleman. New York: Scribner's Sons, 1920.
Michaud, Marius. *La Contre-Révolution dans le canton de Fribourg (1789–1815): Doctrine, Propagande et Action*. Fribourg: Editions Universitaires, 1978.
Middlekauff, Robert. *The Glorious Cause: The American Revolution, 1763–1789*. New York: Oxford University Press, 1982.
Montmort, Comte de. *Antoine Charles du Houx, Baron de Vioménil, Lieutenant-General of the Armies of the King, Second in Command Under Rochambeau*. Translated by John Francis Gough. Baltimore: Johns Hopkins Press, 1935.
Murphy, Orville T. *Charles Gravier, Comte de Vergennes: French Diplomacy in the Age*

BIBLIOGRAPHY

of Revolution, 1719–1787. Albany: State University of New York Press, 1982.
Myers, Minor, Jr. Liberty Without Anarchy: A History of the Society of the Cincinnati. Charlottesville: University Press of Virginia, 1983.
Noailles, Amblard Marie Raymond Amedée, Vicomte de. Marins et soldats français en Amérique pendant la Guerre de l'Indépendance des Etats-Unis (1778–1783). Paris: Perrin, 1903.
Nolan, J. Bennett. Lafayette in America, Day by Day. Baltimore: Johns Hopkins Press, 1934.
Ozouf, Mona. La Fête révolutionnaire, 1789–1799. Paris: Gallimard, 1976.
Palmer, Robert R. The Age of Democratic Revolution: A Political History of Europe and America, 1760–1800. 2 Vols. Princeton: Princeton University Press, 1959 and 1964.
Paret, Peter. Yorck and the Era of Prussian Reform, 1807–1815. Princeton: Princeton University Press, 1966.
Patterson, Alfred Temple. The Other Armada: The Franco-Spanish Attempt to Invade Britain in 1779. Manchester: University of Manchester Press, 1960.
Peckham, Howard H. The War for Independence: A Military History. Chicago: University of Chicago Press, 1958.
Perkins, James Breck. France in the American Revolution. Boston: Houghton Mifflin, 1911.
Pinasseau, Jean. L'Emigration militaire. Campagne de 1792. Armée des Princes, Compagnies de Saintonge, Angoumois et Aunis. Paris: Picard, 1971.
———. L'Emigration militaire. Campagne de 1792. Armée Royale. Composition. Ordres de Bataille. 2 Vols. Paris: Picard, 1957 and 1964.
Proulx, Gilles. Between France and New France: Life Aboard the Tall Sailing Ships. Toronto: Dundurn Press, 1984.
Quoy-Bodin, Jean Luc. L'Armée et la Franc-Maçonnerie: Au declin de la monarchie sous la Rèvolution et l'Empire. Paris: Economica, 1987.
Riley, James C. The Seven Years War and the Old Regime in France: The Economic and Financial Toll. Princeton: Princeton University Press, 1986.
Ross, Steven. From Flintlock to Rifle: Infantry Tactics, 1740–1866. Cranbury, N.J.: Associated University Presses, 1979.
Rothenberg, Gunther E. The Art of Warfare in the Age of Napoleon. London: B. T. Batsford, 1977.
Royster, Charles. A Revolutionary People at War: The Continental Army and American Character, 1775–1783. Chapel Hill: University of North Carolina Press, 1979.
Ryan, Lee W. French Travelers in the Southeastern United States, 1775–1800. Bloomington, Ind.: Principia Press, 1939.
Schama, Simon. Citizens: A Chronicle of the French Revolution. New York: Alfred A. Knopf, 1989.
Scott, Samuel F. French Aid to the American Revolution: An Exhibition in Commemoration of a Victorious Alliance. Ann Arbor: William L. Clements Library, 1976.
———. The Response of the Royal Army to the French Revolution: The Role and Development of the Line Army, 1787–1793. Oxford: Clarendon Press, 1978.
Shy, John. A People Numerous and Armed: Reflections on the Military Struggle for American Independence. New York: Oxford University Press, 1976.
Six, Georges. Dictionnaire biographique des généraux et amiraux français de la Révolution et de l'Empire (1792–1814). 2 Vols. Paris: Saffroy, 1934.

BIBLIOGRAPHY

Stinchcombe, William C. *The American Revolution and the French Alliance.* Syracuse: Syracuse University Press, 1969.

Stone, Edwin Martin. *Our French Allies, Rochambeau and His Army, Lafayette and His Devotion, D'Estaing, De Ternay, Barras, De Grasse, and Their Fleets in the Great War of the American Revolution, From 1778 to 1782, Including Military Operations in Rhode Island, the Surrender of Yorktown, Sketches of French and American Officers, and Incidents of Social Life in Newport, Providence, and Elsewhere.* Providence: Providence Press, 1884.

Sullivan, Kathryn. *Maryland and France, 1774–1789.* Philadelphia: University of Pennsylvania Press, 1936.

Tower, Charlemagne. *The Marquis de La Fayette in the American Revolution, With Some Account of the Attitude of France Toward the War of Independence.* 2d ed. 2 Vols. New York: Da Capo Press, 1970.

Van Alstyne, Richard W. *Empire and Independence: The International History of the American Revolution.* New York: John Wiley and Sons, 1965.

Voisin, C. *Historique du 6ᵉ Hussards.* Libourne: Malevillle, 1888.

Vossler, Otto. *Jefferson and the American Revolutionary Ideal.* Translated by Catherine Philippon and Bernard Wishy. Washington, D.C.: University Press of America, 1980.

Ward, Harry M. *Duty, Honor, or Country: General George Weedon and the American Revolution.* Philadelphia: American Philosophical Society, 1979.

Weelen, Jean Edmond. *Rochambeau, Father and Son: A Life of the Maréchal de Rochambeau and the Journal of the Vicomte de Rochambeau.* Translated by Lawrence Lee. New York: Henry Holt, 1936.

Wetzler, Peter. *War and Subsistence: The Sambre and Meuse Army in 1794.* New York: Peter Lang, 1985.

Whitridge, Arnold. *Rochambeau.* New York: Collier, 1965.

Whittemore, Charles P. *A General of the Revolution: John Sullivan of New Hampshire.* New York: Columbia University Press, 1961.

Woloch, Isser. *The French Veteran From the Revolution to the Restoration.* Chapel Hill: University of North Carolina Press, 1979.

Wright, Robert K. *The Continental Army.* Washington, D.C.: U.S. Army Center of Military History, 1983.

SECONDARY SOURCES: ARTICLES

Appleby, Joyce. "America as a Model for the Radical French Reforms of 1789." *William and Mary Quarterly,* 3rd Ser. 28 (1971): 267–286.

Barthold, Allen J. "French Journalists in the United States, 1780–1800." *Franco-American Review* 1 (1936–1937): 215–230.

———. "'Gazette Françoise,' Newport, R.I., 1780–81." *Papers of the Bibliographical Society of America* 28, part 1 (1934): 64–79.

Bertaud, Jean Paul. "Enquête sur les Volontaires de 1792." *Annales historiques de la Révolution française* 60 (April–June 1988): 151–170.

———. "Napoléon, l'armée et la dictature." *L'Histoire,* no. 30 (January 1981): 46–54.

———. "Les officiers de carrière et l'armée nationale à l'époque de la Révolution française." In *Le Métier militaire en France aux époques de grandes transformations*

BIBLIOGRAPHY

sociales, by Commission d'Histoire Militaire. Vincennes: Service Historique de l'Armée de Terre, 1980, 79–87.

———. "Les Soldats de l'an II." *L'Histoire*, no. 13 (June 1979): 22–30.

Bien, David D. "The Army in the French Enlightenment: Reform, Reaction, and Revolution." *Past and Present*, no. 85 (November 1979): 68–98.

———. "La Réaction aristocratique avant 1789: l'exemple de l'armeé." *Annales, Economie, Société, Civilisations* 29 (1974): 23–48 and 505–534.

Bishop, Morris. "A French Volunteer." *American Heritage* 17 (1966): 46–49 and 103–108.

Bodinier, Gilbert. "Etude du comportement des officiers qui ont combattu en Amérique, pendant la Révolution." In *Actes du 102ᵉ Congrès National des Sociétés Savantes. Limoges. 1977.* Vol. 2. Paris: Bibliothèque Nationale, 1978, 107–122.

———. "Les Officiers de l'armée royale et la Révolution." In *Le Métier militaire en France aux époques de grandes transformations sociales*, by Commission d'Histoire Militaire. Vincennes: Service Historique de l'Armée de Terre, 1980, 59–77.

———. "Les officiers du corps expéditionnaire de Rochambeau et la Révolution française." *Revue Historique des Armées* 3, no. 4 (1976): 139–163.

Bowen, Charles A. "A French Officer With Washington and Rochambeau." *Century Magazine* 73 (1907): 531–538.

Campbell, Charles A. "Rochambeau's Headquarters in Westchester County, N.Y., 1781." *Magazine of American History* 4 (1880): 46–48.

Carrez, J. P. "L'Ecole d'Artillerie sous la Convention: 20 septembre 1792–26 octobre 1795." *Revue Historique des Armées* 2, nos. 1–2 (1975): 37–49.

Childs, J. Rives. "French Consul Martin Oster Reports on Virginia, 1784–1796." *Virginia Magazine of History and Biography* 76 (1968): 27–40.

Chuquet, Arthur. "Roture et noblesse dans l'armée royale." *Séances et travaux de l'Académie des sciences morales et politques* 175 (1911): 204–242.

Cilleuls, Jean des. "Jean-François Coste (1741–1819), médecin en chef de l'Armée de Rochambeau, premier maire de Versailles (1790–1792)." *Revue Historique des Armées* 4, no. 1 (1977): 7–27.

———. "Le Service de l'intendance à l'armée de Rochambeau." *Revue Historique de l'Armée* 13, no. 2 (1957): 43–61.

Conner, Susan P. "Les Femmes Militaires: Women in the French Army, 1792–1815." In *Consortium on Revolutionary Europe. Proceedings, 1982*, edited by Warren F. Spencer. Athens, Ga.: Consortuim on Revolutionary Europe, 1983, 290–302.

Contenson, Ludovic de. "Washington et l'amitié franco-américaine à la fin de la guerre de l'indépendance." *Le Correspondant* 308 (August 25, 1927): 566–577.

Corvisier, André. "Hiérarchie militaire et hiéarchie sociale à la veille de la Revolution." *Revue internationale d'histoire militaire* 30 (1970): 77–91.

———. "Le Métier militaire en France aux époques de grandes transformations sociales." In *Le Métier militaire en France aux époques de grandes transformations sociales*, by Commission d'Histoire Militaire. Vincennes: Service Historique de l'Armée de Terre, 1980, 1–21.

Corwin, Edward S. "The French Objective in the American Revolution." *American Historical Review* 21 (1915): 33–61.

Cossé-Brissac, Colonel de. "La France et la guerre de l'indépendance." *Revue Historique de l'Armée* 13, no. 2 (1957): 11–20.

Costantini, E. R. "Le corps Rochambeau face aux difficultés financières et

BIBLIOGRAPHY

économiques du royaume et des Etats-Unis d'Amérique (1780–1782)." *Revue internationale d'histoire militaire* 41 (1979): 108–126.

Crout, Robert Rhodes. "La Fayette and the *Gardes Nationales*: In the Patriarch's Image." In *Actes du 7e Colloque International d'Histoire Militaire*. Manhattan, Kans.: Sunflower University Press, 1984, 448–457.

Dearden, Paul F. "The Siege of Newport: Inauspicious Dawn of Alliance." *Rhode Island History* 29 (1970): 17–35.

De Conde, Alexander. "The French Alliance in Historical Speculation." In *Diplomacy and Revolution: The Franco-American Alliance of 1778*, edited by Ronald Hoffman and Peter J. Albert. Charlottesville: University Press of Virginia, 1981, 1–37.

Defamie, Gérard. "Le mythe américaine à la veille de la Révolution française." *L'Information Historique* 36 (January–February 1974): 59–64.

Depréaux, Albert. "Les Régiments provinciaux et l'ordonnance du 19 octobre 1773." *Revue d'histoire moderne et contemporaine* 13 (1938): 267–286.

Devos, Jean Claude, and Denise Devos. "Opinions et carrière des officiers sous le Directoire et le Consulat." In *Le Métier militaire en France aux époques de grandes transformations sociales*, by Commission d'Histoire Militaire. Vincennes: Service Historique de l'Armée de Terre, 1980, 89–106.

Dinet, Henri. "Craintes, brigandages et paniques inédits des années 1789–1791." *Annales historiques de la Révolution française* 53 (April–June 1981): 304–316.

Doig, Kathleen Hardesty. "War in the Reform Programme of the Encyclopédie." *War and Society* 6 (May 1988): 1–10.

Dull, Jonathan R. "France and the American Revolution: Questioning the Myths." In *Proceedings of the First Annual Meeting of the Western Society for French History, March 14–15, 1974*. Las Cruces: New Mexico State University Press, 1974, 110–118.

―――. "France and the American Revolution Seen as Tragedy." In *Diplomacy and Revolution: The Franco-American Alliance of 1778*, edited by Ronald Hoffman and Peter J. Albert. Charlottesville: University Press of Virginia, 1981, 73–106.

Echeverria, Durand. "Condorcet's *The Influence of the American Revolution on Europe*." *William and Mary Quarterly*, 3rd Ser. 25 (1968): 85–108.

Fiechter, Jean Jacques. "L'aventure américaine des officiers de Rochambeau vue à travers leurs journaux." In *Images of America in Revolutionary France*, edited by Michèle R. Morris. Washington, D.C.: Georgetown University Press, 1990, 65–81.

Fohlen, Claude. "The Impact of the American Revolution in France." In *The Impact of the American Revolution Abroad: Papers Presented at the Fourth Symposium, May 8 and 9, 1975*, by Library of Congress Symposia on the American Revolution. Washington, D.C.: Library of Congress, 1976, 21–38.

Fonteneau, C. R. "La Normandie et la Manche pendant la guerre de l'indépendance américaine." *Revue internationale d'histoire militaire* 41 (1979): 131–140.

―――. "La période française de la guerre d'Indépendance (1776–1780)." *Revue Historique des Armées* 3, no. 4 (1976): 47–86.

Fransson, Frances M. "The French at Lebanon, Connecticut: November 1780–June 1781." *Daughters of the American Revolution Magazine* 108 (May 1974): 454–456.

Fursenko, A. A. "The American and French Revolutions of the Eighteenth Century (An Attempt at a Comparative Characterization)." *Soviet Reivew* 16 (1975): 66–101.

BIBLIOGRAPHY

Girodie, André. " 'Soissonnais' et l'Amérique. Lettres inédites." *Franco-American Review* 1 (1936): 231–239.

Godechot, Jacques. "Les Combattants de la guerre d'indépendance aux Etats-Unis et les troubles agraires en France de 1789 à 1792." *Annales historiques de la Révolution française* 28 (1956): 292–294.

———. "La Gazette françoise, ancêtre des journaux d'armées publiés sous la Révolution." *Annales historiques de la Révolution française* 52 (January–March 1980): 118–125.

———. "La Gazette Françoise: First of the Army Newspapers Published in the World, First French-Language Newspaper Published in the United States." In *Two Hundred Years of Franco-American Relations: Papers of the Bicentennial Colloquium of the Society for French Historical Studies in Newport, Rhode Island, September 7–10, 1978*, edited by Nancy L. Roelker and Charles K. Warner. n.p., n.d., 78–92.

———. "L'Influence de la tactique et de la stratégie de la guerre d'indépendance américaine sur la tactique et la stratégie française de l'armée de terre." *Revue internationale d'histoire militaire* 41 (1979): 141–147.

———. "Revolutionary Contagion, 1770–1825." In *Proceedings of the Fourth Annual Meeting of the Western Society for French History*, edited by Joyce Duncan Falk. Santa Barbara: Western Society for French History, 1977, 245–255.

———. "Robespierre et l'Amérique." *Annales historiques de la Révolution française* 48 (1976): 637–652.

Greene, Jack P. "Social Context and the Causal Pattern of the American Revolution: A Preliminary Consideration of New York, Virginia, and Massachusetts." In *La Révolution Américaine et l'Europe (Colloque international du Centre National de la Recherche Scientifique, 21–25 février 1978, Paris-Toulouse)*, edited by Claude Fohlen and Jacques Godechot. Paris: Editions du C.N.R.S., 1979, 25–63.

Guthrie, William D. "General Count de Rochambeau, Commander of the French Army in America During the American Revolution, 1780–1782." *Franco-American Review* 2 (1938): 230–243.

Harris, Robert D. "French Finances and the American War, 1777–1783." *Journal of Modern History* 48 (June 1976): 233–258.

Higginbotham, Don. "American Historians and the Military History of the American Revolution." *American Historical Review* 70 (October 1964): 18–34.

———. "The American Militia: A Traditional Institution With Revolutionary Responsibilities." In *Reconsiderations on the Revolutionary War: Selected Essays*, edited by Don Higginbotham. Westport, Conn.: Greenwood Press, 1978, 83–103.

Hytier, Adrienne D. "The Decline of Military Values: The Theme of the Deserter in Eighteenth Century French Literature." *Studies in Eighteenth-Century Culture* 11 (1982): 147–162.

Idzerda, Stanley. "When and Why Lafayette Became a Revolutionary." In *Consortium on Revolutionary Europe Proceedings. 1977*, edited by John C. White. Athens, Ga.: Consortium on Revolutionary Europe, 1978, 1–27.

Jones, Colin. "The Military Revolution and the Professionalisation of the French Army Under the Ancien Régime." In *The Military Revolution and the State, 1500–1800*, edited by Michael Duffy. Exeter: University of Exeter Press, 1980, 29–48.

———. "The Welfare of the French Foot-Soldier." *History* 65 (June 1980): 193–213.

Kellogg, Louise Phelps, ed. and trans. "Passerat de la Chapelle in the American

BIBLIOGRAPHY

Revolution." *Mississippi Valley Historical Review* 25 (1939): 535–538.
Kennedy, Michael. "La Société française Amis de la liberté et de l'égalité de Philadelphie (1793–1794)." *Annales historiques de la Révolution française* 48 (October–December 1976): 614–636.
Kennett, Lee. "The American Revolution as a Model of Revolutionary War." In *La Revolution américaine et l'Europe (Colloque international du Centre National de la Recherche Scientifique, 21–25 fevrier 1978. Paris-Toulouse)*, edited by Claude Fohlen and Jacques Godechot. Paris: Editions du C.N.R.S., 1979, 579–588.
———. "Le Bilan d'une rencontre: l'armée française en Amérique, 1780–1783." *Annales historiques de la Révolution française* 48 (October–December 1976): 529–542.
———. "L'expédition Rochambeau-Ternay: un succès diplomatique." *Revue Historique des Armées* 3, no. 4 (1976): 87–105.
Kite, Elizabeth S. "French 'Secret Aid,' Precursor to the French Alliance, 1776–1777." *French American Review* 1 (1948): 143–152.
Kramer, Lloyd S. "America's Lafayette and Lafayette's America." *William and Mary Quarterly*, 3rd Ser. 38 (April 1981): 228–241.
Lane, John E. "Jean-François Coste, Chief Physician of the French Expeditionary Forces in the American Revolution." *Americana* 22 (January 1928): 51–80.
Lefebvre, Georges. "La Révolution française et son armée." *Annales historiques de la Révolution française* 41 (1969): 576–582.
Leith, James A. "Le culte de Franklin en France avant et pendant la Révolution française." *Annales historiques de la Révolution française* 48 (October–December 1976): 543–571.
Lenhart, John M. "German Catholic Soldiers and Their Chaplain in the Revolutionary War." *Central-Blatt and Social Justice* 23 (April 1931): 17–18.
———. "Letters of an Officer of the Zweibrücken Regiment." *Central-Blatt and Social Justice* 28 (January and February 1936): 321–322 and 359–360.
Lombarès, Michel de. "Varennes ou la fin d'un régime (21 juin 1791)." *Revue Historique l'Armée* 16, nos. 3 and 4 (1960): 33–56 and 45–62; and 17, no. 1 (1961): 23–36.
Lynn, John A. "An Aspect of the Political Education of the French Army: The Distribution of Political Journals, 1793–1794." In *Consortium on Revolutionary Europe. Proceedings. 1982*, edited by Warren F. Spencer. Athens, Ga.: Consortium on Revolutionary Europe, 1983, 75–90.
———. "French Opinion and the Military Resurrection of the Pike, 1792–1794." *Military Affairs* 41 (February 1977): 1–7.
———. "A Pattern of French Military Reform, 1750–1790: Speculations Concerning the Officer Corps." In *Consortium on Revolutionary Europe. Proceedings. 1974*. Gainesville: Consortium on Revolutionary Europe, 1978, 113–128.
MacCarthy, M. Dugué. "Reflections on the War of Independence: A French View." *Military Affairs* 46 (1966): 19–25.
Mackesy, Piers. "What the British Learned." In *Arms and Independence: The Military Character of the American Revolution*, edited by Ronald Hoffman and Peter J. Albert. Charlottesville: University Press of Virginia, 1984, 191–215.
Marion, M. "De la participation financière de la France à la guerre d'indépendance américaine." *Revue du dix-huitième siècle* 3 (January–April 1916): 1–7.
Martin, James Kirby. "Benedict Arnold's Treason as Political Protest." *Parameters:*

Journal of the U.S. Army War College 11 (September 1981): 63–74.

Maspero-Clerc, Hélène. "Une 'gazette anglo-française' pendant la guerre d'Amérique: le 'Courier de l'Europe' (1776–1788)." *Annales historiques de la Révolution française* 48 (October–December 1976): 572–594.

McDonald, Forrest. "The Relation of the French Peasant Veterans of the American Revolution to the Fall of Feudalism in France, 1789–1792." *Agricultural History* 25 (October 1951): 151–161.

McKee, Kenneth. "The Popularity of the 'American' on the French Stage During the Revolution." *Proceedings of the American Philosophical Society* 83 (September 1940): 479–491.

Michon, Georges. "L'armée et la politique intérieure sous la Convention." *Annales historiques de la Révolution française* 4 (1927): 529–546.

Montross, Lynn. "François-Louis de Fleury: Fort Mifflin, 1777–Stony Point, 1779." *Revue Historique de l'Armée* 13, no. 2 (1957): 21–28.

Murphy, Orville T. "The American Revolutionary Army and the Concept of Levée en Masse." *Military Affairs* 23 (1959): 13–20.

———. "The French Professional Soldier's Opinion of the American Militia in the War of the Revolution." *Military Affairs* 32 (1969): 191–198.

———. "The View From Versailles: Charles Gravier Comte de Vergennes's Perception of the American Revolution." In *Diplomacy and Revolution: The Franco-American Alliance of 1778*, edited by Ronald Hoffman and Peter J. Albert. Charlottesville: University Press of Virginia, 1981, 107–149.

Palásti, Ladislas. "Soldats de la Révolution française en captivité à Szeged." *Annales historiques de la Révolution française* 57 (July–September 1985): 353–364.

Palmer, Robert R. "Frederick the Great, Guibert, Bülow: From Dynastic to National War." In *Makers of Modern Strategy: Military Thought From Machiavelli to Hitler*, edited by Edward Mead Earle. Princeton: Princeton University Press, 1973, 49–74.

———. "The Impact of the American Revolution Abroad." In *The Impact of the American Revolution Abroad: Papers Presented at the Fourth Symposium, May 8 and 9, 1975*, by Library of Congress Symposia on the American Revolution. Washington, D.C.: Library of Congress, 1976, 5–18.

Paret, Peter. "Colonial Experience and European Military Reform at the End of the Eighteenth Century." *Bulletin of the Institute of Historical Research* 37 (May 1964): 47–59.

———. "The Relationship Between Revolutionary War and European Military Thought and Practice in the Second Half of the Eighteenth Century." In *Reconsiderations on the Revolutionary War: Selected Essays*, edited by Don Higginbotham. Westport, Conn.: Greenwood Press, 1978, 144–157.

Peronnet, Michel. "Le stationnement des troupes du Roi en 1789." *Mémoires de la Société pour l'Histoire du Droit et des Institutions des anciens pays bourguignons, comtois et romands* 49 (1992): 27–44.

Plumb, J. H. "The French Connection." *American Heritage* 26 (December 1974): 26–57 and 86–87.

Prelinger, Catherine M. "Less Lucky Than Lafayette: A Note on the French Applicants to Benjamin Franklin for Commissions in the American Army, 1776–1785." In *Proceedings of the Fourth Annual Meeting of the Western Society for French History*, edited by Joyce Dunca Falk. Santa Barbara: Western Society for French History, 1977, 263–271.

BIBLIOGRAPHY

Preston, Howard W. "Rochambeau and the French Troops in Providence in 1780–81–82." *Rhode Island Historical Society Collections* 17 (January 1924): 1–23.

Rainbolt, John C. "Americans' Initial View of Their Revolution's Significance for Other Peoples, 1776–1788." *The Historian* 35 (May 1973): 418–433.

Reinhard, Marcel. "Nostalgie et service militarie pendant la Révolution." *Annales historiques de la Révolution française* 30 (1958): 1–15.

Ropp, Theodore. "The General Military Significance of the American Revolution." In *Arms and Independence: The Military Character of the American Revolution*, edited by Ronald Hoffman and Peter J. Albert. Charlottesville: University Press of Virginia, 1984, 216–230.

Rosen, Howard. "Le système Gribeauval et la guerre moderne." *Revue Historique des Armées* 2, nos. 1–2 (1975): 29–36.

Ross, Steven. "French Revolutionary Infantry Tactics." In *Consortium on Revolutionary Europe. Proceedings. 1979*, edited by Warren Spencer. Athens, Ga.: Consortium on Revolutionary Europe, 1979, 149–154.

Rowland, Kate Mason. "Maryland Women and French Officers." *Atlantic Monthly* 66 (November 1890): 651–659.

Schalck de la Faverie, A. "La Révolution américaine et la Révolution française." *Société des Américainistes de Paris. Journal* 11 (1919): 385–401.

Scott, Samuel F. "L'armée royale et la Contre-Révolution." In *Les résistances à la Révolution: Actes du colloque de Rennes (17–21 septembre 1985)*, edited by François Lebrun and Roger Dupuy. Paris: Editions Imago, 1987, 191–201.

———. " 'Careers Open to Talent' in the Armies of the Revolution: Myth and Reality." In *Consortium on Revolutionary Europe. Proceedings. 1982*, edited by Warren F. Spencer. Athens, Ga.: Consortium on Revolutionary Europe, 1983, 60–70.

———. "Le corps de Rochambeau, 1783–1789: microcosme de l'Armée royale." *Mémoires de la Société pour l'Histoire du Droit et des Institutions des anciens pays bourguignons, comtois et romands* 49 (1992): 23–36.

———. "Foreign Mercenaries, Revolutionary War, and Citizen-Soldiers in the Late Eighteenth Century." *War and Society* 2 (1984): 41–58.

———. "Military Nationalism in Europe in the Aftermath of the American Revolution." In *Peace and the Peacemakers: The Treaty of 1783*, edited by Ronald Hoffman and Peter J. Albert. Charlottesville: University Press of Virginia, 1986, 160–189.

———. "The Regeneration of the Line Army During the French Revolution." *Journal of Modern History* 42 (1970): 307–330.

———. "Rochambeau's Veterans: A Case Study in the Transformation of the French Army, 1780–1794." In *Consortium on Revolutionary Europe. Proceedings. 1979*, edited by Warren Spencer. Athens, Ga.: Consortium on Revolutionary Europe, 1979, 155–163.

———. "The Soldiers of Rochambeau's Expeditionary Corps: From the American Revolution to the French Revolution." In *La Révolution américaine et l'Europe (Colloque international du Centre National de la Reclerche Scientifique, 21–25 février 1778, Paris-Toulouse*, edited by Claude Fohlen and Jacques Godechot. Paris: Editions du C.N.R.S., 1979, 565–578.

———. "Strains in the Franco-American Alliance: The French Army in Virginia, 1781–1782." In *Virginia in the American Revolution: A Collection of Essays*. Vol. 2,

BIBLIOGRAPHY

edited by Richard A. Rutyna and Peter C. Stewart. Norfolk: Old Dominion University Press, 1983, 80–100.

Selig, Robert A. "Deux-Ponts Germans: Unsung Heroes of the American Revolution." *German Life* 2 (August–September 1995): 50–53.

———. "Finding Fame in Virginia." *Colonial Williamsburg* 17 (Winter 1995): 55–59.

———. "Georg Daniel Flohr's Journal: A New Perspective." *Colonial Williamsburg* 15 (Summer 1993): 47–53.

———. "A German Soldier in America, 1780–1783: The Journal of Georg Daniel Flohr." *William and Mary Quarterly*, 3rd Ser. 50 (July 1993): 576–590.

———. "A German Soldier in New England During the Revolutionary War: The Account of George Daniel Flohr." *Newport History* 65 (1993): 49–65.

———. "Private Flohr's America." *American Heritage* 43 (December 1992): 64–71.

———. "Private Flohr's Other Life." *American Heritage* 45 (October 1994): 94–95.

———. "Storming the Redoubts." *Quarterly Journal of Military History* 8 (Autumn 1995): 18–27.

Shy, John. "Yorktown, 1781, Personalities and Documents." *The Tocqueville Review/ La Revue Tocqueville* 3 (Fall 1981): 249–348.

Six, Georges. "Fallait-il quarte quartiers de noblesse pour être officier à la fin de l'ancién régime." *Revue d'histoire moderne* 4 (1929): 47–56.

Smith, Fitz-Henry, Jr. "The French at Boston During the Revolution, With Particular Reference to the French Fleets and the Fortifications in the Harbor." *Bostonian Society Publications* 10 (1913): 9–75.

Solovieff, Georges, "Les relations franco-américaines entre 1775 et 1800." *Annales historiques de la Révolution française* 55 (January–March 1983): 114–129.

Stevens, John Austin. "The Allies at Yorktown, 1781." *Magazine of American History* 6 (January 1881): 1–53.

———. "The French in Rhode Island." *Magazine of American History* 3 (1879): 385–436.

———. "The Operations of the Allied Armies Before New York, 1781." *Magazine of American History* 4 (January 1880): 1–45.

———. "The Return of the French, 1782–3." *Magazine of American History* 7 (1881): 1–35.

———. "The Route of the Allies From King's Ferry to the Head of Elk." *Magazine of American History* 5 (July 1880): 1–20.

Stinchcombe, William C. "Americans Celebrate the Birth of the Dauphin." In *Diplomacy and Revolution: The Franco-American Alliance of 1778*, edited by Ronald Hoffman and Peter J. Albert. Charlottesville: University Press of Virginia, 1981, 39–71.

Stourzh, Gerald. "The Declaration of Rights, Popular Sovereignty, and the Supremacy of the Constitution: Divergences Between the American and French Revolutions." In *La Révolution américaine et l'Europe (Colloque international du Centre National de la Recherche Scientifique, 21–25 février 1978, Paris-Toulouse)*, edited by Claude Fohlen and Jacques Godechot. Paris: Editions du C.N.R.S., 1979, 347–364.

Topolski, Jerzy. "Revolutionary Consciousness in America and Europe From the Mid-Eighteenth to the Early Nineteenth Century as a Methodological and Historical Problem." In *The American and European Revolutions, 1776–1848:*

BIBLIOGRAPHY

Sociopolitical and Ideological Aspects, edited by Jaroslaw Pelenski. Iowa City: University of Iowa Press, 1980, 75–93.
Van Tyne, Claude H. "French Aid Before the Alliance of 1778." *American Historical Review* 31 (1925): 20–40.
———. "Influences Which Determined the French Government to Make the Treaty With America, 1778." *American Historical Review* 21 (1916): 528–541.
Whitbridge, Arnold. "Two Aristocrats in Rochambeau's Army." *Virginia Quarterly Review* 40 (Winter 1964): 114–128.
Wick, Daniel L. "The Court Nobility and the French Revolution: The Example of the Society of the Thirty." *Eighteenth Century Studies* 13 (Spring 1980): 263–284.
Willcox, William B. "The British Road to Yorktown: A Study in Divided Command." *American Historical Review* 52 (October 1946): 1–35.
———. "Rhode Island in British Strategy, 1780–1781." *Journal of Modern History* 17 (1945): 304–331.
Wolch, Isser. "War-Widows' Pensions: A Social Policy in Revolutionary and Napoleonic France." *Societas* 6 (Autumn 1976): 235–254.
Wright, Robert K., Jr. " 'Nor Is Their Standing Army to Be Despised': The Emergence of the Continental Army as a Military Institution." In *Arms and Independence: The Military Character of the American Revolution*, edited by Ronald Hoffman and Peter J. Albert. Charlottesville: University Press of Virginia, 1984, 50–74.
Wrong, Charles John. "The *Officiers de Fortune* in the French Infantry." *French Historical Studies* 9 (1976): 400–431.
York, Neil L. "Clandestine Aid and the American Revolutionary War Effort: A Re-Examination." *Military Affairs* 43 (February 1979): 26–30.

UNPUBLISHED SOURCES

Baldwin, William C. "Professionalism and the Old Regime: The Case of the Military: The Marquis de Bouillé." Unpublished paper, 1978.
Carlisle, Ronald C. "Louis-Antoine-Jean-Baptiste, Le Chevalier de Cambray-Digny." M.A. thesis, University of Pittsburgh, 1977.
Clifford, Dale L. "The Real National Guard: Local Culture in Paris, 1789–90." Paper presented at the International Congress on the History of the French Revolution, Washington, D.C., May 5, 1989.
Johnson, Hubert C. "The Role of the Army in the Early Revolution in the Midi, 1789–1793." Paper presented at the tenth annual meeting of the Western Society for French History, University of Winnipeg, Manitoba, Canada, October 14–16, 1982.
Johnson, Mary Durham. "Polly à la Française. A Study of the French Officers' Views of American Women During the American Revolution, 1776–1783." Paper presented at the Salem Conference on Revolutionary Culture, 1776–1828, Salem [Massachusetts] State College, October 29–30, 1976.
Lynn, John A. "The Campaign of Political Education and the Question of Motivation in the Armies of Revolutionary France." Paper presented at the meeting of the Southern Historical Association, Louisville, Kentucky, November 1982.
———. "Structures Versus Standards: Small Unit Cohesion in the Armies of Revolutionary France, 1792–1794." Paper presented at the ninety-sixth annual meet-

BIBLIOGRAPHY

ing of the American Historical Association, Los Angeles, California, December 29, 1981.

Pichon, René Georges. "Contribution à l'étude de la participation militaire de la France à la guerre d'indépendance des Etats-Unis, 1778–1783." Thèse du troisième cycle, Universitè de Paris I, 1976.

Scott, Samuel F. "The French Revolution and the Line Army, 1787–1793." Ph.D. dissertation, University of Wisconsin, 1968.

Selig, Robert A. "The American Campaigns of Georg Daniel Flohr, Fusilier, Regiment Royal-Deux-Ponts, 1780–1784." Paper presented at the annual meeting of the Organization of American Historians, Louisville, Kentucky, April 14, 1991.

———. "Friendly Bayonets? French Losses During the Storming of Redoubt #9 and the Journal of Georg Daniel Flohr, Chasseur, Regiment Royal-Deux-Ponts." Unpublished paper, 1992.

———. "Transatlantic Revolutions? The Case of the Royal Deux-Ponts, 1780–1781." Unpublished paper, 1994.

INDEX

1st Battalion of the Sarthe, 160
2nd Battalion of the Ariège, 159
3rd Battalion of the Bouches-du-Rhône, 160
6th Battalion of the Haute-Saône, 174
25th Demi-Brigade, 197, 198, 203, 205; incorporation of, 178
26th Demi-Brigade, 197, 203, 206; incorporation of, 178
50th Demi-Brigade, 197, 204
75th Demi-Brigade, 201, 202
79th Demi-Brigade, 201, 202
81st Demi-Brigade, 176
108th Demi-Brigade, 203, 206
177th Demi-Brigade, 178, 204
178th Demi-Brigade, 178

Active (frigate), 107
Adams, Samuel, 102
Aigle (frigate), 97
Allégeance (ship), capture of, 108
Amazone (ship), swamping of, 108
Ambercromby, Robert, 70
America (ship), 103
American Journal and General Advertiser, 48

American Revolution: French Revolution and, xii, 139, 141, 146, 214–15; French veterans and, xii, 118, 119, 122, 124, 136, 137–38, 139, 182, 213–15; influence of, 117–23, 126, 146, 182, 214; officers and, 139
Anciaux, Nicolas: resignation of, 104
André, Louis, 200; career of, 191–92
Andromaque (frigate), 73
Anhalt Regiment, 6, 7, 52
Arbuthnot, Marriot, 18, 19, 48
Army of Belgium, 177
Army of the Ardennes, 176
Army of the Midi, revolution and, 170
Army of the North, 154
Army of the Rhine, 176
Army of the Sambre and Meuse, 200
Army of the West, 176
Arnold, Benedict, 42, 47, 48; French measures against, 49; Lafayette and, 59
Asgill, Charles: execution of, 75
Associated Loyalists, Huddy and, 75
Astrée (frigate), 48
Aubry, François: desertion by, 105

INDEX

Auguste (ship), 100, 103
Auvergne Regiment, 52
Auxonne (6th) Artillery Regiment, 6, 7, 8, 41, 52, 53, 68, 76, 83, 85, 171, 173, 175, 181, 202; departure of, 118; desertion from, 151; discharges from, 107, 142, 144; history of, 184n39; losses for, 108; recruitment by, 166; register of, 174; review of, 82; revolution and, 156; soldiers of, 20; tensions within, 167

Babeuf, Conspiracy of Equals and, 195
Bailly, Etienne: desertion by, 203–4
Barollière, Jacques François Alphonse Pilotte de la, 41–42
Barras, Louis Jacques, comte de, 50, 51, 58, 59, 61, 67; Rochambeau and, 55
Barrois Regiment, 52
Barrot (*seigneur*), attack on, 130
Barthélémy, Nicolas, 167
Battle of the Saints, 86, 98
Bauer, Jacob: career of, 196–97
Bayet, Jean Baptiste Aubert du, 165
Beaumarchais, Caron de, 3–4
Beffroy, Louis Henry de, 170; duelling by, 40
Belombre, Camusat de: aristocratic plot and, 135
Beltz, Conrad, 192, 200
Bergeot, Jacques: execution of, 81
Berthier, Charles Louis Jean: death of, 109
Berthier, Louis Alexandre, 14n14, 109, 139; dismissal of, 170
Bertrand, Joseph Pierre Alexandre de: command for, 85
Bertrand, Nicolas: discharge of, 128
Bessonies de Neuville, Lieutenant, 10

Beuzelin (Beuselin), Jean: French Guards and, 137
Béville, Pierre François de, 51, 100
Binet de Marcognet, Pierre Louis: discharge of, 188
Biron, duc de. *See* Lauzun, duc de
Blakely, Josiah: provisions from, 36
Blanchard, Claude, 37, 74, 165; travels of, 25
Blou, Louis Joseph: death of, 202
Bodinier, Gilbert, 14n14, 15n22; on duelling, 46n40
Bonaparte, Napoleon. *See* Napoleon.
Bonichon, Pierre Antoine: execution of, 22
Bonnefon, Joseph de, 157, 167
Bonuses (*gratification*), 40, 74, 87n20
Boredom, problems with, 82, 99
Bosque, Jean Pierre: discharge of, 107
Boston Gazette and Country Journal, 102
Bouillé, François Claude Armour, marquis de, 145, 147, 153; Varennes and, 158
Boulonnais Regiment, 52
Bourbon, Louis Henri Joseph, duc de: execution of, 180
Bourbonnais (13th) Infantry Regiment, 6, 8, 10, 18, 48, 53, 57, 60, 157, 178, 180, 188, 197, 201, 205, 206; departure of, 118; desertion from, 142, 143, 145, 150n36, 151; discharges from, 142, 143, 146; history of, 184n39; Hocheim and, 176; problems for, 108; problems within, 167–68; punishment in, 42; recruitment by, 166; register of, 174; revolution and, 156
Bourgogne (ship), wreck of, 108, 144, 168, 190
Bourrot, Nicolas, 107
Brandmayer, Hubert: career of, 197
Bret, Sulpice: death of, 201

INDEX

Broglie, Charles Louis Victor, prince de, 97, 109, 139, 140, 165, 168
Broglie, Marshal de, 97

Carnot, Lazare, 187
Castries, duc de. *See* Charlus, Armand Charles de
Catherine the Great, 140
Catholic Church: prejudices against, 122; reorganization of, 154
Chabanier, Claude: career of, 191
Champcenetz, Louis Pierre de Quentin de Richebourg de, 170
Chandelier, Jean Baptiste, 127–28
Charleston, 72, 86; evacuation of, 103
Charlotte (schooner), 82
Charlotte Courthouse, 76; controversy at, 93–94
Charlus, Armand Charles de (duc de Castries), 39, 139, 141, 165; travels of, 25
Chasseurs, 126, 168
Chastellux, Jean François de Beauvoir, marquis de, 39, 44n13, 77, 97, 119–20, 154; command for, 102; travels of, 25
Choisy, Claude Gabriel de, 51, 57, 58, 59, 61, 76, 94, 98; Lauzun's Legion and, 79; at Newport, 52; runaway slaves and, 79–80; at Yorktown, 69
Church, John Barker, 36
Clairet, André, 205
Clermont-Crèvecoeur, Jean François Louis de Lesquevin de, 53, 54; on casualties, 68
Clinton, Henry, 19, 43, 46n49, 87n7; Hessian reinforcements for, 58; Yorktown and, 72
Collier, Pierre: punishment for, 83
Colonial Artillery, 128
Colonial Committee, 154
Colowsky, Zachaire: discharge of, 107

Comartin, baron de. *See* Dezouteux, Pierre Marie Félicité
Committee of Public Safety, 187
Common Council (Williamsburg), 93
Concorde (ship), 50
Condé, Louis Joseph Henri, prince de, 157, 167, 168
Conspiracy of Equals, 195
Contades, Marshal de, 127
Continental Army, 123, 126
Continental Journal and Weekly Advertiser, 102
Convention, 181; dismissals by, 194
Cooper, Samuel, 21, 28n18
Cordeliers Club, 198
Coriolis, chevalier de, 78
Corn du Peyroux, Zacharie Jean de, 157
Cornevin, Claude: execution of, 41–42, 51
Cornwallis, Charles, 53, 58, 59, 67, 87n7; Rochambeau and, 75; at Yorktown, 60, 61, 68–72, 74
Corny, Dominique Louis Ethis de, 17, 139
Coste, Jean François, 77, 119
Craik, James, 18
Crubilier d'Opterre, Henry, 165
Cuisinier, Sebastien: at Invalides, 204
Curien, Jean Georges: resignation of, 104
Custine, Adam Philippe, comte de, 39, 41, 139, 158, 165, 176; career of, 9; execution of, 179; travels of, 25
Custine Dragoons, 9
Customs, differences in, 33–34

Dabney, Charles, 94
D'Aboville, François Marie, 9
D'Aigrefeuil, Louis, 7–8

241

INDEX

Damas, Joseph Louis César, comte de, 155; travels of, 25
Dandridge, William, 79
Dapre, Pierre: desertion by, 105
D'Arlande de Salton, Louis François, 168, 178
Dartus, Jean Baptiste, 180; revolution and, 179
Deaths: causes of, 90n57; number of, 64n55; rate of, 50, 90n57, 128, 146
Declaration of the Rights of Man and Citizen (1789), 125, 214; officers and, 140
De Grasse, François Joseph, comte, 50, 51, 52, 59, 67, 75, 77, 85; Battle of the Saints and, 86; casualties for, 33; at Chesapeake Bay, 60; Hood and, 60–61; loan for, 58; at Yorktown, 70
De Lancey's Tories, 57
De Lauberdière, Captain: duelling by, 40–41; on punishment, 42
Delmard, Louis François: at Invalides, 204
Demi-brigades, amalgamation of, 178
Denox, Augustin Rouxelin, 78
D'Epinousse, Jean Baptiste Coriolis, 170
De Prez de Crassier, Louis Aimable, 52, 59; supplies and, 81
Deratz (priest), 106
Desandrouins, Jean Nicolas, 9
Desertion, 55–56, 90n69, 141, 142, 146, 147, 175; American, 57, 128; discouraging, 143; by enlisted men, 32; excessive, 128, 144, 145; French, 25, 41, 57, 77, 103, 128, 138; German, 32, 84, 106; increase in, 154, 167; by long-term veterans, 203–4; problems with, 83–84, 85, 104–5; punishment for, 35; rate of, 105, 106, 128, 144, 145, 149n33, 150n36, 152, 168, 169; reasons for, 84, 105, 136

Des Forêts, André de Bertier: suicide of, 41
Desprez de la Gralière, Jean Philippe: execution of, 180
D'Estaing, Charles Hector, comte, 18, 125; expeditions of, 4–5
Destouches, Charles René, chevalier, 47, 49; expedition by, 48
Des Vignes, Pierre, 166, 183n5
Dette, Ignace Joseph: National Guard and, 137
Deux-Ponts, Christian Forbach, comte des, 25, 153
Deux-Ponts, duc de (Charles II), 153
Deux-Ponts, Guillaume de: departure of, 73
Devrigny, Denis Félix, 188, 193
Dezouteux, Pierre Marie Félicité (baron de Comartin), 155
Dietz, Anton, 177
Digby, Robert, 67; POWs and, 74
Diggs, Dudley, 80
Dillon, François Théobald (Frank), 10
Dillon, Guillaume Henri (Billy), 10
Dillon, Robert Guillaume, comte de, 10, 12, 83; duelling by, 40; Franco-American relations and, 94, 95; travels of, 25
Directory, 191, 197; coup d'état by, 189, 216; health care and, 200; political crises of, 196; ratification of, 194
Discharges, 104, 107, 142, 143–44, 146, 170–71, 180, 194, 206; reasons for, 196
Discipline, 84, 142, 154; examples of, 21–22, 41–42, 51; maintaining, 198–99; problems with, 145, 152, 157, 167–68
Diseases. *See* Illnesses
Dôle, Claude: career of, 197
D'Olonne, Pierre François Gabriel, comte, 180

INDEX

D'Opterre, Henry Crublier: retirement of, 196
Drinking, prohibitions on, 41
Du Bayet, Aubert, 178; arrest/imprisonment of, 179
Dubet, Jean Baptiste: death of, 145
Du Bouchet, Denis Jean Florimond de Langlois, marquis, 121; duelling by, 40–41; resignation of, 157
Duc de Bourgogne (ship), 11, 58
Duchesne, Léonard: death of, 202
Duelling, 40–41, 46n40, 82, 109
Duffraine, Mathieu: hardships for, 201
Duffy, Captain, 75, 88n33
Du Fort, Jean Aymard Josserand, 170
Du Hainaut, Claude Théodore, 147, 178
Dulany, Ann, 75
Dumas, Mathieu, 21, 165, 170, 189, 195, 208n8; travels of, 25
Dumouriez, Charles François, 177, 185n44; overthrow attempt by, 173; revolution and, 179
Duplessis, Marie Athanase Riffault: career of, 159
Du Plessis, Thomas Antoine, chevalier de Mauduit (Thomas Duplessis Mauduit), 154; death of, 155
Dupont, Gilles François, 166
Duportail, Louis Le Begue, 123
Du Rosel, Gilles, 166
Du Rosel, Louis, 166
Dussart, Fidel, 146
Du Teil, Lieutenant Colonel, 144

Eblé, Jean Baptiste, 208n21
Egyptian expedition, 202, 215
Emeraude (frigate), 81, 107
English language, coping with, 24, 33, 84
Enlisted men, 7–8, 127, 197, 198, 215; death rate for, 50, 90n57; desertion by, 32; discharge of, 104; supplemental jobs for, 129
Erpelding, Pierre, 177
Escelent, Henry: arrest of, 82; duelling by, 40
Estates General, 119, 139, 140, 214
Estheimer, Christophe: desertion by, 104–5

Fauvel, Charles, 211n79; at Invalides, 205
Ferrier, Etienne: commission for, 161
Ferrier, Jean: dismissal of, 146
Fersen, Hans Axel de, 21; on American cupidity, 37; morale problems and, 39; travels of, 25
Feyolard, Jacques, 8
Fischer, Johannes: demotion of, 147
Flet, Claude: career of, 191
Fleurus, 175, 177
Fleury, François Louis Teissedre de, 123
Flohr, Georg Daniel, 23–24; death of, 106; on slavery, 132n23
Folmer, Jean, 107
Fontaine, Pierre: discharge of, 104
Foodstuffs, 68; concerns about, 36, 38
Forage, problems with, 34
Fort Knyphausen, attack at, 55
Fort Louis, 177
Franck, Joseph: execution of, 35
Franco-American relations, 43, 65n66, 84, 94, 95, 102–3; POWs and, 75; problems in, 49, 77–80; in Rhode Island, 101–2
François, Pierre: death of, 203
Franklin, Benjamin, 4, 77
French Guards, 135, 137
French Revolution: American Revolution and, xii, 139, 141, 146, 214–15; French veterans and, 143,

243

INDEX

182, 190, 213; impact of, 215–16; influences on, 117–18; officers and, 153–54; opposition to/support of, 162

Gabel, Adam, 54
Gálvez, Bernardo de, 97
Ganiard, Michel, 177
Gardel, Jacques: career of, 159
Gardiens du feu, work of, 35
Garnier, Jean Pierre: National Guard and, 137
Gazette de France, 120
Gazette de Leyde, 120
Gazette de Paris, 157
Gazette françois: announcements in, 24; publication of, 23
General Assembly (Rhode Island), 101, 102; desertion and, 18
General Assembly (Virginia), gratitude from, 93
George III, 72
Gerard (Girard), Marin: at Invalides, 205
Gilbert, Jean: career of, 201–2
Girault, Philippe René, 174, 175; complaints by, 200–201; imprisonment of, 82
Gloire (frigate), 96, 97
Gloucester, 70, 71, 72; POWs at, 74
Gogue, François, xi, xiiin1
Gourbil, Pierre, 127
Graves, Thomas, 61
Great Fear (1789), 138
Greene, Nathanael, 123
Greene, William, 58, 76, 93; Corny and, 17; supplies and, 29
Grellé (Grelay), Jean, 212n89; pension for, 207
Grouchy, Emmanuel de, 175
Guichard, Antoine: promotion for, 171

Guidez, François, 198, 209n44
Guillet, Joseph, 146
Guinez, Jean Baptiste: at Invalides, 205

Haacke, Frédéric Charles de: travels of, 25
Hamilton, Alexander, 70, 123
Hancock, John, 49
Hand, Christophe: execution of, 35
Harris, Mary, 79
Harrison, Benjamin, 77, 82; deserters and, 83; Franco-American relations and, 94–95; runaway slaves and, 79, 80
Hartmann, Jacques, 57
Health conditions, problems with, 25–26, 38, 81, 200–201
Heath, William, 18, 19, 21, 59
Hector (ship), 97
Hell, François Xavier de, 170
Hessian mercenaries, enlistment of, 32
Hiton, Jean Jacques de, 168
Hoffmann, Paul: career of, 192
Holker, John, 36, 37
Hood, Samuel: De Grasse and, 60–61
Hospital of Saint Laurent: Girault at, 200–201
Hôtel des Invalides, 196, 211n75; admission to, 204–5
Huddy, Joshua: execution of, 75
Hugau, Claude Etienne, 139, 165; arrest of, 82; on duelling, 40
Huntington, Andrew, 57
Huntington, Ebenezer: on French Army, 57
Hygiene problems, 25–26, 38, 81, 200, 201
Hyvert, Armand: French Guards and, 137

INDEX

Illnesses, 204; dealing with, 20, 51, 18, 81–82, 96, 109, 110, 128, 200
Insubordination, 141, 142, 196; problems with, 82–83, 144, 147, 157
Isle de France (ship), 18

Jacobins, 154, 167, 173, 195, 196
Jefferson, Thomas, 77, 82
Jemappes, 175, 176, 177, 215
Jennings de Kilmaine, Charles Edouard, 175, 179, 185n44; on Varennes/Bouille, 158
Jeriez, Henry: discharge of, 107
Joseph II, 42
Jourdan, Mathieu Jouve, 152
Jourdan Law, 198
Journal Militaire, on order/discipline, 154
Jousselin, Louis Gabriel François de: execution of, 180
Jujardy, Jean Baptiste de: arrest of, 83

Kennett, Lee: on French officers/ Southern planters, 89n43; on Rochambeau, 27n12
Kerdaniel, Jean Marie Le Météier de: resignation of, 156–57
Kimball, Stephen, 58
King George's War, 215
King William's War, 215
Klein, Jacob: death of, 203
Klein, Jean: desertion by, 32
Kreps, Jean: career of, 197, 209n40

La Brue, Jacques Joseph de, 168
Lacey, John, 123
La Chau, Michel Giraud de, 85
La Chesnaye, Claude François Bernardin: duelling by, 40

La Fage, Bernard: career of, 159
Lafayette, Marie Joseph Paul Yves Roch Gilbert du Motier, marquis de, xi, 6, 17, 21, 58, 60, 67, 68, 126, 170; American Revolution and, 122, 139; Arnold and, 48, 59; morale problems and, 39; in Newport, 19, 23; revolution and, 179; Rochambeau and, 27n10, 31; at Yorktown, 70
La Forest, Thomas: desertion by, 107
Lagache, Ambroise: death of, 201
Lagrange, Adélaïde Blaise de, 175
Lahogue, François: National Guard and, 137
La Luzerne, Anne César, chevalier de, 39, 42, 44n14, 77, 99; Lafayette and, 19; Rochambeau and, 32, 80
La Marck Regiment, 52, 143
Lameth, Alexandre de, 139, 140, 158, 170; flight of, 189
Lameth, Charles de, 139, 141, 158, 190; arrest of, 170; flight of, 189
Lameth, Théodore de, 75
Langeron, Louis Alexandre Andrault, comte de, 190
Languedoc Regiment, 52
La Pérouse, Jean Françoise de, 48, 49, 50
Laprun, Pierre, 193, 195–96
La Serre, Arsène Gillaume Joseph Barbier de: resignation of, 104
Lauberdière, Louis François Bertrand Dupont d'Aubervoye de, 74, 189
Lauliot, Pierre, 161
Launay, Bernard René, marquis de, 140
Laurens, John, 71
Lauzun, Louis Armaud, duc de (duc de Biron), 35, 96, 100, 103, 107, 139, 140, 154, 165; departure of, 73; execution of, 179; travels of, 25
Lauzun (6th, 5th) Hussars, 35, 118, 135, 153, 155, 171, 175, 179, 206,

245

INDEX

207, 212n88, 212n90; American Revolution veterans in, 174; conduct of, 145; desertion from, 128, 145, 151, 169; discipline of, 142; reconstitution of, 169; recruitment by, 166; revolution and, 156. See also Lauzun's Legion

Lauzun's Legion, 6, 7, 8, 12, 25, 32, 39, 53, 57, 60; changes in, 118, 126; cohesion of, 152; controversy for, 78–79, 93; desertion from, 105, 142; discharges from, 107, 144; duelling in, 40; forage for, 34; history of, 184n39; length of service in, 14n13; Lincoln and, 55; officers of, 10; runaway slaves and, 79; in Virginia, 62; at Yorktown, 69, 71. See also Lauzun Hussars

La Valette, Georges Balthazar Edme Chandron, chevalier de, 10, 95, 96, 100, 107; duelling by, 40; resignation of, 158; at Yorktown, 94

Lavit, Jacques: discharge of, 104
Leblanc, Jean: death of, 201
Le Bret, Jean François, 139
Le Breton, Pierre: at Invalides, 204
Le Brun, Jean: death of, 177
Le Courier de l'Europe, North American news in, 120
Lee, Charles: Washington and, 126
Lefebvre, Pierre: resignation of, 205–6
Le Gardeur de Tilly, Captain, 47
Legislative Assembly, 170; revolution and, 165–66
Lehetre, Jean Baptiste, 146
Lemière, Guillaume Pierre, 178; career of, 190–91
Le Monier (Le Monnier), René Nicolas, 184n33, 196, 208n21; career of, 193; commission for, 172
Lenoir, Nicolas: career of, 191
Leroy, Jean Baptiste, 8

Les Affaires de l'Angleterre et de l'Amérique, North American news in, 120
Levée en masse, 173
L'Halle, Jacques Joseph: arrest of, 82
Limousin, François, 206, 207
Lincoln, Benjamin, 5, 61, 68; at Charleston, 71; Lauzun and, 55
Lindel, Jean: at Invalides, 204
Lippincott, Richard: Huddy and, 75
Lodging, problems with, 34–35
Louis Philippe, 175
Louis XIV, Invalides and, 204
Louis XVI, 4, 6, 28n18, 42, 49, 103, 106, 120, 157, 162, 171; Estates General and, 119; popular violence and, 135; support for, 170; Te Deum and, 72, 77; Varennes flight by, 151, 155, 180
Louis XVIII, 192, 195

Mackenzie, Frederick, 57; Franco-American relations and, 49
MacNamara-Hussey, Caroline, 189
Marcognet, Pierre Louis Binet de, 178
Maria Theresa, 42
Mariscaille (Mariscal), Joseph: at Invalides, 205
Marneur, Claude: French Guards and, 137
Martel, Joseph, 56
Martraire, Charles, 172, 195
Masieu, Paul, 205
Maubourg, Marie Charles de la Tour, 152
Menonville, François Louis Thibault de, 139
Messerte, Henrich: desertion by, 104–5
Milice, 124
Military advancement: by merit, 127, 129; by privilege, 125, 127, 193
Military Committee, 140

INDEX

Military hospitals, problems with, 200–201
Militia, 123, 125; defects in, 124; National Guard and, 141
Miller, John: deserters and, 83
Milliard, Ignace, 201, 210n62
Miollis, Sextius Alexandre François: career of, 160
Mirabeau, Gabriel Honoré de Riquetti comte de, 121
Mitier, Jacques, 129, 161
Momeril, Charles Georges Calixte Deslon de, 155
Monsieur (13th) Dragoons, 155
Montchoisy, Antoine Louis Choin de Montgay, baron de, 195
Montesquieu, Charles Louis de Secondat, baron de, 21, 25, 97; morale problems and, 39
Montmorency-Laval, Anne Alexandre de, 8, 48; travels of, 25
Montmort, Claude Bernard Loppin, marquis de: resignation of, 158
Morale: bolstering, 31; problems with, 23–24, 39, 82, 91n72, 99, 105, 108, 123, 145, 199 201
Morgan, Daniel, 123
Morge, Alexis, xi–xii, 202
Mosny, Louis François Philippe de: execution of, 180
Mutiny, 35, 144, 145, 154, 215

Napoleon (Bonaparte), 6, 139, 160, 189, 190, 194, 195, 197, 207; Egyptian expedition of, 202; health care and, 200
Narbonne, André, 178
National Assembly, 140, 158, 159, 165, 166, 214
National Convention, 170, 187, 191; armed forces and, 172; military reorganization by, 173

National Guard, 137, 154, 159, 214; French Revolution and, 124; militia and, 141; Paris, xi, 137, 139, 140; Versailles, 139
NCOs: commissions for, 129, 161, 171, 192; work of, 129, 172
Neerwinden, 175, 177, 215
Nelson, Thomas, 47, 62n2, 68, 76, 77, 82; POWs and, 74
Neptune (ship), 51, 109
Neustrie Regiment, 6, 7, 52, 205
Newport: British blockade of, 18; desertions at, 25; French at, 3, 5, 12, 21–23, 39, 44n13, 52, 101
Newport Mercury, 112n48; announcements in, 24; French advertisements in, 23; on Rochambeau, 52; on Yorktown capitulation, 72
Ney, Michel, 206
Noailles, Louis Marie, vicomte de, 71, 139, 140, 158, 165; duelling by, 40; travels of, 25; at Yorktown, 71

Officers: accommodations for, 107; American Revolution and, 139; peacetime service for, 110; political motives of, 167; punishments and, 42; resignation of, 104, 158, 161; rivalry among, 40–41; routine for, 99; social distinctions among, 8–11
Officers de fortune, 11, 104, 147; revolution and, 171; work of, 129
O'Hara, Charles: at Yorktown, 72
Olmy (Ohny), Jeremiah, 98–99
Ordinaire (mess), described, 198–99

Pandoua, Jean Baptiste, 89n51; desertion by, 106; runaway slaves and, 80
Paradise, John, 80

INDEX

Pelletier, François, 210n66; death of, 202
Pensions, 84, 204, 206, 207
Perche (30th) Infantry, 174, 175
Pericot, Jacques: death of, 203
Perrucheau, Jean, 143
Petitjean, Antoine: death of, 52
Phillips, William, 59
Pichon, Jean: career of, 197
Pichon, Martin, 172
Pollerescky, Jean Ladislas, 39, 82
Poulnot, Jean Baptiste: retirement of, 84
POWs: death rate among, 202–3; deprivations for, 74, 203; Franco-American disagreement over, 75
Practonel, Joseph François Dalmas de, 170
Pradelles, Benoît François van, 104
Prevost, Augustin, 5
Professionalism, increase in, 194–95
Providence Gazette and Country Journal, 112n48; on desertion, 105
Punchelet, Frédéric Wilhelm: desertion by, 32
Punishment. *See* Discipline

Queen Anne's War, 215
Queyssat, Gabriel de, xi, xiii, 170

Rations: distribution of, 38; limits on, 56
Reade, Thomas, 79
Redoubts no. 9 and 10, 70, 71, 75
Regiment of Béarn, 10
Regiment of Flandre, 141
Regiment of Toul Artillery, 105
Regneauld, François Denis: death of, 20
Reinforcements, lack of, 85, 118
Religious tolerance, 20, 122

Remy, Jacques, 168
Resignations, 104, 158, 160, 161, 180
Retirements, 84, 146, 196, 204
Revolutionary Tribunal, xi
Rhode Island Council of War, Corny and, 17
Riccé, Gabriel de, 170
Richard, Georges, 202, 210n66
Rignatz (priest). *See* Deratz (priest)
Robespierre, 188, 194
Robin, Charles César, 21, 119, 121; Estates General and, 140
Rochambeau, Donatien Marie Joseph de Vimeur, vicomte de, 10, 32, 50, 141; career of, 188–89
Rochambeau, Jean Baptiste Donatien de Vimeur, comte de, 42, 43, 62–63n16, 67, 77, 78, 156; on American regiments, 56–57; American Revolution and, 119, 121, 124, 139, 182; appeal by, 32; Army of the North and, 154; blockade and, 18, 47–48; budget for, 33; Cornwallis and, 75; desertion and, 83, 84, 106, 128, 136, 137; discipline and, 21–22, 41, 84; enlisted men and, 7–8, 127, 197, 198, 215; expedition of, 6–7, 12, 13n6, 40, 214–15; Franco-American relations and, 26, 31, 49, 84, 94; French Revolution and, 171; German troops and, 213; gratitude for, 52, 73, 93, 95; income for, 74; Indian leaders and, 24; marching orders by, 53, 54–55; at Newport, 3, 12, 17–22, 24–25, 31, 36, 101; officers of, 8–12, 110, 124, 127, 158, 165, 187, 213; POWs and, 74; problems for, 32–33, 34, 36–39, 95; return of, 100, 117; review by, 24, 98; slaves and, 80; social life and, 35; *Te Deum* and, 77; in Virginia, 60, 80, 86, 93;

Washington and, 32, 49–51, 59, 73, 76, 86, 91n77, 95–96, 100, 102; at Williamsburg, 61; at Yorktown, 69, 71, 72, 74, 94, 95, 119
Roderique Hortalez and Company, 3
Romulus (ship), 47
Rossel, Chrétien: career of, 206
Roussy, Jean: desertion by, 203–4
Roy, François: desertion by, 56
Royal Army: American Revolution and, 182; disintegration of, 151
Royal Deux-Ponts (99th) Infantry Regiment, xi, 6, 7, 11, 23, 32, 52, 53, 54, 55, 57, 59, 60, 152, 160, 175, 177, 179, 181, 191, 204, 215; bonuses for, 74; changes for, 153; conditions within, 168–69; demi-brigades and, 178; desertion from, 83, 104–5, 128, 143, 146, 147, 150n36, 151; discipline in, 144, 147; discipline of, 142; history of, 184n39; problems in, 144; recruitment by, 166; register of, 174; resignations from, 104; revolution and, 156
Royal Liégeois (101st) Infantry, 206
Rühl, Charles Guillaume, 147
Rupplin, Jean Népomucène: deserters and, 83

Saint-Cyr, Georges Cyr Antoine de Bellemare de: discharge of, 181
Saint-Hilaire, Charles Marie Martial Bessonies de, 10; discharge of, 170–71
Saint-Just, Louis Antoine, 187
Saint-Maisme, Jean Baptiste d'Allière, comte de, 37; arrest of, 83; travels of, 25
Saint-Martin, Pierre-Charles Tuffet de, 8
St. Pierre, Paul de, 106. *See* Deratz (priest)

Saint-Simon, Claude Anne, marquis de, 67, 75; at James Island, 60
Saintonge (82nd) Infantry Regiment, 6, 9, 10, 20, 39, 41, 53, 60, 76, 78, 97, 173, 180, 205; deaths in, 128; demi-brigades and, 178; departure of, 118; desertion from, 142, 143, 145, 150n36, 151; discharges from, 142, 144, 146; duelling in, 40, 46n40; at Halfway House, 76; history of, 184n39; reconstruction of, 176; recruitment by, 166; register of, 174; review of, 81–82; revolution and, 156
Savannah, 19, 72, 96
Saxe, Maurice de, 126
Schauenbourg, François André de, 178, 179
Scherrer, Henry, 161
Schumacher, Jean: desertion by, 203–4
Schwartz, Georges: death of, 203
Schwartz, Jean: discharge of, 107
Second Amalgam, 178, 196
Ségur, Henri Philippe, marquis de: Rochambeau and, 43, 49, 55, 56
Ségur, Louis Philippe, comte de, 97, 98, 99, 109, 140
Selig, Robert, 26n6, 106; on French officers/Southern planters, 89n43
Service: average length of, 14n13; preserving records of, 183n8
Seven Years' War, 3, 85, 119, 215; lessons from, 126
Sheldon, Dominique: travels of, 25
Sibaud, Jacques François: career of, 159
Sicard, Jean: discharge of, 104
Silly, Gabriel François de, 10, 14n18
Silly, Hyacinthe Joseph de, 157
Sinéty, François Bernard, 139
Sirjacques, Henry, 169, 172
Six, Georges, 208n21

INDEX

Slaughter, Captain, 94
Slaves, 122; French army and, 79–80, 132n23
Society of the Cincinnati, 121, 140
Society of Thirty, 139
Soissonnais (40th) Infantry Regiment, xi, xiiin1, 6, 10, 37, 48, 53, 55, 60, 76, 80, 83, 85, 97, 179, 201, 202; demi-brigades and, 178; deserters from, 151, 183n17; discharges from, 118, 142, 144; discipline in, 144; duelling in, 40; history of, 184n39; police work by, 130, 152; recovery for, 177; recruitment by, 166; register of, 174, 184n29; revolution and, 156, 169–70; tensions within, 167; at Toulon, 109, 110; at Villefort, 130
Sonnette, Lieutenant: promotion of, 73
Stack, François Joseph de: command for, 85
Steil, Joseph: career of, 192
Stenger, Jean: career of, 191
Stevens, Edward, 94
Stoertz, Jean, 143
Stone, Edward Martin, 27n7
Strategies, 5, 68
Suffren, Pierre André, bailli de, 5, 85
Sugg, Jacob: desertion by, 143
Sullivan, John, 4
Supplies: payment for, 36–37, 39; problems with, 36, 37, 38, 78, 80–81, 93, 95, 199; transportation of, 38, 68
Surveillance (ship), 73
Swiss Guards, 135

Talleyrand-Périgord, Jacques Boson, comte de, 9, 97
Tallmadge, Benjamin, 49
Tarlé, Benoît Joseph de, 38, 53; finances and, 36

Tarleton, Banastre: at Gloucester, 70; at Yorktown, 71
Te Deum celebrations, 72, 77
Ternay, Charles Louis d'Arsac de, 19, 24, 31; death of, 47
Thiriat, Pierre: National Guard and, 137
Thirre, Laurent, 177
Thomas, Louis, 143
Tilton, James: health problems and, 81
Treaty of Alliance, 4
Treaty of Amity and Commerce, 4
Tressan, Claude Marie, chevalier de, 37
Tribout, Nicolas, xxi, xiii, 191, 200
Tricot, Antoine, 200, 201, 210n63
Troupes provinciales, 124
Trumbull, Jonathan, 100; lodging and, 34–35
Tucker, St. George, 68
Tuo, Pierre: career of, 197–98

Uzdowsky, Georges: death of, 145

Valmy, 175, 176, 177, 215
Vareilles, Alexis Dujuast de: Custine and, 41
Varennes, flight to, 153, 155–57, 162, 162n10, 180, 215
Vauban, Jacques Anne de, 9, 97
Vaudreuil, Jean Louis de Rigaud, vicomte de, 140, 154
Vaudreuil, Louis Philippe Rigaud, marquis de, 97, 99, 103, 106, 108; Battle of the Saints and, 98; departure of, 107
Verdier, Jean Pierre, 57
Verette, Dominique, 20
Verette, François, 20
Vergennes, Charles Gravier, comte de, 6, 43; La Luzerne and, 42

INDEX

Verger, Jean Baptiste Antoine de: on bonuses, 74
Ville de Paris (flagship), 67
Villey, François Joseph Donatien de Grivel de: suspension of, 181
Vioménil, Antoine Charles du Houx, baron de, 37, 39, 41, 48, 100, 108, 158; death of, 170; French Revolution and, 155; review by, 81–82
Vioménil, Charles Gabriel du Houx, 10
Vioménil, Joseph Hyacinthe, comte de, 157, 180; at Yorktown, 78; command for, 102; enlisted men of, 127
Von Closen, Captain, 82, 107; on social/recreational activities, 77
Von Steuben, Fredrich, 68, 123
Voves, Joseph François Gau de, 195

Wadsworth, Jeremiah: supplies from, 36, 37
Washington, George, 24, 25, 40, 47, 55, 60, 67, 82, 123, 140; admiration for, 125; After Order of, 72; French and, 17–18, 19, 49; Lauzun and, 79; in Newport, 48; Rochambeau and, 31, 32, 49–51, 59, 73, 76, 86, 91n77, 95–96, 100, 102; at Williamsburg, 61; at Yorktown, 69, 71, 72
Washington, Lund, 49
Wasservas, Philippe François Roch de: career of, 188
Wayne, Anthony, 59
Weather conditions, problems from, 199–200
Weedon, George, 69, 123
Wenger, Phillip, 147
Wervy, Mathias, 207, 212n90
Williamsburg, 67, 68
Wisch, Jean Christophe, baron de, 181, 187
Wolff, Philippe: commission for, 161
Wounds, 204; treating, 200–201

Yorktown, 19, 62, 68–70, 78

Zabe, Joseph, 206

www.ingramcontent.com/pod-product-compliance
Lightning Source LLC
Chambersburg PA
CBHW062046290426
44109CB00027B/2743